UNDERSTANDING 'SECTARIANISM'

FANAR HADDAD

Understanding 'Sectarianism'

Sunni–Shi'a Relations in the
Modern Arab World

HURST & COMPANY, LONDON

First published in the United Kingdom in 2020 by
C. Hurst & Co. (Publishers) Ltd,
41 Great Russell Street, London, WC1B 3PL

Printed in India

A Cataloguing-in-Publication data record for this book is available from the British Library.

ISBN: 9781787382060

www.hurstpublishers.com

CONTENTS

ACKNOWLEDGEMENTS

There is no clear starting point to when the idea for this book or the thinking behind it first emerged. Rather, it is the product of over a decade's worth of work spent on the subject. As such, it has benefited from the insights, comments, thoughts and suggestions of a number of friends and scholars over the course of many years. Be it through academic symposia or casual conversation, I am thankful for all that I have learnt from them.

My thanks to the members of Aarhus University's Sectarianism in the Wake of the Arab Revolts Project – Morten Valbjorn, Ray Hinnebusch, Martin Reixinger and Thomas Fibiger – for allowing me to share my research and exchange ideas with students and faculty at Aarhus. I would also like to thank Ali Allawi, Madawi al-Rasheed, Keiko Sakai, Zoltan Pall, Eskandar Sadeghi-Boroujerdi, Ahab Bdaiwi, Farid al-Attas and Sajjad Rizvi for lending an analytical ear and indulging my interest in this subject – this book would have been a very different and undoubtedly inferior one without their ideas and input. My gratitude and appreciation as well to Wayne Yeo for his research assistance and feedback. Special thanks also to the late Professor Peter Sluglett – a gentleman and a scholar but above all a dearly missed colleague who always welcomed my intrusive requests for feedback and discussion during our time working together at the Middle East Institute, National University of Singapore, from 2012 until his unfortunate passing in 2017.

ACKNOWLEDGEMENTS

I am especially grateful to Nader Hashemi, Morten Valbjorn, Ray Hinnebusch and Simon Mabon for being so generous with their time and providing such extensive, thoughtful and constructively critical feedback on various chapters of this book. Likewise, special thanks to Toby Dodge for his much-appreciated support, guidance, advice and encouragement over the years. I am especially indebted to him for his help and input on chapter 4, an earlier version of which was presented in 2018 at a workshop he organized at the London School of Economics on the comparative politics of sub-state identities. In that regard I also owe thanks to Charles Tripp and John Hutchinson for their feedback on the draft submitted to that workshop.

Spouses are always deserving of special mention in authors' acknowledgements given how inordinately taxed their capacity for love, generosity, indulgence and kindness becomes when their other halves are immersed in the maddening obsession that is a book project. They go through the pain of reading sub-standard ur-drafts too poor to be shared with colleagues. They have to tolerate sudden absences whenever the writer-partner suspects that an irregularly timed visit from the muses may be upon them. They endure having to endlessly listen to, discuss and bounce ideas about their partner's pet subject for longer and more repeatedly than they would do with their own. They have to allay the writer-partner's repetitive bouts of self-doubt. But above all, they have to suffer listening to the writer-partner incessantly talk about their bloody book! For all of that and so much more, I am forever grateful to Farah, who not only had to put up with all of the above but did so with more love, encouragement, patience and support than anyone deserves and all while carrying and giving birth to our Mizna. To Farah and Mizna: I love you both.

INTRODUCTION

Is there any call for yet another book on 'sectarianism'? After all, over the past two decades or so, few subfields of Middle Eastern studies or Islamic studies have attracted more scholarly, and some not so scholarly, attention than 'sectarianism', particularly in relation to the Sunni–Shi'a divide. Anyone with a sustained interest in the subject cannot but notice the enormous growth – not just quantitatively but thankfully in qualitative terms as well – of the literature; so why burden the bookshelves with another volume on a subject that has attracted no end of analysis, column inches and, in some cases, outright hot air? To begin with, while this book is about sectarian identity (specifically and exclusively Sunni–Shi'a identities) this is not a book about 'sectarianism': in fact one of the primary and more ambitious – pie in the sky, some might say – purposes of this book is to finally liberate the study of sectarian identity and sectarian relations from the cognitive shackles of the term 'sectarianism'; a term so opaque, circuitous, negatively charged, politically controversial and emotive as to be meaningless (hence the quote marks). As will be discussed in the opening chapter, my objection to the term 'sectarianism' should not be taken to mean a rejection of the study of sectarian identities, sectarian relations or any other sect-coded process or phenomenon; rather, in rejecting 'sectarianism' I am proposing the abandonment of an absurdly catch-all phrase that encompasses so much as to stand in

1

the way of coherent debate – how can a debate adequately cohere if its parameters are so hazy? In conferences, in commentary and in the literature, one all too often gets the impression that discussants are talking past each other in the absence of agreement as to the basic terms of reference and their meaning. While there is no shortage of studies problematizing the term 'sectarianism' there has been little in the way of serious theorization of alternatives that go beyond yet more definitions of 'sectarianism', thereby ultimately making an already circuitous debate all the more labyrinthine. In this book I try to go beyond just admiring the problem, or what Kieran Healy critiqued as the tendency to "equate calling for a more sophisticated approach to a theoretical problem with actually providing one."[1] To that end, this book attempts to formulate a theoretical framework that might enable us to cut the conceptual umbilical cord that is 'sectarianism' and to start exploring the innumerable phenomena that the term encompasses and how these relate to each other.

The many ways in which 'sectarianism' is framed, used and understood and the bewildering array of things that it is used to refer to – from innocuous sectarian insularity all the way to sectarian murder – will be covered in chapter 1. For now, it suffices to point out that, however the term is used and however it is understood, 'sectarianism' is necessarily a function of, or is related to, sectarian identity. Yet despite that, surveying the literature, one notices a surprising lack of attention given to sectarian identities. Rather, their meaning, contours, inner dynamics and so forth are assumed and then obscured by the analytical black hole that is 'sectarianism'. In other words, the *ism* has overshadowed the root, creating a ripple effect of confusion as to the parameters, content and drivers of sectarian dynamics. A central contention of this book, therefore, is that we firstly need to discard the cumbersome and entirely unnecessary frame of 'sectarianism' and, secondly, that we should instead direct our analytic focus towards understanding sectarian *identity*. The failure to do so thus far, and our obsession with the *ism* at the expense of the identity, have left us chasing the chimeric shadows of the former at the cost of understanding the latter.

---

[1] Kieran Healy, "Fuck Nuance," *Sociological Theory*, 35:2 (2017): 121.

In attempting to consign the term 'sectarianism' to terminal redundancy, this book tries to introduce a new theoretical framework that might better enable us to understand sectarian identity and to more effectively unpack the plethora of subjects, dynamics and processes that are covered by 'sectarianism'. One of the reasons that the term has proven so difficult to define is that it has, practically speaking, become shorthand for the many facets of sectarian identity and sectarian relations. This, it seems to me, is the reason that, as already mentioned, scholars of the subject often end up speaking past each other: one assumes 'sectarianism' to refer to matters of doctrinal incompatibility, while another would understand it to mean the instrumentalization of sectarian categories in geopolitics; yet another supposes it refers to the institutionalization of sectarian identities in governance and national politics, while another presumes the phrase to indicate hatred between sects, and so on and so forth. It is not that any one of these is right or wrong, it is that they are each focusing on a different aspect of the same multidimensional subject. Accordingly, rather than trying to identify which individual approach is (in)correct, what is needed is for us to redefine the subject in a way that reflects the inherent multidimensionality of sectarian identity. The failure to do so is especially problematic where it becomes definitional: unidimensional definitions of 'sectarianism' end up painting sectarian dynamics, and by extension sectarian identity, in unrealistically monochrome ways. We can avoid this and help move the debate forward by acknowledging that 'sectarianism' is a reductionist and sloppy way of referring to the many facets of sectarian identity; at this point we can then start thinking about the layered nature of sectarian identities and the multiple ways they are imagined and manifested. For example, on one level, Sunni and Shi'a identities clearly signify adherence to or association with a doctrinal belief system or a set of metaphysical or religious truths underpinning a group's normative understanding of authority, community, spirituality and the relation to a higher power. In this framing, sectarian identity comes to mean membership in the collective that subscribes or professes loyalty to, and is defined by, these religious truths – be they metaphysical (for example, beliefs regarding creation, salvation or eschatology) or temporal (as in the divergent readings of post-Prophetic Islamic history). By extension, in this framing, sectarian division and sectarian contestation become functions of incompatible doctrines with the sectarian other being othered for their doctrinal heterodoxy if not heresy: the other is defined, accepted or rejected on the basis of their beliefs and the extent to which they accord with or diverge from a given conception of truth and orthodoxy. This is a self-evidently valid and relevant framing of sectarian identity, one that is often overlooked in the literature perhaps as a function of our secular biases. However, and herein lies the point, there are limits to this validity and it would simply be counterfactual to adopt such an understanding as the sole definer of, or frame for, sectarian identity, or to reduce sectarian dynamics to a matter of clashing doctrines.

To illustrate, a fundamentalist cleric may define and reject the sectarian other based on their beliefs and their reading of Islamic history, yet how relevant is that to the way that Sunni–Shi'a prejudices are governed in, say, the Lebanese context today? How relevant have doctrinal matters been to Sunni–Shi'a contestation in the Lebanese political system after the Taif Accord of 1989 or indeed how relevant were they to broader Muslim and non-Muslim sectarian competition during the civil war that preceded it? Is the fact that Hizbullah, Lebanon's most powerful and relevant Shi'a actor today, is an adherent of Iran's revolutionary doctrine of *wilayat al-faqih* the sole determinant of Sunni–Shi'a relations and Sunni–Shi'a competition in Lebanon? Or is something more tangible and less abstract also at stake: the respective shares of, and access to, the Lebanese state that the supposed representatives of Sunnis and Shi'as have and the relations of power governing sectarian relations in Lebanon perhaps? Likewise, does the unmistakable overlap between class prejudice and sectarian prejudice (in Lebanon and elsewhere) render matters of doctrine superfluous to sectarian prejudice? Or, alternatively, is the matter one of competing transnational visions? Does not Hizbullah's role in the region and relations with Iran (even prior to the Syrian conflict) feed sectarian (Sunni–Shi'a) competition and resentment in Lebanon? Needless to say, rather than having to choose any one of these frames or debating which is more important, we ought to accept the obvious fact that all are relevant and all are essential to how sectarian identity is imagined, experienced and projected. Accordingly, rather than viewing these as separate approaches to the understanding of sectarian dynamics, we should instead view them as integral in that they collectively form the contours of sectarian dynamics.

The theoretical approach introduced in this book frames sectarian identity as the sum of its parts; specifically, it will be argued that sectarian identity is simultaneously formulated along four overlapping, interconnected and mutually informing dimensions: doctrinal, subnational, national and transnational. Which of these is more relevant, which helps us better understand causality or which better explains sectarian dynamics is entirely context-dependent – with the proviso that no single dimension can be taken in complete isolation from the others. By thinking of sectarian identity in this way we can better appreciate its malleability: not *just* a tool of political elites seeking to secure their power and privilege; not *just* a matter of dogma and belief; not *just* a political issue or a frame for intergroup competition at the subnational level. An appreciation of this malleability and multidimensionality is important to understanding the dynamics of sectarian identity, what is at stake from one context to another, and what drives the waxing and waning of sectarian competition. To illustrate the tangible relevance of these dimensions and the differences between them: a Sunni-centric politician in Iraq or Lebanon for example, can still have ties to and even intermarry with Shi'as on the basis of shared economic interests or other commonalities such as shared socio-economic or ideological background; however, in contexts where doctrine matters more – say, in the case of a Sunni fundamentalist cleric – such interlinkages would be less likely. Put simply, that a Sunni-centric Iraqi politician would be married to a Shi'a is fairly unremarkable (and indeed there are several such cases today); however, it would be downright astonishing if it were to emerge that Saudi Arabian fundamentalist cleric Nasir al-Omar is married to a Shi'a given his visceral hostility to Shi'ism and to Shi'as *qua* Shi'as.[2] This is not just a question of degree between moderate Sunni-centric politicians and a far more extreme fundamentalist cleric. Rather, it is a matter of substantive difference in how the meaning and significance of sectarian identity and how the lines of contestation in

---

[2] For al-Omar's views of Shi'ism, see Nasir al-Omar, *Waqi' al-Rafidha fi Bilad al-Tawhid* (The Reality of the Rafidha [Shi'a] in the Land of Monotheism), self-published, available at https://eldorar.net/science/article/13802.

sectarian competition are differently formulated from one dimension to another. Sectarian competition for a mainstream sect-centric politician in a context of acknowledged and accepted sectarian plurality is a matter of contested national truths, contested hierarchies of power, and differential access to and ownership of the nation-state; for someone like al-Omar, however, it is a matter of religious truths and doctrine. We need to be able to identify, understand and account for these and other manifestations of sectarian dynamics, and it is hoped that the multidimensional framework introduced in this book can help further that kind of conceptual flexibility.

At a more fundamental level, greater awareness of sectarian identity's multidimensionality is needed for greater accuracy and better understanding of sectarian dynamics. The importance of this can scarcely be exaggerated given the policy relevance of the subject and the reckless way in which the terminology is used in relation to conflict and politics in the contemporary Middle East. Urgently needed is a demystification of sectarian categories. This cannot be done while continuing to use the term 'sectarianism', a term so hazy that it goes beyond being merely an "essentially contested concept" (like democracy or social justice, for example) and rather becomes the subject of a definitional free-for-all in which all manner of personal preferences and political agendas can be projected onto the word.[3] To give an extreme example, in 2016 I heard a North American scholar argue, at an academic conference, that contemporary Muslim 'sectarianism' in the Middle East was a function of white supremacy. Such bizarre linkages reflect the unconstrained way in which understandings of the term are formulated. Moreover, as will be seen, the term's opacity facilitates a fetishization of sectarian identity whereby it is endowed with far more causal and explanatory power and socio-political relevance than is necessary or reasonable. In the process the term 'sectarianism' reinforces the essentialization of the Middle East as somehow different, if not aberrant, while also reinforcing conventional fallacies about the role of religion in the region. On a practical level this often leads to

---

[3] Walter Bryce Gallie, "Essentially Contested Concepts," *Proceedings of the Aristotelian Society*, 56 (1955–1956): 167–198. My thanks to Morten Valbjorn for drawing my attention to Gallie's work.

analytic misdirection towards symptoms rather than causes. A typical case in point is the tendency to view the sect-coding of patronage networks as a function of sectarian identities and sectarian loyalties while ignoring structural drivers such as under-institutionalization, endemic corruption, lack of transparency and the like. In this way sectarian identity – or more commonly 'sectarianism' – undeservedly steals the analytic limelight. Why are Donald Trump's antics and messaging considered examples of populism while his sect-centric equivalents in the Middle East are examples of 'sectarianism'? Why are patron-client networks called 'sectarianism' in Lebanon but clientelism elsewhere? Why are discriminatory, personalized hiring practices referred to as patrimonialism in some settings but 'sectarianism' where Sunnis and Shi'as are involved? Why is an Iraqi politician forming webs of personalized interest regarded as an example of 'sectarianism' while the same is referred to as 'big man politics' in sub-Saharan Africa? Not all interactions between Sunnis and Shi'as – conflictual or otherwise – are a function of sectarian dynamics and, even where they are, the relevance and role of sectarian identity need to be correctly contextualized rather than unthinkingly assumed. To paraphrase a similar critique of the concept of race, so long as we fetishize sect, we ensure we will never be rid of the hierarchies it imposes.[4]

Another aim of this book and of the multidimensional framework it introduces is to help move the discussion of sectarian relations and sectarian identity beyond the rather dated and circuitous debates that continue to dominate the field – for example, the classic and largely redundant binary between instrumentalists and primordialists or that between 'sectarianism' as religion and 'sectarianism' as politics. As will be seen in chapter 2, a lot of these are a function of the problematic nature of the term 'sectarianism' and the result of an insufficiently agile and multidimensional framing of sectarian dynamics. One such binary, one that is rarely challenged, is that between sectarian harmony and sectarian division or conflict. While reductionists will adopt a minimalist position that emphasizes the former and alarmists

---

[4] Thomas Chatterton Williams, "How Ta-Nehisi Coates gives whiteness power," *New York Times*, Oct. 6, 2017, https://www.nytimes.com/2017/10/06/opinion/ta-nehisi-coates-whiteness-power.html.

will adopt a maximalist position that overplays the latter, few consider the obvious: rather than explicit division or consciously performed ecumenism, a far more common setting in Sunni–Shi'a relations is sectarian irrelevance. Not every act of kindness or act of enmity between a Sunni and a Shi'a is animated by their sectarian identities, and not every interaction lends itself to positive or negative value judgements or sect-coding. Like other people across the world, most Sunni–Shi'a interactions are banal or transactional. Affirmations of sectarian harmony or of sectarian hate are more a feature of times of crisis; otherwise, what is more commonly being affirmed in Sunni–Shi'a interactions is mundane coexistence. As with many of the binaries that dominate the field, the unity–division binary is a false one, one that will be revisited at several junctures in this book. More broadly, the layered framework introduced here will allow us to better grasp the fluidity of sectarian identity and to encourage us to think of sectarian dynamics in terms of an ever-evolving process of identity formation and interrelation rather than a reflection of static conceptions of identity encapsulated in unhelpful binaries and meaningless terms like 'sectarianism'.

A few cautionary words as to what this book is not. It is not a history of Sunni–Shi'a relations nor is it a history of sectarian dynamics in the twenty-first century. The book is an attempt to formulate a clearer conceptual framework with which such histories can be written. In doing so, I will not be delving into the early history of the Sunni–Shi'a divide for the simple reason that I do not believe that events and disputes in the early centuries of Islam are what animate sectarian relations today. Of course, basic familiarity with this foundational background is essential but it is not the subject of this book: as will be argued, early Islamic history and the genesis of the Sunni–Shi'a divide may furnish modern sectarian competition with some of its discursive and symbolic props and some of its mobilizational tools but they are neither a causal nor an explanatory variable in Sunni–Shi'a dynamics today.[5] That is not to dismiss the relevance of history, and chapters 2

---

[5] For the early emergence of the Sunni–Shi'a divide, see, among others, Barnaby Rogerson, *The Heirs of Muhammad: Islam's First Century and the Origins of the Sunni–Shia Split* (New York: Overlook Press, 2008); Lesley Hazleton, *After the Prophet: The Epic*

to 4 make regular forays into the later medieval and, more so, early-modern periods in search of roots of and parallels to contemporary sectarian relations. However, again, this is not a work of history and I make no claim to being a medievalist or an Ottomanist. The temporal and geographic scope of this book is very specific: as already mentioned, the sects referred to throughout are only Sunni and (Twelver) Shi'a Muslims – the spectral nature of both notwithstanding – and my primary interest is in modern sectarian relations. Geographically the book is similarly restricted: while examples and parallels from beyond the Arab world and beyond Sunni–Shi'a relations will be drawn upon for comparative purposes, the book nevertheless restricts its focus to Sunni and Shi'a Muslims in the modern Arab world. Despite this relatively restricted scope there will inevitably be an element of generalization when discussing categories as immense as these. This is unavoidable but, while it is something we should approach with caution, it need not be a bar to examining Sunni–Shi'a dynamics. In other words, while nothing can be said about *all* Sunnis or *all* Shi'as, we can nevertheless sensibly identify context-dependent dominant trends in ever-fluctuating perceptions of self and other, and contingent modes of identity formation among self-professed Sunnis and Shi'as (or critical masses thereof). More to the point, even if 'Sunnis' and 'Shi'as' do not exist as coherent groups, they certainly exist as identity categories – no matter how contested, fluid, ambiguous or variously perceived – and have existed for centuries: not for nothing did Sunni medieval chroniclers – from Ibn Kathir to Ibn al-Athir to the storied Ibn Battuta – refer to Shi'as (usually by using what by then had become the derogatory term *rafidha*).[6] This does not primordialize sectarian

---

Story of the Shia–Sunni Split (New York: Anchor Books, 2010); Najam Haider, *The Origins of the Shi'a: Identity, Ritual and Sacred Space in Eighth-Century Kufa* (Cambridge: Cambridge University Press, 2014); John McHugo, *A Concise History of Sunnis and Shi'is* (London: Saqi Books, 2017).

[6] *Rafidha* (also rendered *rawafidh*, singular *rafidhi*) is a derogatory term for Shi'as. Its root is *rafdh*, meaning rejection, and is a reference to the Shi'a rejection of the first three caliphs. For the earlier, intra-Shi'a use of the term to distinguish proto-Zaydiyya from proto-Imamiyya, see Etan Kohlberg, "The Term 'Rafida' in Imami Shi'i Usage," *Journal of the American Oriental Society*, 99:4 (Oct.–Dec., 1979): 677–679. My thanks to Ahab Bdaiwi for drawing my attention to this.

identities nor is recognizing their medieval antecedents equal to essentializing them. As will be repeatedly argued throughout, while sectarian identities may have existed for centuries, their salience, relevance, meaning and content have continuously fluctuated in response to the broader context. The issue therefore is not their age or longevity, but how they have been variously constructed and mediated over time and space.

The Sunni–Shi'a divide is of course not equally relevant across the region, and the book is primarily, though not entirely, informed by the examples of Iraq, Lebanon, Bahrain and Syria. Using the conceptual framework outlined above, I try to shed light on how sectarian identities are formulated and experienced – how they 'work' – in these contexts. I should also point out that, despite my previous work on Iraq, this book is not an 'Iraq book'; rather than painting the other countries with an Iraqi brush, I endeavour to treat Iraq as one of a handful of primary points of reference (chapter 7 notwithstanding). The opening chapter of the book interrogates the term 'sectarianism' and makes the case for its abandonment. In doing so I survey the field and highlight the various ways in which the term is used and understood. The chapter will also outline why the term 'sectarianism' is not just unhelpful but actually distortive. This is fundamentally a result of the term's lack of definition and lack of boundaries combined with its assumed negativity. The chapter outlines an alternative semantic framework that does away with 'sectarianism' and also restricts the usage of 'sectarian'. Briefly, it will be argued that 'sectarian' should only be used as a prefix to other terms rather than as a stand-alone adjective ('sectarian hate', 'sectarian identity' rather than accusing someone or something of *being* 'sectarian'). Chapter 2 examines the main debates in the field and particularly the stultifying binaries that have prevented the discussion from moving on to more fertile ground. Essentially, this chapter demonstrates the need for a fundamental shift in how we think about sectarian identity. Having made the case for dropping the term 'sectarianism' and having examined the problems that characterize its attendant discussions, in chapters 3 and 4 I propose an analytical shift in focus to sectarian identity. In doing so, the two chapters outline the multidimensional, four-sided framework with which sectarian identity is best captured. Chapter 3 looks at three dimensions, doctrinal, subnational and transnational, while chapter 4 looks at the national dimension. The reason that the national dimension is given a whole chapter is partly a reflection of my own research interests but is also a reflection of the immediacy and centrality of the nation-state in political perception and socio-political contestation in the modern world. Having set the theoretical stage, in the remaining chapters I employ this framework to better understand modern sectarian dynamics. Chapter 5 examines the overlooked question of demographics and how conceptions of minorities and majorities have influenced sectarian identity formation and sectarian relations. In doing so, this chapter challenges the false equivalence that is often assumed to apply across the spectrum of Sunni–Shi'a relations. The last two chapters are more case study focused. Chapter 6 looks at the sectarian wave that followed the invasion of Iraq in 2003 and how it transformed sectarian relations and inflated the relevance of sectarian categories in the Middle East and beyond. The final chapter takes modern Iraq as a case study with which to demonstrate many of the themes of the book and with which to illustrate the variable, multidimensional and context-dependent nature of sectarian dynamics. It will also discuss not just the drivers of sectarian entrenchment after 2003 but also the drivers of its retreat in recent years. In this way, the multidimensional model introduced here will help us not just understand the manner in which sectarian relations come to be inflamed but also shed light on the reverse: the de-escalation of sectarian conflict, how sectarian identities lose relevance and how banal coexistence is recaptured.

Finally, to pre-empt criticism of what some may see as an omission: the Islamic State or ISIS does not feature in any significant way in this book – neither conceptually nor in the chapters looking at the post-2003 Middle East. As will be argued throughout, a key characteristic of modern sectarian relations is the paradoxical dialectic between unity and division: the normative value attached to Islamic or national unity versus the imperatives of sect-specificity. This furnishes sectarian relations with both centripetal and centrifugal characteristics, with the dialectic relation between Islamic unity and sect-specificity placing limits on the conceivable extent of both unity and division. Such contradictions are hardly unique to Sunni–Shi'a relations. A pertinent parallel can be found in the way national identities and regional variances in the Arab world interact with the concept of pan-Arab identity. The late philosopher Muhammad al-Jabiri's summation of the dialectic nature of Arab unity–division is equally applicable to the sectarian divide: "regional [or, for our purposes, sectarian] idiosyncrasies compete with the pan-national [pan-Islamic] whole – but without either the parts or the whole seeking to cancel or negate each other. Such a negation would be a self-defeating act, because the existence of one is dependent and conditional on that of the other."[7] The countries and cases surveyed in this book illustrate the intertwinement of sectarian plurality with normative conceptions of Islam and of nationalism that ultimately serve to position sectarian identities as subsidiary to larger religious and national frames that are themselves subject to internal contestation. As will be seen, this inner tension between unity and division, between sect-specificity and Islamic oneness or sect-blind conceptions of nationalism, is highly elastic in that sectarian relations can be calmed or inflamed but remain highly resistant to a definitive break between Sunnis/Sunnism and Shi'as/Shi'ism without a significant redefinition of what constitutes the parameters of mainstream modern, global Islam and barring a major redefinition of what constitutes acceptable forms of nationalism in the countries surveyed. The extreme case of the Islamic State and their unequivocal, genocidal even, rejection of sectarian plurality is what makes them unusual, though not necessarily unprecedented, in the history of sectarian relations and particularly in the contexts of modern Iraq and Syria.[8] Ultimately, the Islamic State was a symptom of

---

[7] Muhammad al-Jabiri, *Takwin al-Aql al-Arabi* (The Formation of the Arabic Mind) (Beirut: Centre for Arab Unity Studies, 2006), p. 52. Quoted in Tim Mackintosh-Smith, *Arabs: A 3,000 Year History of Peoples, Tribes and Empires* (New Haven: Yale University Press, 2019), p. 456.

[8] The rise of Wahhabism in the Arabian Peninsula in the eighteenth to twentieth centuries is a case in point. For the parallels with the Islamic State/ISIS, see Cole Bunzel, "The Kingdom and the Caliphate: Saudi Arabia and the Islamic State," in *Beyond Sunni and Shia: The Roots of Sectarianism in a Changing Middle East*, ed. Frederic Wehrey (London: Hurst & Co., 2017). The term Wahhabi is derived from eighteenth-century Islamic scholar Muhammad ibn Abd al-Wahhab. He advocated an extreme form of Hanbali Sunni Islam that condemned all but a narrowly defined conception of Islam and was intrinsically anti-Shi'a. Abd al-Wahhab was instrumental in the rise of the first Saudi state following his alliance with Muhammad bin Saud. That alliance

a broader enabling environment that empowered what was otherwise an anomaly in sectarian relations. My interest lies in understanding the evolution of that environment rather than the exceptional demons that it created.

---

continued and aided in the survival and resurrection of the Saudi Arabian state. The term Wahhabiyya (or Wahhabism) and its derivative Wahhabi are derogatory terms that are not used self-referentially. The term is better understood as a reference to a political formation (the extreme Hanbalism of the Saudi clergy and the political patronage they receive) rather than a clearly demarcated doctrinal current. In practice, however, and especially in common Shi'a parlance, Wahhabism is often used as a synonym for anti-Shi'a Sunnism and for Salafis more generally.

1

WHAT IS 'SECTARIANISM'?

Given the ubiquity of the concept of 'sectarianism' (and its Arabic equivalent 'ta'ifiyya') in commentary and opinion on the contemporary Middle East – be it as an all-purpose explainer for the region or as an example of the nefarious machinations of Orientalists and neo-imperialists – it is astounding how little attention has been paid to defining what exactly is entailed by 'sectarianism'. Particularly since the invasion of Iraq in 2003, there have been a number of intense debates involving 'sectarianism'. Does it exist? What are its drivers? What role does it play? How much can it explain? And so forth. Yet in the vast majority of cases, no attempt is made to first identify what 'sectarianism' actually is. How can we possibly pin down the causes, drivers and associated variables of a phenomenon if we neglect to define it? It is this oversight that renders 'sectarianism' one of the most commented upon yet understudied subjects today. With no agreement as to what it is that is being analysed, trying to understand 'sectarianism' today, as it relates to the modern Middle East, is akin to trying to understand a slogan, the meanings of which are left to the beholder.

It is therefore scarcely surprising that the terms 'sectarianism' and 'ta'ifiyya' are versatile to the point of incoherence. They can be used as nouns, for example: the Arab world in the twenty-first century is "characterized by open and discomforting sectarianism."[1] They can be used to describe an act, as in "practising sectarianism."[2] Similarly, for some scholars, 'sectarianism' is a state policy, something to be implemented rather than a social or religious phenomenon. For example, one study defines 'sectarianism' as "the promotion and deliberate deployment of sect-based allegiance in the pursuit of political ends."[3] In other cases the terms are used to refer to a system of government whereby 'sectarianism' becomes "the division of the state into separate communities based on their ethnic and/or religious affiliations."[4] This highly restrictive understanding of 'sectarianism' is particularly prevalent in the Arabic literature on Lebanon where *'ta'ifiyya'* is often a byword for the Lebanese political system.[5] Some scholars portray elites manipulating and politicizing a pre-existing 'sectarianism' while others frame the matter as the end result of the politicization of sectarian identities.[6] And so the various usages of 'sectarianism' continue to proliferate.

More than just a matter of academic interest and semantics, the term 'sectarianism' is not just incoherent but dangerously distortive.

---

[1] Rainer Brunner, "Sunnites and Shiites in Modern Islam: Politics, Rapprochement and the Role of al-Azhar," in *The Dynamics of Sunni–Shia Relationships: Doctrine, Transnationalism, Intellectuals and the Media*, ed. Brigitte Marechal and Sami Zemni (London: Hurst & Co., 2012), p. 27.

[2] For example, "a person ... practises sectarianism [*yumaris al-ta'ifiyya*] in service of ends that may not be sectarian." Yassin al-Haj Salih, "al-Ta'ifiyya wa-l-Siyasa fi Syria" (Sectarianism and Politics in Syria), in *Nawasib wa Rawafidh*, ed. Hazim Saghiya (Beirut: Dar al-Saqi, 2009), p. 77.

[3] Fatima Ayub, "Introduction," in European Council on Foreign Relations, *The Gulf and Sectarianism*, Gulf Analysis, Nov. 2013, p. 2.

[4] Orit Bashkin, "'Religious Hatred Shall Disappear from the Land': Iraqi Jews as Ottoman Subjects, 1864–1913," *International Journal of Contemporary Iraqi Studies*, 4:3 (2010): 306.

[5] Whereby "*al-ta'ifiyya fi Lubnan*" refers to the system of communal apportionment in politics. See, for example, the term's usage in Ahmed al-Zu'bi, "al-Ta'ifiyya wa Mushkilat Bina' al-Dawla fi Lubnan" (Sectarianism and the Problem of State-Building in Lebanon), in *Al-Ta'ifiyya: Sahwat al-Fitna al-Na'ima* (Sectarianism: Awakening the Dormant Discord), al-Mesbar Studies and Research Centre (Beirut: Madarek, 2010).

[6] See, for example, Abd al-Khaliq Nasir Shuman, *Al-Ta'ifiyya al-Siyasiyya fi-l-Iraq: al-Ahd al-Jumhuri, 1958–1991* (Political Sectarianism in Iraq: The Republican Era, 1958–1991) (London: Dar al-Hikma, 2013), pp. 12–15.

This is primarily a function of ambiguity combined with emotive negativity: the ambiguity maximizes the term's usages, thereby lending it a shape-shifting quality that allows it to be deployed in all manner of contexts, while the negativity sharpens the term's utility as a political tool. As will be shown, this combination of ambiguity and negativity has allowed the term 'sectarianism' to be used to marginalize enemies, delegitimize political opposition, mobilize supporters, punish nonconformity and stigmatize sectarian outgroups. Moreover, its lack of definition coupled with its recklessly widespread usage has seen 'sectarianism' used to stigmatize what are in fact perfectly legitimate expressions of sectarian identity and legitimate forms of sect-centricity. Furthermore, the field's barely critical reliance on 'sectarianism' has hindered our understanding of sectarian identity and the dynamics of sectarian relations. Finally, the boundless quality of the term has allowed it to obscure other variables in the study of state and society in the contemporary Middle East whereby anything that could be even remotely associated with sectarian identity is likely to be consumed by the gravitational pull of a negatively charged, value-laden and undefined 'sectarianism'. In that way, an ever-multiplying set of variables – socio-economic inequalities, regional variations, local dynamics, religious dogma, geostrategic considerations and so the list goes on – is liable to be subsumed by the presumptively self-explanatory illustrative power of the term 'sectarianism'.

Despite the patently problematic, accusatory and morally charged nature of the term, relatively few scholars and even fewer commentators see any need to explore the definition of 'sectarianism' or to try to ring-fence what the term means. Surveying over 200 studies on 'sectarianism' or 'ta'ifiyya', I found that close to 70 per cent made no attempt to define the term.[7] Beyond what might be regarded as benign laziness or intellectual inertia, one sometimes encounters resistance to attempts to define or find alternatives to 'sectarianism'.

---

[7] This is a continuation of an earlier survey I conducted for my article in the *Middle East Journal* (2017) on which this chapter is based. The original survey looked at 125 works (63 in Arabic and 62 in English) and found that 83 left the terms undefined. The extension of that survey takes in 202 studies (80 in Arabic and 122 in English), 138 of which leave the terms undefined.

At an academic gathering not too long ago, a senior scholar dismissed the need to define 'sectarianism' by paraphrasing an American judge's opinion of what constituted 'hard-core pornography': "when you see it, you will know."[8] While it succeeded in getting a laugh from those in attendance, this simplistic quip was highly misplaced: unlike hard-core pornography, 'sectarianism' is a term that pervades policy discussions of the Middle East and is a concept whose meaning has proven highly divisive within the region. To illustrate, the divided popular response in the Arab world towards mass demonstrations in Bahrain and Syria in 2011 showed that there clearly was considerable disagreement as to what constituted 'sectarianism'. Likewise, there have long been differences over whether or not, and in what context, certain sect-specific rituals and expressions of sectarian identity constitute 'sectarianism'. These examples have had a real impact on identity formation and sectarian relations in the Arab world. Rather than being as obvious as hard-core pornography, the term 'sectarianism' is as multifaceted and ambiguous as identity itself. As will be amply illustrated, that ambiguity, coupled with the unrelenting negativity associated with the term, has turned it into a tool for political exclusion and social division. Like the above-mentioned senior scholar, many people are inclined to breathe a sigh of despondency when the matter of defining 'sectarianism' comes up, primarily because the concept seems so clear in their own heads. The obvious thing to point out is that no matter how clear and uncontested a concept might be to one's own mind, we cannot assume that others share our understanding of such an elastic term. Most importantly, however, it is the tangible consequences of the policy relevance and misuses of 'sectarianism' that make the issue of its definition so important.

Rather than trying to define 'sectarianism', I believe that the term urgently needs to be discarded: it is too politicized, overused, mired in

---

[8] The comment was made at a workshop in a North American institution in 2015. The quote is from *Jacobellis v. Ohio* (1964): "I shall not today attempt further to define the kinds of material I understand to be embraced within that shorthand description [hard-core pornography]; and perhaps I could never succeed in intelligibly doing so. But I know it when I see it, and the motion picture involved in this case is not that." For full details, see https://supreme.justia.com/cases/federal/us/378/184/case.html

negativity, and emotionally charged for it to be salvageable. In today's usage, 'sectarianism' can cover anything from benign sect-specificity to intercommunal violence, and the term leaves too much room for subjective interpretation and personal whim for it to be useful as a category of scholarly inquiry.[9] It is important to note that what is being questioned here is not the relevance of sectarian identities and their associated meanings, relationships and dynamics to the study of the contemporary Middle East, but the vocabulary used in relation to the subject. As such, what is being suggested is an alternative lexical framework that can help us better unpack the catch-all term 'sectarianism'. In most cases, this can easily be done by using the word 'sectarian' as a qualifier: sectarian relations, sectarian harmony, sectarian cooperation, sectarian conflict, and so forth. However, some aspects of sectarian identity can be more clearly identified. For example, if we want to refer to a symbol associated with a sect, we should refrain from using the term 'sectarian symbol', lest we tar what may be a perfectly legitimate symbol of a particular sect with the stigmatizing, hate-associated brush of 'sectarianism'. In such cases, the term 'sect-specific' would be more accurate and less ambiguous. Likewise, in other contexts, 'sect-centric' can serve the same purpose of increasing clarity and avoiding what could be misconstrued as value judgements: referring to a political party that represents a sect-specific constituency as a 'sect-centric party' is far less problematic than referring to it as a 'sectarian party', which can mean anything from a party marked by sect-specificity to one that promotes hatred of others.

It should be highlighted from the outset that what follows is not a critique of the scholars cited; rather, it is a critique of the term 'sectarianism' itself. The usage of the term does not detract from the value of the scholarly contributions examined here; indeed, many of

---

[9] An interesting example can be found in the comments of one of Pierret's Syrian informants in which 'sectarianism' is used in the same breath to refer to both the burning of mosques and to the commemoration of the first intra-Muslim battle in 657 CE: "In two days, around two hundred mosques have been burnt in Iraq ... I have received an invitation to attend the celebration of the battle of Siffin in Raqqa! [He yells] Siffin!! ... Sectarianism infiltrates from the East ..." Thomas Pierret, "Karbala in the Umayyad Mosque: Sunni Panic at the 'Shiitization' of Syria in the 2000s," in *The Dynamics of Sunni–Shia Relationships*, ed. Marechal and Zemni, p. 108.

the works cited are among the most valuable scholarly works on the dynamics of Sunni–Shi'a relations. Rather than detracting from the work of the scholars cited here, the aim is to question the validity of the term 'sectarianism' in scholarly inquiry and to question the term's coherence, relevance, utility and applicability.

'Sectarianism' / 'Ta'ifiyya': A Definitional Free-for-All

The literature on 'sectarianism' has grown exponentially since 2003. Today, we perhaps have a better understanding of sectarian dynamics in the Middle East than ever before. Yet even the most valuable contributions, though they might excel at exploring a specific mechanism of sectarian relations or some of the ways in which sectarian dynamics come to gain political relevance, are nevertheless stymied by their failure to adequately define 'sectarianism'. At times 'sect' and the Arabic *'ta'ifa'* are defined at great length, while 'sectarianism' and *'ta'ifiyya'* escape scrutiny. We have a clear example of this in Khalil Osman's 2015 study of sectarian relations in Iraq wherein he states, "the obvious question that now arises is: what is sectarianism?" He then provides us with a masterful treatment of the terms 'sect' and *'ta'ifa'* before seamlessly switching to 'sectarianism', which is left undefined.[10] One can only surmise that in such cases scholars assume that, having defined 'sect', the meaning of 'sectarianism' becomes self-evident. Indeed one author explicitly makes this very point by arguing that "*ta'ifiyya* as it relates to *ta'ifa* is the same as Egypt in relation to Egyptian."[11] However, the multiple manifestations of sectarian identity and sectarian relations are far too vast to be subsumed by one elastic and highly charged term. To illustrate, if we were to agree that 'sectarianism' is that which relates to 'sect', then it would naturally follow that the word's meaning would encompass a spectrum stretching from beliefs, rituals, symbols and solidarities all the way to sect-based discrimination, active hatred and violence.

---

[10] Khalil F. Osman, *Sectarianism in Iraq: The Making of a Nation since 1920* (London: Routledge, 2015), pp. 39–42.

[11] Ahmed Rasim al-Nifis, "al-Ta'ifiyya al-Unsuriyya" (Racist Sectarianism), *Shu'un Mashriqiyya*, 1:1 (Summer 2008): 44.

While attempts to define 'sectarianism'/*ta'ifiyya* are relatively rare or superficial, it is nevertheless possible to identify, through direct or inferred meaning, several conflicting ways in which the terms are employed. One approach involves a very expansive understanding, using the terms to encompass virtually everything related to sectarian identity.[12] In some of these cases, one finds 'sectarian' and 'sectarianism' being used synonymously. In other instances the scope is broadened to encompass much more than religious or subreligious categories, with 'sectarianism' being used to refer to antagonisms between any set of subnational groups – be they religious, subreligious, ethnic, political or regional – thereby rendering the term meaningless.[13] Another less restrictive use of the term refers to varying forms of sect-centricity.[14] Another approach uses 'sectarianism' in a more restrictive fashion that

---

[12] Osman, *Sectarianism in Iraq*; Harith Hasan al-Qarawee, "Heightened Sectarianism in the Middle East: Causes, Dynamics and Consequences," Italian Institute for International Political Studies, Analysis no. 205, Nov. 2013; Issam Nu'man, "al-Munaqashat" (Debates), in *Al-Ta'ifiyya wa-l-Tasamuh wa-l-Adala al-Intiqaliyya: min al-Fitna ila Dawlat al-Qanun* (Sectarianism, Tolerance and Transitional Justice: From Discord to the State of Law), ed. Abd al-Ilah Bilqiz (Beirut: Centre for Arab Unity Studies, 2013); Farian Sabahi, "Iran, Iranian Media and Sunnite Islam," in *The Dynamics of Sunni–Shia Relationships*, ed. Marechal and Zemni.

[13] Al-Nifis, "al-Ta'ifiyya al-Unsuriyya" and Mahdi al-Shar', "al-Mukawinat al-Siyasiyya li-l-Ta'ifiyya fi-l-Iraq" (The Political Components of Sectarianism in Iraq), *Shu'un Mashriqiyya*, 1:1 (Summer 2008); Tareq Y. Ismael and Jacqueline S. Ismael, "The Sectarian State in Iraq and the New Political Class," *International Journal of Contemporary Iraqi Studies*, 4:3 (Dec. 2010); Rashid al-Khayyun, *Dhid al-Ta'ifiyya: Al-Iraq – Jadal ma Ba'd Nisan 2003* (Against Sectarianism: Iraq – The Post-April 2003 Debate) (Beirut: Madarek, 2011); Lawrence G. Potter, "Introduction," in *Sectarian Politics in the Persian Gulf*, ed. Lawrence G. Potter (London: Hurst & Co., 2013).

[14] Sulayman Taqi al-Din, "al-Ta'ifiyya wa-l-Mathhabiyya wa Atharuhuma al-Siyasiyya" (Sectarianism, *Mathhabiyya* and their Political Influences), in *Al-Ta'ifiyya wa-l-Tasamuh*, ed. Bilqiz; Elisheva Machlis, *Shi'i Sectarianism in the Middle East: Modernisation and the Quest for Islamic Universalism* (London: I.B. Tauris, 2014). Peter Sluglett wrote that the term refers to "a state of mind in which the religious or sectarian affiliation into which an individual was born ... has come to dominate his or her other identities and in which he/she may join together with 'co-religionists' against members of 'other' religions or sects, usually in order to obtain, or deny, political representation or political rights." From "The British, the Sunnis and the Shi'is: Social Hierarchies of Identity under the British Mandate," *International Journal of Contemporary Iraqi Studies*, 4:3 (Dec. 2010): 258 n1.

frames it as the sect-based equivalent of racism.[15] More narrowly still, there is a body of literature – particularly but not exclusively pertaining to Lebanon – that takes 'sectarianism' to mean a political system based on religious or ethnic identities.[16] Finally, some scholars have approached defining 'sectarianism' by providing multilayered definitions for the term.[17] These works often include a typology that differentiates between different kinds of 'sectarianism' and do not restrict themselves to a singular definition.[18] While such attempts may have enriched

---

[15] Abbas Kadhim, "Efforts at Cross-Ethnic Cooperation: The 1920 Revolution and Sectarian Identities in Iraq," *International Journal of Contemporary Iraqi Studies*, 4:3 (Dec. 2010): 275–294; Muhammad al-Sadr, *Al-Ta'ifiyya fi Nadhar al-Islam* (Sectarianism in the Eyes of Islam) (Beirut: Dar wa Maktabat al-Basa'ir, 2013); Antun Daw, "al-Munaqashat" (Debates), in *Al-Ta'ifiyya wa-l-Tasamuh*, ed. Bilqiz; Roel Meijer and Joas Wagemakers, "The Struggle for Citizenship of the Shiites of Saudi Arabia," in *The Dynamics of Sunni–Shia Relationships*, ed. Marechal and Zemni; Hasan bin Musa al-Saffar, *Al-Ta'ifiyya Bayn al-Siyasa wa-l-Din* (Sectarianism between Politics and Religion) (Casablanca: al-Markaz al-Thaqafi al-Arabi, 2009).

[16] One study defines *ta'ifiyya* as referring to "a confessional order in which a system of proportional power sharing between different religious groups is instituted as in Lebanon." Brigitte Marechal and Sami Zemni, "Introduction: Evaluating Contemporary Sunnite–Shiite Relations; Changing Identities, Political Projects, Interactions and Theological Discussions," in *The Dynamics of Sunni–Shia Relationships*, ed. Marechal and Zemni, p. 253 n4. Other works that adopt a similar approach include Bashkin, "Religious Hatred Shall Disappear"; al-Zu'bi, "Al-Ta'ifiyya wa Mushkilat Bina' al-Dawla fi Lubnan" in *Al-Ta'ifiyya*, ed. al-Mesbar.

[17] Abd al-Ilah Bilqiz, "Muqadima" (Introduction) and "al-Munaqashat" (Debates) in *Al-Ta'ifiyya wa-l-Tasamuh*, ed. Bilqiz; Farhad Ibrahim, *Al-Ta'ifiyya wa-l-Siyasiyya fi-l-Alam al-Arabi: Namudhaj al-Shi'a fi-l-Iraq* (Sectarianism and Politics in the Arab World: The Example of the Shi'a in Iraq) (Cairo: Madbouly, 1996); Justin J. Gengler, "Understanding Sectarianism in the Persian Gulf," in *Sectarian Politics in the Persian Gulf*, ed. Potter; John Warner, "Questioning Sectarianism in Bahrain and Beyond: An Interview with Justin Gengler," *Jadaliyya*, April 17, 2013, www.jadaliyya.com/pages/index/11267/questioning-sectarianism-in-bahrain-and-beyond_an-n; Vali R. Nasr, "International Politics, Domestic Imperatives, and Identity Mobilization: Sectarianism in Pakistan, 1979–1998," *Comparative Politics*, 32:2 (Jan. 2000): 171–190.

[18] Max Weiss, *In the Shadow of Sectarianism: Law, Shiism, and the Making of Modern Lebanon* (Cambridge: Harvard University Press, 2010), pp. 2–3, 11–15; Fanar Haddad, *Sectarianism in Iraq: Antagonistic Visions of Unity* (London: Hurst & Co., 2011), pp. 25–29.

our understanding of sectarian dynamics, the term remains too problematic to pin down. For instance, some scholars have tried to identify different types of 'sectarianism', such as 'social sectarianism', 'violent sectarianism', and so forth. However, this inevitably leaves us wondering what 'sectarianism' is, without the modifier.

Some have attempted to resolve this lexical awkwardness by restricting their portrayal of 'sectarianism' to the intersection of sectarian identities and politics. This is by far the most popular approach to the subject: it is neat and manageable and highlights the fact that much of what is referred to as 'sectarianism' is indeed a function of modern politics rather than ancient religions. This approach can yield elegant, clearly demarcated understandings of 'sectarianism' such as in Makdisi's definition: "sectarianism refers to the deployment of religious heritage as a primary marker of modern political identity."[19] As appealing as this approach might be however, it cannot rein in the inherent unwieldiness of the term 'sectarianism' nor can it unpack its many meanings. There are at least three issues with any definition of 'sectarianism' that strictly focuses on the intersection between politics and sectarian identity. Firstly, it immediately raises a chicken-or-egg conundrum: does 'sectarianism' exist *outside* politics and prior to politicization or is it the *product* of politics? For example, Rashid al-Khayyun writes of "the political utilization of sectarianism," thereby suggesting that 'sectarianism' exists independently of and prior to politicization.[20] More commonly, other writers would suggest that 'sectarianism' is the product of the politicization of sectarian identities. Rather egregiously, there is nothing to suggest that this divergence forms two sides of a debate; rather, it is a result of the incoherence of the vocabulary and the careless way in which it is employed in the field. Secondly, this approach carries an inherent tendency to view sectarian dynamics from above: since it focuses on politics and politicization, one sees this approach often – though by no means always – overly focusing

---

[19] Ussama Makdisi, *The Culture of Sectarianism: Community, History, and Violence in Nineteenth-Century Ottoman Lebanon* (Berkeley: University of California Press, 2000), p. 7.

[20] Rashid al-Khayyun, "al-Iraq: Tawdhif al-Ta'ifiyya Siyasiyyan," in *Al-Ta'ifiyya*, ed. al-Mesbar.

on political power. Hence it is often suggested that 'sectarianism' is a product of this or that nefarious state power that has utilized sects for political ends.[21] Framing 'sectarianism' as something wielded by powerful political actors and unleashed upon helpless people may account for some of the popularity of this approach in that it exonerates society (and religion) from the grievous (though largely undefined) charge of 'sectarianism'.

Finally, the third problem with restricting our understanding of 'sectarianism' to the confluence of sectarian identity and politics is that it can end up excluding religion, religious dogma, questions of religious orthodoxy, and religious ideas. For example, could a strict interpretation of 'sectarianism' as political instrumentalization of sectarian identities explain popular sect-based prejudices or clerical injunctions urging sectarian enmity on the basis of *doctrinal* otherness?[22] If we insist on retaining the term, is it feasible to exclude such instances from our understanding of 'sectarianism'?[23]

Sectarian dynamics are not restricted to politics any more than they are restricted to faith and doctrine: too narrow a focus on politics ends up overlooking important factors in the realm of perceived religious truths just as too narrow a focus on religious dogma ends up overlooking the political dimension of sectarian relations and sectarian competition. This is well illustrated in a 2014 op-ed by political scientist Thomas Pierret, which criticized a leaked

---

[21] See overview of Arabic commentary on the subject in Frederic M. Wehrey, *Sectarian Politics in the Gulf: From the Iraq War to the Arab Uprisings* (New York: Columbia University Press, 2014), pp. x–xi.

[22] For example, the concept of *al-wala' wa-l-bara'* (loyalty and disavowal; i.e., embracing that which upholds Islam and opposing that which opposes it) has been used by some religious scholars to frame the sectarian other as an enemy of the faith who, at the very least, must be ostracized. Likewise, in some Shi'a circles, enmity toward many of the Prophet Muhammad's companions is seen as a religious duty. In turn, this is used by some Sunni scholars as grounds for obligatory enmity towards Shi'as.

[23] To illustrate, one scholar wrote of "the rise of sectarianism (as opposed to religious rivalry)." This entails the exclusion of intense, often poisonous and widely prevalent Sunni–Shi'a religious polemics from the study of 'sectarianism'. Bassam Yousif, "The Political Economy of Sectarianism in Iraq," *International Journal of Contemporary Iraqi Studies*, 4:3 (Dec. 2010): 357.

report by journalist Nir Rosen for writing that the Syrian regime was "not sectarian."[24] The elasticity of the term 'sectarianism' allowed Rosen to argue that the Syrian regime is not sectarian because it is not composed of sect-centric religious fanatics while simultaneously allowing Pierret to argue that the point is irrelevant given the Syrian regime's routine manipulation of sectarian divides. In the absence of clear definitions, both positions can seem coherent: the more one associates 'sectarianism' with doctrinal religion, the more Rosen's view makes sense; and the more one includes the social and political existence of religious communities, the more cogent Pierret's becomes. Ultimately, as with much relating to 'sectarianism', the absence of clear definitions means that such questions are often left to the individual's personal preference.

Here an important point presents itself. When trying to identify what is sectarian and what is 'sectarianism', the oft-paraded dichotomy between the religious and the secular is of little use. This is particularly true with regard to sectarian dynamics in the age of the nation-state, when sectarian competition can be animated by contested *national* truths as much as, if not more than, religious ones – hence the redundancy of the presumed polarity between national/nationalism and sectarian/'sectarianism' (see chapter 4). As witnessed in modern Syria, Iraq, Lebanon and Bahrain, sectarian solidarities and sectarian prejudices can be influenced far more by considerations of class, regionalism and locality rather than by dogma or jurisprudence. In that sense, secular people, even committed atheists, can be 'sectarian' in the sense of harbouring deep prejudices against a particular sect.[25] If we reconsider Makdisi's definition, not only can political behaviour be sect-centric (and thereby perceived as 'sectarian') without "the deployment of religious heritage as a primary marker of modern political identity," it can also be sect-centric while standing militantly against any such deployment.

---

[24] Thomas Pierret, "On Nir Rosen's Definitions of 'Sectarian' and 'Secular'," *Pulse*, Dec. 23, 2014, https://pulsemedia.org/2014/12/23/on-nir-rosens-definitions-of-sectarian-and-secular/

[25] For more on this theme, see Fanar Haddad, "Secular Sectarians," Middle East Institute, Middle East–Asia Project, *Sectarianism in the Middle East and Asia*, June 17, 2014, www.mei.edu/content/map/secular-sectarians

This is most vividly demonstrated in the make-up and policies of the Arab Socialist Ba'th Party regimes in both Syria (1963–) and Iraq (1968–2003). In both cases, religious heritage was not deployed as a marker of political identity, nor were conceptions of religious orthodoxy a precondition for political inclusion; on the contrary, both regimes displayed a paranoid aversion to displays of sect-specificity. Yet this aversion did not prevent the ruling parties of both Syria and Iraq from exhibiting various degrees of sect-centricity. This was not solely a function of sectarian identity as the misnomers "Alawi regime" and "Sunni regime" would suggest; rather, it was a function of tribal, regional and class solidarities as well. Both regimes have been accused of sect-centricity and of 'sectarianism', but less because they have asserted a particular sectarian identity and more because they sustained a set of power relations that favoured one sectarian group (or, more specifically, tribal and regional subsets thereof), while suppressing and stigmatizing others.[26] In short, the cases of the Syrian and Iraqi Ba'th parties illustrate how neither a professed secularism nor an aversion to displays of sect-specificity could, in and of themselves, prevent sect-centricity or stifle perceptions of 'sectarianism'.

Perhaps to overcome such issues, some scholars have opted for an expansive understanding of the terms 'sectarian' and 'sectarianism'. While this ensures that all facets of sectarian dynamics are included, it also serves to further obscure our understanding of the terminology. In this we are reminded of anthropologist Jack Goody's lament that

---

[26] For a nuanced treatment of the role of sectarian identity in the Syrian and (post-1968) Iraqi Ba'th parties, see Nikolaos van Dam, "Middle Eastern Political Cliches: 'Takriti' and 'Sunni Rule' in Iraq; 'Alawi Rule' in Syria; A Critical Appraisal," *Orient: German Journal for Politics and Economics of the Middle East*, 21:1 (Jan. 1980): 42–57. For more on this theme in the Syrian context, see Nikolaos van Dam, *The Struggle for Power in Syria: Sectarianism, Regionalism and Tribalism in Politics, 1961–1980* (London: Croom Helm, 1981), pp. 25–27; Raymond Hinnebusch, "Syria's Alawis and the Ba'ath Party," in *The Alawis of Syria: War, Faith and Politics in the Levant*, ed. Michael Kerr and Craig Larkin (New York: Oxford University Press, 2015), pp. 114–15. On the Iraqi context, see Hanna Batatu, *The Old Social Classes and the Revolutionary Movements of Iraq: A Study of Iraq's Old Landed and Commercial Classes and of Its Communists, Ba'thists and Free Officers* (Princeton: Princeton University Press, 1978), pp. 1078–1093.

the term 'ethnic' had lost meaning by becoming a catch-all phrase. Or as he put it:

> The term 'ethnic' has become a cant word in the social sciences and often in everyday speech, where it is frequently used in a blanket fashion to refer to any collective grouping with a semblance of homogeneity ... The concept of ethnicity has been so widely taken up because it gets around the problem of defining what it is that makes a people – that is, an ethnos – distinctive ... Ethnicity covers all as well as covering up all.[27]

The terms 'sect', 'sectarian', and particularly 'sectarianism' are similarly shape-shifting and have been used to refer to all manner of phenomena and groups, not just religious subdivisions. For example, one 2013 analysis states that "Regional events this year necessitated a sharp swing from Shi'ism to Sunni political Islam as the target of Saudi state sectarianism..."[28]

This blurring of the contours of 'sectarianism' is far from atypical. Some scholars have used the term to refer both to subreligious divisions (Sunni–Shi'a for example) and to ethno-linguistic or ethno-national divisions such as the Arab–Kurdish divide.[29] Some scholars have even included political divides (such as fascists versus leftists) alongside religious or subreligious divisions in their usage of 'sectarianism'.[30] Others have extended the term's meaning to include any intolerance shown toward any group, "be it on the basis of social class, on the basis

---

[27] Jack Goody, "Bitter Icons," *New Left Review*, no. 7 (Jan.–Feb. 2001): 8.

[28] Andrew Hammond, "Saudi Arabia: Cultivating Sectarian Spaces," in European Council on Foreign Relations, *The Gulf and Sectarianism*, 2013, p. 9.

[29] For example, Eric Davis, "Introduction: The Question of Sectarian Identities in Iraq," *International Journal of Contemporary Iraqi Studies*, 4:3 (Dec. 2010): 234. Michael Mitchell, "Iraq Is Collapsing: It's Time to Reshape the Middle East Map," Canadian Defence and Foreign Affairs Institute, Policy Update, Nov. 2014; Zack Beauchamp, "America's Kurdish Problem: Today's Allies against ISIS Are Tomorrow's Headache," *Vox*, April 8, 2016, www.vox.com/2016/4/8/11377314/america-kurds-problem; Tom Coghlan and Lucinda Smith, "Kurd Land Grab Deepens Sectarian Divide in Syria," *The Times*, Aug. 18, 2016, www.thetimes.co.uk/article/kurd-land-grab-deepens-sectarian-divide-in-syria-lc7mjh7hp

[30] Brigitte Marechal and Sami Zemni, "Conclusion: Analysing Contemporary Sunnite–Shiite Relationships," in *The Dynamics of Sunni–Shia Relationships*, ed. Marechal and Zemni, p. 308 n39.

of profession or colour or even opinion, tribe, gender."[31] In one case, we see three different definitions given for 'sectarianism' in a single study: firstly, as "strict, extreme adherence to a sect, party, or group"; secondly, as the use of religious diversity for political, economic or cultural goals; and, most egregiously, 'sectarianism' is finally defined as "the politicization of sectarianism (*tasyis al-ta'ifiyya*)."[32] Even in some of the most analytically valuable cases, the term's malleability sees it used with reference to myriad manifestations of sectarian identities and sectarian dynamics. An insightful 2013 examination of sectarian dynamics in the contemporary Middle East by Harith Hasan al-Qarawee offers an illustrative example. While al-Qarawee did not clarify the criteria for what constitutes 'sectarianism', it is clear that at the most basic level, he used the term to denote both sect-specific mobilization and heightened sectarian solidarity. However, when the existence and relevance of 'sectarianism' in pre-2003 Iraq is mentioned in the article, it is not clear whether the term entails sect-centricity or whether it is restricted to active sectarian mobilization. Is it only *antagonistic* sectarian solidarities that define 'sectarianism' or would a rising tendency to self-identify according to sectarian categories also qualify, even if the identifications were not hostile? In places, belligerence across sectarian lines is emphasized as a defining feature, while in others solidarity within sects is emphasized.[33]

As already mentioned, some scholars take an approach to 'sectarianism' that mirrors popular understandings of racism. An illustrative example of this paradigm defines 'sectarianism' as "feelings of narrow-minded prejudice, which often result in intolerance,

---

[31] Khayyun, *Dhid al-Ta'ifiyya*, p. 7. More often, this expansive approach is restricted to religious, ethnic and tribal divisions; see Potter, "Introduction," pp. 1–2.

[32] Shar', "al-Mukawinat al-Siyasiyya," pp. 95, 102, 113. The final definition highlights an additional complication in our understanding of the Arabic word *ta'ifiyya* in that it is both the word for 'sectarianism' and the feminine singular (and also nonhuman plural) form of *ta'ifi* (sectarian) – as in *qadhiyya ta'ifiyya* (sectarian issue) and *qawanin ta'ifiyya* (sectarian laws).

[33] Al-Qarawee, "Heightened Sectarianism," pp. 4, 5, 10, 12. Another example of an excellent treatment of sectarian dynamics that nevertheless uses the term 'sectarianism' to refer to a range of issues relating to sectarian relations is Nasr, "International Politics, Domestic Imperatives," pp. 171–190.

discrimination and hatred towards people of other religious sects or ethnic groups."[34] This approach might one day potentially yield fruit to the study of sectarian relations, if and when it catches up with the sophistication of the far more developed literature on race, race relations, and critical race theory. For example, studies of racism not only take into account its vulgar manifestations such as violence or overt discrimination, but the literature also draws our attention to its more subtle manifestations, including institutional racism, structural racism, and the role of law and power in race relations.[35]

If we are to understand 'sectarianism' as the sect-based equivalent of racism, then the study of sectarian relations should match the sophistication of the study of race relations. Indeed, it is precisely the absence of deeper analysis of sectarian identities and sectarian relations that has allowed some to maintain that 'sectarianism' in the Middle East is a post-2003 phenomenon.[36] The reality is that the complexity of sectarian relations means that our understanding of 'sectarianism' cannot be restricted to the blunt example of the post-2003 Middle East any more than a plausible understanding of racism can be restricted solely to its violent manifestations. Otherwise, we risk blinding ourselves to the more subtle aspects of sectarian or race relations and obscuring the role of power relations, economic conditions, memory, prejudice, personal and group bias, and so forth.

Despite the best efforts of numerous scholars and despite the abundance of the literature in recent years, the meaning of 'sectarianism' remains as elastic as good and bad, as subjective as beauty,

---

[34] Kadhim, "Efforts at Cross-Ethnic Cooperation," p. 276.

[35] For useful surveys of scholarship on race, see Richard Delgado and Jean Stefancic, *Critical Race Theory: An Introduction*, 3rd edn (New York: New York University Press, 2017); Les Back and John Solomos (eds), *Theories of Race and Racism: A Reader* (London: Routledge, 2000).

[36] This is especially pronounced in the press. For examples, see Sami Ramadani, "The sectarian myth of Iraq," *The Guardian*, June 16, 2014, www.gu.com/commentisfree/2014/jun/16/sectarian-myth-of-iraq; Musa al-Gharbi, "The myth and reality of sectarianism in Iraq," Al Jazeera America, Aug. 18, 2014, http://america.aljazeera.com/opinions/2014/8/iraq-sectarianismshiassunniskurdsnourial malaki.html; Dahr Jamail, "The Myth of Sectarianism: The Policy Is Divide to Rule," *International Socialist Review*, 57 (Jan.–Feb. 2008), www.isreview.org/issues/57/rep-sectarianism.shtml

and as indefinable as evil. To conclude this survey of the literature, the many uses, definitions and understandings of 'sectarianism' can be condensed into six broad approaches spanning a spectrum from expansive to restrictive ones:

1. As a catch-all for all that is related to sectarian identity.
2. As a catch-all for all that is related to inter-sect antagonisms (sometimes extended to include antagonisms between any groups regardless of their ascriptive marker – sects, tribes, races, ethnicities and so forth).
3. As a term for various forms of sect-centricity, benign or otherwise.
4. As the sect-based equivalent of racism.
5. As the intersection of sectarian identity and politics.
6. As a multilayered and multidimensional concept that cannot be contained in any single definition – hence, sometimes, the reliance on typologies of 'sectarianisms' in this approach.

As already mentioned, this is not a case of mere semantics. That a subject as policy relevant as 'sectarianism' should lack clear definitions is bad enough; but when this definitional ambiguity is coupled with the widespread normative assumptions regarding the negativity of 'sectarianism', the term goes beyond being merely incoherent and becomes analytically distortive, politically dangerous and socially divisive.

Not Just Useless, but Dangerously Distortive

Amid the cacophony of understandings and misunderstandings regarding the nature of 'sectarianism' there seems to be only one constant: a near consensus regarding the term's negativity.[37] This negativity extends to the usage of 'sectarian' to refer to an organization, message or person.

---

[37] A very Lebanon-specific exception in that regard is those who, taking 'sectarianism' as a referent to the Lebanese political system, defend it as the consociational sect-coded power sharing system that prevents Lebanon from returning to civil war. My thanks to Rima Majed for drawing my attention to this point.

If 'sectarianism' and 'sectarian' were solely used to refer to hatred, discrimination or violence, then the negativity would be justified; however, this is far from the case. Indeed, the terms' uses have often seen perfectly legitimate aspects and expressions of sectarian identity tarred with the same brush of negativity that is applied to 'sectarian' and 'sectarianism'. Here we are confronted with a basic problem: it is often difficult, if not impossible, not to sect-code some issues and actors. For example, can we avoid the turbulent lexicon of sectarian relations when discussing a movement advocating the political rights of one sect or another? Can a disturbance, demonstration or uprising escape sect-coding if one or all sides display elements of sect-centricity? Indeed, *should* it escape sect-coding if sectarian identities are driving factors in the event, as they occasionally are? The problem is that the negativity associated with the terms 'sectarian' and 'sectarianism' is such that merely coding a movement or event with the name of a specific sect (e.g. a Shi'a movement or a Sunni party) conveys negative connotations – as amply illustrated by the fate of the 'Shi'a protests' in Bahrain and Syria's 'Sunni demonstrations' in 2011. Whether in Arabic or English, it is exceedingly difficult to dissociate 'sectarianism' or *ta'ifiyya* and kindred terms like sectarian or *ta'ifi* from their deeply ingrained negative connotations, rooted in etymological, historical and political factors.

In his study of sectarian relations in Iraq, Osman notes that Western sociology always associated sects – and, by extension, 'sectarianism' – with schismatic groups that had broken away from a larger, more established, religious category, thereby equating the concept with "aberrant or deviant religious groups."[38] Needless to say, the church–sect dichotomy as formulated by Max Weber and his successors with reference to Christianity is of questionable applicability to the Islamic context: in addition to the absence of an official church, what is referred to by the term 'sect' differs vastly in the two contexts.[39]

---

[38] Osman, *Sectarianism in Iraq*, p. 39. On the following page, Osman convincingly challenges the conventional wisdom: "Ultimately, not only breakaway groups but also the entire religious community becomes imbued with a distinct sectarian ethos."

[39] This of course makes the term 'sectarianism' all the more problematic. For a discussion of the inapplicability of Weber's church–sect dichotomy to the Islamic context, see Michael Cook, "Weber and Islamic Sects," in *MaxWeber and Islam*, ed. Toby

Yet there is at least one similarity between 'sect' and what is most commonly regarded as its Arabic equivalent, *ta'ifa*, and that is that both are associated with parts of a larger whole.[40] While this association seems to be a value-free matter of group size, this definition still fits within an intellectual and religious history of framing the concept of *ta'ifa* in terms of factionalism, internal conflict and strife – the more that conceptions of orthodoxy cohered, the more this became the case. Whether in earlier Islamic history or in the age of the modern nation-state, the term *ta'ifa* (and, by extension, *ta'ifiyya*) has been liable to negative interpretations in that it is associated with deviation from either religious or national norms. As analyst and commentator Yusuf al-Dini argues with regard to the etymology of *ta'ifa*, "We are therefore dealing with a quantitative concept denoting a minority that differs from what is predominant [*sa'id*]."[41] One of the consequences of this – intended or otherwise – is that 'sectarianism' (with all its negative connotations) has often been disproportionately associated with minorities and outgroups.

In the name of secularism, modernity, anti-colonialism or the need for unity, modern authoritarian Arab nation-states tended to vilify assertions of a differentiated sectarian identity (a pattern seen with regard to differentiated ethnic and religious identities as well). Lebanon was the exception in this regard, yet the violent consequences of this exceptionalism may have served to further entrench the stigma associated with differentiated sectarian identities elsewhere in the region. The underlying assumption seems to have cast identification along sectarian lines as the polar opposite of successful nation-building

---

E. Huff and Wolfgang Schluchter (New Jersey: Transaction, 1999); Adam Gaiser, "A Narrative Identity Approach to Islamic Sectarianism," in *Sectarianization: Mapping the New Politics of the Middle East*, ed. Nader Hashemi and Danny Postel (London: Hurst & Co., 2017), pp. 65–68.

[40] In the early centuries of Islam, *ta'ifa* referred to a group with fewer than 1,000 people. For a discussion of the meanings of *ta'ifa*, see Taqi al-Din, "al-Ta'ifiyya wa-l-Mathhabiyya," in *Al-Ta'ifiyya wa-l-Tasamuh*, ed. Bilqiz, pp. 60–61; Osman, *Sectarianism in Iraq*, pp. 40–41; Khayyun, *Dhid al-Ta'ifiyya*, p. 16.

[41] Yusuf al-Dini, "Mafhum al-Ta'ifiyya bayn al-Tajathub al-Dini wa-l-Siyasi" (An Understanding of Sectarianism between Religious and Political Dynamics), in *Al-Ta'ifiyya*, ed. al-Mesbar, p. 10.

of the modern, progressive and secular variety.[42] As will be discussed in chapter 5, while the twentieth-century regimes of places like Syria, Egypt or Iraq officially celebrated pluralism, the reality was that authoritarian regimes across the Arab world sought to transcend demographic cleavages not through inclusion, but through dilution. In this way, pluralism often came to be seen as a threat to a very restrictively framed and coercively imposed state-defined 'unity' that would pay lip service to its population's diversity while actively trying to marginalize and silence differentiated group identities (see chapter 5). One of the many detrimental legacies of this mismanagement of communal heterogeneity is a widespread popular allergy towards differentiated group identities. In the post-2003 environment, this has been particularly pronounced where sectarian identities are concerned, to the extent that some are more comfortable with a rather contrived and counterfactual avoidance of all that is related to sects. For example, in his discussion of identity in Iraq, legal scholar Abd al-Hussain Sha'ban argued that Iraq's demographic pluralism can be defined along the lines of "national and ethnic divisions" (most notably, between Arabs and Kurds) or on the basis of religion, specifically the country's Muslim majority and its smaller religious minorities. He then concludes, "This is the true picture of a historical, united, inclusive [jami'] Iraq. Not a presumptive Iraq [of] ... statelets, regions, sects and ethnicities..."[43] The proverbial elephant in the room is Iraq's sectarian groups, particularly Shi'as and Sunnis, all mention of whom is painstakingly avoided. This omission neither helps the reader understand Iraq nor does it help ameliorate Iraq's intercommunal issues.

Another counterproductive reaction to the negativity of 'sectarianism' can be found among those who try their utmost to isolate 'sectarianism' from society and, particularly in the Arabic literature, from religion, in order to exonerate the latter. The most common way that such attempts are made is either through blaming external actors

---

[42] For more on this theme, see Makdisi, *Culture of Sectarianism*, pp. 5–8; Weiss, *In the Shadow of Sectarianism*, pp. 5–6.

[43] Abd al-Hussain Sha'ban, *Jadal al-Hawiyat fi-l-Iraq: al-Dawla wa-l-Muwatana* (The Identity Debate in Iraq: The State and Citizenship) (Beirut: Arab Scientific Publishers, 2010), pp. 50–52.

and factors for fanning the flames of an undefined 'sectarianism' or through outlining the contours of a 'political sectarianism' of which religion and society are ostensibly innocent. Leaving aside the obvious problems with assuming too clear a delineation between politics and society, this assumption also seems to wilfully ignore historical, intellectual and juridical realities. Society and religion are similarly excluded in studies that adopt an overly instrumentalist approach that frames 'sectarianism' in almost entirely top-down terms.[44] Yet even if elites were indeed the puppet masters that some of the more extreme examples would have us believe, the fact remains that elites reflect and are products of their societies. Similarly, attempts at dissociating religion from 'sectarianism' are equally problematic.[45] This invariably requires a highly selective reading of religious doctrine and history, ignoring the fact that the Abrahamic faiths – including each of Islam's major branches – have traditions explicitly calling for division and condemnation of the other, even if they do so alongside and in contradiction to other more permissive traditions.[46] The point to be made here is that the perceived need by some to exonerate religion and society from the charge of 'sectarianism' stems from the term's toxicity and its careless usage – something that has been facilitated by its lack of definition.

The negative connotations of 'sectarianism' are such that they have, at times, contributed to the demonization of sect-specific symbols and rituals and of sectarian identity itself. Here it has to be noted that we

---

[44] For examples, see Bassel Salloukh, "The Sectarianization of Geopolitics in the Middle East," and Madawi al-Rasheed, "Sectarianism as Counter-Revolution: Saudi Responses to the Arab Spring," in *Sectarianization*, ed. Hashemi and Postel; Elizabeth Shakman Hurd, "Politics of Sectarianism: Rethinking Religion and Politics in the Middle East," *Middle East Law and Governance*, 7:1 (2015): 61–75; F. Gregory Gause III, "Beyond Sectarianism: The New Middle East Cold War," Brookings Doha Center, Analysis Paper no. 11, July 2014.

[45] For example, one account notes that when it comes to religion, "Sectarianism is a political tendency that has no relation to religion but has exploited denominational differences for reasons of self-interest." Abd al-Khaliq Hussain, *Al-Ta'ifiyya al-Siyasiyya wa Mushkilat al-Hukum fi-l-Iraq* (Political Sectarianism and the Problem of Governance in Iraq) (Baghdad: Dar Mesopotamia, 2011), p. 16.

[46] For another example of such attempts at exonerating religion from 'sectarianism', see Shar', "al-Mukawinat al-Siyasiyya", pp. 100–101.

are not dealing with a level playing field: as will be seen in chapters 5 and 6, the fact that until recently there was hardly a Sunni identity to contend with – certainly not in any fashion that would parallel various forms of Shi'a identity – has meant that the issue of the expression of sectarian identity was primarily a Shi'a issue. Be it through Ashura rituals, images of the Shi'a Imams or any other aspect of the pantheon of Shi'a iconography, the assertion of Shi'a identity has been problematic in much of the Arab world and is often labelled as 'sectarian' or an example of 'sectarianism'. Indeed, there has often been a tendency to view organized expressions of Shi'a identity as more than just problematic, but rather with alarm and as a security issue. In large part this is due to the intertwining of the geopolitics of Arab–Iranian rivalry with sectarian identity. The relations of power underlining these dynamics will be discussed later, but what concerns us here is how an amorphous 'sectarianism' can lead to the stigmatization of otherwise legitimate expressions of sectarian identity. This is a fairly routine matter and the examples are endless. To name a few, there is the frequent media condemnation of Iraqi security forces displaying 'sectarian banners' and 'sectarian flags' (these depict Shi'a symbols such as images of their Imams). Such instances are commonly framed in a negative way, often being presented as evidence of 'sectarianism'. Yet a more context-dependent reading would recognize that such displays can sometimes be examples of the talismans that soldiers the world over display for luck and safekeeping.[47] What this points to is, again, the securitization of differentiated sectarian identities – particularly those of minorities and outgroups. The same pattern can be found in some unlikely places as well: in 2015 the Egyptian Ministry of Endowments closed the al-Imam al-Hussain mosque in Cairo (one of the purported burial sites of the Prophet Muhammad's grandson and third Shi'a Imam) for three days to prevent Egypt's minuscule Shi'a population from commemorating al-Hussain's death.[48] More recently,

---

[47] Underlining the point, the same 'sectarian flags' were in evidence during the mass protests against the Iraqi political system in late 2019. Yet this was neither controversial nor did media coverage sect-code the protests or such instances of sect-specific expression.

[48] For details: Walid Abd al-Rahman, "Al-Awqaf Tughliq Masjid al-Hussain fi-l-Qahira wa Tatawa'ad al-Shi'a bi-Ijra'at Hazima Hal Mukhalafatihim al-Qanun" (The

in 2017 footage of Shi'as commemorating the *Arba'in* (the fortieth day after the Battle of Karbala) in Damascus proved controversial. One commentator tweeted, "The new Syria is sectarian and ugly," with a link to footage of the event (a 49-second clip of bare-breasted men beating their chests to rhythmic chants of "Hussain").[49] This is symptomatic of a broader aversion to expressions of the other's sectarian identity, which has complicated sectarian plurality in the Arab world inasmuch as the expression of otherness comes to be treated as an expression of belligerence.

It is hardly practical to demonize the veneration of sect-specific symbols and rituals or the championing of sect-specific issues in a context of sectarian heterogeneity. At most, the above examples can be labelled as sect-centric, but sect-centricity need not be problematic as long as it is not adversarial; indeed it seems fairly obvious that some degree of sect-centricity is perfectly natural for those who subscribe to a sectarian identity. Hence, to lump benign or innocuous forms of sect-centricity into the definitional vortex that is 'sectarianism' implicitly stigmatizes sectarian identity and sectarian ritual. The above examples echo the pattern of silencing outgroups witnessed throughout much of the twentieth-century Arab world, and it is a pattern that will likely persist so long as we continue using an undefined term of such inescapable negativity. Most damagingly, this perpetuates the blurring of the line between acceptable sectarian identity (particularly that of outgroups) and unacceptable 'sectarianism'. In this we have a near-perfect parallel from Barbara Fields's critique of how 'racism' and 'racial identity' are often treated: "The vagueness of the concept of identity and its usually undetected incursions back and forth across the border between individual and collective, subjective and objective, optional and compulsory, have tempted scholars to collapse racism — a

---

Endowments Closes the al-Hussain Mosque in Cairo and Warns Shi'as of Stringent Measures if They Violate the Law), *Al-Sharq al-Awsat*, Oct. 23, 2015, http://aawsat. com/node/480636. For the broader context behind the rise of Egyptian anti-Shi'ism in recent years, see Alam Saleh and Hendrik Kraetzschmar, "Politicized Identities, Securitized Politics: Sunni–Shi'a Politics in Egypt," *Middle East Journal*, 69:4 (Autumn 2015): 545–562.

[49] See @hxhassan, Nov. 10, 2017, https://twitter.com/hxhassan/status/929067738995322881

forcible and authoritative assignment of race – into racial identity."[50] This is doubly problematic when we recall that race-coding and sect-coding are not level playing fields: who is racialized, who is sect-coded, and how these matters are normalized are ultimately questions to do with social and political relations of power. As amusingly illustrated by Richard Dyer: "An old-style white comedian will often start a joke: 'There's this bloke walking down the street and he meets this black geezer,' never thinking to race the bloke as well as the geezer."[51] Likewise, as seen above, the vocabulary of 'sectarianism' is commonly associated with minorities and outgroups – indeed the concept of a politically salient Sunni sectarian identity is a rather recent one.[52]

The negative connotations of 'sectarianism' have also allowed states and politically conservative social elements to delegitimize otherwise legitimate political activism by association with the term. This was dramatically illustrated in the Bahraini and Syrian regimes' reactions to the protests of 2011. In both cases, the regimes correctly judged that there was no surer way of neutralizing the political threat they faced, delegitimizing protesters and rallying pro-regime sentiment than by conflating the growing protest movements with 'sectarianism'. While this label amounted to little more than an implicit reference to the protesters' sectarian affiliation, it found a receptive audience in broader society, reflecting the reality that, whether looking from above or from below, we find a significant body of opinion that is ever ready to believe that members of the other sect are capable of an undefined (yet undoubtedly nefarious) 'sectarianism'. This raises the question of how sectarian outgroups can pursue their interests or agitate for greater rights without being vilified as purveyors of 'sectarianism'? As Matthiesen argued with regard to Bahrain in 2011: "Was this a 'Shi'a' protest right from the start...? The majority of the protestors were Shi'a – but the majority of citizens in Bahrain are Shi'a. The demographic mix should not come as a surprise. More important are

---

[50] Barbara J. Fields, "Whiteness, Racism and Identity," *International Labor and Working-Class History*, 60 (Fall 2001): 49.

[51] Richard Dyer, "The Matter of Whiteness," in *Theories of Race and Racism*, ed. Back and Solomos, p. 50.

[52] Fanar Haddad, "A Sectarian Awakening: Reinventing Sunni Identity after 2003," *Current Trends in Islamist Ideology*, 17 (2014): 70–101.

the demands of the protestors that, at least in the early days, were not sectarian."[53]

In some cases, it can be necessary to highlight sectarian identity in politics. The intersection of politics and sectarian identity need not be a case of negatively charged 'sectarianism'; rather, it can be a legitimate effort to address sect-specific discrimination or injustice. Advocacy groups and political movements around the world campaign for group-specific issues, yet, for example, we would not typically think of applying the term 'racism' to race-specific issues and organizations before examining the content and discourse of the people in question – otherwise 'racism' could be used to describe everything from the Ku Klux Klan to the National Association for the Advancement of Colored People. The presumed virtues of sect-blindness and the normative assumption that sectarian identity and politics are always best kept apart are inherently problematic in that they can end up ignoring – if not actively concealing – the often skewed relations of power that underline sectarian relations. Intentionally or otherwise, the supposedly sect- or religion-neutral modern Middle Eastern state can end up exacerbating religious or sectarian differences and reifying and protecting hierarchies of power.[54] In practice this obliges sectarian minorities and outgroups to accept a secondary role, if not secondary status, in the national framework and prevents them from mobilizing or seeking redress without having to contend with accusations of 'sectarianism' regardless of the manner of their mobilization, the content of their discourse, or the legitimacy of the issues they are championing. These dynamics and the equivocal effects of sect-blindness are almost perfectly mirrored in the concepts of gender-blindness and colour-blindness. As one study argued with regard to the latter: "Part of this new colour-blind ideology is the presumption or assertion of a race-neutral social context. It stigmatizes attempts to raise questions about

[53] Toby Matthiesen, *Sectarian Gulf: Bahrain, Saudi Arabia and the Arab Spring That Wasn't* (Stanford: Stanford University Press, 2013), p. 12.

[54] For a broader discussion of the paradoxical impact of the modern state and secularization on religious identities and communal relations in the Middle East, see Saba Mahmood, *Religious Difference in a Secular Age: A Minority Report* (Princeton: Princeton University Press, 2016), especially Introduction and chapter 2.

redressing racial inequalities through accusations such as 'playing the race card' or 'identity politics'...”[55]

The incoherence of 'sectarianism' is often mirrored in diagnoses and proposed cures for critically important issues relating to sectarian dynamics. For example, a particularly bizarre analysis sees an otherwise insightful discussion of sectarian identities drawing a direct link from the struggle between the shepherd and the farmer in ancient Mesopotamia to the struggle between the Qahtani and Adnani Arab tribes in the Abbasid era to the struggle between Sunnis and Shi'as in twenty-first-century Iraq.[56] Were the concept of 'sectarianism' less amorphous such mystifications might be avoided. Equally problematic, the term's incoherence is often reflected in proposed solutions. For example, the Iraqi Da'wa Party's 1992 platform (*"Barnamijuna"* – "Our programme") included the phrase "With the aim of addressing the anomalous conditions that have characterized the governing order in Iraq that is based on the hegemony of the governing sectarian minority [*al-aqaliyya al-ta'ifiyya al-hakima*]..."[57] Needless to say, this can be taken to mean a minority of Iraqis who are sectarian (in the common negative sense of the term) or a minority sect. In other words, given the history and identity of the authors, it could also be interpreted as a stigmatization of Sunnis. Ironically, this very issue came to pass thirteen years later when the preamble to the first draft of the new Iraqi constitution lamented the "sectarian oppression carried out by the despotic clique against the majority," which some interpreted as implicitly vilifying not only the Saddam regime but Sunnis generally.[58]

---

[55] Amanda E. Lewis, "'What Group?' Studying Whites and Whiteness in the Era of 'Color-Blindness'," *Sociological Theory*, 22:4 (Dec. 2004): 635.

[56] Fadhil al-Rubay'ie, "Al-Harb wa-l-Ta'ifiyya" (War and Sectarianism), in Fadhil al-Rubay'ie and Wajih Kawtharani, *Al-Ta'ifiyya wa-l-Harb* (Sectarianism and War) (Damascus: Dar al-Fikr, 2011), p. 48.

[57] Salah Abd al-Razzaq, *Masharee' Izalat al-Tamyiz al-Ta'ifi fi-l-Iraq: Min Muthakarat Faisal ila Majlis al-Hukum, 1932–2003* (Projects to Remove Sectarian Discrimination in Iraq: From Faisal's Memorandum to the Governing Council, 1932–2003) (Beirut: Ma'aref Forum, 2010), pp. 80–81.

[58] *"Al-qam' al-ta'ifi min qibal al-tughma al-mustabidda dhid al-aghlabiyya."* The ending 'against the majority' was eventually scrapped and does not appear in the final

Similarly incoherent and counterproductive proposed cures can be found in common calls for blanket bans on 'sectarianism'.[59] The danger here is not just that such calls will remain meaningless so long as 'sectarianism' is left undefined but that the lack of definition will allow officials to put the power of the law behind a malleable and easily manipulated term. In this way the criminalization of violent or destructive manifestations of sectarian relations can then be extended to the expression of sectarian identity itself. In the annexure to his study of identity in Iraq, legal scholar Abd al-Hussain Sha'ban presents a detailed outline for a law aimed at "outlawing [*tahrim*] sectarianism and reinforcing citizenship in Iraq." In introducing his proposed bill, Sha'ban states, "The first indispensable step towards reconstituting Iraqi society's cohesion ... begins with the abolition [*ilgha'*] and outlawing of sectarianism in all its forms and manifestations..."[60] While the text's 17 articles include some sensible recommendations, such as banning sectarian apportionment in governmental and non-governmental hiring (article 4), or the need to bring religious schools under the purview of the Ministry of Education (article 12), it nevertheless suffers from the same problem that has plagued most commentary on the subject: nowhere in the proposed law are we given a definition of 'sectarianism'. Without clear definitions, it is difficult to see how any such legislation could avoid targeting sectarian identities and criminalizing their expression. Does the 'sectarianism' that is to be 'abolished' and 'outlawed' include sect-specific symbols and rituals? After all, as we have seen, in some contexts such rituals can lead to fears of exclusion or encirclement among the sectarian other. Does a secular historical understanding of the legitimacy or falsehood of the

---

document. See Yahya al-Kubaisi, "Al-Iraq: al-Ihtijajat wa Azmat al-Nidham al-Siyasi" (Iraq: The Protests and the Crisis of the Political System), Arab Center for Research and Policy Studies, Case Analysis, Feb. 2013, p. 6.

[59] Article 95 of the Lebanese constitution, amended in 1990 after the civil war, calls for the establishment of a committee with the goal of 'nullifying political sectarianism' (*ilgha' al-ta'ifiyya al-siyasiyya*). See text on the Lebanese Parliament website at https://www.lp.gov.lb/CustomPage.aspx?id=26&. The term's use is less problematic in the Lebanese context as it is widely understood to refer specifically to the country's system of communal apportionment in politics.

[60] Sha'ban, *Jadal al-Hawiyat fi-l-Iraq*, p. 98.

first three caliphs or of the Twelve Imams constitute 'sectarianism'? Is a latent, normatively held inherited belief in the legitimacy or otherwise of such figures a marker of 'sectarianism'? Sha'ban's proposed bill adopts a maximalist approach to the subject; for example, article 2 states: "All work or political activism under any political, party, social, professional or any other guise for the purposes of spreading sectarianism or *mathhabiyya*,[61] whether openly or implicitly, is to be banned particularly if its membership was restricted to a specific sectarian group or if it claimed to represent or aid it."[62]

Needless to say, such a law would be widely open to abuse: would simply being a cleric constitute "spreading sectarianism or *mathhabiyya*"? After all, clerics often do social and political work, and such roles are usually restricted to a specific sectarian group. Furthermore, and crucially, what if there really was a case of sect-specific discrimination? Would it be a crime to violate sect-blindness and advocate the rights of a disadvantaged sectarian group? At times, the proposal seems to suggest that its intention is precisely to marginalize and vilify sectarian identities. Article 3 states, "It is forbidden to use religious rituals, practices and symbols for sectarian or *mathhabi* purposes,"[63] leaving unanswered the question of what distinguishes a 'sectarian' purpose from a non-sectarian one.

Even when accompanied by an attempt to define the term, proposals for blanket bans on 'sectarianism' have been patently unworkable. In his suggested cure for 'sectarianism', the Saudi Arabian Islamic intellectual Muhammad Mahfuz aimed at the protection of each group's sanctities: "We will not be able to end the dilemma of sectarianism and the discourse of *takfir* [i.e., charging others with

---

[61] Sometimes used interchangeably with *ta'ifiyya* to mean 'sectarianism', *mathhabiyya* derives from the word *mathhab*, most often used to refer to one of the major schools of thought within religious legal opinion (Shafi'i, Ja'fari, Hanafi, etc.). It may be argued that the only practical difference between *ta'ifiyya* and *mathhabiyya* is that the latter suggests that the sects in question are more likely to be Islamic and that the pertinent issue is one of religious legal opinion. The fact that it is a question of connotations rather than clearly demarcated definitions is what has allowed the terms to be used interchangeably.

[62] Sha'ban, *Jadal al-Hawiyat fi-l-Iraq*, p. 99.

[63] Ibid.

apostasy] and the propagation of hate other than through legislating clear and frank laws that punish anyone who participates in abusing the sanctities of others ..."[64] Yet what if one group's sanctities include elements that directly violate the cherished beliefs of others? Would praising Mu'awiya, the first Umayyad caliph, or denigrating his son Yazid, who defeated Hussain ibn Ali at the Battle of Karbala in 680 CE – unavoidable positions in some Sunni and Shi'a circles, respectively – be considered 'sectarianism'? Would speaking ill of clerical figures be criminalized in the name of ending 'sectarianism'? If so, one need look no further than the Iraqi parliament to see that, far from addressing sectarian tensions, such laws would in all likelihood exacerbate them: on more than one occasion, Iraqi parliamentarians squabbled over real and perceived slights against Iraqi and foreign religious figures.[65] It would seem that 'sectarianism' is so negative and convoluted a concept that it defies resolution.

Defining the Indefinable: What Is to Be Done?

What does it mean to be 'sectarian'? Depending on which of the scholars cited here one happens to agree with, a 'sectarian person' could be one who is biased toward one's own sect; they might actively hate people from other sects; it could mean that the person in question consumes or propagates religious polemics attacking others; it could mean that one belongs to sect-specific organizations or that one is intellectually insular and closed off from all that is beyond the horizons of one's own

---

[64] Muhammad Mahfuz, *Dhid al-Ta'ifiyya* (Against Sectarianism) (Casablanca: al-Markaz al-Thaqafi al-Arabi, 2009), p. 12.

[65] For example, see the controversy that was caused in 2012 over Iraqi parliamentarian Muhammad al-Alwani's comment about the leader of the Lebanese Shi'a group Hizbullah, Hasan Nasrallah. Ali Abd al-Amir, "Hadathan fi isbu' yakshifan ikhtilalat 'al-Iraq al-jadid'" (Two incidents in a week reveal the imbalances of 'the new Iraq'), *al-Hayat*, Aug. 9, 2012, www.alhayat.com/Details/425331. More recently a fist fight broke out in the Iraqi parliament over derogatory remarks made about the late Iranian Supreme Leader Ruhollah Khomeini. See "Irak bi-l-aydi khilal jalsa li-majlis al-nuwab al-Iraqi bi-sabab al-Khomeini" (Fist fight during Iraqi parliament session because of Khomeini), *Alhurra*, Aug. 26, 2013, www.alhurra.com/content/Iraq-fight-inside-parliament-khomeini/231389.html.

sect. This ambiguity is a product of the inherent incoherence of the term 'sectarianism'.

I have tried to outline the various ways in which the term has been approached and the detrimental impact that common understandings and usages of 'sectarianism' have had, both intellectually and practically. First, the absence of clear definitions has accorded the term a shape-shifting quality that allows it to apply to a vast spectrum of issues, behaviours, forms of expression, organizations, people and events. Second, the assumed negativity of the term has turned the allegation of 'sectarianism' into an effective tool with which some manifestations of sectarian identity can be silenced, marginalized, and even criminalized as and when needed. This has been particularly damaging where matters of political participation and political activism are concerned. Regimes have repeatedly and successfully neutralized the political opposition and political mobilization of sectarian outgroups by purposely conflating them with an undefined but universally reviled 'sectarianism'. Third, the definitional free-for-all that characterizes common understandings of the term has often seen analytic focus diverted away from underlying issues, whether socio-economic or political, drawing the focus instead to a mercurial 'sectarianism' so elastic that it can stand in as a scapegoat or explainer for any problem or issue even remotely related to sectarian identities. Finally, the convoluted and multi-headed way in which 'sectarianism' is conceived has marked the study of sectarian relations in the Middle East with a pervasive incoherence – indeed, it may have prevented its emergence as a recognized field of study on a par with the study of race or ethnicity. Once again, it should be stressed that, far from being yet another case of an academic's obsession with semantics, addressing our garbled understanding of 'sectarianism' is a matter of some urgency, given how the term pervades discussions of policy toward the Middle East.

Justin Gengler is correct in his criticism of those who dismiss 'sectarianism' as a useless concept, because to dismiss the term in its current usage often means dismissing sectarian dynamics.[66] There can be no denying the potential relevance and impact of sectarian or any other mass-group identities, and being allergic to the subject is as

---

[66] Gengler, "Understanding Sectarianism," p. 33.

counterproductive as being obsessed with it. Sectarian relations do not explain the Middle East nor is their relevance the figment of Orientalist imaginations. Accordingly, my interrogating the term 'sectarianism' in no way denies the centrality of sectarian dynamics to many issues that have pervaded several societies in the twenty-first-century Middle East. What is being contested is not the various phenomena that fall under the ever-malleable umbrella term 'sectarianism', but rather the fact that the term is used as shorthand for what are in reality complex manifestations of sectarian identities and relations. Several scholars have tried to present definitional frameworks that account for the complexity of the subject at hand.[67] Often, this has entailed a typology of 'sectarianisms', each applying to a particular context. An alternative approach is that which seeks to apply a simplified understanding of the word 'sectarianism' free from value-laden connotations such as violence or hatred. In such cases, 'sectarianism' can simply mean sect-centricity or alternatively the adoption of sectarian identity as a marker of modern political identity, without presuming anything about possible outcomes.[68]

Without detracting from the validity of these approaches, I would nevertheless suggest that the term 'sectarianism' needs to be permanently discarded. In 2011, I argued for the term's redundancy – even called it 'useless' – but nevertheless felt obliged at times to surrender to what I then believed was the term's linguistic inescapability. The typology I suggested back then (assertive, passive and banal sectarianism)[69] would have worked far better had I completely discarded the term and gone with assertive, passive and banal *sectarian identities*, for in essence that is what I was referring to. This is as good an illustration as any of the merits of abandoning the usage of 'sectarianism' and instead unpacking and identifying whichever of the many phenomena that the

---

[67] Some original attempts at resolving the definitional issues surrounding 'sectarianism' would include: Bilqiz, "Muqadima" and "Munaqashat" in *Al-Ta'ifiyya wa-l-Tasamuh*, ed. Bilqiz; Taqi al-Din, "al-Ta'ifiyya wa-l-Mathhabiyya," in *Al-Ta'ifiyya wa-l-Tasamuh*, ed. Bilqiz, pp. 9–18 and 78–81; Ibrahim, *Al-Ta'ifiyya wa-l-Siyasiyya*, pp. 23–24.

[68] Makdisi, *Culture of Sectarianism*, p. 7; Sluglett, "The British, the Sunnis and the Shi'is," p. 258 n1; Gengler, "Understanding Sectarianism," pp. 33, 42, 64.

[69] Haddad, *Sectarianism in Iraq*, pp. 25, 53.

term encompasses concerns us. There is simply no manifestation of sectarian relations or identities that mandates the usage of the term.[70] I would suggest that a more coherent lexical framework would start by specifying what type of group is intended by the term 'sect'. Once sects have been identified, and rather than using 'sectarianism' to refer to all or part of that which relates to them, we need to delineate precisely which aspects of these groups concern us. In most cases this is easily done by using the term 'sectarian' only as a modifier relating to sects or the relationships between or within them: sectarian identity, sectarian dynamics, sectarian mobilization, and so forth. However, as mentioned at the outset, some facets of sectarian identity can be further clarified by using the terms 'sect-specific' and 'sect-centric' to denote that which relates to or revolves around a specific sect.

In many ways, this all renders the word 'sectarian' meaningless unless it is modifying another term, and indeed the word is sufficiently laden with negative connotations to be considered impractical. To revisit an earlier example: what is usually meant when a person is described as sectarian? In its common usage, the term usually suggests feelings of disdain toward people affiliated with this or that sect that can lead to harmful intentions, feelings and acts. However, the term can also mean little more than sect-centricity: a kind of narcissistic attachment to one's own sectarian identity that may or may not be accompanied by belligerence toward the sectarian other. People, organizations or policies that are sect-centric (and hence confusingly labelled 'sectarian') are not necessarily hateful of or belligerent towards others: one may have a skewed view of the world that is characterized by strong bias toward one's own sect, accompanied by a non-belligerent obliviousness bordering on disregard for the views of others. This is a far cry from what is normally associated with a person being sectarian.

I am not the first to suggest that the term 'sectarianism' may hinder more than advance our understanding. Though falling slightly short of

---

[70] It is notable that one of the earlier and more cogent treatments of Sunni–Shi'a relations in Iraq never used 'sectarianism'. Peter Sluglett and Marion Farouk-Sluglett, "Some Reflections on the Sunni/Shi'i Question in Iraq," *British Society for Middle Eastern Studies Bulletin*, 5:2 (1978): 79–87.

total abandonment of the term, Dina Rizk Khoury pointed out that "sectarianism as a category of analysis of identity formation conceals as much as it reveals. Its use by political actors as well as producers of knowledge needs to be at all times analysed within specific contexts..."[71] More forceful and to the point is Lebanese scholar Antoine Messarra's rejection of the word, which he believes is "not a [comprehensible] notion and is unsuitable for use when diagnosing, analysing or curing ... Ultimately, the term 'sectarianism' expresses an intellectual laziness in analysis and in most cases expresses prior ideological positions..."[72]

I have tried to highlight the intellectual and practical problems caused by the rudderless usage of an undefined 'sectarianism'. I hope that my suggested framework may act as a first step towards starting a broader debate as to how best to reformulate a relevant vocabulary for the study of the dynamics of sectarian relations. Messarra's apt and colourful description of the term 'sectarianism' may hopefully underline the urgency of that much-needed debate: "Since the 1920s, the term 'sectarianism' has turned ... into a wastebasket into which everyone discards that which displeases them. The contents of this wastebasket are scattered and contradictory and are devoid of classification and coordination, thereby turning the phrase into a landfill of ideologies, disputes, and disagreements."[73]

In chasing a chimeric 'sectarianism' and treating it as a singular phenomenon, individual studies are always likely to be incomplete: often 'sectarianism' is framed as a political *or* a social phenomenon; as a function of religion *or* of geopolitics; driven from above *or* from below. In other words, when taken together in all of its contradictions, the literature ends up reflecting the many ways and many plains on which sectarian identity can be imagined, driven, utilized and projected. The

---

[71] Dina Rizk Khoury, "The Security State and the Practice and Rhetoric of Sectarianism in Iraq," *International Journal of Contemporary Iraqi Studies*, 4:3 (Dec. 2010): 325.

[72] Antoine Messarra, "Munaqashat" (Debates) in *Al-Ta'ifiyya wa-l-Tasamuh*, ed. Bilqiz, p. 92.

[73] Antoine Messarra, "Ma Ma'na al-Ta'ifiyya wa Kayfa Nadrusuha al-Yawm" (What Is the Meaning of Sectarianism and How Can We Study It Today?) in *Al-Ta'ifiyya wa-l-Tasamuh*, ed. Bilqiz, p. 51.

reality is that 'sectarianism' – however understood – is not something that identifiably exists; rather, it is shorthand for a variety of symbols, behaviours, actions, attitudes and other phenomena related to sectarian identity. Thus, what is actually being discussed in the rapidly expanding literature on 'sectarianism' is in fact sectarian identity and its many facets; hence, sectarian *identity* should be our conceptual starting point.

As will be explained in the following chapters, sectarian identity and sectarian relations operate on several fields or along several dimensions: on the level of religious doctrine and religious truths; on a local, subnational level; on the level of the nation-state, nationalism and national identity; and finally on the level of transnational politics. The conception and contours of sectarian identity – and indeed the analytical tools required to understand it – will differ from one dimension to another; however, as will be seen, no single dimension can be treated in complete isolation from the others given the dialogical nature of their relation. In this way, rather than something that can be understood through any one prism, sectarian identity becomes the sum of its parts, as will be shown in the following chapters.

2

THE STUDY OF SECTARIAN RELATIONS
KEY DEBATES

The previous chapter argued that there is no such thing as 'sectarianism' – at least not in the sense of anything remotely resembling a clearly identifiable phenomenon or analytically useful concept. Unshackled from this burdensome phrase, we can now aim for a clearer and more accurately segmented understanding of the myriad phenomena to which 'sectarianism' refers. More to the point, unhindered by the fog of 'sectarianism', we can aim for a better understanding of modern sectarian identities and sectarian relations (here referring to Sunni and Shi'a Muslims). Even a cursory glance at popular commentary on 'sectarianism' reveals an urgent need for a broader demystification of sectarian identity. This requires us to stop treating it as *sui generis* and instead framing it as another modern form of collective identity – whatever its specificities, it remains similar in many ways to other mass-group identities that are regarded as 'primordial' (race, tribe, ethnicity and so forth).

As argued in the previous chapter's closing, to understand Sunni or Shi'a identities and Sunni–Shi'a relations we must first identify and explore the multiple dimensions of sectarian identity. These will be the subject of the next two chapters. Before that, in an attempt to further demystify sectarian identity, this chapter will address some of the more persistent debates and (mis)conceptions that have characterized this relatively new field of study. This will better set the ground for a discussion of the dimensions of sectarian identity in chapters 3 and 4.

The Role of Religion in Sectarian Identity

Much of the mystification of sectarian identity referred to above is often a function of the fact that 'sect' is ordinarily a referent to a religious or, more commonly, a subreligious category. Particularly in popular commentary, this simple fact seems to throw observers off or, more perniciously, it is used to reinforce ideological prejudices regarding the Middle East. Either way, the result is that we often find sectarian identity being suspended beyond the parameters of modern identity – indeed, beyond modernity and beyond the present. This habitually leads to what Makdisi aptly labels as 'medievalization': the belief that the dynamics of 'sectarianism' are best understood through the prism of early Islamic history.[1] This of course fits into a broader and older pattern of 'medievalization' of Islam and the Middle East in general. A fairly typical example is the *New York Times* columnist Thomas Friedman declaring that "the main issue [in the war in Yemen] is the 7th century struggle over who is the rightful heir to the Prophet Muhammad – Shiites or Sunnis."[2] In one stroke, Friedman manages to misinform his readers not just about the nature and drivers of the Yemeni conflict but also about the sectarian composition of Yemeni Muslims and the nature of Zaidi Islam – whose views on the succession to the Prophet are actually closer to mainstream Sunni than to Twelver Shi'a Islam.[3] Far from unique, this example is symptomatic of a broader pattern: by fixating on matters of religious doctrine, observers end up fetishizing and exoticizing modern sectarian identities and reducing them to

---

[1] Ussama Makdisi, "The Problem of Sectarianism in the Middle East in an Age of Western Hegemony," in *Sectarianization*, ed. Hashemi and Postel, p. 25.

[2] Thomas Friedman, "Tell me how this ends well," *New York Times*, April 1, 2015. www.nytimes.com/2015/04/01/opinion/thomas-friedman-tell-me-how-thisends-well.html.

[3] For an interesting discussion of how and why the (Zaydi) Houthis came to be framed as Shi'a, see Anna Gordon and Sarah E. Parkinson, "How the Houthis Became 'Shi'a'," Middle East Research and Information Project, Jan. 27, 2018. http://merip.org/mero/mero012718.

their religious or doctrinal dimension to the point that Sunni and Shi'a identities become irrelevant to, and beyond the comprehension of, modern politics and sociology. In the process, any chance of understanding how sectarian identities operate in the modern Middle East is completely lost. Yet as will be shown, differences over religious doctrine, jurisprudence and spirituality – in other words, 'religion' in a relatively narrow but conventional sense of the term – in fact play a somewhat marginal role in modern sectarian dynamics. Indeed, a central argument of this book, one that will be more fully explored in the following chapters, is that modern sectarian competition, rather than necessarily reflecting contested religious truths, is in fact just as likely, if not more so, to be a function of contested *national* truths – as modern and as political as the nation-state itself.

This is something that observers seem capable of intuitively comprehending when it comes to Western cases of 'sectarianism' but not where the Middle East or Islam are concerned. It is, for example, commonly understood that sectarian identities in Scotland are not driven mainly, let alone solely, by questions of religious truth and orthodoxy: after all, how relevant are these to Scottish 'sectarianism', particularly given that its most visible avatar is the football hooligan who, one can reasonably assume, is less than concerned with differences over Christian catechisms.[4] Likewise, to take the more prominent example of recent Western European sectarian conflict, public commentary on 'The Troubles' in Northern Ireland (1968–98), never reduced the issue to questions of Papal authority or Christian liturgy despite the fact that the violence was sect-coded. In other words, sectarian dynamics in Scotland and Ireland are readily recognized as modern social and political conflicts that are fundamentally *not* about competing religious truths even if, superficially, the protagonists self-identify and are coded along religious or sectarian lines.

Put simply, religion as doctrine is not needed to make 'religious conflict'; it is far more likely for such conflicts to be driven by religion

---

[4] On sectarian dynamics in Scotland and their intersection with football see for example, Steve Bruce et al., *Sectarianism in Scotland* (Edinburgh: Edinburgh University Press, 2011), chapter 4; Tom Gallagher, *Divided Scotland: Ethnic Friction and Christian Crisis* (Glendaruel: Argyll Publishing, 2013), chapter 9.

as *identity* – in other words, religion less as a metaphysical truth and more as a marker of group solidarities and group boundaries. To refer to Makdisi once again, his description of 'sectarianism' as part of a process that sees "religious identity politicized, *even secularized*" aptly captures the often incidental nature of doctrinal differences to modern sectarian conflict.[5] Nor is this solely a feature of the twentieth to twenty-first centuries; the outsizing and exaggeration of the role of religious doctrine in religious conflict is also evident in popular perceptions regarding sixteenth-century Europe's wars of religion. While the relevance of religious doctrine to these conflicts is undoubted and seldom paralleled, it is nevertheless not without limits. As Mark Greengrass has argued:

> This period is commonly called the time of Europe's 'wars of religion'. In reality, these were political contentions in which religion was the way by which conflicts in the commonwealths of state and Church manifested... Calling the later sixteenth century the era of the wars of religion underestimates the polymorphy of religious dissent and the degree to which religion became the prism through which questions of power and identity were viewed...[6]

The very same can be said of sect-coded conflict in the twenty-first-century Middle East. Religion can certainly act as a mobilizational force, and religious doctrine, belief and symbols are capable of inflaming popular emotion, but this does not mean that religion has a hypnotic or maddening effect upon believers. Indeed, what is viewed as the irrational hatred and passion of religious conflict is often driven by a lot more than religious belief and encompasses a much wider web of interests, beliefs and solidarities. Again this is particularly true today but is also applicable to early-modern religious conflict as well: in a description that particularly recalls today's instrumentalization of sectarian identities (and how widely recognized such strategies are), Greengrass notes with regard to sixteenth-century Europe:

---

[5] Ussama Makdisi, "Pensee 4: Moving Beyond Orientalist Fantasy, Sectarian Polemic and Nationalist Denial," *International Journal of Middle East Studies*, 40:4 (Nov. 2008): 559. Emphasis added.

[6] Mark Greengrass, *Christendom Destroyed: Europe 1517–1648* (London: Penguin Books, 2015), pp. 394–396.

"Religious dissent did not necessarily lead to conflict. Contemporaries appreciated that religion was a superficial rallying cry for people's loyalties, a smokescreen behind which people could pursue their individual interests."[7]

And so it has been ever since. Several Ottomanists – Stefan Winter, Karen Kern, Bruce Masters and others – have noted the pragmatic and essentially political approach of the Ottoman authorities to questions of religious doctrine and sectarian dynamics.[8] Consequently, it has been argued that when matters of religious orthodoxy did gain prominence, it was for reasons of state rather than of faith – and while we should not overlook the overlap between the two, there is nevertheless an important distinction between them. For example, as Kern has shown with regard to the long history of Ottoman proscriptions on marriages between Ottoman and Persian subjects – or between Muslims and *rafidha*, to echo the anti-Shi'a language often used by Ottoman officials in this regard – one frequently finds domestic and geopolitical concerns relating to Ottoman–Persian rivalry dictating the ebbs and flows of what are nominally static doctrinal issues.[9] As will be seen in chapter 4, even explicit anti-Shi'a heresiography in the Ottoman Empire was not as ideological as one would assume. In other words, just as described by Greengrass with regard to religious conflict in early-modern Europe and just as is commonly the case today, anti-Shi'ism and its underlining body of jurisprudence were invoked by the Ottoman authorities more for reasons of political expediency than religious conviction.

None of this is meant to suggest that differences over religious doctrine and notions of religious orthodoxy or heterodoxy are of

---

[7] Ibid., p. 396.

[8] See Stefan Winter, *The Shiites of Lebanon under Ottoman Rule, 1516–1788* (Cambridge: Cambridge University Press, 2010). For an illustration of the transactional and pragmatic Ottoman–Persian management of Shi'a shrines in late nineteenth-century northern Iraq, see Reidar Visser, "Sectarian Coexistence in Iraq: The Experiences of the Shia in Areas North of Baghdad," in *The Shi'a of Samarra: The Heritage and Politics of a Community in Iraq*, ed. Imranali Panjwani (New York: I.B. Tauris, 2012).

[9] Karen Kern, *Imperial Citizen: Marriage and Citizenship in the Ottoman Frontier Provinces of Iraq* (Syracuse: Syracuse University Press, 2011).

no relevance. They can be, but even then this would usually be as part of a larger constellation of factors and frames of reference that together make up sectarian dynamics. Hence, even the most notorious examples of doctrinaire proponents of sectarian division are products of a context that goes beyond questions of doctrine. As Farouk-Alli points out, Ibn Taymiyya's infamous *fatwa* of 1317 in which Nusayris (what are today also called Alawis) were condemned as "more disbelieving than the Jews and Christians" was not just the product of dogma: it was a response to the 1317 Nusayri rebellion in coastal Syria led by a millenarian figure who rejected the authority of the Mamluk state, proclaimed contemporary Muslims to be unbelievers, and declared himself the Mahdi (the redeeming figure of Islamic end times).[10] Likewise, the role of context is no less important in the case of ecumenical *fatwas* such as that of the Grand Mufti of Jerusalem, Haj Amin al-Hussaini, who in 1936 issued a *fatwa* recognizing Alawis as Muslims. Rather than being solely a product of abstract doctrinal considerations or a tendency towards toleration, the *fatwa* reflected al-Hussaini's pan-Arabist tendencies and the need to maintain unity in the face of the Mandate powers' attempts to rule through division.[11] Here we should be careful not to repeat the common mistake of dismissing religion as mere cover for supposedly more concrete drivers – Ibn

---

[10] Aslam Farouk-Alli, "The Genesis of Syria's Alawi Community," in *The Alawis of Syria*, ed. Kerr and Larkin, pp. 32–33. For the rebellion of 1317, see Sato Tsugitaka, *State and Rural Society in Medieval Islam: Sultans, Muqta's and Fallahun* (Leiden: E.J. Brill, 1997), pp. 162–176. For an analysis of Ibn Taymiyya's anti-Nusayri *fatwas* see Yaron Friedman, "Ibn Taymiyya's Fatawa against the Nusayri-Alawi Sect," *Der Islam*, 82:2 (2005): 349–363. Friedman points out that, of Ibn Taymiyya's three anti-Nusayri *fatwas*, only one can be definitively dated to the 1317 rebellion but he argues that at least another of the three should be similarly understood. In any case, the *fatwas* not associated with the rebellion were nevertheless similarly responding to a specific contingency, namely the need to repel the Mongols and the Crusaders.

[11] Yvette Talhamy, "The Fatwas and the Nusayri/Alawis of Syria," *Middle Eastern Studies*, 46:2 (2010): 185–187. Talhamy charts the history of *fatwas* relating to the Nusayris/Alawis: three by Ibn Taymiyya; one in the sixteenth century; one in the 1820s; and three in the twentieth century including that of Haj Amin al-Hussaini. The twentieth-century *fatwas* were embracing of the Alawis while the earlier ones attacked them. However, as Talhamy points out, these differences and the varying content of the *fatwas* were shaped by the prevailing political climate of the time.

Taymiyya's hatred of Nusayris was hardly just a product of a Nusayri rebellion in 1317. Rather, the point to be derived from this and other examples is that, in line with the multidimensionality of sectarian identity, sectarian dynamics are the alloyed product of several factors and drivers only one of which might be religious doctrine. To illustrate, its attendant heresiography notwithstanding, the Ottoman–Safavid war of 1578–90 was driven in large part by Ottoman fears of a Russian–Iranian alliance and hence the need to establish a stronger presence in the Caucasus by annexing resource-rich Azerbaijan.[12] However, this does not mean that religious doctrine was irrelevant or that its role was purely instrumental. Rather than imposing unnecessary binaries, we are better served viewing the relation between politics and religion or doctrine in such cases as one of intertwinement as opposed to a religious smokescreen providing cover for the supposedly more 'real' political and economic considerations. This is as true of the contemporary Middle East as it was of Ottoman–Persian rivalry: at the Peace of Istanbul which concluded the Ottoman–Safavid war of 1578–90, Sultan Murad not only insisted on Safavid recognition of Ottoman rule over all annexed Iranian territories but, despite the economic and geostrategic rationale for the war, he also demanded that the Safavids abandon the practice of *tabarru'* (in which the first three caliphs and the Prophet's wife Aisha are publicly cursed).[13] Even when religious or doctrinal drivers are secondary to a sect-coded conflict, religious doctrine can still be relevant in and of itself as an expression of belief, as a legitimizing tool, as a tool for the assertion of identity or for establishing dominance.

At times doctrinal differences can be completely incidental to sectarian division. An interesting illustration of this comes courtesy of Matthew Allen's study of sectarian relations and temperance movements in mid-nineteenth-century Sydney, Australia. Contrary to common assumptions, temperance movements were not a cause

---

[12] Max Sherberger, "Confrontations between Sunni and Shi'i Empires: Ottoman–Safavid Relations between the Fourteenth and the Seventeenth Century," in *The Sunna and Shi'a in History: Division and Ecumenism in the Middle East*, ed. Ofra Bengio and Meir Litvak (New York: Palgrave Macmillan, 2011), pp. 60–65.

[13] Ibid., pp. 60–61.

promoted by the Protestant middle classes; rather (in Sydney at least) they drew strength from Irish Catholics from all levels of society who were reacting to the negative stereotype of the drunken criminal Irishman. The Protestant counter-reaction is telling: the more that temperance was perceived as a vehicle for Catholic political action – "an assertion of their respectability" – the more Protestants were inclined to withdraw their support for temperance movements.[14] Here we have a fascinating illustration of how even the unlikeliest of domains can come to be sect-coded and turned into a site of sectarian competition and assertion or counter-assertion of sectarian identities. Indeed, the fact that, "respectability," rather than issues of religious doctrine or the rights of religious groups (say, sect-specific schooling or the codification of sect-specific religious strictures, for example), became a vehicle for sectarian competition is itself noteworthy and mirrors more recent class and regional drivers of 'sectarianism' in the modern Middle East – a recurring theme in modern sectarian relations and something that will be discussed at length in this book.

Faith and religious doctrine are but one dimension of sectarian identity. They can potentially drive sectarian dynamics but, as counterintuitive as it may sound to the casual observer, in practice they are seldom a causal factor in modern sectarian discord. A 2018 study of Sufi-Salafi relations in Libya came to much the same conclusion. The authors critiqued the fact that Salafi animosity towards Sufis is often framed by observers in purely doctrinal or theological terms. While religious or doctrinal otherness is undoubtedly a factor, it is questionable whether it can, on its own, animate sectarian dynamics. As the authors argue, "there are often deeper socio-economic and political drivers. As case studies from across the Islamic world highlight, anti-Sufism is sometimes a proxy for class-based tensions…"[15] Here,

---

[14] Matthew Allen, "Sectarianism, Respectability and Cultural Identity: The St Patrick's Total Abstinence Society and Irish Catholic Temperance in mid-Nineteenth Century Sydney," *Journal of Religious History*, 35:3 (Sept. 2011): 374–392.

[15] Katherine Pollock and Frederic Wehrey, "The Sufi-Salafi Rift," *Diwan*, Carnegie Middle East Center, Jan. 23, 2018, http://carnegie-mec.org/diwan/75310. Likewise a recent study argues that, despite its emphasis on doctrinal purity, in practice militant Salafism attracts adherents for a variety of reasons that are just as likely to be socio-political as they are doctrinal. See Raphael LeFevre, "The

reaching the correct diagnosis is particularly important not just as an academic pursuit but also as a first step towards finding solutions. Rather than reconciling doctrines, what is needed in such cases is often more structural and grounded in social and political issues: economic reform, building inclusive institutions, upholding social justice, defending the rule of law, and so forth. Again, the point here is not to stress one factor over another but to illustrate that a number of factors will have varying degrees of relevance depending on context. In this way, rather than being any one thing, sectarian identity becomes an amalgam or an umbrella for several identities, social structures and processes. As one study notes with regard to Alawi identity in modern Syria: "Being Alawi was more of a communal cultural symbol than a deeply held religious phenomenon … [that] meant being part of a network that facilitated social mobility, political opportunity and economic advancement."[16] In other words, what is lazily referred to as 'sectarianism' is not simply about sectarian identity per se, much less solely about differences in religious belief; indeed, it is seldom, if ever, manifested in such monochrome forms. As one study on sectarian division in Scotland notes: "A whole bundle of distinguishing characteristics – race and accent, religion, occupation, residence and politics – set the Catholic Irish portion of Glasgow's population apart from the rest."[17] A similarly broad nexus of factors marks and animates sectarian boundaries in the Middle East. This should be borne in mind as a corrective to those accounts that view sectarian identity in the region mainly, if not solely, through the prism of religious doctrine, for it is precisely that prism that leads to the medievalization pervading popular commentary on the subject.

To bring the discussion back to Sunni–Shi'a relations, on the one hand there are important points of doctrinal divergence (the Imamate, the Prophet's Companions, the nature and role of religious authority, and so forth) that give the lie to the simplistic and formulaic insistence

---

Sociopolitical Undercurrent of Lebanon's Salafi Militancy," Carnegie Middle East Center, March 26, 2018, https://carnegie-mec.org/2018/03/27/sociopolitical-undercurrent-of-lebanon-s-salafi-militancy-pub-75744.

[16] Michael Kerr, "Introduction: For 'God, Syria, Bashar and Nothing Else'?" in *The Alawis of Syria*, ed. Kerr and Larkin, pp. 3–4.

[17] Gallagher, *Divided Scotland*, p. 24.

of some that there is no substantive difference between Sunni and Shi'a interpretations of Islam. On the other hand, this cannot be taken a priori as a driver of sectarian dynamics – let alone sectarian conflict – in the contemporary Middle East. As is being increasingly recognized, the existence of theological or jurisprudential divergences has yet to feature as a central driver of *any* modern sect-coded conflict. As one study argues, we cannot focus on doctrinal formulations and intellectual history alone without recognizing that "power, community and identity are simultaneously embedded in any claim to orthodoxy." Commenting on the historical evolution of Sunni identity, the same study notes that the excessive focus on "the way particular elites (*ulama*) formulated positions on hair-splitting issues" fails to explain the endurance of religious identity as a socio-political force and collective identity.[18] The same point reveals itself when one considers the irrelevance of the same hair-splitting *ulama* to, for example, the Lebanese civil war (1975–90), which was never driven by matters of religious orthodoxy or fantasies of religious homogeneity despite it being a sect-coded conflict. The same can be said about more recent episodes from Lebanon, Iraq, Syria and Bahrain. In each of these cases doctrinal otherness was, at most, a rhetorical device and never a central driver of conflict. This does not mean that sectarian identity was not relevant to these conflicts; rather, it means that other aspects of sectarian identity besides the doctrinal component were in play. Thus, when trying to understand modern sectarian dynamics we need to look at other grounds for sectarian othering and otherness in addition to the realm of religious doctrine. Indeed, one study urges us to think of sectarian othering as a process that may begin with religious doctrine but then moves on to permeate other levels of society: "Over the course of time, othering rhetoric has expanded beyond theology to become a decisive part of political, social, religious and economic reality ..."[19] Again, while we should be wary of

---

[18] Abbas Barzegar, "The Persistence of Heresy: Paul of Tarsus, Ibn Saba' and Historical Narrative in Sunni Identity Formation," *Numen*, 58:2/3 (2011): 209. A similar argument can be found with regards to the study of contemporary jihadi movements in Olivier Roy, *Jihad and Death: The Global Appeal of Islamic State* (London: Hurst & Co., 2017), pp. 41–42.

[19] Naser Ghobadzdeh and Shahram Akbarzadeh, "Sectarianism and the Prevalence of 'Othering' in Islamic Thought," *Third World Quarterly*, 36:4 (2015): 700.

exaggerating the role of religious doctrine, we should also be careful not to dismiss its potential as a driver. In particular, religious leaders and religious structures can potentially play a role in setting norms of intergroup relations. Again, nothing is predetermined: in some instances (say the 2nd Vatican Council of 1962) doctrinal shifts and clerical initiatives can set the stage for a more ecumenical atmosphere at the social level;[20] in other instances (say the Amman Message of 2005), even the highest levels of clerical buy-in may fail to bridge sectarian division in moments of acute sectarian entrenchment.[21]

To ask if sectarian dynamics are driven by religion *or* politics is to ask the wrong question. Seldom is it clearly one or the other: when it comes to how sectarian identities and sectarian relations are produced, both religious doctrine and politics are inescapable factors, with the balance between the two being dictated by context. A particular facet of sectarian identity – for example, personal status codes – may become a political issue, but this is neither inevitable nor impossible. Indeed, rather than a strict binary, politics and religion exist often in a reciprocal relationship characterized by circularity rather than antagonism or exclusivity – two separate but nevertheless intertwined concepts, to borrow from Brubaker's analysis of religion and nationalism.[22] Commenting on the relationship between religion and politics in the United States, Mark Farha argues: "Politicians exhibit a penchant to legitimize their ruling mandate with religious rhetoric and symbols, while confessions need access to the levers of political power to institutionalize their tenets. Not every leader is endowed with the self-confidence to wholeheartedly subscribe to Ataturk's maxim that 'a ruler who needs religion to help him rule is a weakling'."[23] It is for this reason that drawing too stark a dividing line between religion and politics is unhelpful. Likewise the inherent ambiguity of identity mandates that we be intellectually flexible enough

---

[20] For the impact of the 2nd Vatican Council on sectarian relations in Scotland, see Gallagher, *Divided Scotland*, p. 116.

[21] For details of the Amman Message, see http://ammanmessage.com/.

[22] Rogers Brubaker, "Religion and Nationalism: Four Approaches," *Nations and Nationalism*, 18:1 (2012): 2–20.

[23] Mark Farha, "Global Gradations of Secularism: The Consociational, Communal and Coercive Paradigms," *Comparative Sociology*, 11 (2012): 380.

to go beyond conceptions of sectarian identity as *either* religious *or* political or any other one thing. Here, again, the literature on race relations and critical race theory is of use: rather than framing race as a product of symbolic issues (identity, ideology, culture) *or* material ones (economic and political resources, for example), the scholarship has moved beyond framing race as a unitary concept and scholars now seek a better understanding of the different components of race and how they interact. In this way, "the interesting question is [no longer] 'which is it' but how do the symbolic and material dimensions of race interact and how are they reproduced or challenged in the everyday."[24] By framing sectarian identity as the multidimensional sum of its parts – doctrinal, subnational, national, transnational – we can adopt a similar approach to the study of sectarian dynamics.

One of the questions this raises is the uniqueness of sectarian identities. Rogers Brubaker's extensive work on religion and politics is informative in this regard. He rejects the dichotomy between what he labels as the 'particularizing' and 'generalizing' stances towards religion – the former treating it as a *sui generis* identity, the latter as little if at all different from other mass-group markers – opting instead to explore the synergy between the two.[25] For example, he argues that certain contexts are best understood by subsuming religion under the rubric of politicized ethnicity – whereby even if competing actors are religiously coded, they may be competing not over religious stakes but over more profane goals such as economic resources or territorial boundaries[26] (the entire political systems of contemporary Iraq and Lebanon could serve as examples). However, he counterbalances this seemingly 'generalizing' stance with what should be an obvious point: in some ways religious (or sectarian) identity is at once both similar to and different from other mass-group identities. On the one hand, religion has a "boundary-defining" aspect that delineates group members from outsiders; in this way religion operates in much the same way as tribe, ethnicity, race and so forth. However,

---

[24] Lewis, "'What Group?'," p. 625.

[25] Rogers Brubaker, "Religious Dimensions of Political Conflict and Violence," *Sociological Theory*, 33:1 (2015): 1–19.

[26] Ibid., p. 4.

Brubaker points out that what sets religion somewhat apart from these otherwise comparable categories is its "normative ordering power" – the religious understandings of a right order, not just on the level of the individual believer or the religious community but, in some cases, on the level of wider society and the polity.[27] This indeed makes religious and sectarian identities potentially different from other mass-group identities, but such potential should neither be overstated nor its realization presumed. After all, religious identity's "normative ordering power" is only as potent as the religious doctrines from which it is derived are relevant at a given moment. As already mentioned, in most cases it is highly questionable just how relevant doctrine is to modern sectarian dynamics. In that sense, sectarian identity again comes to resemble other mass-group identities: as one early formulation put it, "it is the ethnic boundary that defines the group, not the cultural stuff that it encloses."[28] Replace 'ethnic' with 'sect' and 'cultural stuff' with 'doctrine' and the parallel becomes obvious. In many cases, sectarian identity is not defined by doctrine nor experienced through it; rather, any number of frames – national, political, social, economic, symbolic – can form the 'cultural stuff' that furnishes sectarian identity with meaning and sectarian competition with content.

Sectarian Identity and the Middle East: Between Allergy and Obsession

The question of religion versus politics is not the only restrictive binary one encounters when surveying the literature on 'sectarianism' in the Middle East. Equally myopic is the remarkably common tendency to frame Sunni–Shi'a relations in starkly absolutist and unrealistic terms, with Sunnis and Shi'as portrayed as either perpetually at each other's throats or forever in each other's embrace. Unfortunately, much of what is said and written about sectarian identity and 'sectarianism' falls into one or the other side of this unhelpful yet pervasive binary thereby

---

[27] Ibid., p. 5.

[28] Frederik Barth, "Introduction," in *Ethnic Group and Boundaries: The Social Organization of Culture*, ed. Frederik Barth (Boston: Little, Brown, 1969), p. 15. Quoted in Krishan Kumar, *The Making of English Identity* (Cambridge: Cambridge University Press, 2003), pp. 60–61.

creating two equally unhelpful approaches: alarmist and reductionist or, more straightforwardly, maximalist and minimalist. The alarmist or maximalist position (commonly referred to as primordialism) is a staple of political and journalistic commentary on the subject and it is rare to encounter it in the scholarly literature – though there are exceptions.[29] It holds sectarian identity as all-important and 'sectarianism' as one, if not *the*, defining characteristic of the Middle East and particularly of those countries where it has, at one point or another, been a source of contention. In this alarmist or maximalist view, political causality is traced to sectarian identity (and 'sectarianism') whose relevance is inflated to the extent that it subsumes much if not all of that which relates to the Middle East. This maximalist position has had a highly damaging effect not just because of its pervasiveness but because of its influence in policy-making circles – something abundantly evident in the long history of political and imperial interests inflating, instrumentalizing and deepening sectarian cleavages.[30]

Whether because of its ubiquity in the popular press or its considerable historical role in fostering an exploitative, paternalistic and condescending Western policy towards the Middle East, this simplistic maximalist position has been met with considerable resistance in recent years in the form of its inverse twin: an equally simplistic minimalist view. Instead of obsessing over an assumedly all-important and Middle East-defining 'sectarianism', the minimalist position does the opposite by seeking to deny sectarian identity and

---

[29] For an example of a primordialist take on sectarian relations from academia, see Ze'ev Maghen, "Unity or Hegemony? Iranian Attitudes to the Sunni–Shi'i Divide," in *The Sunna and Shi'a in History*, ed. Bengio and Litvak; Mark Tomass, *The Religious Roots of the Syrian Conflict: The Remaking of the Fertile Crescent* (New York: Palgrave Macmillan, 2016).

[30] Most recently this has been evident in the conversation on Iraq and Syria. Interestingly, the maximalist belief in perennial and perennially relevant sectarian identities governing the Middle East can lead to opposing, albeit equally reductionist, conclusions. For an example of a maximalist stance forming the basis of interventionist US policy recommendations in Iraq, see Daniel Byman, "Let Iraq Collapse," *National Interest*, 45 (Fall 1996): 48–60. For an example of the same maximalist stance as the basis for non-interventionist policy recommendations in Syria, see David Rieff, "History Resumes: Sectarianism's Unlearned Lessons," *World Affairs*, 175:2 (July–Aug., 2012): 29–38.

'sectarianism' any social, political or historic relevance beyond, possibly, its manipulation (if not creation) by foreign powers and nefarious politicians. In other words, one side sees sectarian identity as all-important – a fountain of causality – while the other seeks to reduce it to a myth fabricated by imperialists and other political actors. Pushback is certainly needed against the maximalist position but the minimalist position is no less problematic: being allergic to the concept of sectarian identity is just as simplistic, inaccurate and unhelpful as being obsessed by it. Interestingly, one finds a similar awkwardness and similar polarization between minimalists and maximalists in the way sectarian identity and 'sectarianism' are framed in the Scottish context: between hysterical inflations and unrealistically total denials of their relevance.[31] To illustrate, in responding to sensationalist reporting regarding sect-coded football violence, one minimalist retort argued: "Scotland was disgraced not by bigotry but by the unthinking way that its existence was assumed."[32]

As is often the case with extremes, the minimalist–maximalist divide contains many similarities. For example, both positions employ similar methods to back up their claims. They will invariably take a recent example of sectarian harmony or conflict and pair it with an analogous historical episode, thereby creating the illusion of uninterrupted non-'sectarianism' or 'sectarianism'. In the process, both positions effectively write out the intervening period from their narrative. To give one example, pointing to communal fears and sect-coded political organization in Mandate-era Syria as an explainer or harbinger of the Syrian civil war after 2011 erases the better part of seven decades' worth of social, political, economic and national history. Similarly, and far more egregiously, framing contemporary sectarian competition as part of a 1,400-year-old conflict effectively writes out 1,400 years of history from the story. The obverse is equally ahistorical: anchoring one's understanding of sectarian identity in a moment of sectarian

---

[31] For an interesting discussion of the debate on 'sectarianism' in Scotland, see the essays in Thomas Martin Devine (ed.), *Scotland's Shame? Bigotry and Sectarianism in Modern Scotland* (Edinburgh: Mainstream Publishing, 2000).

[32] Steve Bruce, "Scottish sectarianism? Let's lay this myth to rest," *The Guardian*, Apr. 24, 2011, https://www.theguardian.com/commentisfree/belief/2011/apr/24/scotland-sectarianism-research-data.

unity or an era in which sectarian identities had lost their relevance, and supposing that this snapshot view of history can be standardized as 'the real' of identity in the Middle East, is no more accurate than the 1,400-year-old-conflict trope.

Both the minimalist and maximalist positions are self-reinforcing in several ways: from the echo chambers that have emerged around them to the ways in which historical and contemporary data are selectively read. The inescapable difficulties in trying to 'measure' identity often exacerbate the problem. Opinion surveys, anecdotal evidence and personal experience, unavoidable and valuable tools of the trade, are especially susceptible to confirmation bias. Further, without a record of several years, such sources often provide snapshots of public sentiment towards a particular issue at a specific time. This is useful when examining a particular context but is not a solid foundation for an attempt to make generalizations or normative assumptions about sectarian identity and sectarian relations. Quite the opposite, snapshot vision reinforces the zero-sum dichotomy of minimalists and maximalists by encouraging us to wed our perceptions to a specific context, thereby leading us to a monochrome and static understanding of sectarian relations. This feeds into an all-too-human tendency of believing that "wherever we happen to be is where we always have been and always will be."[33] As I have argued elsewhere, the default setting of modern sectarian relations, particularly in places with significant Sunni and Shi'a populations, is characterized by banality: Sunnis and Shi'as interact, coexist, intermarry, fight and argue without doing so in a self-consciously *cross-sectarian* way. In other words, more often than not, they interact as people who happen to be Sunnis or Shi'as rather than as Sunnis or Shi'as. This is precisely why we remember instances of explicitly sect-coded cooperation or sect-coded conflict: they are exceptional occurrences and should not be used as the foundation on which to build an ahistorical, unchanging and inaccurate picture of either eternal sectarian harmony or ceaseless sectarian division.

The maximalist and the minimalist positions are attractive because of their simplicity but, beyond that, both also validate a certain

---

[33] Stephen Reicher, "The Context of Social Identity: Domination, Resistance and Change," *Political Psychology*, 26:6 (2004): 926.

perception of the Middle East and of sectarian identity. As with much relating to modern sectarian identities, the minimalist–maximalist divide is in large part rooted in divergent views regarding nationalism and the nation-state in the modern Middle East. The alarmist or maximalist take fits into a broader discourse that juxtaposes a normatively Western form of nationalism that is modern and secular with a Middle East composed of artificial states, fragmented peoples and stubborn resistance to modernity. Ultimately, therefore, the fixation of maximalists on sectarian identity goes hand in hand with their dismissal of the viability of the nation-state and of modern nationalism in places like contemporary Syria, Iraq, Lebanon and other parts of the Middle East. Hence the already noted difference in how contemporary 'sectarianism' is viewed in Western as opposed to Middle Eastern contexts: the former as a function of modern and intrinsically contemporary political and social processes, the latter as a sort of pre-modern ghoul whose 1,400-year-old echo continues to stalk the Middle East in the form of inescapably and irrationally divided Sunnis and Shi'as whose perennial and obscurantist divisions prevent the region from embracing modernity. This unhelpful binary rests on the unfounded assumption that sectarian identity is a handicap that needs to be overcome or neutralized by the modern nation-state. Yet, as will be explored in chapter 4, the widely presumed distinction and mutual exclusivity between a modern and 'good' national identity or nationalism, on the one hand, and a pre-modern 'bad' sectarian identity or 'sectarianism', on the other, is extremely misleading.[34]

Unity and Division, Aspirations and Reality

Be it in Europe or the Middle East, the performative rejection of 'sectarianism' is a common theme. As we discussed in the previous

---

[34] In her excellent study of Lebanese Shi'as, Shaery-Eisenlohr laments: "Studies of Lebanon continue to be informed by a normative dichotomy, in which identification with the nation and religious belonging are at odds with each other … [and] public expression of religion (often referred to as sectarianism) is imagined as an antithetical force to the nation." Roschanack Shaery-Eisenlohr, *Shi'ite Lebanon: Transnational Religion and the Making of National Identities* (New York: Columbia University Press, 2011), p. 6.

chapter, the overwhelming negativity of the term means that it is viewed with such revulsion that even sectarian identity itself is often approached with considerable awkwardness. The dominant form of political correctness in the Middle East holds unity – religious or national unity – as the Manichaean good opposing the evil of 'sectarianism'. In fact one could go as far as saying that it is near impossible to find someone defending 'sectarianism' or portraying it in positive terms. To draw on an imperfect Western parallel, as with 'sectarianism' in the Middle East there is widespread consensus in Western countries against racism and it is difficult to find mainstream voices openly embracing it. Even pedlars of race-hate and racial division tend to avoid self-identifying as racists, opting instead for less incriminating euphemisms such as nationalists or identitarians (the term of choice for the white nationalist and public face of the American alt-right, Richard Spencer).[35] In the Middle East, the toxicity of 'sectarianism' and 'sectarian' is far more pronounced, but this rejection of 'sectarianism', as sincerely held as it is, can obscure a more complicated reality if taken at face value. As former Lebanese prime minister Salim Hoss observes: "No one calls himself a liar in much the same way that no one calls himself sectarian."[36] Or as an old Arabic joke puts it: "The two things that I hate most are sectarianism and Shi'as!" The first step towards grasping the paradox of near-universal revulsion at 'sectarianism' alongside the perpetuation of sectarian divides is to move beyond stark, all-or-nothing binaries of either implacable hate or inseparable unity. Societal rejection of 'sectarianism' does not guarantee that sectarian divisions are not being perpetuated, sometimes unwittingly, by the very people who so loudly condemn them – the same can be said with regard to racism for that matter. Beyond the headline-grabbing instances of sectarian violence

---

[35] For an interesting discussion of the terminology of Western racial politics, see Thomas Chatterton Williams, "The French Origins of 'You Will Not Replace Us,'" *New Yorker*, Dec. 4, 2017, https://www.newyorker.com/magazine/2017/12/04/the-french-origins-of-you-will-not-replace-us.

[36] Quoted in Hussain Abdul-Hussain, "Hoss book touts secular credentials in sectarian world," *Daily Star*, Nov. 14, 2003, http://www.dailystar.com.lb/News/Lebanon-News/2003/Nov-14/44469-hoss-book-touts-secular-credentials-in-sectarian-world.ashx.

or explicit sectarian hate, it is far more common for sect-centric grievances to be produced in a variety of opaque ways.

Put simply, the genuinely and broadly held ideal against 'sectarianism' is not always matched in reality. Generally speaking, people in the Middle East and particularly those in contexts of high sectarian heterogeneity have been thoroughly socialized into accepting the principle of sectarian plurality. However, the ambiguity inherent in sectarian relations means that negative stereotypes, imbalances in the relations of power, and sect-centricity (potentially turning into sectarian division) are as much a reality as is the commonly encountered mantra 'we are all brothers'. This is perfectly illustrated in a Pew Research Center study that found that Sunnis in the Middle East are more likely to view Shi'as as non-Muslims in countries with few if any Shi'as. Lebanon and Iraq were in fact the most accepting of sectarian plurality among the Middle Eastern countries surveyed, thereby reflecting the reality that cross-sectarian interactions and connections are not a bar to sectarian competition or even, in extreme cases, sectarian conflict.[37] Again there is no shortage of parallels from across the world: good intergroup relations can break down, either permanently (Yugoslavia or Partition in South Asia) or temporarily (Lebanon or Rwanda).

None of this is unique to sectarian relations or to the Middle East; rather, the discrepancy between social ideals and messier social realities, and the paradoxical relationship between coexistence and competition or conflict, are common features of intergroup relations generally. In times of tension or crisis, the gap between the ideal of intergroup relations and the reality widens as does the gap between what people claim and how they feel. In this way people can end up over-emphasizing the extent to which they are guided by socially desirable views. We see this in how political correctness plays out in Western contexts or in what one study of sectarian relations in Northern Ireland described as 'hidden sectarianism'.[38] A more basic

---

[37] Pew Research Center, *The World's Muslims: Unity and Diversity*, Aug. 9, 2012, chapter 5.

[38] Ulrike Niens, Ed Cairns and Suzanne Bishop, "Prejudiced or Not? Hidden Sectarianism among Students in Northern Ireland," *Journal of Social Psychology*,

point, however, is that coexistence, intermarriage and even kinship are unfortunately not a bar to periodic outbreaks of intergroup antagonisms or even hostilities.[39] To explain this apparent paradox, some scholars have looked to Freud's 'narcissism of minor differences' theory according to which people, both as individuals and collectives, form an exaggerated sense of their own uniqueness to differentiate themselves from others, making similarity and coexistence a fickle barrier against conflict. As anthropologist Anton Blok informs us, the Mae Enga of the western highlands of Papua New Guinea have a saying: "We marry the people we fight."[40] Or as Turkkaya Ataov put it with regard to conflict in Central Asia: "When relations are pleasant, their desirable parts come to the fore. When disagreements rise, differences get the upper hand, and minor differences are then magnified. Even if there are no minor differences, groups tend to create them."[41]

In short, notions of unbreakable unity and aeonian division are equally absurd: sectarian intermarriage and popular rejection of 'sectarianism' are not proof of the former any more than sectarian competition or instances of sectarian conflict are evidence of the latter. No one in their right mind would frame interracial marriage or the cross-racial appeal of many African-American celebrities as evidence that racial categories do not matter in the United States. By the same token, racial controversies and race riots are not grounds for dismissing

---

144:2 (2005): 163–180. For the discrepancy between what people say and what they believe in the context of American race relations, see Adam J. Berinsky, "Can We Talk? Self-Presentation and the Survey Response," *Political Psychology*, 25:4 (Aug. 2004): 643–659; Daniel Corstange, "Ethnicity on the Sleeve and Class in the Heart," *British Journal of Political Science*, 43:4 (Oct. 2013): 889–914.

[39] Yugoslavia offers a tragically apt illustration. For a moving account of the breakdown of communal relations in Yugoslavia, see Peter Maass, *Love Thy Neighbor: A Story of War* (New York: Random House, 1999).

[40] Anton Blok, "The Narcissism of Minor Differences," *European Journal of Social Theory*, 1 (1998): 33–56.

[41] Quoted in Pal Kolsto, "The 'Narcissism of Minor Differences' Theory: Can it Explain Ethnic Conflict?" *Filozofija I Drustivo*, 2 (2007): 161. Kolsto adds to Ataov's comments by suggesting that hostilities do not stem from the minor differences themselves; rather, the conflicts are caused by something else but that "members of different groups will seize upon the minor differences in order to expand the identity gap between them and justify their mutual hostility." Ibid.

the concept of an American people, much less grounds for believing that US borders need to be redrawn.[42] The same self-evident logic applies to sectarian relations in the Middle East and needs to be recognized as such. In that sense, sectarian identities are little different from other mass-group identities. Asking if Sunni–Shi'a relations are amicable or antagonistic is asking a non-question in that it demands an answer devoid of the most basic element of intergroup relations: context.

Context, Flexibility, Salience

Both alarmists and reductionists are partially correct yet both miss the mark for the same reason: they insist on framing sectarian identities and sectarian relations in *either* positive *or* negative terms. In other words, they overlook the importance of context and deny the fluidity, flexibility and ambiguity of identity. In the process they overlook the fact that neither the meaning, salience, relevance nor even the content of sectarian identities are fixed. Furthermore, sectarian identity cannot be taken in isolation in that it inescapably sits alongside, and is mediated through interaction with, a number of other identities several of which can transcend Sunni–Shi'a division: national identity, local or city identity, class identity, tribal identity, Muslim identity and so forth. How sectarian identity is positioned with regard to these other categories depends on context. Sunni and Shi'a identities share enough in common for them to be framed as two amicable parts of a united whole; conversely, they have enough points of contention and difference between them for the relation to be imagined in

---

[42] For a recent iteration of the evergreen fallacy that the Middle East is best served and sectarian competition is best resolved by redrawing national borders, see Jim Hanson, "To bring peace to Syria and Iraq, allow them to break apart," *Fox News*, Feb. 18, 2018, http://www.foxnews.com/opinion/2018/02/16/to-bring-peace-to-syria-and-iraq-allow-them-to-break-apart.html. For a corrective to such views, see Sara Pursley, "'Lines Drawn on an Empty Map': Iraq's Borders and the Legend of the Artificial State," *Jadaliyya*, June 2, 2015, http://www.jadaliyya.com/Details/32140/%60Lines-Drawn-on-an-Empty-Map%60-Iraq%E2%80%99s-Borders-and-the-Legend-of-the-Artificial-State-Part-1; Fanar Haddad, "Political Awakenings in an Artificial State: Iraq, 1914–1920," *International Journal of Contemporary Iraqi Studies*, 6:1 (2012): 3–26.

confrontational terms. In other words, there is enough symbolic raw material for both frames – it all depends on context.

An awareness of the spread of history – as opposed to snapshot vision – easily illuminates the sometimes drastic changes in how sectarian identities are imagined. The sharp relief into which Sunni–Shi'a differences have been thrown by events since 2003 has seen the reformulation of sectarian identity as a causal factor and historical explainer, thereby creating an often false sense of continuity. For example, the sectarian element of the Syrian conflict has been inflated to the extent of dominating understandings not just of the Syrian civil war but also of Syrian and regional history more broadly. This is well illustrated by the assumption that the Assad regime, Iran and Hizbullah are allies today because of supposed religious affinities that pit them (as 'Shi'as') against 'Sunnis'. Such a view obscures a far more complicated history, to say nothing of the shifting relevance and meaning of sectarian identities over the decades. Iran's fostering of proxies, clients and allies is far from perfectly aligned with sectarian boundaries: Shi'a credentials are not a recipe for a strategic relation with Iran any more than Sunni identity is a bar to such relations.[43] In particular, the affinity of the Assad regime for Twelver Shi'ism is neither constant nor preordained, and the presumed synonymity of Alawism and Shi'ism is misplaced. As Kerr notes, while the Alawi community in Syria went through a process of "Shi'aization," under Hafez al-Assad, his son and successor attempted a "Sunnification" of the community.[44] Even more jarring is the evolution of the relationship between Hizbullah and Damascus. Far from being the natural, inevitable bedfellows that their alliance in the Syrian conflict would suggest, the relationship was in fact strained early on under Hafez al-Assad and the

---

[43] For an examination of Iran's patron-client relations in the region and the relevance of sectarian identities to them, see Afshon Ostovar, "Iran, Its Clients, and the Future of the Middle East: The Limits of Religion," *International Affairs*, 94:6 (Nov. 2018): 1237–1255.

[44] Kerr, "Introduction," in *The Alawis of Syria*, ed. Kerr and Larkin, p. 6. He goes on to suggest that the community has been going through a process of "re-Alawization" over the past decade or so. For a broader discussion of the relationship between the Syrian state and religion and particularly Sunni religious structures, see Thomas Pierret, *Religion and State in Syria: The Sunni Ulama from Coup to Revolution* (Cambridge: Cambridge University Press, 2013).

Syrian regime was initially uncomfortable with Hizbullah in the 1980s as they were seen as a threat to Damascus's 'secular' Lebanese Shi'a client Amal. Indeed, what appears to be an ironclad relationship between Hizbullah and the Assad regime in fact only dates to the 1990s.[45]

In a word, what sectarian identity means and how it is expressed and imagined at a given point will inevitably change. The reduced relevance of sectarian identities in, for example, the mid-twentieth century is no more the 'real' face of sectarian relations than is the sectarian violence and competition that have been witnessed in the early twenty-first century: neither frame invalidates the other; rather, they are two points on an ever-shifting continuum. To illustrate with an example from Cairo's al-Azhar University, one of the main centres of Sunni religious learning: in 1959, the Rector of al-Azhar, Shaikh Mahmud Shaltut, issued his famous statement declaring the legitimacy of Twelver Shi'ism as an Islamic school of thought (*mathhab*). Much like the earlier-mentioned example of Haj Amin al-Hussaini's *fatwa* on Alawism, some of Shaltut's motives were eminently political, relating to Gamal Abd al-Nasser's regional policies and ambitions; nevertheless, the pronouncement marks a highpoint in Sunni–Shi'a ecumenism at the doctrinal level.[46] However, it would be disingenuous to use this example as a template for making positive generalizations about the nature of Sunni–Shi'a relations. Doing so would fly in the face of a more ambivalent history that also includes less conciliatory episodes involving al-Azhar and Shi'ism. For example, in a reflection of the times, al-Azhar ran an essay competition in December 2015 entitled "The spread of Shi'ism in Sunni society: its causes, dangers and how to confront it."[47]

---

[45] Farouk-Alli, "The Genesis of Syria's Alawi Community," in *The Alawis of Syria*, ed. Kerr and Larkin, p. 45.

[46] For an in-depth study of Azhar University engagement with Shi'a scholars over the course of the twentieth century, see Rainer Brunner, *Islamic Ecumenism in the 20th Century: The Azhar and Shiism Between Rapprochement and Restraint* (Leiden: Brill Academic Publishers, 2005).

[47] Lu'ay Ali, "Mashyakhat al-Azhar tu'lin 'an musabaqa li-l-talaba a-wafidin 'an 'al-tashayu' fi-l-mujtama' al-Sunni" (Shaikhs of al-Azhar announce competition for foreign students on 'Shi'ism in Sunni society'), *al-Yawm al-Sabi'*, Dec. 11, 2015, http://www.youm7.com/story/2015/12/11/للطلبة-مسابقة-عن-تعلن-الأزهر-مشيخة/2485142#.VoJGfxV96M9.فى-التشيع-عن-الوافدين

Even seemingly straightforward cases of sect-specific or sect-neutral symbolism cannot be treated independently of context. In many cases, whether a symbol is 'sectarian' and offensive or not depends on who is invoking it and in what climate. To illustrate with a simple example, Hussain ibn Ali, the Prophet's grandson, third Shi'a Imam and a figure revered by all Muslims was invoked by Saddam Hussain during the Iran–Iraq war when a recently unveiled Scud missile was christened 'al-Hussain'. This was not only a nod to Iraq's Shi'a population, it was a pan-Islamic and, above all, a nationalist appeal. If we fast-forward to May 2015, we find the same symbol used for similar reasons but, unlike the example of Saddam's Scuds, 'al-Hussain' proved controversial when Prime Minister Nouri al-Maliki named the newly launched anti-ISIS operations in Anbar '*labayk ya Hussain*' (which roughly translates as 'we are here for you / we are at your service, O Hussain'). The matter proved controversial enough to force a change in the operation's name to '*labayk ya Iraq*'. In other words, despite the fact that, objectively, 'Hussain' is a cross-sectarian symbol, the context of the 1980s allowed 'Hussain' to be used by the Iraqi regime as a nationalistic symbol, but its usage was too sect-coded in the context of 2015.[48]

Even the sect-specificity of a symbol is subject to interpretation as are its salience and impact. At first glance, few things could be as inoffensively Christian as making the sign of the cross in a Christian majority country. Yet in Scottish football, a player crossing himself is grounds for a red card in that it can be interpreted as a display of sectarian affiliation and hence possibly a sect-coded taunt against the other side.[49] This is but an extreme illustration of the broader reality that the meaning of symbols, the way they are perceived, and their potential for instrumentalization can differ across time and place. For example, the bombing of the Askari Shrine in the Iraqi city of Samarra in February 2006 is correctly identified as a pivotal turning

---

[48] Al-Hussain has proven to be an especially elastic symbol: in addition to being a Shi'a Imam, an Islamic figure and an Iraqi nationalist trope, he has also served as a prop in narratives of Kemalist secularism and as a symbol for anti-capitalist critiques by Middle Eastern Marxists and others. For a brief overview, see Jean-Francois Bayart, *The Illusion of Cultural Identity* (London: Hurst & Co., 2005), p. 101.

[49] Patrick Reilly, "Kicking with the Left Foot: Being Catholic in Scotland," in *Scotland's Shame?*, ed. Devine, p. 29. Also see Gallagher, *Divided Scotland*, pp. 186–187.

point in post-2003 Iraq's civil war – either as the inaugural event or as a significant escalator. Here was a holy, primarily Shi'a, pilgrimage site that was subject to a devastating attack which unleashed a terrible spiral of sect-coded violence. The causality seems obvious; yet what is often overlooked is that the same shrine was struck again the following year with little consequence. Needless to say, it is not that the shrine had lost emotional importance to Shi'as, but the climate of 2007 – plus the fact that a second bombing will never have the same shock value as the first – produced a different reaction. This example calls into question the commonly encountered instrumentalist–primordialist dichotomy: the differing reactions to the two bombings show that the value, meaning and relevance of identities and their symbols are prone to fluctuations and are not frozen in primordial stasis; likewise, they show that those seeking to instrumentalize sectarian identity are not puppeteers operating in a vacuum nor do they have free rein with events and people.

From Above, from Below and the Role of Foreign Powers

Intertwined with the debates between minimalists and maximalists, instrumentalists and primordialists, are the related debates surrounding the role of foreign powers in sectarian relations and whether sectarian identity is driven from above or from below. To one degree or another, all of these questions boil down to the issue of agency. Is the relevance of sectarian identity created from above, instrumentalized by local or foreign actors, and forced upon society, thereby creating something akin to a false (sectarian) consciousness? Or is it something innately held by Sunnis and Shi'as – a primordial form of solidarity extending across time and space periodically and irresistibly rising from below? The problem with these questions is the impossible binaries they impose: binaries that are completely incompatible with the inherent ambiguities of identity. An instrumentalism that imagines omnipotent elites manipulating people devoid of agency is no less absurd than a primordialism that portrays sectarian identity as an insurmountable operating system deeply embedded in Sunnis and Shi'as and dictating their perceptions across time the world over. Ultimately these positions are of little analytical use and are often encountered as vehicles for the advancement of ideological predispositions regarding the Middle East. More broadly, the from above–from below dichotomy is unhelpful in that it forces us to divert our analytical attention to one or the other rather than examining the interaction between elites and people. Rather than a binary, the drivers of sectarian relations come both from above and from below in a circular, mutually reinforcing fashion.[50]

To take the role of foreign powers, there can be no denying the pivotal role that foreign interests can play in fostering sectarian entrenchment and endowing sectarian identity with added political relevance. This is as plainly evident in the impact of Ottoman–Persian rivalry on sectarian relations as it is in how Western imperial interests drove the politicization of sectarian identity in the nineteenth-century Levant or, more recently and no less nakedly, post-2003 Iraq. Yet while divide-and-rule strategies are well-documented parts of the imperial foreign policy toolkit, they are not deployed in a vacuum. Rather than *creating* sectarian divides or sectarian antagonisms, foreign powers will have to be mindful of local agency and the history of sectarian relations in a given place when charting their policies.[51] This again highlights the limits of adopting too strict an instrumentalist approach. For instance, in a discussion of the relation between state power and tribal or ethnic identity formation, James C. Scott cautions against an overly top-down approach: "it is striking how often a tribal or ethnic identity is generated at the periphery almost entirely for the purpose

---

[50] For example, in his study of sectarian relations and Shi'a identity in Lebanon, Max Weiss argued that sectarianization of the Lebanese Shi'a community during the French Mandate era was being pushed both from below in the form of Shi'a demands for sect-specific rights and religious recognition and from above in the form of elite and colonial divide-and-rule strategies. Of course the two dynamics were linked in a circular fashion. More broadly, he makes the argument that it is unsustainable to claim that colonialism alone created 'sectarianism'. Weiss, *In the Shadow of Sectarianism*, p. 11.

[51] For a nuanced treatment of the role of foreign powers that strikes a balance between the role of sectarian identity and local agency on the one hand and the role of foreign powers and elite manipulation of sectarian identities on the other, see Mark Farha, "Searching for Sectarianism in the Arab Spring: Colonial Conspiracy or Indigenous Instinct," *MuslimWorld*, 106:1 (Jan. 2016): 8–60.

of making a political claim to autonomy and/or resources."[52] This highlights the basic circularity between elite-led and mass-led factors: it plainly makes sense for people to adopt frames of reference that carry political relevance when advancing political claims just as it makes sense for elites or foreign powers to employ frames of reference that resonate with a critical mass of the population or with a specific target audience among them. As Scott explains with reference to tribal identities, even if such categories are inventions of state power, "once invented ... the tribe took on a life of its own. A unit created as a political structure of rule became the idiom of political contestation and competitive self-assertion. It became the recognized way to assert a claim to autonomy..."[53] Today's colonial imposition can become tomorrow's normative basis for perceptions of self and other – all the more reason not to anchor our conceptions of sectarian identity in any one time or era.

None of this is to denigrate instrumentalism per se or to deny its relevance. The instrumentalization of religious categories and religious (and sectarian) identities is well documented and easily demonstrated. For example, states have tried to exert a monopoly on *fatwa* production in the service of state interest.[54] Lebanon's uniquely sect-centric political system was, from the very beginning, the product of a top-down push to serve the interests of local elites and imperial powers. A century later, foreign powers were again instrumental in setting up and sustaining post-civil war Lebanon's political system.[55] Still in Lebanon, Suad Joseph has shown how a deliberate effort was made to reorganize neighbourhoods along sectarian lines in the run-

---

[52] James C. Scott, *The Art of Not Being Governed: An Anarchist History of Upland Southeast Asia* (New Haven: Yale University Press), pp. 258–259.

[53] Ibid.

[54] Abdullah Alaoudh, "State-Sponsored Fatwas in Saudi Arabia," Carnegie Endowment for International Peace – Sada, Apr. 3, 2018, http://carnegieendowment.org/sada/75971.

[55] "It was clear that the Taif Agreement [of 1990 that helped end the Lebanese civil war] could function only because it had an external regulator, Syria, that could enforce decisions thanks to its domination." Joseph Bahout, "The Unravelling of Lebanon's Taif Agreement: Limits of Sect-Based Power Sharing," Carnegie Endowment for International Peace, May 2016, p. 19.

up to and during the civil war as heterogeneity came to be regarded as a threat by some leaders concerned with their ability to maintain their control and influence.[56] Nor are these exclusively Lebanese phenomena, and examples of sectarian divides being used as regime-maintenance tools can be found across the region, from Iraq to Syria, Bahrain, Saudi Arabia and elsewhere.[57] Further, beyond individual regime interests, Makdisi argues that top-down dynamics in the form of American interest in and domination of the region make the study of sectarian identities and 'sectarianism' in the Middle East inherently more problematic than is the case with the study of similar dynamics in Ireland or South Asia.[58] Of course the tendency of foreign imperial powers to view the region in primordial terms has an especially long history; hence, just as the sect-coding of Iraq helped to frame and justify the US-led invasion of 2003, so we find the French doing much the same in their policy towards the region almost a century earlier. As Benjamin White informs us in his insightful study of the codification of minorities in Mandate-era Syria, "[French] documents on a startling diversity of subjects find it necessary to emphasize the absence of unity in Syrian society, its 'non-nationness' … [but] no mandate functionary ever questioned the (eminently questionable) unity or nationhood of French society."[59]

My intention therefore is not to detract from the validity of instrumentalist approaches but rather to highlight that they only help us explain and understand part of the story: an analysis that focuses solely on top-down factors while ignoring reciprocal bottom-up dynamics will inevitably remain wanting. The drivers of sect-specificity and sectarian entrenchment do not always come from above and,

---

[56] Suad Joseph, "Working-Class Women's Networks in a Sectarian State: A Political Paradox," *American Ethnologist*, 10:1 (Feb. 1983): 1–22.

[57] See, for example, Salloukh, "The Sectarianization of Geopolitics"; al-Rasheed, "Sectarianism as Counter-Revolution"; Toby Matthiesen, "Sectarianization as Securitization: Identity Politics and Counter Revolution in Bahrain," in *Sectarianization*, ed. Hashemi and Postel.

[58] Makdisi, "Pensee 4: Moving beyond Orientalist Fantasy," p. 559.

[59] Benjamin Thomas White, *The Emergence of Minorities in the Middle East: The Politics of Community in French Mandate Syria* (Edinburgh: Edinburgh University Press, 2011), p. 6.

even when they do, at some point such top-down processes will have a normative effect on popular perceptions. More to the point, elites are not always in the driving seat nor is sect-centricity always in their interest; the impetus sometimes comes from below. For example, top-down elite attempts to deconfessionalize personal status laws have often created a backlash in some segments of popular opinion. This was the case in 1950s India just as it was in 1998 Lebanon when Prime Minister Rafik al-Hariri opposed the draft uniform civil code due to popular and clerical Sunni opposition.[60] Alongside the many instances of top-down instrumentalization of sectarian identities, at some junctures and on some issues one finds a popular desire for sect-specificity in which elites will need to acquiesce. The potential for sectarian entrenchment to be driven from below is especially marked in our own times because of the emergence of social media and the decentralization of the production of information. This has enhanced the potential for bottom-up drivers to incentivize sect-centricity at the level of elites. Needless to say, this should not lead us to exaggerate the role of bottom-up drivers: again, circularity is more useful than dichotomization when considering top-down and bottom-up drivers.[61]

What all this underlines is the need for a more nimble approach to the subject that takes circularity rather than top-down or bottom-up flows as its starting point. The Syrian civil war is often regarded as the example *par excellence* of instrumentalist 'sectarianism'. Yet as Thomas Pierret argues, common as it is, the idea that regional powers sectarianized the Syrian civil war is overstated. He goes as far as reversing (to some extent) the presumed causality, arguing instead that the sectarian frame often ran counter to the intentions and interests of major foreign stakeholders. Rather, Pierret suggests that it was the deeply sect-centric character of the conflict that imposed itself on

---

[60] Farha, "Global Gradations," p. 364.

[61] As is well documented, while social media can empower local voices, it is also susceptible to manipulation. See Marc Owen Jones, "Propaganda, Fake News and Fake Trends: The Weaponization of Twitter Bots in the Gulf Crisis," *International Journal of Communication*, 13 (2019): 1389–1415; Marc Owen Jones, "Automated Sectarianism and Pro-Saudi Propaganda on Twitter," *Exposing the Invisible*, 2016, https://exposingtheinvisible.org/resources/obtainingevidence/automated-sectarianism.

regional powers and calculations.[62] This echoes broader research on the interaction of conflict and identity. Again, rather than one shaping the other, circularity seems to be more common. In her study of identity and the Arab–Israeli conflict in Israeli electioneering, Neta Oren found "the relationship between conflict and national identity to be circular; the conflict shapes national identity, while changes in national identity influence the course of conflict."[63] A similarly multidirectional framework would be more fruitful for the study of sectarian relations than the unhelpful binaries that have dominated the debate thus far: instrumentalism versus primordialism; foreign versus local; top-down versus bottom-up. The utility of such a multilayered approach can be seen in Paulo Pinto's lucid analysis of the sectarianization of the Syrian conflict: "a process that has unfolded on multiple levels: top-down (state generated); bottom-up (socially generated); outside-in (fuelled by regional forces); and inside-out (the spread of Syria's conflict into neighbouring states)."[64] The complexity of sectarian identity (to say nothing of the complexity of the Syrian civil war) mandates such a multidirectional and multifaceted approach rather than the unrealistic binaries that have often discoloured the study of sectarian relations.

The intersection of local and foreign or imperial interests, the circular, mutually reinforcing way in which they operate, and the context-dependent fluidity of sect-centricity are perfectly captured in Eugene Rogan's masterful study of intergroup relations and social conflict in nineteenth-century Damascus.[65] Rogan examines the writings of Christian intellectual Mihayil Misaqa (1800–88) and his accounts of the Muslim–Christian disturbances of 1860 and of Muslim–Christian relations in general. What emerges is that over the course of the 1860s and 1870s, Misaqa's position shifts depending on the intended audience, the socio-political climate, the perceived entrenchment of

---

[62] Thomas Pierret, "The Reluctant Sectarianism of Foreign States in the Syrian Conflict," United States Institute of Peace, Peace Brief 162, Nov. 18, 2013.

[63] Neta Oren, "Israeli Identity Formation and the Arab Israeli Conflict in Election Platforms, 1969–2006," *Journal of Peace Research*, 47:2 (2010): 193–204.

[64] Paulo Gabriel Hilu Pinto, "The Shattered Nation: The Sectarianization of the Syrian Conflict," in *Sectarianization*, ed. Hashemi and Postel, p. 123.

[65] Eugene Rogan, "Sectarianism and Social Conflict in Damascus: The 1860 Events Reconsidered," *Arabica*, 51:4 (Oct. 2004): 493–511.

Ottoman power, the vicissitudes of European policy, and the potential for European involvement in the region. When addressing a domestic audience, the language is ecumenical and tolerance dominates his rhetoric. Here the communal (Muslim–Christian) violence of 1860 is portrayed as the work of the unenlightened lower classes. When addressing Europeans, however, the language shifts to one of primordial religious strife to better reflect the language of European analysts of the day who consistently viewed the region in primordial terms. Over the course of 13 years (1860–73) Misaqa's narrative vacillates, depending on the circumstances, between a class-coded ecumenism on the one hand and minority-rights assertiveness on the other. Misaqa's oscillations reflect his perceptions regarding the political circumstances within the Ottoman Empire and the role that Europeans were likely to play, and hence the change they might affect. As Rogan explains, by 1873

> The justification for European intervention had been eliminated by a successful Ottoman reassertion of authority in Damascus ... Vigorous new governors in Damascus played an important role in reinvigorating both the Ottoman administrative presence and the economic well-being of the city ... Such measures, by giving *all* Damascenes a stake in the new Ottoman order, were important in bridging the deep communal divisions provoked by the 1860 massacres ... The communalist and submissive tone of Misaqa's history of 1873 [as opposed to his earlier accounts] may be explained by these changes. Misaqa was now writing for an Ottoman audience...[66]

In other words, what Rogan labels "the European language of sectarianism" chimed to some degree with Misaqa's self-perception as an Ottoman Christian writing not too long after the intercommunal violence of 1860; however, this feeling was prone to fluctuations and could be internalized or weakened depending on bottom-up communal relations, the role and perceived power of local authorities, and the position of foreign powers.

The primordialization of sectarian relations can at times serve both foreign and local interests, and in this the parallels between the above

---

[66] Ibid., p. 509.

account and more recent history are stark. In the case of nineteenth-century Damascus, it was used by Europeans to justify intervention within the Ottoman Empire and it was used by local minorities to attract European assistance. This almost perfectly parallels the run-up to the invasion of Iraq in 2003 and the way both US policy and Shi'a-centric and Kurdish nationalist opposition groups primordialized ethno-sectarian relations in mutually reinforcing ways. A key variable here is the degree to which people feel the political status quo is susceptible to change – something in which foreign powers play a huge role: from 1860 to Mandate-era Palestine to Partition, and so on.

Demystifying Sectarian Identity

The debates and differences addressed above have dogged the study of sectarian relations for far too long. Thankfully there is considerable scholarly agreement on many of the main points, though mainstream and political opinions continue to lag behind. In order to help move the study of sectarian relations forward, we need to revise our conception of sectarian identity. By adopting a more multilayered, segmented understanding of what sectarian identity is and how it operates, we can better address the controversies already discussed and finally move beyond them. There are several dimensions to or fields of sectarian identity: a local subnational dimension, the dimension of the nation-state, the dimension of international or transnational solidarities, competition and calculation, and, finally, sectarian identity as an identity organized around a set of religious truths. As will be shown in the next two chapters, these dimensions are interdependent and mutually reinforcing and cannot be treated in isolation from each other. Combined, they give us a more rounded picture of what sectarian identity constitutes and the roles it can play. This framework also allows us to finally escape the binaries that have long constrained discussions of sectarian identity and sectarian relations.

3

THE MANY DIMENSIONS OF MODERN
SECTARIAN IDENTITY

Many of the debates discussed in the previous chapter are a function
of insisting on too narrow a conception of sectarian identity. Hence
the abundance of unhelpful binaries: from above vs from below;
instrumentalists vs primordialists; religion vs politics; and so forth.
A less constricted understanding of modern sectarian identity allows
us to accept and navigate through these frames rather than forcing
ourselves to choose one or another.

The Complexity of Identity

Identity is one of the most theorized concepts in the social sciences
and it provides us with a useful starting point for thinking about that
most *under*-theorized of concepts: sectarian identity. With identity
as our conceptual starting point for sectarian identity we can begin
developing a multifaceted understanding of sectarian dynamics. The
need for such an approach should be obvious given the varied ways
in which sectarian relations have been studied. Some scholars view
sectarian identity as an expression of Islamic thought (political or
philosophical). Others view it as a political construct or a function
of symbolic politics. Some have focused on class dynamics while
others frame sectarian identity as a tool for regime maintenance or

geopolitical rivalries. Surveying these and many other arguments, one cannot help concluding that they are all partially correct and each holds a piece of the puzzle. Accordingly, we need to broaden our conception of sectarian identity to enable us to identify and understand all of the frames in which sectarian identity operates. To do so we need to view sectarian identity as a composite, multilayered identity: it is not any one thing nor does it operate on any single level (politics *or* religion *or* social identity and so forth); rather, it is all of these and more. Sectarian identity is imagined, formulated, mobilized and expressed on several interdependent, mutually informing and mutually reinforcing levels or dimensions:

1. *Doctrinal*: At the level of doctrine and religious truths; in other words, as an identity organized around a set of religious truths and as a global or anational identity.
2. *Subnational*: At the local level within a given national setting.
3. *National*: At the level of the nation-state and as a prism through which national identity is mediated.
4. *Transnational*: As a prism for international relations, international or transnational solidarities, and geostrategic competition.

Given the interdependency of these dimensions, the fluidity of their boundaries and the constant cross-pollination between them, they should not be viewed in a hierarchical way nor should a fixed causal relationship between them be presumed. Accordingly, rather than a pyramid – a Maslow's hierarchy of sectarian identity, so to speak – this approach holds sectarian identity as the sum of these four constituent parts or dimensions. Rather than onion-like with differently sized layers encasing a core or a heart, sectarian identity operates at these four equally important levels or dimensions. Any one or any combination of these can drive sectarian relations, and the relevance of individual dimensions is completely context-driven. Such a multifaceted conception is hardly unique in the study of identity, and scholars of sectarian relations should likewise avoid monochrome conceptions of what is an inescapably multilayered phenomenon. To give one of many examples, taking issue with the imprecision of the term 'identity', one group of scholars proposed a more complex and segmented approach: rather than being any one thing, they argued that collective identity is "a social category that varies along two dimensions – content and contestation. Content describes the meaning of a collective ID … Contestation refers to the degree of agreement within a group over the content of the shared category."[1] Such a framework, and others like it, enable us to envision the constellation of moving parts that constitute any one form of collective identity. In a similar way, the framework I am proposing here allows us to imagine sectarian identity operating on several interlinked, but very different, fields of perception. And it is questions of perception more than objective facts, cognitive perspectives more than fixed categories, that govern the fluidity of identity. As one study put it, collective identities are "not things in the world but ways of seeing the world. They are ways of understanding and identifying oneself, making sense of one's problems and predicaments, identifying one's interests and orienting one's action."[2] In other words, these identities are lenses through which one variably perceives self and other.

If sectarian identity is one such lens, it has several internal filters of its own: a person's sectarian identity is imagined differently in the context of sectarian relations within the single nation-state from how it is imagined in the context of clerical disputes over dogma or how it is imagined in a transnational context. In that sense, sectarian identity is not just another element (alongside race, gender, class, etc.) in people's multifaceted identities but is itself a multifaceted composite that is subject to similar processes of negotiation and mediation. This recalls broader identity negotiation theory and social identity theory with their emphasis on people's layered identities, the strategies they

---

[1] Rawi Abdelal, Yoshiko M. Herrera, Alastair Iain Johnston and Rose McDermott, "Identity as Variable," *Perspectives on Politics*, 4:4 (Dec. 2006): 696. They go on to further segment the two dimensions they identify; hence, the content of identity – that which described the meaning of collective identity – falls into four interlinked forms: constitutive norms, social purposes, relational comparisons and cognitive models.

[2] Rogers Brubaker, Maria Loveman and Peter Stamatov, "Ethnicity as Cognition," *Theory and Society*, 33:1 (2004): 47.

develop to navigate between them, and the importance of context.[3] Just as self-reflection and social construction processes shape how we negotiate our multiple identities, a similar process governs the inner workings of sectarian identity and the relation between its multiple dimensions. In certain circumstances sectarian identity may gain relevance and, depending on the context, one or more dimensions of sectarian identity may become more relevant and hence privileged over the others. Again, we see a parallel between social identity theory and sectarian identity in the form of the complexity of social identity and that of the inner dynamics of sectarian identity.[4] It is this complexity that makes it insufficient to view the subject through a single prism – be it just as a political system in Lebanon or solely as a religious dispute between clerics or only as a function of Saudi–Iranian geostrategic rivalry.

The nebulous nature of sectarian identity and the need for greater conceptual complexity are well captured in Max Weiss's formulation of 'sectarianism' in Lebanon. Rather than a tangible, clearly identifiable, objective reality, sectarian identity becomes "a way of being in the world that depends upon a set of cultural markers and social practices, a framework capable of holding familial, local, regional and even international loyalties together in a variably defined and shifting communal bloc."[5] Another scholar who has recognized the inadequacy of rigid conceptual compartmentalization of different forms and sites of identity formation is Shaery-Eisenlohr, who argued for a more synergetic conception of national and transnational solidarities: "transnationalism always operates locally

---

[3] For example, Stella Ting-Toomey, "Identity Navigation Theory," in *Sage Encyclopedia of Intercultural Competence*, vol. 1, ed. Janet M. Bennett (Los Angeles: Sage Publishing, 2015); Henri Tajfel and John C. Turner, "The Social Identity Theory of Intergroup Behavior," in *Political Psychology: Key Readings*, ed. John T. Jost and James Sidanius (New York: Psychology Press).

[4] Sonia Roccas and Marilynn B. Brewer, "Social Identity Complexity," *Personality and Social Psychology*, 6:2 (2002): 88–106. Social identity complexity – the degree of overlap perceived to exist between groups of which a person is simultaneously a member – is a useful framework for understanding the overlapping nature of sectarian identity's multiple dimensions.

[5] Weiss, *In the Shadow of Sectarianism*, p. 13.

and ... transnational solidarities ... need to be studied in their national contexts ... transnational ties can help the production of nationalism and appeals to transnational solidarities are often rooted in nationalist agendas."[6] There is no shortage of examples of the applicability of this insight to sectarian relations; however, this needs to be developed into a more structured framework that takes in not just national and transnational frames but doctrinal and local ones as well. To consider one of countless examples: in 2013 Egyptian Shi'a activist Hasan Shehata and three of his companions were lynched in a village in Greater Cairo.[7] The gruesome event, which was filmed and uploaded on YouTube, illustrates the way in which sectarian identity can operate simultaneously at all the levels identified above. On the face of it, the lynching was a local or subnational affair in which anti-Shi'a prejudice was inflamed by Salafi preachers with deadly results. As a result, there is no divorcing the local dynamics of this case from the doctrinal dimension of sectarian relations in that anti-Shi'a hate speech in the prelude to the lynching was rooted in questions of doctrinal or religious otherness. However, the national dimension is equally relevant in that Shi'ism has long been framed as a potential national security threat in the Egyptian context. In that sense, Shi'as are not just doctrinally or religiously alien but they are also antithetical to an 'Egyptianness' that is imagined in strongly Sunni Muslim terms. Finally, there is the crucial backdrop of regional sectarian entrenchment and the perception that sectarian relations in the individual nation-state were linked to the sect-coded conflicts of Iraq, Bahrain, Syria and Lebanon and to Arab–Persian rivalry more generally (see chapter 6).[8] This transnational element was duplicated on the other side of the sectarian divide when Shehata was briefly turned into a martyr among Shi'as in the region. Visitors to Baghdad

---

[6] Shaery-Eisenlohr, *Shi'ite Lebanon*, p. 3.

[7] For details, see: "Egypt: Lynching of Shia Follows Months of Hate Speech," Human Rights Watch, June 27, 2013, https://www.hrw.org/news/2013/06/27/egypt-lynching-shia-follows-months-hate-speech.

[8] On the uses and framing of Sunni–Shi'a relations in Egypt, see Saleh and Kraetzschmar, "Politicized Identities, Securitized Politics" and Steven Brooke, "Sectarianism and Social Conformity: Evidence from Egypt," *Political Research Quarterly*, 70:4 (2017): 848–860.

in 2013 and early 2014 would have seen posters of Shehata in some Shi'a areas of the Iraqi capital.[9]

The above example should not be taken to mean that sectarian identities are always manifested in all four dimensions. If and when sectarian identity becomes relevant – and it is important to reiterate the obvious fact that its relevance is fluid – one or more dimensions will come into play depending on context. This should make us additionally wary of generalizations: for example, competition between Sunnis and Shi'as can be sect-coded and hence be labelled sectarian competition; however, without an understanding of the multidimensionality of sectarian identity and how the different dimensions factor in, this tells us little about the content of that competition beyond the fact that it is being carried out in the name of Sunnis and Shi'as. To borrow an insight from political psychology, intergroup relations are animated by what are perceived to be "valued dimensions of comparison" at any given moment.[10] When it comes to sectarian identity, what constitutes such a valued category will vary according to context as will, by extension, what dimensions of sectarian identity are in play. Accordingly, all manner of interactions can be sect-coded and hence sectarianized but with vastly different implications.

Here, Duncan Bell's notion of 'mythscapes' is instructive. Again, the concept was developed in pursuit of greater clarity regarding commonly used and misused phrases. Specifically, Bell sought to distinguish between myth and memory and to better understand their relation to each other and to national identity. His approach and his insights into mythscapes are equally applicable to sectarian dynamics, particularly given the interaction between modern sectarian identity and national identity – which we will explore in chapter 4. Paraphrasing Bell's words, the mythscape is "the temporally and spatially extended discursive realm wherein the struggle for control of people's memories and the formation of [common] myths is debated, contested and subverted incessantly. *The mythscape is the page upon which*

---

[9] Personal observation. Baghdad, February 2014.
[10] Reicher, "The Context of Social Identity," p. 929.

the multiple and often conflicting [identity] narratives are (re)written; it is the perpetually mutating repository for the representation of the past for the purposes of the present."[11]

If we take the concept of mythscape – or indeed myth–symbol complexes, communal imagination, collective memory or any other similar concept – as the page or canvas on which the past and the present of an identity are constructed, then it stands to reason that, firstly, individuals are simultaneously working on several pages – national, ethnic, religious, racial, sectarian, tribal and so forth – and, secondly, that each individual category can be composed of several pages or canvases of its own. This is especially the case with sectarian identities because they are, by definition, secondary identities that act as subsidiaries to larger ones (religion, nationality, ethnicity). It is the interaction between sectarian identities and the several larger wholes of which they are a part that creates the multiple dimensions, pages, mythscapes and so forth of sectarian identity. 'Persian Shi'ism' is different from an unhyphenated abstract global 'Shi'ism'. Likewise, sectarian relations in Bahrain are marked by a host of issues and are contested and joined along vectors that do not pertain in other contexts. Sunni identity in Lebanon is formulated in a manner that in many regards bears little relevance to or familiarity with, say, Sunni identity in Malaysia. It is in these local and national variations that we can best reveal and examine the intersection of sectarian identity with its many drivers such as class, region, political or economic resources, and nationalism. To take a typical example: in Shaery-Eisenlohr's study of Lebanese Shi'ism we are presented with a student's poem containing an assertion of Lebanese Hizbullah's conception of Shi'a-Lebanese identity. Rather than a religious meditation or an ode to the tenets of Shi'ism or to transnational Shi'a solidarity, the theme of the poem is more an assertion of class identity: a Lebanese underclass whose supposed authenticity, moral high ground and devotion give it more claim to Beirut than others:

---

[11] Duncan S.A. Bell, "Mythscapes: Memory, Mythology and National Identity," *British Journal of Sociology*, 54:1 (March 2003): 66. Emphasis added.

Your Beirut is an old portrait hung on the walls of each house
And my Beirut is a young girl who doesn't know but the silver touch of
the moon and golden glim of the sun

...

Your Beirut is dinner parties full of most delicious food and my Beirut
is a piece of bread in the hand of hungry kids and a doll in the hand of a
poor girl
Your Beirut is sandcastles against the storm
And my Beirut is a tough rock that waves could not and will never erode.[12]

The Dimensions of Sectarian Identity

Just as class intersects with and drives sectarian identity in this poem,
we find similar examples elsewhere of sectarian identity being driven
and imagined along lines that are far removed from religious doctrine
and religious ideas: regional identities, national identities, political
loyalties and so forth. This is a function of the multidimensional
nature of sectarian identity and it is to these dimensions that we now
turn. The remainder of this chapter will deal with three dimensions
(doctrinal, subnational and transnational) while the following chapter
will deal with the national dimension. The model being introduced in
this and the next chapter allows us to sharpen our analytical focus by
identifying which specific aspect of sectarian identity is relevant to a
given situation. As will be seen below, this not only helps us to grasp
the inherent multidimensionality of sectarian identities, it also allows
us to better match the correct analytical tools and the appropriate
bodies of literature to meet the needs of a given context. International
relations theory, for example, can tell us much about sectarian identity
in foreign policy and geopolitics but is completely irrelevant where
the doctrinal dimension of sectarian identity is concerned. Likewise,
the literature on class and critical race theory allows us to better
understand the subnational dimension of sectarian identity but not
the transnational dimension. The point is that, as will be demonstrated
below, the multidimensionality of sectarian identity requires a degree
of conceptual agility and interdisciplinarity that, I hope, will be well
served by this model.

---

[12] Shaery-Eisenlohr, *Shi'ite Lebanon*, p. 67.

Sectarian Identity as a Reflection of Religious Doctrine

As discussed in the previous chapter, the place of religious doctrine, beliefs and truths is not as obvious and certainly not as central to sectarian dynamics as might be thought by the casual observer. A common mistake is to assume that sectarian competition is a function of irreconcilable religious or sectarian doctrines or sets of beliefs. In many cases this is a gross misdiagnosis of the issue – especially in its contemporary, modern form – and it leads to commensurately misplaced remedies. The most common example of this takes the form of over-reliance on inter-faith dialogue to resolve sect-coded political conflict – the failure (indeed irrelevance) of the Amman Message of 2005 and that of the Mecca Declaration of 2006 to stem conflict in Iraq are cases in point. Equally misplaced are calls for nationalism or secularism as natural antidotes to what on the surface appear to be pre-modern, doctrinal, sectarian antagonisms. Yet, as we have already noted and will elaborate further in the following chapter, modern sectarian competition is very often a function of modern nationalism and can be equally at home in supposedly secular settings (Assad's Syria, Saddam's Iraq) as it is in supposedly theocratic settings (Saudi Arabia, post-1979 Iran). Having said that, it is no less problematic to entirely dismiss religious beliefs and questions of religious truths from our understanding of modern sectarian dynamics. Rainer Brunner cautions against reducing Sunni–Shi'a conflict solely to power politics and worldly considerations, arguing that this would inevitably fail to account for the different "and ultimately incompatible" Sunni and Shi'a approaches "to salvation history and the question of the nature and continuity of prophetic charisma."[13] While it is clear that competing religious truths are not the crux of sect-coded violent conflict or sect-coded state rivalries today, Brunner is nevertheless correct to insist that we be mindful of the relevance of contested religious truths when considering modern sectarian dynamics: in some circles and contexts they can act as the primary driver of Sunni–Shi'a competition (consider Salafi anti-Shi'a polemics or the doctrinal anti-Sunnism of the likes of

---

[13] Brunner, "Sunnis and Shiites in Modern Islam," in *The Dynamics of Sunni–Shia Relationships*, ed. Marechal and Zemni, p. 26.

Yasser al-Habib – who we shall meet in chapter 5 – to say nothing of the doctrinal justifications that some militant groups have put forth to justify sectarian violence).[14] Even when questions of religious orthodoxy and religious truths are clearly not at issue, the props of the original schism (such as competing conceptions of salvation history and legitimate authority) can confer a sense of certainty about the legitimacy of one's group and the justice of its claims. By extension, sectarian identity *as doctrine or belief* can potentially play an important – even if residual – role in legitimating sect-coded political and social claims. An obvious parallel here is the ambiguous role and relevance of doctrinal issues as opposed to racial ones in some forms of Western anti-Muslim discrimination today and in some of the ways that Western Muslims have framed their response to it.[15]

In many ways, the doctrinal dimension's often secondary role in modern sectarian dynamics is a blessing that facilitates Sunni–Shi'a coexistence in places of significant sectarian heterogeneity like Lebanon, Iraq and elsewhere. Indeed, one might even go as far as saying that a degree of reciprocal ignorance about the finer points of doctrinal divergence is socially desirable for the purposes of sustainable coexistence. The more prominent the doctrinal level of sectarian identity becomes in sectarian relations, the less bridgeable and more rigid the differences will appear to be. Generally speaking, it is potentially easier to foster sectarian coexistence when matters of religious dogma are relegated below social and political issues and kept to a superficial level which can bear a selective reading that omits controversial points of difference. After all, some elements of dogma do not lend themselves to negotiation in the same way that material interests do. Furthermore, sectarian othering and sectarian

---

[14] For a discussion of doctrinal drivers of sectarian competition, see Jam'iyat al-Tajdid al-Thaqafiyya, *Al-Ta'ifiyya: Radda ila al-Jahiliyya* (Sectarianism: A Return to Jahiliyya) (Manama: Jam'iyat al-Tajdid al-Thaqafiyya, 2010), pp. 47–57; Fu'ad Ibrahim, "Al-Su'udiyya: al-Hiwar al-Masmum" (Saudi Arabia: The Poisoned Discourse) in *Nawasib wa Rawafidh*, ed. Saghiya.

[15] On the ambiguous framing of anti-Muslim prejudice in France, see Caterina Froio, "Race, Religion or Culture? Framing Islam between Racism and Neo-Racism in the Online Network of the French Far Right," *Perspectives on Politics*, 16:3 (2018): 696–709.

exclusion are less absolute and less sweeping when not grounded in matters of faith and doctrine. There is less room for a spectrum of 'good' and 'bad' Sunnis or Shi'as if inter-sect sensitivities are based primarily on matters of belief.[16] Conversely, political rights, political entitlement and access to the national pie are matters that can be contested and in which culpability does not extend to all members of sect *a* or sect *b*. However, if the issue is primarily one of beliefs and dogma then all members of a given sect are to some extent guilty. This is reflected in the contrast between sectarian relations in Saudi Arabia and those in, say, Lebanon, Iraq or Syria. In the former, the very notion of Islamic diversity is contested in a way that is unfamiliar in the latter cases. Sectarian competition may be inflamed and may even descend into all-out civil war (as in Iraq, Lebanon and Syria) but the concept of sectarian plurality is neither controversial nor is it socially contested (with the exceptional extreme of the Islamic State and its prior incarnations). Rather, what is at issue in such contexts is the relations of power governing state and society and the consequences (real or perceived) these have on the distribution of socio-political and economic goods. The Saudi Arabian example differs in that sectarian identity and perceptions of religious orthodoxy explicitly interact with aspects of national inclusion. As Matthiesen has argued: "Contrary to other cases of sectarian discrimination, the problems associated with being Shi'a in Saudi Arabia are therefore not just about political economy or identity politics, they are also about religious beliefs per se. For the acceptance of Shi'a Islam as a valid school of Islamic law is anathema to the Wahhabi clerics."[17]

---

[16] For a broader discussion of this theme and particularly on the differences between a more selective, ethnically inflected anti-Shi'ism and a more wholesale doctrinally inflected anti-Shi'ism, see Fanar Haddad, "The Language of Anti-Shi'ism," *Foreign Policy*, Aug. 9, 2013, http://foreignpolicy.com/2013/08/09/the-language-of-anti-shiism/.

[17] Toby Matthiesen, *The Other Saudis: Shiism, Dissent and Sectarianism* (Cambridge: Cambridge University Press, 2015), p. 8. There are signs that Saudi Arabian state policy may be working towards a more civic/ethnic approach to Saudi nationalism that removes the tension between sectarian plurality and national inclusion. However, these are only tentative moves and it is too early to definitively assess the extent of the shift. For a discussion of these dynamics as of 2018, see Kirstin Smith Diwan,

By segmenting our understanding of sectarian identity we also get a sense of the varying, context-driven distance between Sunnism and Shi'ism. Commenting on the relation between the two (as doctrines and systems of faith), Marechal and Zemni argue that Islam is characterized by an internal "unity-diversity dialectic," adding that "Today's conflicts between Sunnis and Shiites are perhaps best understood as part of a tension between the dream of unity and the reality of internal divisions."[18] Nowhere is this more applicable than to the doctrinal dimension of sectarian relations. There is little doubt that the vast majority of Muslims place a premium on 'Islamic unity'. Yet this aspirational unity is often based on an unrealistic expectation of relative uniformity and can be upset when confronted with the realities of doctrinal difference or the suggestion that Islam can mean more than one thing.[19] In this way, the belief in unity acts in a paradoxical way. On the one hand it acts as a binding force between Sunnism and Shi'ism and frames unity between them as normatively positive – a notion in which many Muslims, especially those from contexts of high sectarian heterogeneity, are thoroughly socialized. However, on the other hand, downplaying doctrinal differences can render them problematic: by creating a pretence to uniformity, the encounter with doctrinal divergence can be transformed into something potentially offensive and shocking. As one scholar argued with regard to Christian views towards Jews, "The greater the theological proximity, the greater the offence…"[20] In that sense, inter-religious (such as Muslim–Christian) dialogue can be potentially less complicated than Sunni–Shi'a dialogue in one crucial respect: nobody expects or aspires to doctrinal convergence; instead, doctrinal *divergence* is taken as the starting point and the goal becomes respect for irreconcilable differences regarding

---

"Saudi Nationalism Raises Hopes of Greater Shia Inclusion," The Arab Gulf States Institute in Washington, May 3, 2018, http://www.agsiw.org/saudi-nationalism-raises-hopes-greater-inclusion-shias/.

[18] Marechal and Zemni, "Conclusion," in *The Dynamics of Sunni–Shia Relationships*, ed. Marechal and Zemni.

[19] Muhammad Qasim Zaman, "Sectarianism in Pakistan: The Radicalization of Shi'a and Sunni Identities," *Modern Asian Studies*, 32:3 (July 1998): 696.

[20] Andrew Mango, "Minorities and Majorities: Review Article," *Middle Eastern Studies*, 23:4 (Oct. 1987): 512–528.

religious truth. Sunni–Shi'a dialogue (again, on the level of religious doctrine) often falters because of the limits to which people admit to and accept doctrinal difference. An interesting corollary to this is how differently the stakes are perceived in religious competition between the Abrahamic faiths on the one hand and intra-Islamic sectarian competition on the other. For example, following the resumption of Iranian tourism to Egypt in 2013, Egyptian Salafis voiced strong objections to having Iranian tourists in their midst. This led some commentators to criticize them for objecting to Iranian but not to Israeli tourism in Egypt. Apart from instrumental and opportunistic motives, the rationale presented by Salafis for the discrepancy was related to their fear that doctrinal proximity could foster doctrinal permeability. As an MP for the Egyptian Salafi Nour Party put it, "We are not afraid of the Zionist tourists, because Egyptians will not convert to Judaism. However, we are not immune from the threat of Shi'a ideologies. It is more likely for an Egyptian to convert to Shi'ism than to Judaism or Christianity."[21]

The details of doctrinal difference between Sunni and Shi'a readings of Islam and Islamic history need not detain us.[22] For our purposes, what is worth noting is that the perceived need to overcome doctrinal distance and the imperative for unity are powerful yet relatively recent phenomena. This does not mean that conflict was the norm in pre-modern or early-modern sectarian relations; quite the contrary, but there was nevertheless seldom any concerted drive towards unity and little perceived need for bridging theological differences. A notable medieval exception relates to the seventh Abbasid caliph, al-Ma'mun (r. 813–33), who designated Ali al-Ridha, the eighth Shi'a Imam, his heir to the caliphate. The caliph's motives are a subject of debate and, just as with all subsequent attempts at doctrinal rapprochement right down to our own times, they combined the earthly and the spiritual. Though al-Ma'mun's sympathy towards (proto-) Shi'ism and his pro-Alid leanings are a matter of historical fact, the decision seems to have

---

[21] Saleh and Kraetzschmar, "Politicized Identities, Securitized Politics," p. 560.

[22] For an excellent overview of Sunni–Shi'a relations with a particular emphasis on efforts to bridge the doctrinal gap, see Hamid Enayat, *Modern Islamic Political Thought* (New York: I.B. Tauris, 2005), chapter 1.

been aimed at securing the stability of his rule and realm.[23] Whatever the motive, this stands as an early example of attempts at doctrinal ecumenism – though at this early stage it was more between the two branches of the Prophet's descendants, Abbasids and Alids, rather than between Sunnis and Shi'as as we know them today. In the event, nothing came of the episode as al-Ridha died (or was poisoned, according to Shi'a accounts) two years after his designation as successor and the matter was soon forgotten. More recently, a relatively rare early-modern example of such an attempt at ecumenism is the Kubrawiyya Sufi order, which sought to resolve Sunni–Shi'a differences in the thirteenth and fourteenth centuries.[24] However, with the dwindling of the Kubrawiyya, the outbreak of the Kizilbas rebellions in Anatolia, and the rise of the Safavid state, the prospects for Sunni–Shi'a dialogue became more distant.[25] Indeed, after the Kubrawiyya, the next significant attempt at Sunni–Shi'a understanding came almost three centuries later with the rise of Nadir Shah, the founder of the short-lived Afsharid state in Iran. This effort proved fleeting and ended with Nadir Shah's assassination in 1747.[26] It was only in the

---

[23] For an overview of the debates surrounding this event, see Mehmet Ali Buyukkara, "Al-Ma'mun's Choice of Ali al-Ridha as His Heir," *Islamic Studies*, 41:3 (Autumn 2002): 445–466.

[24] Enayat, *Modern Islamic Political Thought*, pp. 37–39.

[25] The Kizilbas were eastern Anatolian tribesmen who followed the Safavid Sufi order of Ardabil. In the late fifteenth century and into the sixteenth century a number of these tribes rebelled against the Ottoman state and lent their support to the Safavids. The Kizilbas rebellions were significant in politicizing notions of heterodoxy and orthodoxy and in lending salience to the notion of Sunni identity in the Ottoman state. For an overview, see Stefan Winter, "The Kizilbas of Syria and Ottoman Shiism," in *The Ottoman World*, ed. Christine Woodhead (New York: Routledge, 2012). Also in the same volume see Derin Terzioglu, "Sufis in the Age of State-Building and Confessionalization."

[26] Nadir Shah was not known for his religious devotion. His pursuit of reconciliation was not an ecumenical effort to establish the legitimacy of mutual disagreements; rather, according to Litvak, his main concern was the divisive impact of anti-Shi'ism on his political and military power. As such his effort aimed to secure Shi'a acceptability by appeasing official Sunnism and diluting Shi'a sect-specificity. See Meir Litvak, "Encounters between Shi'i and Sunni Ulama in Ottoman Iraq," in *The Sunna and Shi'a in History*, ed. Bengio and Litvak, pp. 71–74. On Nadir Shah's pursuit of ecumenical rapprochement with the Ottomans, see Ernest S. Tucker, *Nadir Shah's Quest for Legitimacy in Post-Safavid Iran* (Gainesville: University Press of Florida, 2006), chapters 4 and 7.

1800s and the rise of what Enayat describes as Islamic modernism that interest in Sunni–Shi'a dialogue gained momentum. In Enayat's view, the emergence of modernistic trends in religious circles allowed for a softening of doctrinal boundaries and hence the creation of cross-sectarian mobilization and cooperation towards political ends, not least of which were those relating to the newly emerging nation-state: by the late nineteenth century, Islamic modernists such as Jamal al-Din al-Afghani and Muhammad Abduh were dedicating their energies towards Islamic unity in order to establish modern polities that could better resist Western colonialism.[27] Here we find a temporary convergence between the political thinking of Muslim modernists and the political interests of Sultan Abd al-Hamid II who took an interest in pan-Islamism and Sunni–Shi'a unity in the late nineteenth to early twentieth century. The Sultan's motives were entirely related to state interests and were less about building bridges and more about neutralizing threats – especially those relating to Ottoman–Iranian rivalry and, more so, those emanating from Western encroachment and the need to resist the "tyranny and rule of the Christian states."[28]

The twin phenomena of Western imperialism and the rise of the nation-state were crucial in the shift of sectarian dynamics away from religious polemics and more towards political goals, in the process reifying the perceived benefits of, and need for, Islamic unity. These trends were accelerated in the early twentieth century with the demise of the Ottoman Empire and the creation of multi-confessional, ostensibly civic nation-states such as Iraq, Lebanon and Syria, which meant that sectarian cooperation now became "not so much a requirement of Islamic solidarity as a practical necessity."[29]

---

[27] Not coincidentally the same period and the same drivers saw the emergence of the concept of 'the Muslim world'. See Cemil Aydin, *The Idea of the Muslim World: A Global Intellectual History* (Cambridge: Harvard University Press, 2017).

[28] Gokhan Cetinsaya, "The Caliph and Mujtahids: Ottoman Policy towards the Shiite Community of Iraq in the Late Nineteenth Century," *Middle Eastern Studies*, 41:4 (July 2005): 563, 565–567; Juan R.I. Cole, "Shaikh al-Ra'is and Sultan Abdulhamid II: The Iranian Dimension of Pan-Islam," in *Histories of the Modern Middle East: New Directions*, ed. Israel Gershoni, Hakan Erdem and Ursula Wokock (Boulder: Lynne Rienner Publishers, 2002).

[29] Enayat, *Modern Islamic Political Thought*, p. 42.

Beginning in the early twentieth century, Sunni–Shi'a cooperation and ecumenism reached unprecedented heights. More than that, there was a widespread normative belief, particularly among the urban educated classes, in the necessity and benefits of Sunni–Shi'a solidarity – though this was by no means an uncontested issue as illustrated by the example of late nineteenth- and early twentieth-century Islamic reformer Rashid Ridha's critical views of Shi'ism.[30] In any case, as Ende notes, the spirit of ecumenism which societies in much of the Arab world take for granted today as a normatively positive and necessary good did not have deep roots in the early twentieth century and was very much a product of the rise of the nation-state and the ever-increasing penetration of Western imperialism following the demise of the Ottoman Empire.[31]

The modernity of the ecumenical tendency in Sunni–Shi'a relations does not detract from its validity nor does it make it any less real. However, it does highlight the potentially complicating role of religious doctrine and the ways in which it can hold back ecumenism. In that sense this may go against the venerable assumption that sectarian relations only sour when they interact with politics. History would suggest that the manner in which sectarian identities meet and interact with politics dictates whether or not politics and sectarian identity yield benign consequences (Sunni–Shi'a cooperation in the wake of the demise of the Ottoman Empire) or malign ones (the instrumentalization of sectarian or religious identities in nineteenth-century Ottoman Mount Lebanon).

The complicating role of religious doctrine is illustrated in the vicissitudes of twentieth-century efforts at doctrinal rapprochement – or *taqrib*. The most prominent example of this is the *Jama'at al-taqrib bayn al-mathahib al-Islamiyya* (Society for rapprochement between the Islamic schools of thought). This was established in Cairo in the late 1940s by a young and relatively unknown Iranian Shi'a cleric, Muhammad Taqi al-Qomi. Perhaps recognizing the unbridgeable

---

[30] See for example, Brunner, *Islamic Ecumenism*, pp. 89–92.

[31] Werner Ende, "Sunni Polemical Writings on the Shi'a and the Iranian Revolution," in *The Iranian Revolution and the Muslim World*, ed. David Menashri (Boulder: Westview Press, 1990), pp. 220–224.

nature of some elements of doctrinal difference (and perhaps also recognizing the benefits of a degree of popular reciprocal ignorance too), the society opted to sweep such matters under the carpet and restrict its energies to examining points of convergence. This opened them to attacks from more hard-line elements who criticized the society's reluctance to address points of difference between Sunnis and Shi'as. The society's greatest success – and indeed one of the historic highpoints of Sunni–Shi'a ecumenism – was the February 1959 statement from the Rector of the al-Azhar in Cairo, Mahmud Shaltut, authorizing religious instruction in Shi'a jurisprudence. This statement was seminal in that it was a frank acceptance of Twelver Shi'ism as a legitimate school of Islamic thought on a par with its Sunni counterparts. Consequently, it is often referred to as proof that Sunnism and Shi'ism are in fact potentially bridgeable in fairly unproblematic ways were it not for the malign influence of politics. Yet, again, this masks a more complicated reality. As mentioned in the previous chapter, the successes of the society and the crowning achievement of the Shaltut statement were themselves intrinsically a product of the prevailing political climate and, more specifically, the Egyptian regime's interest in investing in pan-Islamism. Likewise, the demise of the society's role was also a function of the Egyptian regime's changing priorities: one year after the Shaltut statement, Shah Muhammad Reza Pahlavi's acknowledgement of his country's recognition of Israel led to a severing of relations between Egypt and Iran and, with it, an end to the Egyptian regime's interest in Sunni–Shi'a ecumenism.[32]

This episode reminds us that, firstly, political instrumentalization of sectarian identities is not always malign nor is fostering division always the aim. Secondly, and more importantly, it shows the difficulty, if not impossibility, of treating any single dimension of sectarian identity in isolation; hence the inadvisability of drawing too clear a line between 'religion' and 'politics' – be it politics at the level of the nation-state and

---

[32] For more details on the society, see Brunner, "Sunnis and Shiites in Modern Islam," in *The Dynamics of Sunni–Shia Relationships*, ed. Marechal and Zemni, pp. 31–37; Ende, "Sunni Polemical Writings on the Shi'a," in *The Iranian Revolution*, ed. Menashri, pp. 224–225; Enayat, *Modern Islamic Political Thought*, pp. 48–51.

its internal dynamics or transnational geostrategic politics. In the case of the Shaltut statement we have an explicitly, seemingly unambiguous, religious and doctrinal issue that was nevertheless ultimately driven and subsequently derailed by political exigencies. Again, it bears repeating that this does *not* mean that religion or doctrine are a fig leaf or a false facade concealing the supposedly 'real' drivers of Sunni–Shi'a relations. Rather, what it does mean is that matters of faith and doctrine cannot alone explain modern Sunni–Shi'a dynamics any more than the paradigm of the nation-state, class or international relations can alone explain sectarian relations. Even if we were to focus specifically on the foundational divisions between Sunnism and Shi'ism, we would find an inextricable intersection between politics and doctrine in the sense that it was a highly political issue (the legitimacy of post-Prophetic authority) that gave rise to doctrinal differences which were subsequently codified as Sunni and Shi'a schools of thought.[33] This highlights that, rather than there being a false dichotomy of religion *or* politics, the two are inescapably linked. To paraphrase Marechal and Zemni, the Sunni–Shi'a divide is as much a discursive tool of power that naturalizes certain political realities as it is a neutral description of religious phenomena.[34]

A final word on doctrinal difference relates to its fluctuating salience in sectarian relations. Just as sectarian identities lose or gain relevance according to context, so too there is an elasticity to the relevance of doctrinal difference between Sunnis and Shi'as. Doctrine becomes particularly relevant in a context where either group's Islamic credentials are threatened or questioned by the other. Yet the same differences fade into oblivion when questions of religious truth are challenged by non-Muslim – say, Christian – sources. In such cases it is far more likely for spiritual legitimacy and moral rectitude to be located in an unhyphenated *Islamic* discourse juxtaposed against the Christian other. Likewise, if we step back further, the differences between Muslims and Christians are just as likely to be overlooked in certain contexts, such as when challenged on issues relating to

---

[33] Marechal and Zemni, "Conclusion," in *The Dynamics of Sunni–Shia Relationships*, ed. Marechal and Zemni, p. 227.

[34] Ibid., p. 238.

LGBTQ rights. Legitimacy and moral rectitude would then be located in a discourse of Abrahamic faith and believers juxtaposed with the amoral, godless other.

While sectarian identities are, on the surface, religious identities, it would be misleading to reduce them to their doctrinal component. Religious doctrine and differing conceptions of religious truth are only one dimension of sectarian identities. As the following sections will show, depending on the context this dimension can at times be irrelevant to sectarian dynamics. This leads us to consider a widespread phenomenon that I have previously labelled "secular sectarians,"[35] in which Sunni–Shi'a relations, prejudices and biases are driven by completely secular or non-doctrinal considerations and motives. For example, self-professed secular liberals may associate a particular group (fairly or not) with obscurantist religiosity and hence condemn it as inherently anti-secular and anti-modern. The critique in this case is not aimed at a competing religious doctrine; rather it is a general antipathy to groups perceived as insisting on maintaining a differentiated religious identity that violates the secular norm: Catholicism in Scotland, Shi'ism in some parts of the Arab world, the near-total synonymization by their critics of Sunni Arab Syrian oppositionists with radical jihadism, the portrayal of Islam by liberal, secular, atheist anti-Islamic voices in the West, and so on.[36] As Mark Farha argues, the waning or otherwise of personal piety and the rise of 'social secularism' are of little relevance to sectarian relations. Taking Lebanon as a case study, Farha concludes that "the vigour of *communal identity* has little to do with the *extent of religious observance and faith*; rather, there is sufficient occasion to differentiate between personal piety and confessional sentiment."[37] In this way, secular people, even atheists, can harbour prejudice against, and advocate the exclusion of,

---

[35] Haddad, "Secular Sectarians."

[36] An interesting example from Scotland: "In 2010, it was not the Orange Order but these secularists who mounted the liveliest opposition to Pope Benedict XVI's visit to Scotland. In 2011, it was the supposedly ultra-modernist Scottish Green Party which included in its manifesto the promise to abolish Catholic state schools. Seculars and humanists view Catholicism as a backward belief system that should not be permitted to influence public life." Gallagher, *Divided Scotland*, pp. 11–12.

[37] Farha, "Global Gradations," p. 358.

this or that sectarian group. However, this should not be taken to mean that doctrinal differences are to be ignored when considering sectarian dynamics; rather, their relevance should not be assumed and should instead be correctly contextualized as part of a multidimensional conception of sectarian identity. As has been stressed throughout, it is important not to draw too clear a line between the various dimensions of sectarian identity. As we have seen above, the all-too-common dichotomization of religion and politics presents us with a false binary that cannot account for the intertwinement of the two concepts. Indeed, even where the doctrinal dimension does not directly animate sectarian relations, it may still be relevant in that it can furnish the symbolic props of sectarian relations (in all their dimensions) in the form of legitimating narratives, drivers of group cohesion, the raw material of group boundaries, and the like.

Sectarian Identity as Subnational Identity

In contexts where articles of faith, doctrinal differences and competing religious truths are the primary drivers of sectarian othering and sectarian competition, a particular body of literature and a certain set of tools are needed to understand the dynamics in play: classical Islamic texts, familiarity with salvation history and theological and jurisprudential disputes, inter-faith dialogue, and so forth. These can, however, be reduced to irrelevance when we consider how sectarian competition unfolds in other dimensions. For example, thinking of sectarian relations at the subnational or local level requires a different body of literature and different conceptual tools. After all, with this dimension we are dealing with the intersection of sectarian identities with class dynamics, regional and tribal discrepancies in resource allocation and power relations, the workings of clientelistic and patrimonial networks, and so forth. These issues are the essence of sectarian identity at the subnational level: basically it is about the governing social and political order within a given national setting and how one's sectarian identity is perceived to fit into the underlying relations of power. Before outlining some of the ways in which this works, we need to make two cautionary comments. Firstly, as with any dimension of sectarian identity and indeed with the very concept of sectarian identity, none of the following or the preceding should be taken to mean that sectarian identities are perpetually relevant to how people view their socio-political horizons; sectarian identities lose or gain relevance according to context. What is being described here is how sectarian identity operates on the various levels identified *when sectarian identity gains relevance and is brought into play*. Secondly, while the line between all four dimensions is blurred and while there is constant interplay between them, this is perhaps most pronounced when considering the subnational and national levels given the relation between national policy and the establishment and maintenance of hierarchies of power, networks of privilege, and so forth. For our purposes, the dimension of the nation-state, which will be dealt with separately in the next chapter, relates more specifically to the intersection between sectarian identity and national identity and nationalism whereas the local or subnational dimension is more concerned with power relations *within* the national setting. At the very least, this segmentation may help us to think about the role of class and local identities in how sectarian relations are framed and how these vary across different settings. The localized, particularistic dynamics of the subnational level are essential to understanding the broader picture of sectarian identity in that, firstly, they have a more tangible, direct impact on the lives of those concerned and, secondly, they indirectly feed into and further intertwine with the other dimensions by, for example, nurturing a greater degree of sect-centricity (and hence perhaps augmenting the doctrinal dimension's relevance) or incentivizing those with a local sense of sect-coded victimhood or sectarian awareness to seek redress through appeal to international co-religionists (thereby potentially bringing the transnational dimension into play).

In the previous section, the Gordian knot of sectarian identities on the doctrinal dimension was, generally speaking, that between politics and religion. With respect to the local or subnational dimension, it is between economics, sectarian identity and other subnational cleavages (particularly class, region, tribe). In many ways, contexts of institutional weakness, endemic corruption, and systemic clientelism and patrimonialism can, in and of themselves, heighten *perceptions* of 'sectarianism'. In an environment where patronage networks are the order of the day, the identities of the political elites will be reproduced in patterns of privilege and networks of patronage in a cascading way throughout society, thereby inevitably privileging a particular set of identity markers. This is why in chapter 1 the Ba'th of Syria and Iraq were not described as representing or privileging one sectarian group (Alawis and Sunnis) but rather a particular regional and tribal subset of a sectarian group.[38] The point is that in such settings, perceptions of sectarian discrimination become all the more likely given that the ruling elite will enforce a set of power relations that, to some extent, are based on personal links and solidarities.[39] In this way, sectarian identity can come to be seen (even if indirectly) as a determinant of personal, political and socio-economic fortunes – either as a source of social capital or as a glass ceiling. Once such perceptions take hold, and regardless of whether they are entirely justified or not, it is very difficult to dispel them from popular perception. For example, one study from 2013 found that, contrary to conventional wisdom, Lebanese Shi'as were not as economically far behind Sunnis and Christians as is often presumed: "Shiites were no longer as economically disadvantaged as the discourse about 'disinheritance' and the stereotypes of the past made them out to be. Yet the stereotypes persist …"[40] Even when changes are occurring, it often takes generations for them to be internalized and regarded as normative.

The importance of patrimonialism and clientelism as structural drivers of sectarian identity is noted by Raymond Hinnebusch, who argues that "class-consciousness is discouraged and small group identity encouraged by the exceptional availability in MENA [Middle East and North Africa] of rents concentrated in state hands, accessed via kin,

---

[38] Alawis in Syria are divided along tribal and regional lines and the same goes for Sunnis and Shi'as in Iraq. That does not mean that a certain set of power relations are not built around subsets of these sectarian groups but it does make labels such as 'Sunni regime' and 'Alawi regime' problematic. For more, see Leon T. Goldsmith, "Alawi Diversity and Solidarity: From the Coast to the Interior," in *The Alawis of Syria*, ed. Kerr and Larkin.

[39] For a discussion of the interaction of personal links and power relations in authoritarian regimes, see Joseph Sassoon, *Anatomy of Authoritarianism in the Arab Republics* (Cambridge: Cambridge University Press, 2016), chapter 5.

[40] Corstange, "Ethnicity on the Sleeve and Class in the Heart," p. 898.

tribal and sectarian *wasta* (clientele connections)."[41] In short, a weakly institutionalized and under-proceduralized system will see political actors relying on personal networks, relations and solidarities (one of which is sectarian identity) to further their interests. If this political culture becomes institutionalized it inevitably pervades society. To take the case of Ba'thist Iraq, while Saddam Hussain's regime continues to be mislabelled as a 'Sunni regime', the logic of its discriminatory politics was driven more by tribe and region than by sectarian identity though the latter inevitably followed on, at the very least in popular perception: being Shi'a added one more hurdle for those trying to tap into elite patronage networks in that it potentially created one extra degree of separation from the geographic and tribal centres of power. The way in which reliance on personal solidarities can drive sectarian entrenchment was far more starkly demonstrated in post-2003 Iraq as former Sadrist parliamentarian and former deputy prime minister Baha' al-A'raji candidly explained in an interview with Iraqi news channel al-Sumaria in 2016:

Baha' al-A'raji:	With regard to the political leaderships and the parties, when we came to Iraq [in 2003], we were leaderships without a base.
Interviewer:	So the easiest way [to build a base] was sectarianism.
Baha' al-A'raji:	[Yes] So as a result, for example from the Iraqi [National] Alliance, Baha' al-A'raji would speak in a sectarian way in order to attract [followers] and create a base.[42]

This interview again highlights the ways in which sectarian identities, when operating at the local or subnational level, can gain relevance and meaning because of their role in broader channels of patronage. This is key to understanding the institutionalization and operationalization of sectarian identities in many Middle Eastern settings. For example, given that the Lebanese system interweaves sectarian identity and patronage networks, disparities and inequalities will inevitably impact

---

[41] Hinnebusch, "Syria's Alawis," in *The Alawis of Syria*, ed. Kerr and Larkin, p. 108.

[42] "Na'ib ra'is al-wuzara' al-Iraqi al-sabiq al-sayyid Baha' al-A'raji – Hiwar Khas – al-halaqa 4" (former deputy prime minister of Iraq Mr Baha' al-A'raji – Hiwar Khas – episode 4), uploaded July 8, 2016, https://www.youtube.com/watch?v=Gz6119ybGLU.

on intergroup relations as one's sectarian identity becomes a key factor in shaping one's access to the state. Sectarian identity is never the be-all and end-all in such systems but it is an important part of a nexus of identities and signifiers – tribe, region, sect, class, political affiliation – that together animate the system of power relations. In Suad Joseph's words:

> *Wasta*, the modus operandi of the ruling class, became the means to political survival for all social classes. Indeed, everyone, even the poorest peasant, participated in this political culture, constructing complex, egalitarian and hierarchical, instrumental and normative networks – built from and legitimated by kin, friendship, neighbourhood and sect idioms and identities. The polity – a system of personalism – consisted of webs of overlapping informal personal networks connecting all social classes.[43]

This is as good an illustration as any of how sectarian identity on the local or subnational level interacts with patronage, and how one comes to inform the other and together they reproduce broader categories such as class distinctions.[44]

Analyses of the Lebanese system, which in many ways is unique in its official institutionalization of sectarian identities,[45] raise an important question: is sectarian identity (or 'sectarianism') really the issue here or is the heart of the matter clientelism and patronage? On the one hand one can argue that sect is not needed to produce these channels of patronage and, by extension, the governing system in Lebanon. Would matters be all that different if a similar logic was at play but operating along regional, party-political or tribal lines rather than sectarian ones? Put another way, there is nothing inherently, let alone uniquely, insidious about sectarian identities and even their institutionalization in that they are far from being the only form of subnational identity that can distort citizenship

---

[43] Joseph, "Working-Class Women's Networks," p. 11.

[44] In this we can borrow from older theories regarding the differences between vertical and horizontal ethnic differentiation and the degree to which ethnic identity maps onto class. For example, Donald L. Horowitz, "Three Dimensions of Ethnic Politics," *World Politics*, 23:2 (Jan. 1971): 232–244.

[45] For a recent treatment of the subject, see Bassel F. Salloukh et al., *The Politics of Sectarianism in Postwar Lebanon* (London: Pluto Press, 2015), especially chapters 1–2.

and the distribution of state resources. This is not to defend the institutionalization of sectarian identities but to caution against its fetishization as somehow uniquely different from neo-patrimonial models elsewhere, such as the manner in which 'tribal identity' intersects with 'big man politics' and economic distribution in many sub-Saharan contexts. Equally important, however, is the fact that, be it sect, tribe or any other ascriptive marker, once institutionalized it becomes pervasive. Rather than a uniquely Lebanese disease, the role of sectarian identity in sectarianized contexts recalls one study's findings regarding race relations: "Participation in race is not voluntary ... within racialized social systems."[46] Nor are race and sect unique in this regard; the same point holds for gender: "Insofar as a society is partitioned by 'essential' differences between men and women and placement in a sex category is both relevant and enforced, doing gender is unavoidable."[47]

The association – never accurate – of a sectarian group with a particular class is another way in which sectarian barriers are maintained even while being cross-cut by other categories. This latent sect-class prejudice is found across the Arab world. An ethnography of Bahrain from 1984, for example, "conceptualized a 'traditional Sunni' perspective of the *Baharna* Shi'a as dirty, revolutionary, uncivilized, animalistic and inbred ... In this the Bahraini represents the urban, civilized Sunni, while *Baharna* is the Shi'i antithesis."[48] In Syria, Alawi identity often carries class as well as religious connotations.[49] "The Alawites were our servants, but now some [Sunni] guys on campus take on the Alawi accent, a gruff accent, to show that they are connected

---

[46] Lewis, "What Group?" p. 629.

[47] Ibid., quoting Candace West and Don Zimmerman, "Doing Gender," *Gender and Society*, 1:2 (1987): 137.

[48] Marc Owen Jones, "Contesting the Iranian Revolution as a Turning-Point Discourse in Bahraini Contentious Politics," in *Gulfization of the Arab World*, ed. Marc Owen Jones, Ross Porter and Marc Valeri (Berlin: Gerlach Press, 2018), p. 95. The term *Baharna* (sing. *Bahrani*) refers to the original inhabitants of the Bahraini archipelago who are mostly Shi'a today. The term differentiates them from later migrants (both Shi'a and Sunni).

[49] Christa Salamandra, "Sectarianism in Syria: Anthropological Reflections," *Middle East Critique*, 22:3 (Oct. 2013): 305.

to power," was the lament of one of Nibras Kazimi's informants.[50] In his classic study of Iraq's social classes, Hanna Batatu likewise found a significant, though far from complete or static, coincidence between the sectarian divide and socio-economic cleavages in early twentieth-century Iraq.[51] In Lebanon the term *metwali* (pl. *metawla*) is a derogatory term used to refer to Shi'as who are stereotyped as lacking taste and refinement.[52] As with similar social prejudices from across the world, such sect or class stereotypes have given rise to a genre of sect-coded jokes of which Corstange gives us a good example: "Another Shiite friend came in dressed sharply in a suit, and joked that he was camouflaged as a Christian."[53] Shaery-Eisenlohr makes an important observation about these jokes when she notes that one of their central messages is that the underclass status of the targeted group is impervious to changes in financial status. Rich or poor, a *metwali* is always a social eyesore with poor taste and vulgar manners. In this we are reminded of how the Iraqi term *shrūgi* (pl. *shrūg*) is used to refer to working-class migrants from the Shi'a south and how the term's elasticity makes it shorthand for (depending on the context) Shi'as in general, southerners in general or the tasteless in general.[54] Such sweeping prejudices that combine class with other collective identities are easily found in other contexts; the term 'guido' (pronounced *gweedo*) is used in the United States to denote both class and ethnic markers associated with Italian-American

---

[50] Nibras Kazimi, *Syria through Jihadist Eyes: A Perfect Enemy* (Stanford: Hoover Institution Press, 2010), p. 66.

[51] Batatu, *The Old Social Classes*, part 1, chapter 4.

[52] Shaery-Eisenlohr, *Shi'ite Lebanon*, pp. 44–45. According to Stefan Winter, the term was used by Maronites as far back as the seventeenth century as a derogatory reference for Shi'as. Winter, *The Shiites of Lebanon*, p. 177. The term's etymology seems to be related to Alid loyalties. See Khalid Sindawi, "Jawla fi-Ma'jam Mustalahat al-Shi'a" (A Journey through the Dictionary of Shi'a Phrases), The Arabic Language Academy, http://www.arabicac.com/content.asp?id=97.

[53] Corstange, "Ethnicity on the Sleeve and Class in the Heart," p. 898.

[54] In the Iraqi dialect, *shrūg* is originally a term used to refer to those from east of the Tigris – the term is derived from *sharq* meaning east. However, it acquired a derogatory association with the working class, particularly those with links to, or who are from, the southern governorates. See Ali al-Wardi, *Dirasa fi-Tabi'at al-Mugtama' al-Iraqi* (A Study of the Nature of Iraqi Society) (Baghdad: Matba'at al-Ani, 1965), pp. 135–136; Batatu, *The Old Social Classes*, pp. 134–137.

stereotypes, and the word 'hillbilly' evolved from a term specific to certain regions of the Appalachians to a marker of white poverty in general, again with connotations of poor taste and vulgarity. Closer to the Middle East, one is reminded of urban stereotypes of rural folk and of Levantine stereotypes of people from the Gulf States. All of these illustrate the intersection of class prejudice and other collective identities. The examples from Iraq, Lebanon, Syria and Bahrain point to the interplay between class and sect and how this can factor into the way in which structurally upheld and privileged conceptions of respectability, political correctness, national authenticity, good taste and social status are determined.

Beyond being just a source of interesting social commentary and inappropriate jokes, the relation between class and sectarian identity has at times distorted the dynamics and perceptions of both. Most obviously, the interchange between sect and class has at times stood in the way of class solidarity in the same way that race has done in other contexts.[55] In such cases, class solidarity is precluded by the poor identifying more readily with the rich of their sectarian group than with the poor of another sectarian group.[56] Even more pervasive and divisive is how the intersection of class and sect can foster the sort of secular sectarian prejudice mentioned earlier. In extreme circumstances we have seen this used as the basis for normative assumptions regarding political inclusion and the suitability of certain sections of society for political office. This was vividly apparent in some of the ways in which rejection of the post-2003 order in Iraq was manifested. Opponents of the new order attacked its legitimacy on a number of grounds (ties to the occupation, ties to Iran, the sect-centricity of the new political order and its elites, and so forth). However, in some corners, the familiar class-sect prejudices were used to question the suitability of

---

[55] Nancy Isenberg, *White Trash: The 400-Year Untold History of Class in America* (New York: Viking, 2016), pp. 248–249. Isenberg drives the point home throughout her study. For example (p. 264), Lyndon Baines Johnson is quoted as saying: "If you can convince the lowest white man he's better than the best colored man, he won't notice you're picking his pockets. Hell, give him somebody to look down on, and he'll empty his pockets for you."

[56] Badr Eddin Rahimah, "The Class Oriented Rationale: Uncovering the Sources of the Syrian Civil War," *Muslim World*, 106:1 (Jan. 2016): 169–186.

a certain kind of Shi'a for political office and political power. Long-standing prejudices against the *shrūgi* and against working-class Shi'a as sect-centric, religious, uncouth, superstitious, provincial and so forth were readily applied to the new Shi'a Islamist elites to question their eligibility for political office and political power.[57] This blends a disdain for religious otherness, public piety and the presumed socio-economic inferiority of an undefined (and hence easily inflatable) subgroup within Iraqi Shi'ism. It ultimately aims at the marginalization and political exclusion, not of Shi'as per se, but at least of sect-centric Shi'as.

This blending of sect and class prejudices was perfectly encapsulated in how some chose to delegitimize Iraqi Prime Ministers Nouri al-Maliki and Haider al-Abadi. A remarkably persistent rumour was put forth that al-Maliki had sold prayer beads for a living prior to his return to Iraq in 2003, leading those who subscribe to this view to mock him with the derogatory label of Abu-l-Sibah (*sibah* means prayer beads).[58] When al-Abadi took over the premiership in 2014 the same circles came up with an even more improbable, and far less successful, rumour that al-Abadi had sold *kubbah* for a living while in exile in London, and hence they referred to him as Haider Abu-l-Kubbah.[59] Both examples

---

[57] A common avatar of this sentiment was that "they [Shi'as] are [good] for chest-beating, not for ruling" (*mal latum, mu mal hukum*). Needless to say, the post-2003 political elites have proven themselves uniquely unqualified for political office but the point to be made is that this was not a function of their class or sectarian backgrounds.

[58] For example, this account from 2010 on *Shabakat al-Difa' 'an al-Sunnah* (Network for the Defence of the Sunnah) makes the claim, complete with a less than convincing photograph (allegedly from 1997) of al-Maliki purportedly selling prayer beads at the Sayyida Zainab shrine in Damascus: http://www.dd-sunnah. net/forum/showthread.php?t=96249&page=3. For a profile of al-Maliki, including an overview of his clandestine political activities prior to 2003, see Ned Parker and Raheem Salman, "Notes from the Underground: The Rise of Nouri al-Maliki," *World Policy Journal*, 30:1 (2013): 63–76.

[59] *Kubbah* is a ubiquitous part of Iraqi (and Middle Eastern) cuisine. It is a kind of dumpling that comes in many forms but is most commonly made of bulgur and stuffed with minced meat. Perhaps reflecting the vast difference in divisiveness and popularity between the two prime ministers, the attempt to launch *Haider Abu-l-Kubbah* failed to gather momentum whereas the *Abu-l-Sibah* story continues to have a loyal following of sorts. An example of the *Abu-l-Kubbah* story can be found on the pro-Saddam blog Ghar Ishtar, "Al-Iraq fi Intiqal: min Abu-l-Sibah ila Abu-l-Kubbah" (Iraq in

show how a particular form of a particular sectarian identity (in this case a visible Shi'a-centricity) is conflated by its critics with class prejudice (as embodied in this case by the menial labours of the prayer bead and *kubbah* sellers). The purpose of this conflation is to fashion a sect/class-based commentary on what constitutes suitability for public office and political power. We see similar examples from across the Arab world and not just as a function of Sunni–Shi'a divisions, as illustrated by the extremes of the 'liberal' backlash against the Muslim Brotherhood in Egypt and how this was linked to perceptions regarding 'progressive' Egyptianness and suitability for high office.[60] Likewise, in Syria, the dynamics of class have frequently informed sectarian prejudices. For example, anti-Alawi resentment often has an element of class prejudice in that Alawis are framed as an impoverished rural community that has usurped wealth and political power. As Nir Rosen informs us, one anti-regime chant promised to send Bashar al-Assad "back to the farm."[61] Both the chant and the outrage it elicited in Rosen's Alawi informer are indicative of the role and interaction of class and sect in political discourse. As Shaery-Eisenlohr puts it with regard to Lebanon and Lebanese Shi'as: "What is provocative in religious dogma is assessed through standards of respectability that are, in turn, part of a nexus of class and politics. Both middle-class respectability and the political discourse of coexistence are social dimensions from which Shiites have traditionally considered themselves marginalized."[62]

It is worth noting that these dynamics are not only driven negatively as a function of political exclusion. These frames have also been used

---

Transition: From Abu-l-Sibah to Abu-l-Kubbah), Aug. 11, 2014, http://ishtar-enana.blogspot.sg/2014/08/blog-post_97.html. For a less obscure example, see Salah al-Furaiji, "Haider Abu-l-Kubbah Tashree' li-l-Fasad wa Ta'ziz li-l-Dhulm al-Ijtima'i wa Mu'aqaba li-l-Mutadhahirin" (Haider Abu-l-Kubbah is a legalization of corruption, a reinforcement of social injustice and a punishment of protesters), Iraq News Network, Oct. 24, 2015, http://www.aliraqnews.com/للظـ-تعزيز-للفساد-تشريع-الكبة-ابو-حيدر.

[60] For more on this theme, see Taufiq Rahim, "Is Hypernationalism the New Islamism?" *Al-Monitor*, Aug. 23, 2013, http://www.al-monitor.com/pulse/originals/2013/08/violence-arab-nationalism.html#.

[61] Nir Rosen, "Assad's Alawites: The guardians of the throne," Al Jazeera, Oct. 11, 2011, http://www.aljazeera.com/indepth/features/2011/10/20111-1-122434671982.html.

[62] Shaery-Eisenlohr, *Shi'ite Lebanon*, p. 155.

as a legitimating tool by those positioning themselves as champions of the subaltern. Few examples better capture this than the messaging of Lebanese Hizbullah and Iraq's Sadrists. Both claim to represent the disempowered and revel in an underclass identity that is presented as pure, committed and loyal as opposed to the corruption and immorality of the rich. In other words, rather than grounds for exclusion, the conflation of sect and lower-class status becomes a driver of political mobilization and is internalized as a source of communal pride. As one Sadrist poet put it, "the poor are my [military] beret" (*al-fuqra beiriti*).[63] This of course reflects competing narratives of nationalism and national authenticity, which are often misinterpreted as evidence of the mutual exclusivity of sectarian identity and national identity. However, as can be seen in the case of Lebanon, "Shiite activism from the 1960s, often depicted as sectarian activities at odds with a commitment to the nation, is an effort to break the Maronite-centred national narrative and to create an alternative nationalism in which Shiites inhabit a central position."[64] This is the very essence of the national dimension of sectarian identity, and it will be the subject of the following chapter.

To conclude this section on the local or subnational dimension of sectarian identity, it is important to point out, firstly, that considerations of class, patronage and local power relations should not be seen as alternatives to sectarian identity but as defining features of it – and vice versa. Therefore, rather than insisting on sectarian conflict being an illusion masking the reality of, say, class struggle,[65] it is more fruitful to think of class and sect as potentially intertwining registers. Put simply, sect is no less 'real' than class, and sectarian solidarities are not a form of 'false consciousness' nor should they be viewed as mutually antagonistic to considerations of class; on the contrary, in some contexts and at certain times, sect and class become mutually forming and reinforcing. However, the correspondence between the two is never complete: even the most disadvantaged sectarian

---

[63] See "Al-Sha'ir al-Mujahid Jawad al-Hamrani" (The Mujahid Poet Jawad al-Hamrani), uploaded Apr. 14, 2008, https://www.youtube.com/watch?v=oPoMk8OuKe0.

[64] Shaery-Eisenlohr, *Shi'ite Lebanon*, p. 49.

[65] An example of this argument can be found in Rahimah, "The Class Oriented Rationale," p. 176.

group will have its wealthy and well-connected members and even the most privileged sectarian group will have its impoverished and marginalized component. Often the pursuit of profit acts as a cross-sectarian glue among the former, and socio-economic grievance can similarly act as a potentially unifying force among the latter.[66] In any case, the importance of including the local or subnational dimension of sectarian identity in our analysis of sectarian relations lies in its ability to shed light on the ways in which sectarian dynamics are affected by material interests, patronage networks and economic distribution within a national setting and *alongside* other emotional and ideational factors. Understanding the subnational dimension of sectarian identity also better enables us to get around the false dichotomy of secular versus sectarian: by incorporating this dimension into our analysis we can better identify and understand secular, non-religious forms of sectarian bias and hostility which can be based, not on religion per se, but on grounds of class, access to state resources and privilege, and normative assumptions about political and social respectability. More broadly, an awareness of the subnational dimension (as part of a broader multidimensional framework) adds clarity and helps us avoid some of the more common pitfalls that so often mar discussions of sectarian dynamics. For example, subnational factors relating to class and to regional cleavages and how these intersect with sectarian relations shed light on intra-sectarian dynamics: to illustrate, no amount of Shi'a political domination in post-2003 Iraq could negate intra-Shi'a divisions. These need not be spectacular instances of armed clashes between political factions. Rather, the subnational dimension reveals more banal divisions such as that between people from the capital and those from beyond,[67] or the traditional division between rural and urban circles, or the competition between various regions and cities – examples from Iraq would include the rivalry between Samarra and Tikrit, Najaf and Karbala, the extreme south and the mid-Euphrates. To end this section with an illustration of the importance of

---

[66] Corstange, "Ethnicity on the Sleeve," pp. 898–899.

[67] Speaking to a couple of young Najafis in 2016, I was surprised to hear them say that they tried to avoid visiting Baghdad as they felt that the people of the capital looked down on them and regarded them as country bumpkins.

recognizing the multidimensionality of sectarian dynamics, the 2005–7 civil war in Baghdad was very clearly a sect-coded war for dominance and a conflict over the very nature of post-2003 governance – a matter that was of concern to the region and that, alongside the presence of occupation forces, lent the conflict an international dimension. Yet at a localized level, there were baser, more personal and material motivations alongside these grander drivers. As Joel Rayburn and others have argued, there was an element of class struggle to the violence as "the Shi'a lower classes [broke] out from their slums in Rusafa to colonize the roomier Sunni-majority neighbourhoods of Baghdad."[68] This is as good an example as any of the need to refrain from viewing Sunni–Shi'a dynamics as being driven by any one thing.

Sectarian Identity as a Frame for Transnational Solidarity and Geostrategic Competition

Apart from the multilayered way in which they operate, one of the most complicating features of modern sectarian identities is the international or transnational dimension of sectarian relations. This should not be confused with the *anational* doctrinal dimension. Rather, what is being referred to here is the intersection of sectarian categories with international relations, international or transnational solidarities, and geostrategic competition.[69] To be sure, this characteristic is not unique to sectarian identity: other religious categories, Catholicism

---

[68] Joel Rayburn, *Iraq after America: Strongmen, Sectarians, Resistance* (Stanford: Hoover Institution Press, 2014), p.85. Another study that sheds much light on the relevance of class to sectarian dynamics in the early post-2003 period is Nicholas Krohley, *The Death of the Mehdi Army: The Rise, Fall and Revival of Iraq's Most Powerful Militia* (London: Hurst & Co., 2015). See also "Iraq's Civil War, the Sadrists and the Surge," International Crisis Group, Middle East Report no. 72, Feb. 7, 2008, pp. 2–7.

[69] Some studies that look at sectarian identity at the inter-state level include Salloukh, "The Sectarianization of Geopolitics in the Middle East," in *Sectarianization*, ed. Hashemi and Postel; Gause, "Beyond Sectarianism"; Pierret, "The Reluctant Sectarianism of Foreign States"; Geneive Abdo, "The New Sectarianism: The Arab Uprisings and the Rebirth of the Shi'a-Sunni Divide," The Saban Center for Middle East Policy at Brookings, Analysis Paper, no. 29, April 2013; Mari Luomi, "Sectarian Identities or Geopolitics? The Regional Shia–Sunni Divide in the Middle East," Finnish Institute of International Affairs, Working Paper 56, Feb. 2, 2008.

and some forms of Islamism for example, and other ideological currents, Arabism or twentieth-century communism, have at one point or another had very powerful transnational dimensions.[70] That modern sectarian identities are rendered somewhat more problematic in our own times than other identities is due less to the uniqueness of the transnational dimension and more to its inflated salience. In the case of Sunni–Shi'a relations in the Arab world this is rooted in, and is a product of, Arab–Iranian political rivalry. While the Iranian Revolution of 1979 and the establishment of an aggressively revolutionary Islamic Republic seriously complicated this rivalry, its origins are far older. As Olivier Roy and others have argued, Ottoman–Persian boundaries nurtured the creation of an imagined border between Arab Sunnism and Iranian Shi'ism.[71] This counterfactually clean-cut division allowed many to think of Shi'ism as a distinctly Iranian phenomenon, thereby further complicating sectarian relations by conflating them with ethnic and political divisions.

The chief driver of the transnational dimension of sectarian identity has been Saudi–Iranian rivalry.[72] This has been especially acute since 2003 and more so since the Arab uprisings of 2011 and the regional upheaval that has followed. Here we see all four dimensions of sectarian identity brought into play in a destructive cycle. A geostrategic contest between two regional powers and would-be regional hegemons is inescapably sect-coded owing to Saudi Arabia's association with a puritanical and explicitly anti-Shi'a strain of Sunnism and owing to Iran's role as political patron of global Shi'ism and as the proponent of a revolutionary ideology of Shi'a political Islam. While this draws on the transnational dimension of sectarian identity, the doctrinal

---

[70] My thanks to Morten Valbjorn for drawing my attention to this point.

[71] Olivier Roy, *The Politics of Chaos* (London: Hurst & Co., 2007), p. 80.

[72] For a useful overview, see Simon Mabon (ed.), *Saudi Arabia and Iran: The Struggle to Shape the Middle East*, The Foreign Policy Centre, 2018, https://fpc.org.uk/wp-content/uploads/2018/11/Saudi-Arabia-and-Iran-The-Struggle-to-Shape-the-Middle-East-Report.pdf. For an in-depth study of Saudi–Iranian relations, see Banafsheh Keynoush, *Saudi Arabia and Iran: Friends or Foes?* (New York: Palgrave Macmillan, 2016); Simon Mabon, *Saudi Arabia and Iran: Power and Rivalry in the Middle East* (London: I.B. Tauris, 2016); Dilip Hiro, *Cold War in the Islamic World: Saudi Arabia, Iran and the Struggle for Supremacy* (London: Hurst & Co., 2018).

dimension is actively enlisted as a result of the centrality of Islam (as doctrine and also as identity) to the construction of political legitimacy in both states. This overlaps with the national and, by extension, the subnational dimensions of sectarian identity as well as with the turmoil of the twenty-first-century Middle East and the internationalization of sect-coded conflicts in Iraq, Syria, Bahrain and (to a lesser extent) Yemen and Lebanon, allowing these dynamics to be mirrored and amplified across the region (see chapter 6).

By framing sectarian identity in this multidimensional way we can better grasp its varying roles in regional politics and help avoid what Marc Lynch memorably described as the all-too-common fallacy of viewing 'sectarianism' as "power politics dressed up in sectarian drag."[73] Sectarian relations (including regional sect-coded conflict) cannot be reduced to their international dimension divorced from the broader, multilayered reality of sectarian identity. Having said that, the importance of the international dimension lies in its impact on the other dimensions of sectarian identity and how this ultimately complicates Sunni and Shi'a identities in a way that is not easily replicated with other collective categories. For one thing, it lends the subnational or national dimensions of sectarian identity an at times inescapable and unwelcome international aspect. This internationalization can help to prolong and deepen sect-coded crises and conflicts. More than just potentially fuelling sect-centricity, the international dimension can end up distorting sectarian relations in a given context by the introduction of competing international interests to local and national settings – few examples are more illustrative in that regard than the Syrian conflict. One manifestation and facilitator of this lies in the creation of sect-coded or sect-specific transnational public spheres.[74] Be it through sect-coded social media echo chambers or privately owned satellite channels whose primary mission is the deepening of

---

[73] Marc Lynch, "The War for the Arab World," in *The Politics of Sectarianism*, POMEPS Briefing 21, Nov. 13, 2013, p. 10, https://pomeps.org/wp-content/uploads/2014/06/POMEPS_Studies4_Sectarianism.pdf.

[74] Toby Matthiesen, "Transnational Diffusion between Arab Shi'a Movements," in *Transnational Diffusion, Cooperation and Learning in the Middle East and North Africa*, POMEPS Studies 28, 2016, http://pomeps.org/2016/08/16/transnational-diffusion-between-arab-shia-movements/.

sectarian divisions, this can potentially strengthen sectarian solidarities across national borders, thereby fostering competing Sunni and Shi'a lenses through which regional politics are filtered.[75]

Another problematic side effect of the instrumentalization, and consequently the relevance, of sectarian identity in international relations is that it often ends up securitizing domestic sectarian plurality – something that will be examined in more detail in chapter 5. In this we have a parallel in how the Papacy was viewed by early-modern Protestant authorities and how this securitized the latter's views towards their Catholic citizens or subjects and complicated domestic sectarian relations.[76] Catholics in Protestant countries were suspected of dual loyalties because of the theoretically transcendent nature of Papal authority. In his 1689 treatise on toleration, John Locke famously cautioned against toleration of Catholics given the political and security implications. In his words:

> That Church [Catholicism] can have no right to be tolerated by the magistrate which is constituted upon such a bottom that all those who enter into it do thereby ipso facto deliver themselves up to the protection and service of another prince. For by this means the magistrate would give way to the settling of a foreign jurisdiction in his own country and suffer his own people to be listed, as it were, for soldiers against his own Government.[77]

Locke's words offer us a perfect precursor of how the transnational dimension of Sunni–Shi'a identities has at times complicated and securitized domestic sectarian relations in the modern Arab world. Time and again, the geopolitics of Arab–Iranian rivalry have enabled the instrumental conflation (cynical or otherwise) of the Sunni–Shi'a divide with the Arab–Iranian divide. A common manifestation of this sees charges of collusion with Iran or Saudi Arabia being used to discredit, isolate and vilify Shi'a activism in the Arab world and Sunni activism in

---

[75] For an examination of the proliferation of sect-coded satellite channels, see BBC Arabic, *Freedom to Broadcast Hate*, Sept. 18, 2014, https://www.bbc.com/news/av/world-middle-east-29257524/freedom-to-broadcast-hate.

[76] Gallagher, *Divided Scotland*, pp. 26–27.

[77] John Locke, *A Letter Concerning Toleration*, ed. James H. Tully (Indianapolis: Hackett Publishing Co., 1983), p. 50. My thanks to Nader Hashemi for drawing my attention to this.

Iran respectively;[78] the fact that the Arab world is an overwhelmingly Sunni majority political construct means that the former is especially pronounced – no less a figure than former Egyptian president Hosni Mubarak frankly stated that Arab Shi'as are more loyal to Iran than to their own countries.[79] Likewise, the intersection of sectarian identity and Arab–Iranian rivalry has seen regional strategy (particularly in the contexts of the Iraqi and Syrian conflicts) instrumentalizing markers of sectarian identity to foster sectarian solidarity and mobilization by portraying geopolitical issues as existential threats confronting all Sunnis or Shi'as – for example, Iran framing its military support for the Assad regime as a defence of Shi'a shrines in Syria.[80]

Here it is worth pondering the matter of causality. It is very easy to assume that, when wedded to geostrategic rivalries, differences in sectarian identity *cause* conflicts and instability such as in Iraq since 2003 or Syria since 2011. Likewise, it is all too easy to assume that transnational sectarian solidarities *dictate* the behaviour of the likes of Iran and Saudi Arabia in internationalized conflicts. Such assumptions underlie the genre of reporting that frames the twenty-first-century Middle East as being torn between Sunni and Shi'a camps. Indeed, the obsession with sect-coding the region can be so relentless that some

---

[78] For example, see Hasan al-Alawi, *Al-Shi'a wa-l-Dawla al-Qawmiyya fi-l-Iraq, 1914–1990* (The Shi'a and the National State in Iraq, 1914–1990) (Qom: Dar al-Thaqafa, 1991); Ali Babakhan, "The Deportation of Shi'as During the Iran-Iraq War: Causes and Consequences," in *Ayatollahs, Sufis and Ideologues: State, Religion and Social Movements in Iraq*, ed. Faleh A. Jabar (London: Saqi, 2002); Stephane A. Dudoignon, *The Baluch, Sunnism and the State in Iran* (London: Hurst & Co., 2017), especially chapter 6.

[79] "Mubarak's Shia remarks stir anger," Al Jazeera, April 10, 2006, https://www.aljazeera.com/archive/2006/04/200849132414562804.html. For more on this theme, see Wehrey, *Sectarian Politics*, parts 2 and 3 for Saudi Arabia and Bahrain; al-Rasheed, "Sectarianism as Counter-Revolution," in *Sectarianization*, ed. Hashemi and Postel; Haddad, *Sectarianism in Iraq*, pp. 40–43.

[80] Maysam Behravesh, "How Iran Justifies Its Costly Syria Intervention," *Middle East Eye*, March 23, 2017, https://www.middleeasteye.net/columns/how-iran-justifies-its-costly-syria-intervention-home-643289507; Afshon Ostovar, "Sectarian Dilemmas in Iranian Foreign Policy: When Strategy and Identity Politics Collide," Carnegie Endowment for International Peace, Nov. 30, 2016, http://carnegieendowment.org/2016/11/30/sectarian-dilemmas-in-iranian-foreign-policy-when-strategy-and-identity-politics-collide-pub-66288.

commentary would sooner turn Sunnis into Shi'as than recognize intra-sectarian competition and hence the limits of the prism of 'sectarianism'. For example, commenting on the divided regional response to the Israeli war against Gaza in 2008–9 (Operation Cast Lead), one scholar inadvertently transformed Hamas and Qatar into Shi'as by arguing that it "highlighted the Muslim cold war between Shiites and Sunnis or between the moderate Arab camp – Saudi Arabia, Egypt and Jordan – and the radical Islamic axis led by Iran, whose other members were Hizbullah, Syria, Hamas, Qatar."[81] Rather than according sectarian dynamics causality in international relations and rather than assuming a sectarian logic where it does not necessarily exist, we would be better served if we held sectarian identity as a variable whose utility to regional statecraft (be it diplomacy or proxy conflict) is far from predetermined and hence should not be assumed. If we take the Iraqi and Syrian conflicts, the role of Saudi Arabia, Iran and other regional actors has ultimately been driven by the pursuit of their interests in a context of state collapse and political vacuum. Within that, the 'sectarian card' is one tool among many and is not always the preferred option of 'Sunni Saudi Arabia' and 'Shi'a Iran' nor is its instrumentalization guaranteed to yield beneficial results.[82] Indeed, as already mentioned, some scholars have argued that regional powers, including both Iran and Saudi Arabia, were reluctantly drawn into sect-coded proxy war in Syria and that the logic of sect was not their preferred strategy.[83] This is not to deny the relevance of sectarian categories to regional dynamics but to highlight its limits.

---

[81] Yehuda U. Blanga, "Saudi Arabia's Motives in the Syrian Civil War," *Middle East Policy*, 24:4 (Winter 2017): 49.

[82] On Iran's use of clients and proxies, see Eskandar Sadeghi-Boroujerdi, "Strategic Depth, Counterinsurgency and the Logic of Sectarianization: The Islamic Republic of Iran's Security Doctrine and Its Regional Implications," in *Sectarianization*, ed. Hashemi and Postel; Ostovar, "Iran, Its Clients, and the Future of the Middle East."

[83] Pierret, "The Reluctant Sectarianism of Foreign States"; Christopher Phillips, "Sectarianism as Plan B: Saudi–Iranian Identity Politics in the Syria Conflict," The Foreign Policy Centre, Nov. 12, 2018, https://fpc.org.uk/sectarianism-as-plan-b-saudi-iranian-identity-politics-in-the-syria-conflict/; Christopher Phillips and Morten Valbjorn, "'What Is in a Name?': The Role of (Different) Identities in the Multiple Proxy Wars in Syria," *Small Wars and Insurgencies*, 29:3 (2018): 414–433.

The Arab–Iranian angle and, by extension, the transnational dimension of sectarian identity have perhaps been the most complicating aspects of modern sectarian relations. That is not to say that Sunni–Shi'a relations would have necessarily been problem-free had fate scripted a Sunni Iran. Likewise, that history has decreed a Shi'a Iran is not a recipe for perpetually problematic sectarian relations, as the long periods of irrelevance of sectarian categories attest to. Nevertheless, it is worth pondering how differently modern sectarian identities (especially in the Arab world) might have evolved without Iran's conversion to Shi'ism following the rise of the Safavid state. For one thing the securitization of sectarian plurality would not have been as prevalent as has often been the case, nor would the conflation of sect and ethnicity have been as common. Sect-coded controversies or political contestation may emerge for a variety of reasons, but it would be far less likely for sectarian plurality to be susceptible to being framed as a national security threat in the Arab world without a Shi'a Iran. The 'Iran factor' heightens the volatility, inflammability and sensitivity of modern sectarian identities and, particularly since 1979, has expanded their political utility by adding an international, geopolitical dimension to sectarian relations. In this way the international dimension of sectarian relations complicates domestic sectarian relations: having a sect-coded, foreign political rival facilitates the superimposition of geopolitics on sectarian identity, thereby blurring the line between the two and adding fears of hidden transnational dual loyalties and fifth columns.

The transnational aspect of sectarian identity fits into and perpetuates a long-standing feature of politics in the Arab world, namely the intersection and overlap between internal and external spheres of politics. Scholars of the international relations of the Middle East have long recognized the permeability of Arab states to trans-state identity discourses such as Arab nationalism, Islamic revivalism or sectarian solidarity. Referring to Bassel Salloukh, Michael Barnett, Marc Lynch and others, Hinnebusch links an older literature on the international relations of the Middle East to the heightened political relevance of sectarian identity in the twenty-first century. As has long been noted, one of the characteristics of the Middle Eastern regional state system is the extent to which rival states compete with each other using transnational discourses of identity that resonate with both domestic and foreign audiences. In this way, Hinnebusch argues, identity and foreign policy come to be shaped and constructed in a transnational public space that generates political norms, interests and constraints (the framing of the Palestinian cause in the twentieth century being the paradigmatic example of this).[84] This furthers the permeability of national boundaries and incentivizes what Roger Owen described as "a habitual willingness to act across international borders that seems unparalleled elsewhere in the non-European world."[85] In this way Arab states are tied together in a supra-state community based on being part of an 'Arab world'. In his treatment of the subject, Morten Valbjorn referred to Egyptian President Gamal Abd al-Nasser's Arab nationalist speeches as the classic example of this: broadcast to a pan-Arab audience, they were seen "by other Arab leaders as a greater security threat than Egyptian tanks and guns."[86] Much the same can be said about how Al-Jazeera and Qatari tanks and guns are viewed today by regional rivals. In any case, this blurring of internal and external spheres means that elites speak to both domestic and regional audiences and, with the existence of shared interests, symbols and causes, have every incentive to meddle in the domestic affairs of other states.

In Valbjorn's analysis, this creates an inner tension between what he refers to as a narrow *raison d'état* and a broader *raison de la nation Arabe*.[87] However, what is often overlooked is the fluidity of the content of these frames. To take the latter, the fact that the Palestinian cause or revolutionary pan-Arabism of the mid-twentieth-century variety are no longer as salient as they once were does not invalidate Valbjorn's point

---

[84] Raymond Hinnebusch, "The Sectarianization of the Middle East: Transnational Identity Wars and Competitive Interference," in *Transnational Diffusion and Cooperation in the Middle East*, POMEPS Studies 21, Aug. 24, 2016, p. 71. See also Raymond Hinnebusch, "The Sectarian Surge in the Middle East and the Dynamics of the Regional States-System," *Tidsskrift for Islamforskning*, 13:1 (2019): 35–61.

[85] Roger Owen, *State, Power and Politics in the Making of the Modern Middle East* (London: Routledge, 2000), p. 74.

[86] Morten Valbjorn, "Arab Nationalism(s) in Transformation: From Arab Interstate Societies to an Arab-Islamic World Society," in *International Society and the Middle East: English School Theory at the Regional Level*, ed. Barry Buzan and Ana Gonzalez-Pelaez (London: Palgrave Macmillan, 2009), p. 146.

[87] Ibid., p. 145.

about a *raison de la nation Arabe*. Within the transnational Arab public space identified earlier, there are new issues and forms of contestation playing out with domestic and regional audiences being targeted in equal measure. This has been as evident in how the fragmentation of the Gulf Cooperation Council (the 'Qatar crisis') has unfolded as it has been in how the 'Arab Spring' has been framed, perceived and contested. Likewise, and more importantly for our purposes, there is an inseparable pan-Arab element to how sectarian identities and sectarian relations have evolved in the twenty-first century. From the invasion of Iraq to the Arab uprisings to the civil war in Syria to Arab–Iranian competition, these divisive, controversial and sect-coded milestones were a staple of a pan-Arab discourse as mediated through Arab satellite networks and social media. Whereas previous generations of leaders tried to 'out-Arab' each other with reference to Palestine, anti-colonialism and Arab unity, today the language of a greater regional Arab good, though diminished, is still in use but in support of different causes. Examples would include the jihadi mobilizations for Iraq and Syria, the need to counter Iran, or the claim to guarantee regional stability. What the twenty-first century has seen therefore is not the disappearance of the 'Arab world' but a shift in its orientation and internal divisions. At several junctures since 2003, sectarian identity was often recast as one of the central props of regional discourse and competition – consider Jordanian King Abdullah's 2004 warning of a 'Shi'a crescent'.[88] This should not be seen as one transnational identity (sectarian) displacing another (Arab); the heightened relevance of sectarian frames of reference in a pan-Arab public sphere should be regarded as one more contradiction and one more internal line of contestation in what is nevertheless an *Arab* public sphere. Just as with Arab nationalism or the Palestinian cause previously, the discourse of sectarian solidarities acquired relevance in the early twenty-first century and was used in a regional Arab public space for similar ends: regime maintenance, mobilization of support, neutralizing opposition, undermining rival regimes and extending national interests. Whatever

---

[88] Robin Wright and Peter Baker, "Iraq, Jordan see threat to election from Iran," *Washington Post*, Dec. 8, 2004, http://www.washingtonpost.com/wp-dyn/articles/A43980-2004Dec7.html.

its lifespan, this particular change in the content of the *raison de la nation Arabe* is new and is a direct result of how the invasion of Iraq in 2003 disturbed the balance of power between sect-centric actors in the region. Subsequent events in Lebanon, Bahrain, Syria and Yemen only deepened the trend. In recent years the intersection of internal and external, regional and national has seen such dynamics spreading to unlikely places, for instance the spread of anti-Shi'ism to places lacking any significant Shi'a populations such as North Africa, Jordan and Southeast Asia.[89] As Saleh and Kraetzschmar found in Egypt after the uprisings of 2011, Salafi Egyptians actively tried to securitize sectarian identities by advancing the notion of an imperilled Sunni identity threatened (domestically and regionally) by a malign Shi'ism. In the process they tried to link Egypt's minuscule Shi'a population to broader sectarian tensions in the Middle East.[90] As one informant described it: "Egypt's Shi'a are currently paying the price for what Shi'a in other countries are doing ... the objective of what is happening with Egypt's Shi'a is to send a message abroad."[91]

The unprecedented political relevance of sectarian identities in the twenty-first-century Middle East has naturally been reflected in regional dynamics as well. However, once again it is crucial not to frame the international dimension in a stand-alone or overly influential way. Incentives, threats and opportunities emerge from above and from below, inside-out and outside-in, and interact at the subnational, national and international levels. In the process, sectarian relations are redefined (not necessarily in a permanent way) in all four of its dimensions. For example, local actors are influenced by regional trends of rising or diminishing sect-centricity just as state actors and their foreign policies are likewise influenced by trends at the local level. Local actors might proactively try to link local dynamics to regional trends in order to attract support, protection and resources –

---

[89] For the Jordanian context, see Joas Wagemaker, "Anti-Shi'ism without the Shi'a: Salafi Sectarianism in Jordan," *Maydan*, Sept. 30, 2016. For anti-Shi'ism in Indonesia, see Chiara Formichi, "Violence, Sectarianism and the Politics of Religion: Articulations of Anti-Shi'a Discourses in Indonesia," *Indonesia*, 98 (Oct. 2014): 1–27.

[90] Saleh and Kraetzschmar, "Politicized Identities, Securitized Politics," pp. 550–551.

[91] Ibid., p. 554.

much in the same way that the discourse of minority rights was used by various groups to attract European patronage in the nineteenth and early twentieth centuries. This multidirectionality is at odds with the reductionist framing of transnational sectarian dynamics as a case of Saudi Arabian and Iranian state-puppeteers waging proxy war through their regional client-puppets. By framing the transnational dimension as just one among several dimensions that together animate sectarian dynamics, we can better contextualize the role of state actors without ignoring other drivers, be they bottom-up, local, national or doctrinal drivers.

Conclusion

Sectarian identity is too broad, fluid and unwieldy a category to be conceived rigidly as representing any one thing. For it to be analytically useful, the concept of sectarian identity requires a segmented, layered approach such as the one being attempted here. By acknowledging that sectarian identities and sectarian relations operate interchangeably and simultaneously on multiple levels – doctrinal, subnational, national, transnational – we can avoid the unrealistic binaries that have dominated the literature on sectarian relations and that were covered in the previous chapter. This framework also provides us with more clarity by helping us understand which aspect of sectarian identity is brought into relevance in a given context. In that way we can better identify the drivers of sect-coded dynamics (violent or otherwise) – as opposed to seeking clarity in an undifferentiated 'sectarianism' that seems to encompass all while explaining nothing. By extension, where sectarian conflict is concerned, a clearer grasp of drivers allows for better diagnoses and hence more effective and accurate solutions. This can help us avoid the misplaced initiatives that neglect to identify which dimension of sectarian identity actually requires resolution – for example, by focusing on the doctrinal dimension of sectarian identity in what is otherwise a dispute revolving around its subnational or transnational dimensions.

The next chapter will deal with sectarian identity at the level of the nation-state. The resources of the modern nation-state, the identity anchor that it provides, the way that national politics and national policy can shape intergroup relations, and the manner in which nationalism and national identity generate norms of inclusion, exclusion, majorities and minorities, all of these factors and more make sectarian identity's interaction with national identity the chief characteristic of modern sectarian relations and its chief differentiator from sectarian relations prior to the emergence of the nation-state.

Before we move on to the matter of sectarian identity and the nation-state, it is worth re-emphasizing a few points regarding the idea of a layered approach to sectarian identity. It is vital that the dimensions identified are not viewed autonomously. Rather than four separate phenomena they are four sides of one thing: sectarian identity. Drawing strict lines between the four dimensions re-creates the very rigidity that this model is trying to overcome. It is not always a question of *which* dimension is in play but rather a question of the interaction between the different dimensions in a given context. An illustrative example is the sectarian identity of diasporic groups and the way in which it simultaneously resonates on multiple dimensions. As Oula Kadhum has argued with regard to Iraqi-descended Shi'as in Europe, the territoriality of pilgrimage sites connects younger generations with their parents' country of origin and creates fluid national, social and religious conceptions of belonging.[92] This aptly illustrates the limits of viewing sectarian identity as just a matter of religion or simply a frame for political competition or in any other singular way. The example of diasporic communities shows how sectarian identity can simultaneously signify multiple things and resonate in different ways with individuals. This reflects the layered nature of sectarian identity and how its many dimensions interact in multidirectional ways.

To illustrate with a more problematic example, which dimension of sectarian identity would be most relevant to understanding the display of images of the Ayatollah Ruhollah Khomeini in Lebanese and Iraqi public spaces? Is it a matter of Iranian proxies extending Iranian soft power, thereby making it a matter of sectarian identity at the geostrategic or transnational level? Is it an example of local, subnational

---

[92] Oula Kadhum, "The Transnational Politics of Iraq's Shia Diaspora," *Diwan*, Carnegie Middle East Center, March 1, 2018, https://carnegie-mec.org/2018/03/01/transnational-politics-of-iraq-s-shia-diaspora-pub-75675.

dynamics in which the sect-coding of public space allows particular wings of particular sects to lay claim to it? Is it an example of sect-coded state policy attempting to blend the symbols of sect with the symbols of nationalism by erecting sect-specific monuments? Or is it an example of the veneration of a religious figure and the championing of a religious doctrine and religious identity? Clearly the answer is not any single one of these and, depending on the context, it can be all of the above. This degree of ambiguity is an inherent and ubiquitous part of modern Sunni–Shi'a relations. An accurate understanding of sectarian dynamics requires us not to sidestep this ambiguity but to embrace it. One way of ensuring this is to approach the subject with enough conceptual agility to view sectarian identity as the sum of its parts. Having surveyed the doctrinal, subnational and transnational dimensions, we now turn to the national dimension and the interaction between sectarian identity and national identity.

4

SECTARIAN IDENTITY IN THE ERA OF THE NATION-STATE

One of the most common and most misplaced assumptions regarding sectarian relations is that sectarian identity and national identity are opposites or that they are mutually exclusive. The equally misplaced extension of this line of thinking frames a normatively positive, modern, secular and territorialized national identity or nationalism as the antidote to the ills of a normatively negative, pre-modern, religious and transnational sectarian identity or 'sectarianism'. All of which overlooks one of the defining features of modern sectarian identity, namely its interaction with, and refraction through, the nation-state, national identity and nationalism. The preceding chapter looked at the doctrinal, subnational and transnational dimensions of sectarian identity. This chapter will introduce the final level of analysis, namely the national dimension. It bears repeating that sectarian dynamics operate simultaneously on all four fields and that a correct understanding of modern sectarian identity requires us to view it as the sum of these four parts. The varying relevance of these is context-dependent; rather than clearly delineated categories, the four dimensions of sectarian identity are fluid, interdependent, overlapping, mutually reinforcing and mutually defining.

Nationalism and 'Sectarianism'

As already noted and as I will illustrate here, modern sectarian identity and sectarian relations are very often functions of national identity and nationalism. A common manifestation of this is competing sect-centric visions regarding the form, meaning and content of a given national identity. Put another way, such instances of sectarian competition will revolve around competing *national* truths (mediated through the prism of sectarian identity) – something that has been abundantly illustrated in the sect-coded conflicts of Syria, Iraq, Lebanon and Bahrain. Several observations regarding the relation of sectarian identity to nationalism can be made at this point. Firstly, it again highlights the fluid, at times incidental, role of religious doctrine and questions of religious orthodoxy in modern sect-coded political contestation, which is more likely to be driven by contested *national* truths than religious ones. Secondly, and by extension, far from being a negation of nationalism, the national dimension of sectarian identity allows sectarian competition to act as a function of nationalism. Rather than artificial nations breaking up into supposedly more resonant lines of identity, modern sect-coded conflict is more often the product of a contested but nevertheless singular nationalism. Unlike ethnic identities (Amazigh, Kurdish, Baloch, Arab), transnational sectarian solidarities have not developed into sect-coded secessionist or nationalist movements in the Middle East. This is why we have yet to see a serious sect-coded war for secession (with the far from straightforward and far from clearly *secessionist* exception of the Islamic State). None of this negates the transnational dimension of sectarian identity; however, the transnational aspect of modern sectarian dynamics does not equate to the erosion of national boundaries or the de-nationalization of national issues. Rather, transnational sectarian solidarity towards sect-coded political issues or conflicts is more likely to involve a cross-pollination between the transnational and the national dimensions of sectarian identity. In that sense, a transnational public sphere connects different national settings without erasing the boundaries between them. To illustrate, the transnational nature of

Irish-American sympathy and support for Republican Irish militancy did not make Irish Republicans any less Irish nor Irish-Americans any less American.

Thirdly, it follows therefore that what is at stake in modern sectarian conflict in places like Iraq, Syria, Lebanon and Bahrain is not the survival of the nation-state but the nature of its governing order: hierarchies of power, access to and distribution of political and economic resources, the identity of the nation-state, the symbolic content of national identity, and so forth. Through it all, the nation-state itself continues to be accepted and taken for granted; indeed, it is the prize of the contest. More than that, the nation-state also provides the anchor, the legitimacy and popular resonance for competing sect-coded claims. Again with the exception of the likes of the Islamic State and transnational militants, domestic protagonists in sect-coded conflict almost always frame their stance as a nationalistic one that champions the supposedly true, accurate or fair representation of the nation-state. In that sense modern sectarian competition and sectarian conflict are more likely to unfold within, for and in the name of the nation-state. This is well illustrated by the Iraqi, Lebanese and Bahraini political classes: all are obliged to denounce 'sectarianism', all must voice their commitment to the nation-state, and political messaging (even in times of civil war) has consistently framed sect-centric claims in national terms. Even a document as unabashedly sect-centric as *The Declaration of the Shi'a of Iraq* of 2002 is one that is firmly and inescapably anchored in national claims.[1]

Fourthly, another recurring theme – and one that is again contradicted by the exceptional example of the Islamic State – is that though competing, sect-centric visions of the nation-state can drive political competition to the point of civil war, the concept and reality of sectarian plurality are almost never challenged. As was repeatedly seen in the civil wars of Syria and Iraq, and that of Lebanon before them, demographic engineering may occur in particular locations for

---

[1] For an analysis of the Declaration, see Haddad, *Sectarianism in Iraq*, pp. 148–150. For an English translation of the Declaration, see "Declaration of the Shia of Iraq," *AL-BAB*, https://al-bab.com/documents-section/declaration-shia-iraq.

strategic reasons or as a function of wartime vengeance, but national sectarian homogeneity is never the goal. Rather than a rejection of coexistence, sectarian conflict in contexts of high sectarian heterogeneity is more often about who gets to define the terms of coexistence and who gets what within the national framework.[2] This may explain the paradox seen in chapter 2 of far higher acceptance rates of sectarian plurality in countries that had gone through sect-coded civil wars (Lebanon, Iraq).[3] Finally, given the preceding and given the inextricable link between modern sectarian dynamics and matters relating to the nation-state (national identity, narratives of state and people, access to the state, and so forth), it is patently obvious that the considerable literature on nationalism is useful to understanding modern sectarian relations.

The lack of attention to theories of nationalism among scholars of sectarian relations is unfortunate given the striking overlap between the two subjects. Indeed, if we consider the classic division in approaches to the study of nationalism between 'primordialists' and 'modernists' we find that it is almost perfectly mirrored in one of the central debates in the study of sectarian relations, namely that between what was referred to as 'maximalists' and 'minimalists' in chapter 2 (those who inflate the relevance of sectarian identity, sometimes by primordializing it, and those who downplay its relevance, sometimes by adopting an overly constructivist or instrumentalist approach). Put very simply, where the literature on nationalism is concerned, primordialists believe in the antiquity and 'naturalness' of nations while modernists believe in the modernity and 'constructedness' of nations and nationalism.[4] These two approaches (and they are broad approaches, not unified theories) obviously parallel those of maximalists and minimalists respectively.

---

[2] Shaery-Eisenlohr, *Shi'ite Lebanon*, p. 9.

[3] Pew, *The World's Muslims*, chapter 5.

[4] For an excellent and highly accessible introduction to the study of nationalism, see Umut Ozkirimli, *Theories of Nationalism: A Critical Introduction* (London: Macmillan Press, 2000).

Maximalists / Primordialists	*Minimalists / Modernists*
Sectarian / national identity is 'primordial'.	Sectarian / national identity is a construct.
Collective identity (sect / nation) is central to political action, perceptions of self and other, and the formation of political community / interests.	Sectarian / national identity is of little, if any, relevance to understanding the history and politics of a given society or polity.
Sects / nations explain history, politics, conflict and society.	Sectarian / national identity explains nothing.
Sect / nation is the 'natural' basis of social and political organization.	Sectarian / national identity is a political tool created and wielded by elites from above seeking to manipulate society for their own ends (instrumentalism).
Quote: "Ancient hatreds."	Quote: "The myth of sectarianism / national myth."

Minimalists and modernists both focus on modernity, the industrial revolution (and colonialism in the case of sectarian relations), and the advent of the nation-state as key explainers of modern sectarian or national identities.[5] As for the maximalist–primordialist approach, it is not easy to find a frank expression of crude primordialism in the academic literature, be it about nationalism or sectarian relations,

---

[5] Classic modernist theories of nationalism would include Ernest Gellner, *Nations and Nationalism* (Oxford: Blackwell, 1983); Ernest Gellner, *Nationalism* (London: Weidenfeld and Nicolson, 1997); John Breuilly, *Nationalism and the State* (Manchester: Manchester University Press, 1983); Benedict Anderson, *Imagined Communities: Reflections on the Origins and Spread of Nationalism* (London: Verso, 1983). For the more instrumentalist variant that places more emphasis on the role of elites in the creation of nationalism, see Eric Hobsbawm and Terence Ranger (eds), *The Invention of Tradition* (Cambridge: Cambridge University Press, 1983). For parallels from the study of sectarian relations, see the contributions to Hashemi and Postel (eds), *Sectarianization*, especially Introduction and Part I; Wehrey (ed.), *Beyond Sunni and Shia*, especially Introduction, Part I–II.

though there is no shortage of primordialist pronouncements on both in the popular press.[6] A third major approach to the study of nationalism is ethno-symbolism. This approach does not deny the modernity of nations and nationalism but tries to shed light on the pre-modern symbols and roots of what are nevertheless modern identities.[7] In this way ethno-symbolists position themselves as a third way that allows for a compromise between elements of modernism and primordialism. Again, as with the rest of the vast literature on nationalism, ethno-symbolism is similarly useful for students of modern sectarian identities and sectarian relations.[8]

The idea that there is a national dimension to how modern sectarian identities are imagined, practised and contested becomes fairly unremarkable if we discard the widespread normative, and completely misplaced, assumption that national identities are an inherently more benevolent and positive force than sectarian identities or that the two are completely separable. An older body of literature examined the relationship between national and religious identities in a manner precluding the unrealistic binaries that proliferate in

---

[6] For a nuanced and sophisticated example of a primordialist analysis of nationalism, see Azar Gat, *Nations: The Long History and Deep Roots of Political Ethnicity and Nationalism* (Cambridge: Cambridge University Press, 2013). For a fascinating account highlighting the existence of nations in medieval Europe, see Louise R. Loomis, "Nationality at the Council of Constance: An Anglo-French Dispute," *American Historical Review*, 44:3 (April 1939): 508–527. For an example of a primordialist take on sectarian relations, see Maghen, "Unity or Hegemony?" in *The Sunna and Shi'a in History*, ed. Bengio and Litvak; Tomass, *The Religious Roots of the Syrian Conflict*.

[7] For ethno-symbolism, see Anthony Smith, *The Ethnic Origins of Nations* (Oxford: Blackwell, 1986); Anthony Smith, *Chosen Peoples: Sacred Sources of National Identity* (Oxford: Oxford University Press, 2003); John Armstrong, *Nations before Nationalism* (Chapel Hill: University of North Carolina Press, 1982); Adrian Hastings, *The Construction of Nationhood: Ethnicity, Religion and Nationalism* (Cambridge: Cambridge University Press, 1997); Athena S. Leoussi and Steven Grosby (eds), *Nationalism and Ethnosymbolism: History, Culture and Ethnicity in the Formation of Nations* (Edinburgh: Edinburgh University Press, 2007), especially Introduction and Part I.

[8] For the use of ethno-symbolism in the study of sectarian relations, see Haddad, *Sectarianism in Iraq*, chapters 2–3 and 7; Fanar Haddad, "Sectarian Relations and Sunni Identity in Post-Civil War Iraq," in *Sectarian Politics in the Persian Gulf*, ed. Potter; Osman, *Sectarianism in Iraq*, chapter 2.

recent treatments of 'sectarianism'. For example, Brubaker rejects the dichotomization of nationalism and religion by challenging the assumption that the former is an inherently secular phenomenon – something that is echoed in the late Saba Mahmood's work on Egypt.[9] Instead he proposes several ways of viewing religion and nationalism as separate but intertwined concepts.[10] Along similar lines, Kinnvall has argued that identity constructs *combining* religion and nationalism are an especially common response to crises of ontological insecurity.[11] Likewise, Azar Gat (echoing Anthony Smith) notes that, while religion on its own is rarely able to serve as the basis for nationhood, national and religious sources of identity have, more often than not, acted in complementary and mutually reinforcing ways.[12] We see elements of this across the Middle East in the special place reserved for Islam in nominally secular polities (and for Judaism in Israel) thereby recalling Friedland and Moss's observation that it is "difficult to make a clean separation between religion and nationalism in history, whether nationalism is religionized or religion nationalized."[13]

In an earlier study Friedland made an important point that is very useful in helping us understand the interaction between national identity and religious or sectarian or indeed other identities and

---

[9] See Mahmood, *Religious Difference in a Secular Age.*

[10] Brubaker, "Religion and Nationalism." In the same study (p. 16), he cautions against framing religion and nationalism as identical: "intertwining is not identity." Briefly, the four approaches identified by Brubaker are: religion and nationalism as analogous modes of identification and social organization and as ways of framing political claims; religion as an explanatory variable in the origins and power of nationalism (Protestant influences on English nationalism, for example); religion as an integral part of nationalism (the former defining the boundaries, myths and symbols, and discourse of the latter); and finally, religion as the basis for a distinctly religious form of nationalism (for example, variants of nationalism in India or Israel).

[11] Catarina Kinnvall, "Globalization and Religious Nationalism: Self, Identity and the Search for Ontological Security," *Political Psychology*, 25:5 (2004): 741–767.

[12] Gat, *Nations*, p. 223. A similar argument is at the heart of Smith, *Chosen Peoples*.

[13] Roger Friedland and Kenneth B. Moss, "Thinking through Religious Nationalism," in *Words: Religious Language Matters*, ed. Ernst van den Hemel and Asja Szafraniec (New York: Fordham University Press, 2016), p. 434. One of the examples they point to is, aptly for our purposes, "the Islamists who may deride nationalism yet seek to Islamicize the nation-state" (p. 443).

frames of reference: "Nationalism offers a form of representation – the joining of state, territoriality and culture. It has *nothing* to say about the *content* of representation, the *identity* of that collective subject, or its *values*."[14] This insight highlights how all manner of identities, histories, mythologies and so forth come to compete for position in the national narrative. In that sense, in certain circumstances and in certain contexts of heightened political relevance, sectarian identity may be asserted by sect-centric actors in an effort to have it furnish the props of nationalism, thereby achieving a closer alignment between the symbols of state and the symbols of sect. In the process, a group's belief that it embodies the nation-state and vice versa (the Shi'as' 'Iraqiness' and Iraq's 'Shi'a-ness', for example) or a minority group's sense of itself as an integral part of the nation-state is validated and feelings of existential or ontological insecurity are allayed. These dynamics are often misread as a displacement of nationalism; an argument that baselessly presumes nationalism to have a fixed, predetermined content that is necessarily positive and inclusive. To take a far from unusual example, a study by former politician and public intellectual Azmi Bishara frames nationalism (*wataniyya*) and pan-Arab ethno-nationalism (*qawmiyya*) as inherently integrative processes as opposed to 'sectarianism', which is described as a "violation of national unity."[15] In this way nationalism (including pan-Arab ethno-nationalism) is counterfactually framed as an uncontested and unifying concept while a loosely defined 'sectarianism' is presented as inevitably leading to fragmentation. These assumptions reduce national and sectarian identities to caricatures that fail to capture their fluidity and their interaction.

Friedland's point regarding the undetermined content of nationalism allows us to view sectarian identity as one potential ingredient among many in the mix that can supply nationalism with its emotional, symbolic and discursive content. The interaction between religious or sectarian and national identities is self-evident in places

---

[14] Roger Friedland, "Religious Nationalism and the Problem of Collective Representation," *Annual Review of Sociology*, 27 (2001): 138. Emphasis added.

[15] Azmi Bishara, "Madkhal li-Fahm al-Mas'ala al-Ta'ifiyya wa Sina'at al-Aqaliyat fi-l-Mashriq al-Arabi al-Kabir" (An Introduction to Understanding the Sectarian Question and the Creation of Minorities in the Greater Arab Mashriq), *Omran*, 11 (2015): 7.

like India, Poland, Israel, Ireland and any number of other contexts where national identity is closely associated with a privileged religious identity that is officially or unofficially held as a defining characteristic of the nation. Similarly, as I have argued elsewhere with reference to Iraq, the essence of sectarian competition on the level of the nation-state is not to deny sectarian plurality but to centre a particular sectarian identity at the heart of the national narrative.[16] This is echoed in Shaery-Eisenlohr's description of Lebanese Shi'as and their pushback against older, in their eyes more exclusionary, conceptions of Lebanon; a similar framework can be applied to any number of contexts such as Iraq and Bahrain:

> certain social, political and religious activities of Lebanese Muslim Shi'ites since the 1960s, though often viewed as promoting so-called sectarianism, are not antagonistic to the discourse of Lebanese nationalism. Far from posing an opposition to the nation, Shi'ite activities have centred on a set of practices and ideologies that seek to break the hegemony of Christian (mainly Maronite) narratives of Lebanon as a nation, to place the historically marginalized Shi'ites in the centre of Lebanese national politics and self-imagining, and to change sectarian power relations, granting Shi'ites a more prominent position. These alternative visions of nationhood portray Shi'ites as ideal Lebanese competing for political influence and representation.[17]

In addition to allowing us to go beyond the false dichotomies of sectarian–national and sectarian–secular, the focus on the national dimension of sectarian identity is necessary owing to the transformative impact that the advent of the nation-state had on collective identity and intergroup relations. Given its unprecedented capacity for control, its ability to intrude upon and influence our lives, and its role in dictating matters of inclusion, exclusion, minorities and majorities, the modern

---

[16] Fanar Haddad, "Sectarian Identity and National Identity in the Middle East," *Nations and Nationalism*, forthcoming (2020).

[17] Shaery-Eisenlohr, *Shi'ite Lebanon*, p. 2. For a Bahraini parallel, see Justin Gengler, *Group Conflict and Political Mobilization in Bahrain and the Arab Gulf: Rethinking the Rentier State* (Bloomington: Indiana University Press, 2015), chapter 2. For Iraq, see Fanar Haddad, "Shi'a-Centric State-Building and Sunni Rejection in Post-2003 Iraq," Carnegie Endowment for International Peace, Jan. 2016.

state is central to any comprehensive understanding of modern intergroup relations.[18] This does not mean, however, that sectarian identity can be restricted to the prism of the nation-state. As stated at the outset, what is needed is a multidimensional approach that permits us to identify the various aspects of sectarian identity and sectarian relations and to shift our focus between them according to context. The nation-state, colonialism, modernity and so forth did not *create* sectarian competition – let alone sectarian identity – nor did they create the myriad phenomena to which the term 'sectarianism' refers. What the nation-state and other associated concepts such as modernity did was to alter and add new meaning to how collective (including sectarian) identities and intergroup relations or competition came to be imagined and formulated. As such, the emergence of the nation-state should not be treated as a big-bang moment of creation at which history begins – a point well made by Marc Owen Jones in his study of contentious politics in Bahrain:

> Yet part of the problem in studying Bahrain, perhaps, also lies in the application of what has become a Eurocentric phenomenon of modernity to analysis – one in which the creation of the state and its institutions through colonialism is somehow the subject of focus, and one that can result in total disjuncture between a previous era and the 'modern'. In this analysis, concepts such as sectarianism somehow become a neatly packaged and temporally limited product of modernity ... such arguments run the risk of creating the illusion of a pre-imperial utopia.[19]

Sectarian Identity before the Nation-State

Following on from Jones's argument, it is worth inquiring into medieval and early-modern sectarian relations. While this book is expressly focused on the era of the nation-state, our purposes will be better served by contrasting our own times with earlier periods. In

---

[18] A point well illustrated in a review of a collection of excellent studies of religion, sectarian identity and the modern state. Michael Gasper, "Sectarianism, Minorities and the Secular State in the Middle East," *International Journal of Middle East Studies*, 48 (2016): 767–778.

[19] Jones, "Contesting the Iranian Revolution," in *Gulfization*, ed. Jones et al., pp. 93–94.

doing so, perhaps the most important contrasts that emerge are those relating to state–society relations and the greater distance between the vast majority of people and political authority in pre-national times.[20] Furthermore, the pre-national era was marked by a greater fluidity of religious boundaries, which gradually hardened as a result of the homogenizing and codifying tendencies of the modern state. Having said that, and as is the case with our own times, any notion that early-modern or medieval sectarian relations were always benign is as absurd as the idea that they were always inflamed or even that they were always relevant. Then, as today, context was all-important.

Despite the readiness with which casual observers look to medieval Islamic history for explanations of modern sectarian dynamics, categories such as 'Shi'a' and 'Sunni' can be highly problematic when thinking about the evolution of sectarian identities prior to the eleventh century at the earliest.[21] Before that, such terms had yet to evolve into anything resembling what we would take them to mean today; indeed, medievalists tend to use proto-Sunni and proto-Shi'a to refer to what others mistakenly regard as the medieval versions of today's Sunnis and Shi'as.[22] Nevertheless, the heightened relevance of sectarian categories

---

[20] For more on this theme, see Milton J. Esman, *Ethnic Politics* (Ithaca: Cornell University Press, 1994), chapter 1; White, *The Emergence of Minorities in the Middle East*, p. 82.

[21] There is no scholarly consensus on when Sunni and Shi'a identities emerged in any coherent sense of the term. One of the basic points of scholarly difference is between those who argue that such categories emerged as early as the late eighth century, as evidenced, they will say, by the emergence of hadith scholars formulating conceptions of orthodoxy (the original object of the term *ahl al-Sunna*), and those who argue that such categories remained meaningless and elitist without the development of the institutions necessary for the propagation of orthodoxy. Scholars of the latter persuasion would date the emergence of sectarian orthodoxies to no earlier than the eleventh century and in some cases as late as the thirteenth century. For a concise overview of the issue, see Christine D. Baker, *Medieval Islamic Sectarianism* (Leeds: Arc Humanities Press, 2019).

[22] For a discussion of the early emergence of Shi'ism as a distinct sectarian category, see Marshall G.S. Hodgson, "How Did the Early Shia Become Sectarian?" *Journal of the American Oriental Society*, 57:1 (Jan.–March 1955): 1–13; Etan Kohlberg, "From Imamiya to Ithna-Ashariyya," *Bulletin of the School of Oriental and African Studies, University of London*, 39:3 (1976): 521–534.

in our own times has encouraged some to look to medieval sectarian relations in search for explanatory clues. In particular, attention is often directed towards the tenth and eleventh centuries: the so-called 'Shi'a century' and the subsequent 'Sunni revival'. Again, some medievalists take exception to such labels as they convey an artificially tidy picture of early Islamic thought neatly distilled into a Sunni orthodoxy and a Shi'a heterodoxy, thereby obscuring a far more fluid landscape in which such terms meant little. The popular wisdom regarding the tenth or Shi'a century is that a weakened (Sunni) Abbasid state enabled the rise of Shi'a political power, thereby politicizing sectarian identities and sharpening sectarian tensions.[23] The idea of the Shi'a century is primarily a reference to the rise of the Buwayhid state in Iraq and Iran (945–1055) and the Fatimid state in North Africa (909–1171) and the emergence of other proto- or quasi-Shi'a powers such as the Qarmatians in Eastern Arabia. Some of the most well-known Muslim chroniclers such as Ibn Kathir, Ibn al-Athir and Ibn al-Jawzi relate that these events were accompanied by repeated outbreaks of Sunni–Shi'a violence in tenth-century Baghdad.[24] However, these accounts are less straightforward than is assumed by non-specialists, and there are at least three ways to interpret them and, by extension, the broader 'Shi'a century'.

Firstly, there is the primordialist view that would seize upon a medieval episode of Sunni–Shi'a violence to draw a straight line of sectarian antagonism from the tenth to the twenty-first centuries. Such an approach can be dismissed for what should by now be abundantly clear reasons. The second approach would be to view the tenth century as one in which the balance of power between sect-coded actors was shifting, thereby heightening the relevance of sectarian identity and sharpening sectarian tensions, as evidenced by the recurring bouts of sectarian violence in tenth-century Baghdad.

---

[23] From the tenth century to the final destruction of the Abbasid state in 1258, no less than six Shi'a or quasi-Shi'a dynasties emerged in the region in addition to the Ismaili Fatimid state in North Africa. See Moojan Momen, *An Introduction to Shi'i Islam: History and Doctrines of Twelver Shi'ism* (New Haven: Yale University Press, 1985), pp. 304–309.

[24] For an overview, see George Tarabishi, *Hartaqat II* (Heresies II) (Beirut: Dar al-Saqi, 2008), pp. 15–24.

In this reading the tenth century sees a political issue (proto-Shi'a challengers to Abbasid political authority) becoming intertwined with the matter of foreign threats to a weakening state from 'unorthodox' contenders (for example, the Buwayhids and the Fatimids), leading to greater intercommunal violence on the local level in Baghdad itself. To add another dimension to this multilayered picture, the matter of religious doctrine must also be considered given that this rise in violence coincided with a growing puritanical Hanbali presence in Baghdad that saw them harass other Muslims and especially Baghdad's Shi'as in the Karkh quarter, which was burned down several times.[25] Adding to this layered picture (which obviously mirrors the multidimensional formula presented in this and the previous chapter) is another familiar feature of sectarian conflict, namely its potential to act as a vehicle for ethnic competition – something that persists till today. In the later Abbasid era this took the form of conflict and competition between the Abbasid state's (Sunni) Turkic and (Shi'a) Daylamite mercenaries.[26]

The third reading would be to question the accounts and motives of the aforementioned medieval chroniclers none of whom were contemporaries of the events they describe. In Christine Baker's analysis, their accounts reflect the politics of their own time (twelfth to fourteenth centuries) and the profound changes that had taken place in the codification, formalization and politicization of sectarian categories *after* the tenth century. She argues that the few surviving contemporary accounts of Buwayhid-administered Baghdad make no mention of sectarian identity, much less of sectarian strife.[27] As such, the later chronicles reflect the salience of sectarian identity not in the tenth century but in their own times. In the eleventh and twelfth centuries, the region saw an influx of Turkic powers (the Seljuk conquest of Baghdad in 1055, for example). That the forces they overthrew were (proto-) Shi'a encouraged them to emphasize their own Sunni

---

[25] For an overview, see Nimrod Hurvitz, "Early Hanbalism and the Shi'a," in *The Sunna and Shi'a in History*, ed. Bengio and Litvak.

[26] Tarabishi, *Hartaqat II*, pp. 14–15. The Daylamites – from whom the Buwayhids emerged – are an ethnic group from north-western Iran.

[27] Baker, *Medieval Islamic Sectarianism*, pp. 78–88.

identity and to invest in the development of a coherent framework of Sunni orthodoxy. Therefore, rather than anti-Shi'ism per se, the driver behind this orientation was the need to build a legitimating narrative of political authority (rescuing the Abbasid caliph from the Shi'a Buwayhids) based on more coherent ideological foundations in the form of an increasingly codified Sunni orthodoxy.[28]

As I am not a medievalist, I will refrain from expressing a firm opinion on the issue; however, it scarcely matters for our purposes: whether we accept the twelfth-to-fourteenth-century chroniclers' accounts of sectarian conflict in tenth-century Baghdad or if we follow Baker's lead in rejecting them, the multidimensional, context-dependent, fluid nature of sectarian dynamics reveals itself regardless. Even the bluntest reading of the narratives of sectarian strife found in the later medieval chronicles does not support the idea of existential zero-sum conflict or innate sectarian antagonism. Indeed, to take the narration by Ibn Kathir (d. 1373) of tenth-century sectarian strife for example, one often gets the impression that Sunni–Shi'a violence in medieval Baghdad was more a function of local parochialism than anything actually related to sectarian identity per se – much less a function of Sunni resentment against rising Shi'a power. Such local rivalries are a fairly common feature of city life and can arise irrespective of sectarian or ethnic cleavages – for example, the rivalry between the Zgurt and the Shmurt in all-Shi'a Najaf.[29] In that sense, rather than a holy war between mutually exclusive sects, medieval Baghdad's Sunni–Shi'a violence is perhaps better understood as a vehicle for neighbourhood rivalries. This is certainly the impression one gets when Ibn Kathir recounts the sectarian strife of 1045: at some point in the violence between Sunni and Shi'a quarters of Baghdad, the two sides agreed to put their differences aside and instead channel their violent energies

---

[28] Ibid., p. 78.

[29] The Zgurt and the Shmurt were neighbourhood or tribal gangs that dominated the four quarters of Najaf and played an important role in local politics in the nineteenth and early twentieth century. See Peter Heine, "Zgurt and Shmurt: Aspects of the Traditional Shi'i Society," in *Ayatollahs, Sufis and Ideologues*, ed. Jabar; Meir Litvak, *Shi'i Scholars of Nineteenth Century Iraq: The Ulama of Najaf and Karbala* (Cambridge: Cambridge University Press, 1998), pp. 123–125.

towards looting Jewish homes and burning their temple.[30] This again touches on the ambivalent interplay between unity and division that was mentioned in the previous chapter. Even the later medieval accounts that Baker argues paint an exaggerated picture of sectarian division note instances of proactive sectarian ecumenism between episodic outbreaks of Sunni–Shi'a violence in tenth- and eleventh-century Baghdad. For example, Ibn al-Athir tells us that in AH 441, after mediation from an emissary of the caliph, the Sunnis and Shi'as of Baghdad reconciled after several bouts of violence and, in a gesture of ecumenical harmony, the Sunni call to prayer was heard in the Shi'a quarter and the Shi'a call to prayer heard in Sunni quarters.[31] More to the point, when one considers the full scope of these chronicles (Ibn al-Athir's spans almost a century, for example), the larger picture that emerges is that, in most years, sectarian relations were marked more by banal irrelevance than by conflict or ecumenism.

The point to derive from this cursory look at sectarian relations in the medieval period is that, as ever, Sunni–Shi'a relations were prone to fluctuations and dictated by context. To take the account of later medieval chroniclers, a weakened Abbasid state and the rise of the Buwayhids saw a deterioration in sectarian relations and a rise in Sunni–Shi'a violence. In the mid-eleventh century, sectarian conflict in Baghdad begins to ease, and one of the main reasons for this is the decline of the Buwayhids and the rise of the (Sunni) Seljuks. Conversely, in Baker's analysis the chain of causality is turned on its head and the heightened political relevance of sectarian identity only comes after the rise of the Seljuks. In this view it is the Seljuks who actively accentuate the political relevance of sectarian identities for their own political purposes and in pursuit of legitimacy and state stability. Either way, what emerges is a multidimensional, multicausal and very context-dependent backdrop to sectarian dynamics that cannot be reduced to a

---

[30] Ibn Kathir, *Al-Bidaya wa-l-Nihaya* (The Beginning and the End), vol. 12, p. 54. Quoted in Tarabishi, *Hartaqat II*, p. 19 n21.

[31] Abu Suhaib al-Kirami (ed.), *Al-Kamil fi Tarikh Ibn al-Athir* (The Complete History of Ibn al-Athir) (Amman: Beit al-Afkar al-Duwaliyya, n.d.), pp. 1436–1437. A different version with a more extravagant display of ecumenism – including joint shrine visitations and joint praise for the Companions of the Prophet – is quoted in Tarabishi, *Hartaqat II*, p. 20.

single driver, much less to narratives of perpetual sectarian animosity. Likewise, moving beyond the 'Shi'a century', the fall of Baghdad to the Mongols two centuries later and perceived Shi'a complicity in that event led to a sharp rise in anti-Shi'a polemics. This is reminiscent of the explosion in anti-Shi'a publications after the Iranian Revolution of 1979 or, perhaps more so, the sectarian entrenchment and sectarian animosities after 2003 (chapter 7): what we see in all these cases is a shift in the balance of power between rival, sect-coded, political actors fostering sect-centric fears and ambitions that had a direct and destructive impact on Sunni–Shi'a coexistence.[32] As ever, context is all-important.

In searching for historical roots and precedents with which to understand Sunni–Shi'a relations in the modern Arab world, the Ottoman era and particularly the Ottoman Levant and Ottoman Iraq offer us a more relevant area of inquiry given the administrative, societal and political legacies inherited by their successor states. The Ottoman Empire was neither the triumph of multiculturalism that sympathetic voices would have us believe nor was its Islamic or Sunni identity as rigid or as exclusionary as detractors claim. For our purposes, the nominally Sunni Ottoman Empire's stance towards Shi'ism and its own Shi'a subjects is what concerns us. Here we find a fairly widespread but ultimately exaggerated assumption that Ottoman policy was systemically anti-Shi'a. There is no doubt that Shi'as were othered by Ottoman policy: they were Shi'a, they were *rafidha*, they were potentially Iranian fifth columnists, they were not 'normal' Muslims; and this othering was, to a considerable degree, inherited by the Ottoman Empire's successor states.[33] However, none of this meant that Ottoman policy was consistently or systemically anti-Shi'a. Rather, the chief characteristic of the Ottoman stance towards Shi'as was pragmatic ambiguity. This allowed for vacillations

---

[32] The parallel between the fall of Baghdad in 1258 and in 2003 and the way both events impacted on sectarian relations have been explored by Nassima Neggaz, "The Falls of Baghdad in 1258 and 2003: A Study in Sunni–Shi'i Clashing Memories," PhD thesis, Georgetown University, 2013.

[33] For an examination of this theme in the Iraqi context, see Hasan al-Alawi, *Al-Ta'thirat al-Turkiyya fi-l-Mashru' al-Qawmi al-Arabi fi-l-Iraq* (Turkish Influences on the Arab Nationalist Project in Iraq) (London: Dar al-Zawra', 1988).

in policy orientations, from suppression to local accommodations to forms of benign neglect. Even in their wars against neighbouring Iran, the Ottomans never hesitated to cooperate with individual Shi'a communities if the latter opposed the Safavids for their own political and economic reasons.[34] Ultimately, Shi'a communities were dealt with on a case–by-case basis and, as we saw in chapter 2, there was never a singular, clear-cut Ottoman Shi'a policy that was implemented across the board. A similarly pragmatic flexibility governed policy towards religious, sectarian and ethnic diversity in general. In that regard it is interesting to note that Stefan Winter disputes the existence of the oft-mentioned *millet* system – in his words, it is "One of the most durable myths of Ottoman history ..."[35] Rather than a codified system, Winter and others paint a more fluid and fragmented landscape in which individual communities were sometimes charged with collecting taxes or administering their own affairs for practical rather than systemic or institutional reasons. Likewise, the doctrinal position was also marked by ambiguity: provided they did not challenge state authority, Shi'as, Alawis and other non-Sunni communities escaped doctrinal stricture. The exception illustrates the rule: heterodox Kizilbas groups in Anatolia were systemically persecuted after the pro-Safavid rebellions of the early sixteenth century. This led to a clear doctrinal, military and political stance against the Kizilbas that was not replicated in the case of other communities and certainly not with Shi'a communities outside Anatolia.

---

[34] See, for example, Sherberger, "Confrontations between Sunni and Shi'i Empires," in *The Sunna and Shi'a in History*, ed. Bengio and Litvak, pp. 51–57. The Shi'a Gilanis preferred Ottoman-supported autonomy to Safavid domination and the Ottomans were more than happy to oblige.

[35] Stefan Winter, "The Alawis in the Ottoman Period," in *The Alawis of Syria*, ed. Kerr and Larkin, pp. 50–51. Likewise Benjamin White highlights the transactional, pragmatic and often ad hoc approach of the Ottoman authorities to local communities, which means we should not think of the '*millet* system' as an actual system. See White, *The Emergence of Minorities in the Middle East*, pp. 48–54. This follows in the steps of earlier scholarship by the likes of Benjamin Braude in questioning the concept of the *millet* system. See Benjamin Braude, "Foundation Myths of the Millet System," in *Christians and Jews in the Ottoman Empire, vol. I: The Central Lands*, ed. Benjamin Braude and Bernard Lewis (New York: Holmes and Meier, 1982). My thanks to Markus Dressler for drawing my attention to this.

Of course ambiguity towards Shi'ism does not mean that policy oscillated solely between varying shades of benevolence. If deemed necessary for reasons of state, the Ottoman authorities had little compunction in issuing *fatwas* declaring the heresy of Shi'ism. The earliest such *fatwa* was issued in 1512 by Nureddin Hamza Sarigurz, the *qadhi* (judge) of Istanbul. The context was Sultan Selim I's war against the Safavids and the Kizilbas rebellion in Anatolia:

> Muslim people! Note that this group of Kizilbas whose leader Ismail [Shah, founder of the Safavid Empire] the son of Ardabil, disregard the Shari'a and Sunna of our Prophet ... and the incontestable Quran ... [hence, we have] issued a fatwa that the mentioned group are infidels and heretics. To kill them and to destroy their communities is an implicit and essential obligation for all Muslims ... The Sultan of Islam is authorized to kill their men and to distribute their property, women and children among the defenders of religion.[36]

This was not the only case of a *fatwa* justifying war against heretical Safavids and Kizilbas, and, as with subsequent examples, there is some ambivalence in this *fatwa* regarding the official position towards other Shi'a groups and other variants of Shi'ism. The text singles out the Kizilbas and Ismail Shah (and by extension the Safavid state), leaving enough ambiguity for the inclusion or exclusion of other Shi'as and of Shi'ism in general. The more widely cited *fatwa* of Grand Mufti Mehmed Ebu's-Su'ud Efendi in 1548 was also issued in the context of war against the Safavids and was even more ambivalent regarding the status of Shi'as and Shi'ism:

> Their detestable deeds testify that there is no connection between him [Safavid Shah Tahmasp] and those pure ancestors [the family of the Prophet] ... his father Isma'il forced the exalted sayyids [descendants of the Prophet] to enter his name in the register of the sayyids at the place of Imam Ali al-Ridha bin Musa al-Kazim's martyrdom and at the other holy places ... [The Safavids] belong to neither the Shi'a nor clearly to one of those 73 sects about which the Prophet said that they were destined for hellfire, with the exception of his own community. They took from each

---

[36] Sherberger, "Confrontations between Sunni and Shi'i Empires," pp. 54–55. Also see Kern, *Imperial Citizen*, pp. 42–43.

of these sects something evil, sinful and erroneous, and added it to the unbelief, heretic innovations and error which they had chosen. They thus invented a new confession swerving from the truth and degenerated from day to day.[37]

Again the ambivalence is unmistakable. The target of the *fatwa* is obviously not the Shi'a who are clearly distinguished from the Safavids – thereby giving us an early precursor of a tradition that continues to the present, namely ring-fencing a 'bad' (invariably 'Safavid' or some other variant of Iranian) Shi'ism from a 'good' Shi'ism.[38] The Shi'a are also differentiated from the 73 hell-bound sects mentioned by the Prophet, thereby suggesting a degree of legitimacy and recognition. On the one hand, this could be a function of political exigency: a lack of clarity serves practical political and administrative needs in that it creates sufficient room for flexibility when needed – after all, the Ottomans had Shi'a subjects of their own to govern and tax. It would hardly be in the Porte's interests to alienate Shi'as with a rigid, unambiguous and irrevocable declaration of Shi'a heresy. Then as now, rather than excluding the whole, this ambiguity helps state authorities manage sectarian division by facilitating targeted exclusion of those Shi'as deemed threatening or politically problematic. Further, the very same ambiguity allowed for the possibility of the Ottomans gaining allies and clients from within the Safavid Empire. On the other hand, this fluidity may also be a function of the fact that there was no shortage

---

[37] Quoted in Sherberger, "Confrontations between Sunni and Shi'i Empires," p. 59.

[38] An even earlier iteration of this is the Abbasid-era category of *al-tashayu' al-hasan* (good Shi'ism) – my thanks to Ahab Bdaiwi for this insight. *Al-tashayu' al-hasan* referred to Shi'ism without the denigration of the first three caliphs and what critics regarded as the heretical veneration of Ali (*ghuluw*) that was practised by other Shi'as. In modern Arabic commentary the good–bad Shi'a dichotomy is used to distance Arab Shi'as from Iranian Shi'as to better deflect accusations that the former can potentially act as a Trojan horse for the latter. It is also used by those seeking to encourage Sunni–Shi'a doctrinal rapprochement by distancing Shi'ism from its more questionable (in Sunni eyes) aspects. For a recent example, see Nabil al-Haidari, *Al-Tashayu' al-Arabi wa-l-Tashayu' al-Farisi: Dawr al-Furs al-Tarikhi fi-Inhiraf al-Tashayu'* (Arabic Shi'ism and Persian Shi'ism: The Historical Persian Role in the Perversion of Shi'ism) (London: Dar al-Hikma, 2014).

of Alid devotion in Ottoman conceptions of Islamic orthodoxy. For example, given how rigidly maintained ritualistic boundaries have become, it may seem strange to our twenty-first-century sensibilities that the eighth Shi'a Imam, Ali al-Ridha, is mentioned above in reverent terms in what is otherwise a statement of religious intolerance. Yet the fact is that there was considerable fluidity in what constituted Sunni orthodoxy and especially where veneration of Ali and his descendants was concerned – hence the many Alid shrines across the Middle East that were never as firmly associated with Shi'ism in the Ottoman period as is the case today.[39]

This was mirrored in a wider confessional fluidity that was in evidence at all levels of society and particularly in rural settings. The rigidity of confessional and sectarian boundaries to which we are accustomed today was largely unknown in earlier times. Here the advent of the nation-state with its inherently homogenizing tendencies may well deserve the lion's share of the dubious credit for this shift in perceptions. For the vast majority of Muslims in Ottoman and pre-Ottoman times, the lines between Sunnis and Shi'as were blurred, and religious rituals and expressions of popular devotion often defied clear sectarian categorization: "Shi'ite inclinations (*tashayyu'*) and Alid loyalties were not an express negation of Sunni orthodoxy but rather the natural mode of a non-literate, non-sectarian folk Islam."[40] This loosely demarcated folk religiosity extended not just to sectarian (Sunni or Shi'a) religious practice but to inter-religious ritual as well. This syncretism is conveyed in vivid detail in Grehan's fascinating study of folk religiosity in the Ottoman era when Christians and Muslims, especially in rural settings, would often venerate the same shrines and saints. The overall picture that emerges is one perfectly

---

[39] Winter, *The Shi'ites of Lebanon*, p. 29. Winter refers to the Sayyida Zainab shrine in Damascus as an example.

[40] Ibid, p. 8. Underlining the point is the fact that the Janissary corps was heavily associated with the Shi'a-leaning Sufi Bektasi order. "In their military ceremonies the Janissaries would invoke Hacci Bektas as well as Ali and the Twelve Imams and Ali's mythical two-pronged sword Dhu-l-Fiqar was emblazoned on all the corps' standards ... it was only with the suppression of the increasingly mutinous Janissary division in 1826 that it [the state] decided the Bektasi order was too unorthodox as well." Ibid., p. 10.

summed up by Grehan: "They did not believe so much as belong." It was not until the nineteenth century and the transformative pressures of modernity that "worshippers" turned into "believers."[41] In one of the countless anecdotes that Grehan unearths we see how what he refers to as 'agrarian religion' rendered sectarian boundaries and religious codification somewhat superfluous: "In the final decades of the eighteenth century, a Shiite [sic] preacher settled near Homs and began preaching to the local population. To the consternation of the Sunni ulama of the town, the adoring crowds who heard his message could not tell the difference between the sects."[42]

Beyond confessional fluidity and political pragmatism, the Ottoman ambivalence towards Shi'ism is likely a reflection of the fact that they actually lacked a clear scholarly consensus on the issue. Even if Shi'as were officially considered heretics, the record would suggest that, at the very least, the Ottomans regarded Shi'ism as a spectrum that only went beyond the pale if and when it overtly offended Sunni sensibilities or actively worked against the Ottoman state. Otherwise, the Ottoman authorities were generally not concerned with questions of orthodoxy nor were they inclined to actively root out heretics unless there was a pragmatic need to do so (conflict with Iran, for example). In Winter's words: "Heterodox belief, it has been said, becomes heresy only when the authorities find it useful to define it as intolerable."[43] To that end, the Ottomans had recourse to a body of vague anti-Safavid, anti-Kizilbas and anti-Shi'a *fatwas* that, precisely due to their vagueness, did not stand in the way of a transactional coexistence between Sunnis and Shi'as but that could nevertheless be referred to whenever necessary – such as when confronting a belligerent Iran or facing down rebellious Shi'a subjects. Political expediency, not religious ideology, dictated the utility of such *fatwas*. This highlights an important and overlooked point, namely that the focus on textual and official evidence can artificially magnify Ottoman anti-Shi'ism (or indeed modern anti-Shi'ism) in the form of religious edicts and treatises. The informal tolerance and

---

[41] James Grehan, *Twilight of the Saints: Everyday Religion in Ottoman Syria and Palestine* (New York: Oxford University Press, 2014), p. 196.

[42] Ibid., p. 59.

[43] Winter, *The Shi'ites of Lebanon*, p. 15.

pragmatic accommodation that characterized most Sunni–Shi'a and state–Shi'a interactions within the Ottoman Empire did not leave a "literary imprint," the way that Ebu's-Su'ud Efendi's *fatwa* did, for example.[44] Put another way, whether in Ottoman times or in our own, the banality of irrelevance is more difficult to document than the extremes of sectarian conflict and proactive sectarian ecumenism.

Nevertheless, sectarian identities seem to have provided a relatively strong basis for social and political boundaries regardless of doctrinal fluidities. Hence, for example, while at no time were Shi'as and Shi'ism the subject of systematic and wholesale Ottoman persecution, the spread of Shi'ism in nineteenth-century Iraq was viewed with deep concern by the Porte.[45] Again this was primarily a function of the Ottoman rivalry with Iran, which led the former to regard conversions to Shi'ism as a security threat. In an officially commissioned report on the subject, the Palace was informed that while the Iraqi *wilayets* had previously been Sunni, "Now, however, the people of that region [Baghdad *wilayet*] seem to be a natural army for Iran."[46] The latter decades of the nineteenth century saw repeated calls for and attempts at a solution to the matter of Shi'a conversion among the people of central and southern Iraq. However, at no time did the discussion advocate a forceful or even an assertive policy. On the contrary, clerics and officials in Iraq and in Istanbul consistently believed that the solution lay in education, religious instruction and improvements to public amenities. In other words, it was felt that a civilizing effort was needed to stop ignorant tribesmen from falling prey to the erroneous tenets of Shi'ism. Interestingly, the same formula applied to stemming the spread of Wahhabism; indeed, the instructions to an official commission set up in 1906 to examine and reform the Iraq region referred to the two in a single breath: "In order to reduce

---

[44] Ibid., p. 18.

[45] See Selim Deringil, "The Struggle against Shiism in Hamidian Iraq: A Study in Ottoman Counter-Propaganda," *Die Welt des Islams*, 30:1/4 (1990): 45–62; Gokhan Cetinsaya, *Ottoman Administration of Iraq, 1890–1908* (London: Routledge, 2011), chapter 5; Yitzhak Nakash, *The Shi'is of Iraq* (Princeton: Princeton University Press, 1994), pp. 25–43.

[46] Cetinsaya, *Ottoman Administration of Iraq*, pp. 101–102.

and limit the spread of the Shi'i and Wahhabi sects ..."[47] Again one senses a doctrinal ambivalence juxtaposed with a far clearer sense of political and security priorities. A similar example can be found in the Ottoman prohibition on marriages between Ottomans and Iranians dating back to the sixteenth century and variably renewed, modified and applied until the twentieth century.[48] As with the matter of Sunni to Shi'a conversion, the manner in which such intermarriages were viewed by the Ottoman authorities had a doctrinal dimension, a social one and a geostrategic element related to the balance of power vis-à-vis Iran. In some cases the ban on Ottoman–Iranian marriages was framed as necessary to prevent the spread of Shi'ism, which officials feared might lead to conflict between Sunnis and Shi'as. In other cases the matter was framed as an issue of citizenship rather than religion – hence in 1892 the proscription also included *Sunni* Iranians. Often, intermarriage was seen as a security issue, especially in the Iraqi *wilayets* where the Ottomans feared that the spread of Shi'ism could challenge their authority.[49]

Here we find one of the most unfortunate, consequential and durable continuities between the past and the present: the securitization of sectarian plurality.[50] As we saw in the previous chapter when we discussed the transnational dimension of sectarian identity, this securitization frames outgroups and minorities as potential rear bases for foreign powers and regional rivals. This can be born of genuine – even if misplaced – fears or cynical calculation. Either way, it invariably has a trickle-down effect in that it accentuates the otherness, and casts doubts on the loyalties of minorities and outgroups. When it came to Ottoman views towards its own Shi'a subjects, the matter was largely governed by the state of Ottoman–Iranian relations and, by extension, the degree to which the authorities felt that Shi'as could be trusted to

---

[47] Ibid., p. 124.

[48] See Karen Kern's study on the subject: Kern, *Imperial Citizen*.

[49] Ibid., pp. 108–112.

[50] For example, see Guldem Baykal Buyuksarac, "Unheard Voices: State-Making and Popular Participation in Post Ottoman Iraq," *Ethnic and Racial Studies*, 38:14 (2015): 2551–2568; Hamit Bozarslan, "Rethinking the Ba'thist Period," in *Writing the Modern History of Iraq: Historiographical and Political Challenges*, ed. Jordi Tejel et al. (Singapore: World Scientific Publishing, 2012).

identify with the Ottoman Empire;[51] hence the alarm with which the Porte viewed the spread of Shi'ism in Iraq. While Iran is understandably centre stage when it comes to the securitization of Shi'a communities in the Ottoman Empire, the matter was not restricted to Ottoman–Iranian rivalry. The extension of European interests within the Ottoman Empire in the eighteenth and nineteenth centuries, and the way in which this was facilitated by a European discourse of minority rights and the protection of minorities, raised fears that Shi'a communities might provide European powers with yet another channel through which to extend their power and influence.[52] By the same token it was feared that minorities and outgroups might actively try to court foreign interest and patronage – highlighting again the fact that there is often a bottom-up dimension to the foreign instrumentalization of communal divides.[53] In the eighteenth and nineteenth centuries the securitization of sectarian and religious plurality was driven by the decline of the Ottoman Empire in the face of an ascendant Europe. This growing weakness created a sense of insecurity and fear among Ottoman officials, who increasingly distrusted minority communities

---

[51] See Cetinsaya, *Ottoman Administration of Iraq*, pp. 99–103. They were not entirely distrustful of the Shi'a either, as evidenced by the fact that they (successfully) tried to enlist Shi'a clerical support for an anti-British jihad in World War I. See Ali al-Wardi, *Lamahat Ijtima'iyya min Tarikh al-Iraq al-Hadith* (Social Aspects of the Modern History of Iraq) (Beirut: Dar al-Rashid, 2005), 2nd edn, vol. 4, pp. 151–152, 271–284; Werner Ende, "Iraq in World War I: The Turks, the Germans and the Shi'ite Mujtahids' Call for Jihad," in *Proceedings of the Ninth Congress of the Union Européenne des Arabisants et Islamisants, Amsterdam, 1st to 7th September 1978*, ed. Rudolph Peters (Leiden: Brill, 1981); Haddad, "Political Awakenings," pp. 5–15.

[52] Cetinsaya, *Ottoman Administration of Iraq*, pp. 99–100, 106, 123, 128. At this stage the British had a natural link with Shi'a communities in Iraq through the Indian Oudh bequest, which was distributed in Iraq by the British Consul General. The Ottomans, not unreasonably, viewed this as facilitating the spread of Shi'ism and, with it, the spread of British influence. For the Oudh bequest, see Meir Litvak, "Money, Religion, and Politics: The Oudh Bequest in Najaf and Karbala, 1850–1903," *International Journal of Middle East Studies*, 33:1 (2001): 1–21; Juan Cole, "'Indian Money' and the Shi'i Shrine Cities of Iraq, 1786–1850," *Middle Eastern Studies*, 22:4 (1986): 461–480. As for the use of the concept of minorities by European powers, see among many others Makdisi, *The Culture of Sectarianism*, and White, *The Emergence of Minorities in the Middle East*.

[53] As was seen in chapter 2. See Rogan, "Sectarianism and Social Conflict in Damascus." Also see Tarabishi, *Hartaqat II*, pp. 25–29.

as potential Trojan horses – a position that was validated by European powers posing as protectors of non-Muslims. Unsurprisingly, it was in this late period of Ottoman history that we see the state enforcing more overtly Muslim laws that hardened communal boundaries.[54]

Perhaps the last word on the ambivalence of Ottoman views towards Shi'ism should go to Sultan Abd al-Hamid II who, as we saw in the previous chapter, dabbled with pan-Islamism and, by extension, Sunni–Shi'a rapprochement for his own political purposes. Towards that end, Abd al-Hamid wrote to political activist and pan-Islamist thinker Jamal al-Din al-Afghani about the issue of Sunni–Shi'a relations. His comments regarding Iranians and Shi'ism perfectly encapsulate the ambiguity, if not confusion, with which sectarian relations were viewed. The Sultan begins by frankly differentiating Shi'as and Shi'ism from Sunnis as heretics: "The Iranians constantly maintain their heretical beliefs in order to live separately from the Ottoman government, and have endeavoured to convert the Sunnis to their own sect by deceiving ignorant people in Iraq and Baghdad ..." Abd al-Hamid then turns to the protection that Iran was at the time offering Armenian rebels; here the tone suddenly shifts in emphasis from division and difference to unity and sameness: "Even though the Iranians are fundamentally Muslims, and pray, like us, towards the Kaaba at Mecca, [they] support and protect, under the influence of this conflict of sect [between Sunnis and Shi'as], the Armenian villains who work against the Muslims."[55] Two things are especially striking in the Sultan's comments: the malleability of the sectarian divide in the service of political expediency and the manner in which doctrinal ambivalence facilitates this. The Ottoman view seems to frame Shi'as as Muslim enough for the prospect of unity yet different enough to be othered as a threat should the context require it.

With all of this ambiguity, what can we conclude about Ottoman views towards Shi'ism and particularly towards their own Shi'a subjects? On the one hand, Twelver Shi'as were seen as aberrant enough to be different from 'normal' unhyphenated Muslims – different enough to be othered. On the other hand, they were clearly not different enough

---

[54] See Grehan, *Twilight of the Saints*, pp. 202–203.
[55] Quoted in Cetinsaya, *Ottoman Administration of Iraq*, pp. 111–112.

to be considered out-and-out non-Muslims in the way that Babis or Baha'is were. In that sense they were regarded as deviant, schismatic or even heretical Muslims but Muslims nonetheless.[56] This has provided the basis for people to periodically view the sectarian divide as being a fundamentally bridgeable one, as evidenced by the episodic attempts at Sunni–Shi'a doctrinal rapprochement and cooperation. Meir Litvak recounts a revealing incident in that regard. In 1845 a Babi preacher offended Najafi sensibilities through the preaching of what was regarded by Najafi notables as his blasphemous message.[57] He was seized and handed over to the Ottoman authorities in the hope that they would banish him to Iran from whence he came. The matter became controversial when some Sunni clerics got wind of the matter and demanded the man's death. Perhaps to prevent this affair turning into a Sunni–Shi'a dispute, the Ottoman authorities convened an unprecedented joint Sunni–Shi'a court to resolve the matter.[58] For our purposes, what is most relevant about this episode is the fact that, firstly, senior Shi'a clerics and their followers handed the Babi preacher to the Ottoman authorities and that, secondly, a joint Sunni–Shi'a court was convened to address the matter. On both counts we see that, regardless of how deviant, misguided or aberrant Sunnis and Shi'as may have been in each other's eyes, there clearly was mutual recognition between them as fellow Muslims even if of a lower order. The courtesy of a joint court would not have been extended to Jews and Christians, let alone to Babis or Baha'is. It is important not to romanticize this mutual recognition nor to exaggerate its limits. The reality is perhaps closer to the love–hate or unity–diversity dialectic that we have already encountered: the Sunni–Shi'a divide is too deep to be identical to today's innocuous intra-Sunni divisions (between, say, Malikis and Hanafis); however, by the same token, outside extremist

---

[56] See Litvak, "Encounters between Shi'i and Sunni Ulama in Ottoman Iraq," in *The Sunna and Shi'a in History*, ed. Bengio and Litvak.

[57] Babism is a messianic Shi'a movement. In 1844 Ali Muhammad Shirazi declared himself 'the Bab' (literally, the gate) to the twelfth Shi'a Imam – the messianic Mahdi. The Bab eventually declared himself the Mahdi and the Babi movement split off from Twelver Shi'ism.

[58] For details, see Litvak, "Encounters between Shi'i and Sunni Ulama," in *The Sunna and Shi'a in History*, ed. Bengio and Litvak, pp. 77–80.

circles, the divide is nowhere near deep enough to lead to complete separation or for it to resemble the cleavages between the Abrahamic faiths. Such was the case in medieval times and has been so ever since.

The Ottomans' ambivalent and at times securitized view of minorities and outgroups was in some cases and in some ways inherited by the Ottoman Empire's successor states. Ottoman relations with and policies towards outgroups had already been complicated in the nineteenth century as a result of the Porte's attempts at modernization and centralization. This was greatly accelerated in the twentieth century by Western intervention and the Wilsonian discourse of 'peoples' and self-determination; by the collapse of the Ottoman Empire; and by the transformative impact of the nation-state. The centralizing and homogenizing tendencies of the modern nation-state and of various forms of modern nationalism, coupled with the sense of insecurity and dependence that the Ottoman Empire's successor states felt, encouraged the further securitization of plurality and further complicated state–society and intercommunal relations.

The Impact of the Nation-State

The nation-state's revolutionary impact on state–society relations, on intergroup relations and on how people conceptualize their social and political horizons can scarcely be exaggerated. Prior to the advent of the nation-state, political authority was far more distant when compared to the micromanagement and intrusion of the modern state in people's daily lives. Crucially, there was also little pretence on the part of rulers to represent or embody 'the people'; nor did the ruled have any pretence to ownership of, or entitlement to, the state. As Patrick Seale notes, beyond urban centres Ottoman state authority (when in evidence) tended to be coercive and extractive, embodied in the figures of "the tax collector or the mounted gendarme."[59] In

---

[59] Patrick Seale, *Asad: The Struggle for the Middle East* (Berkeley: University of California Press, 1992), pp. 4–5. For state–society relations in urban centres during the twilight of the Ottoman era, see Michael Provence, *The Last Ottoman Generation and the Making of the Modern Middle East* (Cambridge: Cambridge University Press, 2017), especially Introduction and chapter 1.

addition to the rural–urban divide, there was an ethnic dimension (particularly in the later Ottoman period) that served to increase the distance between ruler and ruled outside Turkish-speaking Anatolia.[60] The nature of state–society relations was to gradually change beginning in the mid- to late nineteenth century with colonialism, modernization, nationalism, the idea of representative government, and the rise of the nation-state. These changes also influenced how groups defined themselves in relation to each other and introduced new ways in which to imagine communities, minorities, majorities, inclusion and exclusion. Put more simply, the nation-state altered the way in which people compartmentalized themselves and others and how they perceived community boundaries. Benjamin White has explored these processes with specific reference to the idea of minorities, arguing that the most philosophically important precondition for the emergence of the concept of minorities is the notion of representative government.[61] Needless to say, and as White cautions, representative government should not be confused with democracy; what is important for our purposes is whether state authority claims to represent the people: "whether that representation is democratic or not is irrelevant. Kemal Atatürk was no democrat, but [contrary to his Ottoman predecessors] he based his legitimacy entirely on his claim to represent the Turkish 'people'."[62] In terms of popular views of political authority, these changes created a novel, bottom-up sense of ownership of, and entitlement to, the state. Thereafter, concepts such as citizenship and political and economic rights came to shape collective identities and alter intergroup and state–society relations in ways that had little in

---

[60] For the limits of Ottoman multi-ethnicity and the often overlooked difference in how Ottoman authorities viewed their Turkish and non-Turkish subjects, see Hakan Erdem, "Recruitment for the 'Victorious Soldiers of Muhammad' in the Arab Provinces, 1826–1828," in *Histories of the Modern Middle East*, ed. Gershoni et al.

[61] White, *The Emergence of Minorities in the Middle East*, p. 28. Illustrating just how novel the concept of minorities actually is, White notes (p. 21) that the eleventh edition of the *Encyclopaedia Britannica* of 1910–1911 does not contain an entry for 'minorities' yet the edition of 1929 contained an 11-page entry on the term.

[62] Ibid., p. 29. As for the Ottomans, White notes (p. 31): "The Ottoman state did not – for most of its history – claim a cultural affinity between itself and all groups within the population, any more than it claimed to represent a 'majority'."

terms of a pre-national parallel. The modern state's claims regarding its function, role and responsibility to its citizens radically alter the relations between rulers and ruled:

> While [modern] states clearly seek to govern societies, they are at the same time claiming to represent society as a whole, acting on behalf of 'the people'. The idea of the modern state presupposes that the state represents society, not only in the sense that it acts on behalf of, or in the interest of society, but in the sense that the actions of the state are seen as identical to the actions of society ... The modern idea of the state therefore expresses a unity of ruler and ruled, of the subjects and the objects of government.[63]

Such claims were a novelty of the modern state that made state policy more relevant to subjects and citizens than ever before. Likewise, these changes made the citizenry feel entitled to a say in the identity and policies of *their* state. In this way, an added dimension was introduced to how people perceived their social, political and legal horizons. As far as sectarian relations and sectarian competition are concerned, this was transformative in that it added a previously unknown dimension to sectarian identities: namely, it turned them into a *potential* frame through which competing claims to the nation-state – material, symbolic and ideational – could be made. In this way sectarian identities become intertwined with national identity in that the former can *potentially* act as a filter through which the other is viewed and vice versa.

Another effect of the nation-state was the hardening of collective boundaries. Wherever we look – including, as seen above, the Ottoman Middle East – we find a greater fluidity in identity boundaries prior to the advent of the modern state.[64] In his fascinating study of the

---

[63] Stein Sundstøl Eriksen, "State Effects and the Effects of State-Building: Institution Building and the Formation of State-Centered Societies," *Third World Quarterly*, 38:4 (2017): 774–775.

[64] Grehan, *Twilight of the Saints*. For the impact of the collapse of the Ottoman Empire and the rise of the concept of the nation-state, see Sarah D. Shields, *Fezzes in the River: Identity Politics and European Diplomacy in the Middle East on the Eve of World War II* (New York: Oxford University Press, 2011); White, *The Emergence of Minorities in the Middle East*.

roots of the modern passport, Torpey charts the evolution of this hardening of identity and the nationalization of what were previously far more localized matters. Indeed, one is a function of the other, as nationalization means standardization and hence the levelling, to some extent, of regional variances and the minimization of fluidity. One fairly common example of this is the gradual disappearance of regional accents as a result of the modern state's homogenizing influence.[65] This is an inherent consequence of the concept of the nation-state and its attendant need to distinguish citizen from non-citizen. Combined with the administrative capacity of the modern state, what emerges is a previously unknown level of collective codification and an unprecedented degree of state intrusion into people's lives.[66] One is reminded of Ivo Andric's fictional account of the Bosnian town of Visegrad over the course of some four centuries: as the town passes from Ottoman to Austro-Hungarian control in the late nineteenth century, its denizens are troubled by the new rulers' baffling obsession with documenting and measuring everything, and they worry "what this noting down of houses by number and this counting of men and children might mean."[67] What Andric's fictionalized account portrays is what Torpey described as the "burgeoning 'infrastructural' power to 'grasp' individuals that distinguishes modern states from their predecessors."[68] These processes were augmented by the concepts of representative government, political entitlement and political

---

[65] For example, see Maev Kennedy, "Uncovered: Lost British accents from prison camps of First World War," *The Guardian*, Nov. 9, 2009, https://www.theguardian.com/world/2009/nov/09/world-war-british-accent-recordings.

[66] It has also heightened the salience of questions of orthodoxy at the expense of syncretism. A fairly typical example can be found in the evolution of Shi'ism in Indonesia, where Iranian influence creates a divide between 'true Shi'ism' as opposed to the folk or traditional Shi'ism customarily observed in these communities. See Chiara Formichi, "Shaping Shi'a Identities in Contemporary Indonesia between Local Tradition and Foreign Orthodoxy," *Die Welt des Islams*, 54 (2014): 212–236. Returning Southeast Asian students from al-Azhar and the Islamic University of Madinah have led to similar issues arising between local conceptions of Islamic practice and Middle East-influenced notions of orthodoxy.

[67] Ivo Andric, *The Bridge over the Drina* (London: Harvill Press, 1995), pp. 154–155.

[68] John Torpey, *The Invention of the Passport: Surveillance, Citizenship and the State* (Cambridge: Cambridge University Press, 2000), p. 121.

participation, all of which "led to an intensified preoccupation with determining who is 'in' and who is 'out' when it came to enjoying the benefits – both political and economic – of membership in those [modern] states."[69] The way in which modern states 'cage' social activity within them is important in understanding how sectarian identity comes to acquire a national dimension in which sectarian competition mirrors the territoriality of the nation-state.[70]

When it comes to the Middle East and sectarian identity or relations, these processes of codification, remapping and compartmentalization of society are often attributed solely or overwhelmingly to colonialism and its policies of divide and rule. Yet these processes are as much a function of the modern state as they are of the colonial intrusion. While the rise of the nation-state in the Middle East is inextricably linked to European colonialism, it may be misplaced to attribute the intensified codification of subnational identities and the hardening of identity boundaries to colonialism alone. With or without European patrons, modern Middle Eastern states would have eventually felt the need to note, register, count, stamp, measure, number, assess (and so forth) their people – to paraphrase French anarchist Pierre-Joseph Proudhon.[71] This process is part of what Eriksen calls the creation of state-centred societies: namely, societies that are dependent on, and a product of, the states to which they belong (with or without the backdrop of colonialism).[72] This state-centredness creates a national

---

[69] Ibid.

[70] For more on the notion that the nation-state cages social and political activity and reorients it from the local to the national level, see Michael Mann, *The Sources of Social Power*, vol. 2: *The Rise of Classes and Nation-States, 1760–1914* (New York: Cambridge University Press, 1993), p. 61. Quoted in ibid., p. 12.

[71] Pierre-Joseph Proudhon, *General Idea of the Revolution in the Nineteenth Century* (New York: Haskell House Publishers, 1969, first published 1923), p. 294. "To be GOVERNED is to be watched, inspected, spied upon, directed, law-driven, numbered, regulated, enrolled, indoctrinated, preached at, controlled, checked, estimated, valued, censured, commanded, by creatures who have neither the right nor the wisdom nor the virtue to do so. To be GOVERNED is to be at every operation, at every transaction noted, registered, counted, taxed, stamped, measured, numbered, assessed, licensed, authorized, admonished, prevented, forbidden, reformed, corrected, punished."

[72] Eriksen, "State Effects and the Effects of State-Building."

public sphere that encourages all manner of claims and identities to be framed through the prism of the nation-state and in terms of national belonging, ownership and entitlement. Whether this shift in how collective identities are framed is ultimately a product of colonialism or the modern nation-state becomes largely irrelevant. Once the pattern is established, it develops a self-sustaining logic of its own, as the nation-state becomes the primary medium through which political contestation unfolds. The unparalleled relevance of the nation-state to people's lives inevitably shaped how collective identities – sect, religion, tribe, race and so forth – came to be framed. As we saw in the previous chapter, even religious activism shifted with the onset of Islamic modernism, from questions of religious orthodoxy and practice to political issues. Likewise, the sect-coded conflicts of the twenty-first-century Middle East have been heavily anchored in the contestation of the content and meaning of the nation-state – as will be explored in chapters 6 and 7.

To bring the discussion back to sectarian identity, the processes being described do not mean that the nation-state (with or without colonialism) divided previously united Muslim collectives into competing sects nor did they displace previous conceptions of sectarian identity and older patterns of sectarian coexistence and competition. Rather, these processes and the advent of the nation-state ended up grafting an additional *national* dimension onto sectarian relations. In addition to being cohabitants of a town, city or neighbourhood and adherents of different branches of an Abrahamic faith, at the newly formed national level Sunnis and Shi'as were now also constituent components of, and stakeholders in, *their* nation-state – a concept that came with a host of assumptions, entitlements and expectations that created new forms and frames of sectarian competition, cooperation, unity and division. This most obviously manifested itself in sectarian identities becoming potential vehicles for making political claims relating to the nation-state. For example, the anti-British rebellion of 1920 in parts of central and southern Iraq easily created a heightened sense of political entitlement in the areas that participated. As these were Shi'a majority areas, it was a fairly short leap for this unfulfilled sense of political entitlement to become sect-coded; as a British diplomatic report notes: "Shi'ite frustration with Sunni dominance was … echoed by a Shi'ite student who wondered in 1931, 'Have the Shi'ites sacrificed their men, orphaned their children and widowed their wives in order to set up governmental chairs for the Sunnis on the skulls of their martyrs?'"[73] This kind of political discourse and such political claims would scarcely have made sense in the absence of the idea of representative government and the attendant sense of ownership of, and entitlement to, the nation-state. Indeed, no such sentiment ever followed the many rebellions against the Ottomans in these same areas and beyond. Quite the contrary: rather than seeking a greater share of the state or better representation within it, pre-national rebellion was more often aimed at creating greater distance between local communities and the state.

The dominance of the nation-state in how political perceptions are formulated, and the impact of the nation-state on personal material interests, made sectarian relations at the national level central to how sectarian identity – on all levels – came to be imagined. Indeed, in many ways sectarian relations at the level of the nation-state became the pivot around which all the other dimensions of sectarian identity turn. This reflects the general inescapability of the nation-state in modern politics, something that is well encapsulated in Friedland and Moss's comments on its relationship with resurgent religiosity: "Today we live in a world in which the divine is not only a resurgent

---

[73] Eli Amarilyo, "History, Memory and Commemoration: The Iraqi Revolution of 1920 and the Process of Nation Building in Iraq," *Middle Eastern Studies*, 51:1 (2015): 78. To say the least, the language used in this example is unusually blunt and may well be more the product of careless paraphrasing by the British official. However, there is no shortage of similar examples of veterans of the rebellion of 1920 and of people from the mid-Euphrates region (the centre of the rebellion) expressing political disillusionment but in geographic terms or in terms of their participation in the rebellion. See, for example, Fariq al-Mizhir al-Fir'awn, *Al-Haqa'iq al-Nasi'a fi-l-Thawra al-Iraqiyya Sanat 1920 wa Nata'ijuha* (The True Facts of the Iraqi Revolution of 1920 and Its Consequences) (Beirut: Al-Balagh, 1952). Either way, sect-coded or not, what this example shows is how political action and political dividends acquire an almost inescapable national dimension. For recent examples of sect-coded claims to the mantle of 1920 and the post-2003 anti-American insurgency, see Fanar Haddad, "The Terrorists of Today Are the Heroes of Tomorrow: The Anti-British and Anti-American Insurgencies in Iraqi History," *SmallWars and Insurgencies*, 19:4 (2008): 451–483.

source of individual identity and meaning but also a basis for making claims in the public sphere. And because our political world remains a world of nation-states, claims made in the name of the divine involve some sort of claim about the nation as a form of identity and the nation-state as the ground of bonded societies and sovereignties."[74] This is perfectly encapsulated in how the nation-state altered and politicized sectarian identity at the level of religious doctrine and enmeshed it with questions of national identity and political and representational entitlement. For example, the nation-state creates, intensifies and democratizes vested interests in issues such as the place and form of religion in school curricula, the religious identity of the state, the compatibility of narratives of state with narratives of sect, and whether the state is maintaining an equal distance from all sectarian identities. This is far from restricted to sectarian identities alone; rather, it extends to state–society relations generally. For example, in 1927 the French High Commissioner of the Levant received a petition from self-proclaimed representatives of the Circassian community whose demands were distinctly reflective of the transformative impact of the nation-state and how communal identity came to be refracted through a national lens. The signatories wanted outside powers to guarantee both Circassian representation in Syrian politics and, at the same time, communal control over their own affairs. Yet far from seeking to maximize the distance between the community and the state, the signatories felt entitled to what the modern state had to offer, as expressed in their demand for educational scholarships.[75] Similar examples of communal political actors seeking to maximize, or at least correct, their share of the national pie on the basis that they are entitled stakeholders in the nation-state and its resources are not difficult to find. Hence, from as early as 1922, we find Iraqi Shi'a clerics and political figures objecting to the under-

---

[74] Friedland and Moss, "Thinking through Religious Nationalism," in *Words*, ed. Van den Hemel and Szafraniec, p. 423. Even the expressly anti-national Islamic State failed to escape the logic of the nation-state, as evidenced by one of the more common ways in which their operatives chose their noms de guerre: Abu-*x* al-Amriki (the American), al-Almani (the German) and other national designations.

[75] White, *The Emergence of Minorities in the Middle East*, pp. 89–90.

representation of Shi'as in government and Shi'ism in the judiciary.[76] Likewise, in 1920s Lebanon we encounter calls for equality as an antidote to community-specific complaints against "deprived rights" and communal victimhood.[77] Again, pre-national conceptions of what was due and owed to rulers and ruled would have rendered such questions irrelevant. However, as White has argued, once the premise (or facade) of representative government is established, the question of *how* 'the people' are to be represented becomes all-important and a site of permanent contestation.[78] This of course goes far beyond sectarian identity. In that regard one can argue that, in essence, the controversies surrounding any given Middle Eastern state's sect-centricity have much in common with Europe's debates regarding multiculturalism or America's 'culture wars' between conservatives and progressives in that all are about the identity of a nation-state, who its citizens are, and how they are to be represented.

An added consequence of the national dimension of sectarian identity is territoriality. If Sunnis and Shi'as share a single nation-state and lack secessionist ambitions or an alternative national consciousness, they will define their national identity according to myths and symbols – or a mythscape, to use Duncan Bell's framework once again – rooted in what may be termed a generic view of the nation-state that is relatively sect-neutral alongside group-specific inflections of the same nation-state.[79] In that sense, the national mythscape is itself composed of, and interacts with, several subnational (including sectarian) mythscapes marked by elements both of contradiction and convergence. In this way, the nationalist myth–symbol complex can potentially be refracted through subsidiary sect-specific filters: a Shi'a-centric Lebanese nationalism or a Sunni-centric Syrian nationalism, each incorporating sect-specific symbols and narratives into how the

---

[76] Peter Sluglett, *Britain in Iraq: Contriving King and Country, 1914–1932* (New York: Columbia University Press, 2007), pp. 103–105, 224; Batatu, *The Old Social Classes*, pp. 327–328; Fanar Haddad, "Sectarian Relations before 'Sectarianization' in Pre-2003 Iraq," in *Sectarianization*, ed. Hashemi and Postel, pp. 113–114.

[77] Weiss, *In the Shadow of Sectarianism*, chapter 1, especially pp. 58–69.

[78] White, *The Emergence of Minorities in the Middle East*, p. 151. White is quick to point out that permanent contestation does not make conflict inevitable.

[79] Bell, "Mythscapes."

nation-state is framed. In this way, nationalism becomes the perpetually contested combination of competing reservoirs of symbolic and mythological capital that nevertheless have too much overlap for clear and total separation. To illustrate, an overarching Bahraini national identity does not preclude divergences between Sunni-specific and Shi'a-specific tropes and symbols of Bahraini nationalism – such as sect-specific divergence over what constitutes Bahrain's national symbols and chosen traumas.[80] For instance, the narrative of conquest surrounding the rise of the ruling family would be one such divergence in the Bahraini case as would the memory of the mass demonstrations of 2011 and their suppression.[81] This does not negate the belief in the nation-state or the cross-sectarian appeal of an abstract Bahraini nationalism. Rather, the point is that nationalism is not the same as national consensus. Similarly, communal identity significantly (though not entirely) shaped divergences in Syrian perceptions of the civil war: a survey from 2016 found discrepancies in Syrian opinion about the demonstrations of 2011 with a near consensus among Sunni Syrians that they were a civilian democratic response to tyranny while several minority groups were more likely to echo the regime line and point to anti-Syrian conspiracies.[82] Interestingly, and further underlining the centrality of the nation-state in people's political perceptions, the same survey found that 65 per cent of respondents felt that a political system based on citizenship and equality before the law was the most appropriate form of governance to overcome 'sectarianism' while only 10 per cent countenanced partition as a solution.[83] The point

---

[80] A chosen trauma is a collective memory of a calamity that befell a group. More than just a recollection, it is mythologized into a group-defining event – for example, the Holocaust, Ireland's Great Famine, the Armenian Genocide, to name a few. Vamik Volkan, *Blood Lines: From Ethnic Pride to Ethnic Terrorism* (Boulder: Westview Press, 1998), chapter 3.

[81] See Staci Strobl, *Sectarian Order in Bahrain: The Social and Colonial Origins of Criminal Justice* (New York: Lexington Books, 2018), chapter 1; Gengler, *Group Conflict and Political Mobilization*, chapter 2.

[82] "Sectarianism in Syria: Survey Study," *The Day After*, 2016, pp. 25–28, http://tda-sy.org/en/content/215/279/latest-news/syrian-opinions-and-attitudes-towards-sectarianism-in-syria-survey-study.

[83] Ibid., pp. 82–84.

repeats itself: national consensus is not a correlate of the nation-state and nationalism.

Precisely because sectarian competition in places like Bahrain, Syria, Iraq and Lebanon takes place within, and in the name of, an ostensibly or at least aspirationally sect-neutral national context, sect-specific myth–symbol complexes in such places will locate Sunnis or Shi'as within the nation-state. This further binds Sunnis and Shi'as of a particular country by enhancing the national dimension of their sectarian identity through the creation of added country-specific commonality and contestation. In this way national hyphenation serves to territorialize sectarian relations, anchoring them in a set of issues specific to a particular nation-state; hence the limited utility of doctrinal rapprochement in addressing sect-coded political conflicts. This is particularly important when thinking about the relational aspect of sectarian identity construction and how it differs from one dimension to another. To illustrate, a Lebanese Shi'a debating sectarian issues with an Indonesian Sunni is most likely to focus on religious truths and the doctrinal dimension of sectarian identity because that is the primary site of commonality and hence of contestation between the two. Conversely, the same Lebanese Shi'a debating sectarian issues with a Lebanese Sunni will likely see the discussion shift towards contested national truths: demographics, national narrative and, generally speaking, entitlement and access to the national pie. In other words, the contestation in this case would be primarily between *Lebanese* Shi'ism and *Lebanese* Sunnism. Transnational, non-Lebanese actors are not barred from this contestation but they will have to work through the specificities of the Lebanese context.[84] This dialectic interplay between commonality and contestation among compatriots is hardly unique to the Middle East or to sectarian relations; coexistence and conflict are seldom absolutes, and long-term coexistence can be episodically punctured by instances of tension and possibly violence even among deeply interconnected communities.[85]

---

[84] Of course what is being described here is more of a tendency than an iron-clad rule. Internationalized sect-coded conflicts in Syria and Iraq have seen Sunnis and Shi'as from across the world taking an interest (no matter how ill-informed) in Syrian and Iraqi sectarian dynamics out of a sense of transnational sectarian solidarity.

[85] Blok, "The Narcissism of Minor Differences," p. 37; Kolsto, "The 'Narcissism of Minor Differences' Theory," p. 161.

The importance of the national dimension is magnified by the fact that it often provides the backdrop for sectarian dynamics on the local, doctrinal and, of course, the transnational dimensions. As we saw in chapter 3, the intersection of class and sectarian identity, the relation between clientelistic networks and sectarian ties, to say nothing of the manner in which sectarian identities can factor into geostrategic, inter-state interactions, all of these unfold against the backdrop of the nation-state.[86] They are both facilitated and rendered controversial and divisive by the construct of the nation-state and its associated questions of inclusion, exclusion, minorities and majorities, and ownership of and entitlement to the state – be it having access to national institutions, having influence on and a presence in the national narrative, or being included in dominant conceptions of the *staatsvolk*. More often than not, these issues play out in far more subtle ways than the sledgehammer bluntness of the post-2003 era's sect-centricity – particularly near the epicentres of twenty-first-century sect-coded conflict in Iraq and Syria. A more common manifestation of modern sectarian competition involves differential access to the state and state resources, for example in housing, policing or public services.[87] This is often rooted in deeper sources of modern Sunni–Shi'a contestation relating to competing versions of the national narrative that variously include, exclude, privilege and marginalize – even if only through omission – certain sectarian identities at the expense of others. Elements of this were evident in chapter 3 where we looked at the intersection of class and sectarian identity and how the resultant prejudice ultimately served to marginalize certain sect-coded socio-economic groups "as unsuitable candidates for the

---

[86] Collectively the nation-states of the region form a sovereign state system that, despite being marked by endemic turbulence, has proven remarkably resilient. This resilience further reifies the nation-state and facilitates the interaction of the national and transnational dimensions of sectarian identity. For a discussion of the regional sovereign state system, see Simon Mabon and F. Gregory Gause III, "SEPAD Pod with Gregory Gause," Sectarianism, Proxies and De-sectarianization, Richardson Institute, Dec. 2018, https://soundcloud.com/richardsoninstitute/sepadpod-with-gregory-gause.

[87] See, for example, Gengler, *Group Conflict and Political Mobilization*, chapter 5.

category of the exemplary national."[88] Similarly, myths of origin, authenticity and ethnic purity are used to elevate or demote sectarian identities within the national framework. For example, in Saudi Arabia, in addition to exclusion on the basis of religious or doctrinal othering, certain narratives of state question the origins of Saudi Shi'as by suggesting that they are relative newcomers to Saudi Arabia and were originally of non-tribal or of foreign – Persian or Iraqi – descent.[89] In Bahrain and Iraq one encounters similar contestation around national authenticity and belonging often through the casting of doubts on a community's nativist Arab pedigree.[90] These and other examples may differ in severity but ultimately they are all instances of sect-coded contests for position in the national narrative – either by minorities apologetically trying to gain acceptance or normalization of their place in the nation-state (Shi'as in Saudi Arabia, for example) or of demographically stronger and hence more confident groups trying to position themselves at its centre. To paraphrase Toby Dodge, this competition is ultimately about a struggle to impose one dominant vision of what a country is and who its people are.[91] As will be seen in later chapters, this has been at the heart of the sect-coded conflicts that have afflicted the twenty-first-century Middle East.

---

[88] Shaery-Eisenlohr, *Shi'ite Lebanon*, p. 43.

[89] Toby Matthiesen, "Shi'i Historians in a Wahhabi State: Identity Entrepreneurs and the Politics of Local Historiography in Saudi Arabia," *International Journal of Middle East Studies*, 47:1 (2015): 30–32.

[90] For contested nativism and competing claims to national authenticity in Bahrain, see Gengler, *Group Conflict and Political Mobilization*, chapter 2; Jones, "Contesting the Iranian Revolution," in *Gulfization*, ed. Jones et al., p. 95. For the conflation of sectarian and ethnic identity (and by extension the questioning of one's national credentials) see Haddad, *Sectarianism in Iraq*, pp. 40–51. In Peter Sluglett's words: "The subtext of Iraqi Ba'thism came to be that only Sunni Arabs were 'real' Arabs and thus full members of the rest of the Arab world." Peter Sluglett, "Sectarianism in Recent Iraqi History: What It Is and What It Isn't," in *The Shi'a of Samarra*, ed. Imranali, p. 156. In post-2003 Iraq this trope went both ways: Shi'as were often caricatured as agents of Iran while Sunnis were often vilified as facilitators of foreign jihadis and a threat to the stability of post-2003 Iraq.

[91] Toby Dodge, "'Bourdieu Goes to Baghdad': Explaining Hybrid Political Identities in Iraq," *Journal of Historical Sociology*, 31 (2018): 29.

The Necessity of a Multidimensional Approach

This and the preceding chapter have argued that sectarian identity is too amorphous to be framed in rigid, monochrome ways – be it as just a religious concept or solely as a function of politics and so forth. Rather, the only way to comprehensively understand sectarian identity on its many levels and in its many forms is to view it as the sum of its parts. To that end these two chapters have sought to outline the four dimensions of sectarian identity: doctrinal, subnational, national and transnational. The present chapter has argued that the national level is the most consequential level in modern sectarian relations; indeed, it is the pivot around which the other dimensions revolve and often it is the canvas against which they are formulated. The centrality of the national dimension is a function of the centrality of the nation-state in modern political life. Its emotional content, and its constant reproduction, tie people to it, with national identity forming a basic component of many people's perception of self. Further, its legislative, distributive and legitimating capacities make it both the prize of political contestation and the arbiter of political fortunes and economic distribution. The centrality of the nation-state should be borne in mind when considering the drivers of modern sectarian competition and which frameworks are best suited to preventing sectarian entrenchment and sect-centric political polarization. Rather than doctrinal ecumenism, what is more often required is a political ecumenism capable of building functioning states that can deliver on their supposed promise of representative politics. Contrary to much popular wisdom, the inflated political salience of sectarian identities and the sect-coded civil wars of twenty-first-century Iraq and Syria are not a negation of nationalism; rather, they are signs of its contestation. In that sense, what we have seen in places like Iraq, Syria and Bahrain is not sectarian plurality obstructing the supposedly integrative potential of nationalism, but quite the reverse: it has been political failure and the failure to deliver on the supposed promise of the modern nation-state that have soured sectarian relations. Accordingly, sectarian relations at the national level have been complicated less by doctrinal difference and geostrategic rivalries and more by uneven political development and economic distribution, weak institutions, lack of integrative absorption, personification of rule, fragmentation of the national mythscape, and so forth. It follows that a national political framework that upholds and defends social justice, and in which a critical mass of the citizenry feel that their proximity to the state and its resources is not dictated or influenced by sectarian identity, would go much further in detoxifying sectarian relations and guarding against future inflammation than inter-faith dialogue events or vaguely defined calls for secularism and nationalism as antidotes to 'sectarianism'.

5

SUNNI–SHI'A RELATIONS
AN IMBALANCED DIVIDE

Before we turn to the twenty-first century and the unprecedented politicization of sectarian categories since 2003, it is worth considering some of the structural factors that shaped sectarian relations over the course of the twentieth century and that continue to do so today. Specifically, this chapter will consider how the demographic imbalance inherent in the Sunni–Shi'a divide has shaped sectarian identity formation and sectarian relations in the modern Arab world up to 2003. Of course, the matter of minorities and majorities is ultimately an (often political) abstraction, hence it is important not to think of demographics as predetermining the contours of sectarian relations or regard them as the only factor governing the nature of Sunni–Shi'a relations. Whatever the relevance of demographics, they are but one component in an array of other variables and drivers influencing sectarian dynamics, such as (to take the national and subnational dimensions) economic distribution, political participation, social policy, governance structures, communal rights and so forth. Hence, for example, the Shi'a minority in Kuwait are not othered in the same way that Shi'as are othered in the extreme case of Saudi Arabia, where there is a distinct ideological dimension that is absent in Kuwait and where state–Shi'a relations have charted a very different course.[1] Likewise, power relations may be shaped by demographics but they are also susceptible to contestation, changes and shock — something that has been abundantly demonstrated since 2003, as we will see in the next two chapters. However, while in no way predetermining the minutiae of Sunni–Shi'a relations, demographics (both transnational and national) nevertheless play an important role in structuring many aspects of Sunni–Shi'a interactions and in influencing power relations between them. Further, being mindful of the relevance of demographics can help shed further light on how the different dimensions of sectarian identity come into play. In most Arab countries, Shi'as form too small a minority for sectarian identity to matter much on the national or subnational levels, yet the Sunni–Shi'a divide can still acquire political relevance (contrived or otherwise) in such contexts as a result of transnational considerations relating to Arab–Iranian rivalry. In some cases this has served to reduce the term 'sectarianism' to little more than shorthand for the geopolitical rivalry between some Arab states and post-1979 Iran.[2] However, in countries where the sectarian divide is demographically competitive and politically contested (particularly Iraq, Bahrain, Lebanon) Sunni–Shi'a relations go beyond the transnational dimension and can acquire relevance at the national and subnational levels as well.

This chapter will look at the role of demographics in sectarian dynamics by considering the demographic contradictions that can arise between the various dimensions of sectarian identity — a national minority that is nevertheless part of a transnational majority for example. Secondly, it will look at how demographics have influenced the way that both sectarian bigotry and sectarian rapprochement have

---

[1] On Sunni–Shi'a relations and state–Shi'a relations in Kuwait, see Laurence Louer, *Transnational Shia Politics: Religious and Political Networks in the Gulf* (New York: Columbia University Press, 2008), pp. 45–65; Wehrey, *Sectarian Politics in the Gulf*, pp. 17–20 and part IV; Madeleine Wells, "Sectarianism, Authoritarianism and Opposition in Kuwait," in *Sectarianization*, ed. Hashim and Postel; Lindsey Stephenson, "Ahistorical Kuwaiti Sectarianism," *Foreign Policy*, April 29, 2011, https://foreignpolicy.com/2011/04/29/ahistorical-kuwaiti-sectarianism/.

[2] For a blunt iteration of this line of thinking, see Muhammad al-Sulami, "How to counter Iran's sectarian and terrorist threat," *Arab News*, July 18, 2018, http://www.arabnews.com/node/1341196.

been framed by Sunni and Shi'a actors. Thirdly, it will consider the role of demographics in state–sect relations in the Arab world and how these have been influenced by the normativity of Sunni Islam – itself a function of demographics and empowerment. Finally, this chapter will look at how these factors turned the securitization of sectarian plurality into the securitization of sectarian outgroups.

The Sunni–Shi'a Divide and the Question of Equivalence

It is easy to make the mistake of viewing the Sunni–Shi'a divide as one between two more or less similar if not equal groups. Such a false equivalence leads one to presume a level playing field between Sunni and Shi'a actors with little thought given to power relations between them and how these differ from one context to another. In some cases equivalence is assumed without much forethought – the path of least resistance perhaps. In other cases, however, it is a way to signal neutrality: a safe, politically correct stance to adopt when commenting on sectarian relations in order to spare one the risk of appearing to take sides. In such contentious terrain, failure to uphold equivalence (even if counterfactual) can be seized upon by partisans of sect *a* or sect *b* as proof that the unlucky author is either a champion or an enemy of their cause. The readiness with which charges of prejudice and unfair bias can follow even the most sensible discussions of sectarian dynamics has fostered a dogmatic adherence to equivalence that is more a precaution against the performative outrage that abounds in social media debates than a reflection of the realities of sectarian relations. In this counterfactual equivalence, Sunni and Shi'a militants necessarily become mirror images of each other; Saudi Arabia and Iran must necessarily view and utilize the sectarian divide in identical ways, and anti-Shi'ism and anti-Sunnism become two sides of the same coin. Yet none of this stands up to closer scrutiny: a binary (black and white, Sunni and Shi'a, male and female) is not necessarily balanced. Furthermore, denying equivalence does not have to entail taking sides or making value judgements: exploring differences or imbalances in power relations need not be a commentary on morality, righteousness or virtue. Strength or empowerment is not a priori an incriminating or damning marker any more than relative weakness or disempowerment are title deeds to the moral high ground; ascendant powers are not necessarily villains and embattled minorities are not necessarily heroes. The imposition of false equivalences upon discussions of Sunni and Shi'a sect-centricity – even if well intentioned and driven by a desire for impartiality – can be counterproductive in that it either wrongly assumes equilibrium between the two or wilfully ignores its absence. As will be seen, a long-standing reflection of this can be found in the detrimental impact of the contrived sect-blindness that has long been upheld by state censors, political correctness and social taboo in the Arab world.

Measuring Demographics

Demographic realities and demographic perceptions shape what one scholar calls demographic awareness: a group's sense of its own size and hence the limits of what it can realistically aspire to, fight for or demand.[3] In the case of the Sunni–Shi'a divide, the multidimensionality of sectarian identity is reflected in the multiple and contradictory ways in which demographic awareness can be imagined. At the transnational and the doctrinal levels the matter of demographics between Sunnis and Shi'as is a fairly stable one: the spectrum that constitutes Sunni Islam and Sunni Muslims forms an overwhelming majority of between 85–90 per cent of self-professed Muslims.[4] Consequently, conceptions of what constitutes Sunni Islam understandably play a normative role in

---

[3] Husam Itani, "Khutut al-Fasl wa-Khuyut al-Wasl" (Lines of Separation and Threads of Connection), in *Nawasib wa Rawafidh*, ed. Saghiya, p. 41. Needless to say, this sense of a group's aspirational limits can evolve in line with exceptional shifts in broader relations of power, as abundantly illustrated in Shi'a assertiveness after 2003.

[4] Figures relating to Sunni–Shi'a demographics are imprecise and are almost always based on estimates or extrapolations from dated population surveys. Official censuses generally tend to subsume Sunnis and Shi'as under the category of Muslim. Despite using a very liberal definition of Shi'a, one report by the Pew Research Center estimated the Shi'a population at 10–13% of Muslims globally in 2009. See Pew Research Center, *Mapping the Global Muslim Population: A Report on the Size and Distribution of the World's Muslim Population*, Oct. 2009, pp. 8–11, 38–41, http://www.pewresearch.org/wp-content/uploads/sites/7/2009/10/Muslimpopulation.pdf.

popular views regarding Islam and the 'Muslim world'. By extension, Sunni–Shi'a interactions at the doctrinal and transnational levels are those of a clear majority and a small minority that is readily viewed as aberrant and, were it not for Iran's official adoption of Shi'ism beginning in the sixteenth century, would most likely be viewed as irrelevant as well. However, the nation-state system imposes an additional numerical logic, and if we focus on the national dimension, we find a less uniform and less straightforward picture with Shi'as forming national majorities in Iran, Iraq, Bahrain and Azerbaijan and a plurality in Lebanon. Likewise, the subnational dimension sees significant Shi'a minorities and Shi'a concentrations in many otherwise Sunni-majority or non-Muslim-majority contexts – in fact, the largest national Shi'a populations outside Iran are found in Pakistan and India, where they form small minorities of about 10–15 per cent and only 2 per cent of the respective national populations.[5]

In this way sectarian demographics are inherently contradictory in a very obvious way: majorities at the doctrinal or transnational level can simultaneously be minorities at the national or subnational level and vice versa. This has complex and contradictory implications for sectarian relations in that they are influenced by more than one frame of demographic awareness. At the national level, the political horizons of, for example, Bahraini Shi'as are not the same as those of Emirati Shi'as: the former are those of a majority national group and are shaped by a particular colonial and post-colonial history of sect-coded political contestation and discrimination, while the latter are those of a tiny minority which has been relatively well integrated into a national context that has enough sectarian homogeneity and integrative frameworks to avoid the bane of having a 'sectarian issue'. Yet at the same time, both share a similar demographic awareness when it comes to the doctrinal and transnational dimensions where

---

[5] As with Sunni–Shi'a demographics in other contexts, these are only estimates as official censuses generally tend to subsume both under the category of Muslim. The figure of 10–15% is commonly used for the Shi'a population of Pakistan. As for Indian Shi'as, they are often estimated at between 10% and 15% of Indian Muslims – who in turn form an estimated 14.2% of India's nearly 1.3 billion people. Taking the upper limits of these figures, the total number of Indian Shi'as comes to just over 2% of India's total population.

Shi'ism carries minority and outgroup status. Of course there is a limit to how much demographics can tell us on their own: while Sunnis in Syria are a majority in both national and transnational terms, the hierarchies of power in Ba'thist Syria have nevertheless created a profound sense of Sunni victimhood among significant sections of Sunni society, who resent what they regard as sectarian oppression by an Alawi-dominated regime.

This leads us to a seemingly pertinent but ultimately misleading question: which dimension is more relevant when thinking about demographics and processes of minoritization and majoritization? As we have seen in the previous two chapters, rather than being clearly ring-fenced or mutually exclusive concepts, the dimensions of sectarian identity are best imagined as the interdependently connected moving parts constituting the whole that is sectarian identity. As such, minority or majority status at the national or subnational levels cannot be entirely divorced from the inverse at the transnational and doctrinal levels. Sunni national minorities remain cognizant of the normative role that conceptions of Sunnism play in how Muslims and Islam are imagined. Likewise, no matter the sense of entitlement or political ambition of Shi'a national majorities, they nevertheless retain a sense of themselves as an outgroup given their minority status in respect of the transnational and doctrinal dimensions (as most obviously demonstrated in how Sunni and Shi'a actors have approached doctrinal rapprochement or *taqrib* – as will be seen below). This has proven problematic where Shi'ism's minority status in transnational conceptions of Arab or Islamic community has been transposed onto national settings where Shi'ism is demographically competitive, thereby artificially minoritizing national pluralities and even majorities (Bahrain and pre-2003 Iraq, for example). This again underlines the fact, touched upon in chapter 1, that the term 'minority' is not always an innocuous expression of quantitative value but is often also an expression of power relations. Few examples are more illustrative in that regard than American Vice President Spiro Agnew's response to a question about American policy towards the white supremacist regime in what was then called Rhodesia (today's Zimbabwe): it was no business of the United States how other countries dealt with their minorities, by which Agnew of course meant the country's black majority.[6] This dissonance between demographic realities and cultural or political weight is particularly relevant in the Arab world where, as we discussed in chapter 3, the line between the national and the transnational is especially permeable. This is mirrored both conceptually and practically in how sectarian relations are perceived and specifically in how Shi'a Arabs are framed in a political ecosystem that continues to be imagined as Sunni: no less a figure than Albert Hourani defined minorities in the Arab world as non-Sunni Muslims or non-Arabic speakers.[7]

Minorities, Majorities, Demographics and Power

In many ways the minoritization of Shi'as and the normativity of Sunni Islam in the Arab world are only to be expected given the demographic weakness of Shi'ism. As already mentioned, even the most generous estimates of the global Shi'a population would fall well short of 20 per cent of Muslims. If we restrict our focus to the Arab world, that figure drops significantly: in the 22 countries that constitute the Arab League, the (Twelver) Shi'a population comes to less than 9 per cent of the total population. Even if we include Yemen's sizeable Zaidi community – though it is debatable whether such an inclusion is warranted – the figure would barely exceed 11 per cent.[8] Moreover, Arab Shi'ism is

---

[6] Quoted in Karen E. Fields and Barbara J. Fields, *Racecraft: The Soul of Inequality in American Life* (London: Verso, 2014), p. 28.

[7] Albert Hourani, *Minorities in the Arab World* (London: Oxford University Press, 1947), p. 1, quoted in Laura Robson, "Introduction," in *Minorities and the Modern Arab World: New Perspectives*, ed. Laura Robson (Syracuse: Syracuse University Press, 2016), p. 1. This is part of a broader problem with how minorities are framed in a region that is imagined in exclusionary terms, both ethnically (Arab) and religiously (Sunni Muslim). See Hani Nusseira, "Hawl Kharitat al-Aqaliyat fi-l-Alam al-Arabi" (On the Map of Minorities in the Arab World), in *Al-Ta'ifiyya*, ed. al-Mesbar, pp. 136–138.

[8] As already mentioned, sectarian demographics are an inexact matter of estimation as no official figures are publicly available. The numbers presented here are based on generous estimates of Shi'a populations in the 22 countries of the Arab League: 65% in Bahrain, 55% in Iraq, 40% in Lebanon, 27% in Kuwait, 17% in Saudi Arabia, 12% in the United Arab Emirates, 10% in Qatar and an additional 1% to account for other Shi'a communities in the Arab world. The estimate used for Zaidis in Yemen is 35% of the Yemeni population. I have applied these estimates to the UN ESCWA population

made all the less visible and all the more marginal by the fact that it is heavily concentrated in a few countries: nearly 60 per cent of all Shi'a Arabs are Iraqi.[9] The significance of Iraq to Arab Shi'ism – both in demographic terms and, more so, in historical terms and as a site of pilgrimage – may explain Ali al-Wardi's comment that "It is possible to say that, in no country amongst all Islamic countries, is there one that resembles Iraq where the inflammation of conflict between these two sects [Sunni and Shi'a] is concerned."[10] Taken at face value, Shi'ism's demographic weakness makes the episodic salience of the Sunni–Shi'a divide seem somewhat baffling. However, numbers alone seldom tell the whole story. After all, European anti-Semitism has historically thrived despite the Jewish population of Europe hardly ever exceeding 2 per cent of the whole, while the Jewish population of Germany stood at less than 1 per cent of all Germans in the 1930s.[11] Likewise, for all the hysterics surrounding Muslim migration, the Muslim population of Europe was estimated at less than 5 per cent of Europeans in 2016.[12]

In the case of the Sunni–Shi'a divide, its salience has been disproportionate to its demographic composition chiefly as a result of its intertwinement with political rivalry. Be it in the form of the early challenge to post-Prophetic political legitimacy that proto-Shi'ism presented to the Umayyad state or in the form of the medieval Shi'a and quasi-Shi'a challenges to the late Abbasid state or in the form of

---

figures for 2015: United Nations Economic and Social Commission for Western Asia, "The Demographic Profiles of the Arab States, 2017," https://www.unescwa.org/sites/www.unescwa.org/files/publications/files/demographic-profiles-2017.pdf.

[9] Using the estimates for Twelver Shi'a populations in individual countries listed in the previous note and applying them to UN ESCWA population totals for 2015, Iraqi Shi'as number 19,863,606 (57%) of a total of 34,771,675 Twelver Shi'as in the Arab world. Again, caution is needed with these estimates: 57% may be the upper limit but even the most conservative estimates would still have Iraqi Shi'as making up either a strong plurality or a majority of Arab Shi'as.

[10] Al-Wardi, *Dirasa fi-Tabi'at al-Mugtama' al-Iraqi*, p. 192.

[11] United States Holocaust Memorial Museum, "Jewish Population of Europe in 1933: Population Data by Country," *Holocaust Encyclopedia*, https://encyclopedia.ushmm.org/content/en/article/jewish-population-of-europe-in-1933-population-data-by-country.

[12] Pew Research Center, *Europe's Growing Muslim Population*, Nov. 29, 2017, pp. 4–5, http://www.pewforum.org/2017/11/29/europes-growing-muslim-population/.

Ottoman–Iranian rivalry, we repeatedly see the emotive currency of Sunni–Shi'a ideological difference and group solidarity being enlisted in the service of domestic and regional power politics. In the modern Arab world, this is chiefly manifested through the prism of Iran and threat perceptions relating to it. Indeed, it is difficult to see the Sunni–Shi'a divide being of much relevance outside very localized episodes at the doctrinal or subnational levels were it not for the fact that Iran, an important geostrategic actor with aspirations to regional hegemony, is a Shi'a state. More than anything else, the Iran factor has complicated Sunni–Shi'a (more precisely, state–Shi'a) relations in the modern, pre-2003 Arab world, as will be seen when we turn to the securitization of sectarian plurality below.

Leaving the Iranian factor aside for the moment, the demographic imbalance between Sunnis and Shi'as has several important implications. Firstly, it underpins the normativity of Sunni Islam and Sunni frames of reference in how Islam and Muslims are imagined. Secondly, as a result, the minority or outgroup status of Shi'ism has served to create a far stronger sense of Shi'a identity with little in terms of a Sunni parallel. To put it into perspective, while the emergence of an explicitly Sunni identity as a politically and socially salient frame of reference may be episodically witnessed in times of sect-coded crisis, the Shi'a equivalent is far more consistent and integral to Shi'a conceptions of self. Some scholars argue that even if the terminology of sects and the rigid formalization of sectarian boundaries were to come much later, a Shi'a identity of sorts was in evidence as early as the eighth century when political and intellectual changes affecting early proto-Shi'as served to "create in effect a *sect*, with the purity and zeal of a sect."[13] Over the centuries this has resulted in a far more developed and more relevant sectarian myth–symbol complex among Shi'as than is the case with their Sunni counterparts.[14] To be sure, this is not solely a matter of

---

[13] Hodgson, "How Did the Early Shi'a Become Sectarian?" p. 12.

[14] See, for example, Ala' Hamid, "Al-Ayquna al-Shi'iyya: Qira'ah fi-Dala'il al-Suwar al-Ramziyya li-A'immat al-Shi'a" (The Shi'a Icon: Analysing the Symbolic Images of the Shi'a Imams), *Masarat*, 15 (2011): 116–220; Haddad, "Sectarian Relations and Sunni Identity," in *Sectarian Politics in the Persian Gulf*, ed. Potter. For a fascinating examination of the symbolism of Ali ibn Abi Talib in Shi'a iconography, see Shakir Lu'aibi, *Tasawir al-Imam Ali* (Depictions of Imam Ali) (Beirut: Riad al-Rayyes Books, 2011).

demographics; rather, at heart it is about power relations: historically, political, social and religious dynamics meant that Sunni identity was seldom called upon to fulfil the functions demanded of Shi'a identity (such as the autonomous perpetuation of the group and ensuring the survival of what at times seemed like an encircled identity) – hence the absence of a symbolic heritage similar to that found in Shi'ism.

In modern times the same processes resulted in greater sect-centricity among Shi'as: as seen in the modern examples of Shi'a activism in Iraq, Bahrain, Saudi Arabia and Lebanon, a clearer and more salient Shi'a identity marked by feelings of victimhood or marginalization created Shi'a issues, Shi'a causes, Shi'a organizations and the like – in other words, the markers of political sect-centricity. That the Sunni parallel to such sect-centric activism was so weak in these countries is a reflection of the relations of power underpinning Sunni–Shi'a dynamics within them. The Syrian exception underlines the case: Sunni-centric activism emerged to address real and perceived discrimination against Sunnis in Ba'thist Syria and their political exclusion. Ultimately, the more empowered an identity is and the more its empowerment is secure, the less visible and less forcefully asserted it becomes. An obvious parallel presents itself in the study of white identity or whiteness.[15] Until recently, white identity was often regarded as race-less; in other words, white people tended to see themselves as 'normal' people lacking a racial identity. They saw their viewpoint not as a specifically white one but as a "universally valid one – 'the truth' – what everyone knows."[16] In this way, white becomes the standard or the normative benchmark from which all others are distinguished. At heart this is reflective of and supported by a set of power relations that racialize and thereby minoritize non-white identities. Likewise, there is, generally speaking, a tendency to view sects (along with the incriminating and vilifying language of 'sectarianism') as essentially referring to non-Sunnis. In other

---

[15] See Dyer, "The Matter of Whiteness," in *Theories of Race and Racism*, ed. Back and Solomos; Steve Garner, "A Moral Economy of Whiteness: Behaviours, Belonging and Britishness," *Ethnicities*, 12:4 (2012): 445–464; Lewis, "'What Group?'" For a critique that questions the analytical utility of the concept of whiteness, see Fields, "Whiteness, Racism and Identity."

[16] Delgado and Stefancic, *Critical Race Theory*, p. 80.

words, just as whites were often viewed as race-less, there is a tendency to view Sunnis as sect-less – or, to take the terminology's basic (and, for the Islamic context, largely incompatible) meaning in its original Christian setting, Sunnis become 'the church' and non-Sunnis become sects.[17]

Demographics are also important when considering how sectarian polemics are framed in that they lend anti-Shi'ism and anti-Sunnism fundamentally different characteristics. Shi'a identity is grounded in a minority mindset that is integral to Shi'a conceptions of self. In contrast to the emphasis that Sunni schools of jurisprudence place on consensus (*ijma'*), Shi'ism regards the minority status that comes with going against the grain as something of a virtue – evidence of moral righteousness standing fast in the face of a conformist consensus created and upheld by corrupt, illegitimate political power.[18] Of course this narrative is selectively and hypocritically deployed: it may be used to validate Shi'ism's claims in relation to the broader Islamic world when necessary, but it does not translate into a greater acceptance of dissent within Shi'ism's own ranks.[19] It also creates an inherent contradiction in the form of the conflicting priorities of defending, on the one hand, "the moral excellence of an embattled minority" – to use Enayat's words – and, on the other, the modern normative belief in the virtues of Islamic unity.[20] In any case, what matters for our purposes is how

---

[17] On the incompatibility of Weber's church–sect dichotomy with the Islamic context, see Cook, "Weber and Islamic Sects," in *Max Weber and Islam*, ed. Huff and Schluchter; Gaiser, "A Narrative Identity Approach to Islamic Sectarianism," in *Sectarianization*, ed. Hashemi and Postel, pp. 65–68.

[18] For examples of Shi'a traditions that explicitly frame minority status as a virtue, see Enayat, *Modern Islamic Political Thought*, pp. 20–21.

[19] Litvak, "Encounters between Shi'i and Sunni Ulama," in *The Sunna and Shi'a in History*, ed. Bengio and Litvak, p. 83. Also relevant is the treatment of Sunnis in contexts of Shi'a empowerment. See, for example, Sabahi, "Iran, Iranian Media and Sunnite Islam," in *The Dynamics of Sunni–Shia Relationships*, ed. Marechal and Zemni; Shahram Akbarzadeh, "Iran and Daesh: The Case of a Reluctant Shia Power," *Middle East Policy*, 22:3 (Fall 2015): 50 and 53. Far worse is the pronounced anti-Baha'i position commonly taken by conservative Shi'as.

[20] Enayat, *Modern Islamic Political Thought*, p. 19. Enayat points out that the pride that Shi'ism took in maintaining its isolation from the erring majority has largely given way to the exigencies of Islamic unity in modern times. Ibid., p. 47.

this minority mindset differs from a majority or majoritarian mindset in the formation of sectarian polemics and in how conceptions of self and other are constructed.

To begin with, a natural corollary of Shi'ism's minority mindset is Shi'a identity's obsession with victimhood and the construction of a cult of the oppressed. As Michael Cook has argued in his discussion of the synergies between leftist ideology and Islam, Shi'ism provides a ready counterpart to the Marxist proletariat that is lacking in Sunni conceptions of community: "Sunnis were traditionally the victors of history, not its victims."[21] Mythologies of Shi'a victimhood are multilayered and can operate at both the doctrinal and the national levels: a narrative of the victimhood of a uniquely righteous minority in the context of Islamic history alongside a narrative of the victimhood of a uniquely oppressed group in a specific national context. What concerns us here, however, is that whatever dimension we look at, Shi'a martyrology and the obsession with victimhood and oppression do not cast Sunnis per se as a threat, much less as an enemy. Instead, anti-Shi'a religious and political authorities and problematically elastic categories such as *nawasib* and Wahhabi are used to ring-fence 'good Sunnis' from 'bad Sunnis'.[22] In other words, the broader mass of Sunni Islam is not framed in threatening terms; they may be ignored, denigrated, portrayed as lesser Muslims or misguided fools, but Shi'a polemics

---

[21] Michael Cook, *Ancient Religions, Modern Politics: The Islamic Case in Comparative Perspective* (Princeton: Princeton University Press, 2014), pp. 178–182. Interestingly, he extends the argument and highlights its political relevance by pointing out the absence of liberation theology in Sunni Islamism while Shi'a Islamism produced (p. 183) "the greatest political triumph of liberation theology in the entire history of the phenomenon."

[22] The term *nawasib* was initially used in reference to those who oppose or show enmity towards the House of the Prophet. In time this understanding evolved and was broadened to include those who oppose or show enmity to the followers of the House of the Prophet – in other words, Shi'as. For a broader discussion of this and the broader context of anti-Sunni polemics, see Tarabishi, *Hartaqat II*, pp. 63–89; Nasr al-Din bin Ghanisa, "Muqaraba Simya'iyya li-Surat al-Akhar fi Makhyalat al-Ana Bayn al-Sunna wa-l- Shi'a" (Semiotic Comparison of the Portrayal of the Other in Imaginations of Self between Sunnis and Shi'as), in *Al-Ta'ifiyya fi-l-Alam al-Islami: al-Khitab al-Qadim wa-l-Mashhad al-Jadid* (Sectarianism in the Islamic World: Old Discourse and New Scene), ed. Fu'ad Kathim (London: Centre for Academic Shi'a Studies, 2015).

generally do not frame ordinary Sunnis as an inherent threat.[23] Even a figure as unrelentingly and unapologetically anti-Sunni as Shi'a cleric Yasser al-Habib does not frame Sunnis as a threat. For example, in January 2019, US Senator Rand Paul voiced his support for President Trump's intention to withdraw troops from Syria, tweeting: "Sunnis have been killing Shi'a since the massacre at Karbala in 680 AD. If we wait until they stop killing each other, we will stay for a thousand years or more."[24] Predictably, this sort of essentialist, ahistorical nonsense attracted much well-deserved ridicule and criticism. Rather less predictably, however, al-Habib joined the conversation with a 14-tweet thread responding to the Senator, beginning: "We as the Rafida [sic] Shi'a do not support the idea of generalising all from the self-proclaimed 'Sunni' sect to be killers of the Shi'a, as the vast majority of their masses are innocent and peaceful individuals. (1/14)"[25]

This points to an important distinction in the way anti-Sunnism and anti-Shi'ism are framed. As will be seen below, there is a vast genre of anti-Shi'ism that portrays Shi'as and Shi'ism as a threat to Islam and Muslims – one that needs to be unmasked and expunged. Anti-Sunnism, by contrast, is far less likely to adopt such a stance and one of the reasons for this relates to demographics. As a minority group within Islam, and given the immense demographic imbalance between Sunnis and Shi'as, the latter are not in a position to issue unambiguous, wholesale rejections of the former – not as long as they want to be formally represented in expressions of 'the Muslim world' (by having a seat in state-sponsored international Islamic organizations, for example). Put more bluntly, Shi'ism needs the validation of Sunni acceptance in order to survive as a recognized part of mainstream global Islam; needless to say, the reverse does not hold – it is not a mere coincidence that the ecumenical moment of choice for proponents of doctrinal rapprochement is the Rector of

---

[23] Tarabishi, *Hartaqat II*, pp. 63–89; Bin Ghanisa, "Muqaraba Simya'iyya li-Surat al-Akhar," in *Al-Ta'ifiyya fi-l-Alam al-Islami*, ed. Fu'ad Kathim.

[24] See @RandPaul, Jan. 17, 2019, https://twitter.com/RandPaul/status/1085600177682071552.

[25] The tweet came from al-Habib's now defunct English-language Twitter account. Luckily, I retain a screenshot of the tweet: @SheikhalHabib, Jan. 31, 2019, http://twitter.com/SheikhalHabib/status/1090713920308940800.

al-Azhar's statement recognizing Shi'a jurisprudence (see chapter 3) rather than a statement from Qom or Najaf recognizing the various schools of Sunni jurisprudence.[26] The exceptions underline the rule: perhaps the frankest Shi'a rejection of Sunnis and Sunni Islam today comes from 'freelancers', normally based in the West and lacking formal connections to more established Shi'a networks.[27] A paradigmatic example of this breed of Shi'a hate preachers is the above-mentioned London-based cleric Yasser al-Habib.[28] In his line of

[26] An interesting corollary of this is the fact that Shi'as tend to have a better understanding of Sunnism than Sunnis have of Shi'ism. Interestingly this same imbalance in familiarity with the sectarian other was noted by Litvak in his study of Sunni–Shi'a clerical interactions in Ottoman Iraq, where he found a tendency among aspiring Shi'a scholars to attend the classes of leading Sunni jurists – needless to say, the reverse was not the case. Litvak, "Encounters between Shi'i and Sunni Ulama," in *The Sunna and Shi'a in History*, ed. Bengio and Litvak, pp. 75–76. This is again a function of demographics and of the relations of power: as Litvak points out, members of minorities or outgroups have more reason to familiarize themselves with the habits and mores of dominant groups than the other way round.

[27] The concept of 'freelancers' is borrowed from Marius Linge, "Sunnite-Shiite Polemics in Norway," *FLEKS: Scandinavian Journal of Intercultural Theory and Practice*, 3:1 (2016), https://doi.org/10.7577/fleks.1684. In line with its original usage by Michael Walzer with reference to sixteenth-century Puritan clerics (*The Revolution of the Saints: A Study in the Origins of Radical Politics*, 1965), the freelance preacher is estranged from his land and from the traditional structures of religious authorities and he is unconventional and nonconformist. These features are turned into strengths with which to penetrate foreign milieus. Quoted in Louer, *Transnational Shia Politics*, pp. 122–123. In terms of established networks, the Shirazi network (named after the late Muhammad al-Hussaini al-Shirazi) is often regarded as the most polemic in their approach to Sunnism. However, they are defined less by their position towards Sunnis and more by intra-Shi'a disputes regarding religious and political authority. More to the point, their sectarian polemics are almost entirely restricted to the doctrinal dimension: some Shirazis have taken a hard line in maintaining Shi'a doctrinal specificity. This has not prevented political cooperation or sectarian harmony at the national level, as is demonstrated in the evolution of the Shirazis' relation with the state in Saudi Arabia and more so in Kuwait. For a brief historical overview, see Louer, *Transnational Shia Politics*, pp. 88–99.

[28] Al-Habib is a former Kuwaiti national (he was stripped of his citizenship in 2010) now based in London. While a Shirazi in terms of his religious background, he is far more outspokenly anti-Sunni and puritanically Shi'a. His official website: http://www.alqatrah.net/en/index.php.

thinking, the previously noted tension between the need to defend Shi'a specificity and the need to strengthen Islamic unity is resolved by completely rejecting the latter. Hence, al-Habib and his followers are able to reject Sunni Islam wholesale (and vast swathes of Shi'a Islam as well) because they have no interest in being accepted by mainstream variants of Islam nor do they see a virtue in moderating doctrinal differences with ideological opponents for the sake of unity. This, al-Habib argues, would be an unacceptable abandonment of religious principle and a betrayal of religious truth. On the contrary, he insists that true believers should make a point of differentiating themselves from the mass of errant Muslims. For example, as illustrated in his above-quoted tweet, he proudly adopts the normally derogatory term *rafidha* and refers to the '*rafidha* Shi'a' as the only real Muslims in contrast to other Muslims – including what he regards as doctrinally compromised Shi'as. In that sense his thinking mirrors sectarian thinking in the Christian sense of the term.[29] Herein lies the point: this level of openly exclusionary insularity is relatively unusual for contemporary Shi'ism given that it presents itself as a legitimate part of a globally defined Islam (in which it is a small minority) and in view of the primacy that is attached to normative notions of Islamic unity. Instead, the far more common position among Shi'a clerics, activists and public personalities is to try to secure a degree of acceptability for Shi'ism in mainstream conceptions of global Islam.

This is certainly the official Iranian position with the Islamic Republic portraying itself as the vanguard of a united Islamic front transcending the Sunni–Shi'a divide.[30] Ultimately, given Shi'ism's minority status, and given Tehran's pan-Islamic pretensions, sectarian entrenchment does not necessarily serve Iran's interests. Hence Iranian messaging consistently emphasizes sectarian unity while framing sectarian tensions as the product of Zionist, American and imperialist

---

[29] For an overview, see "Is it wrong to call ourselves a sect?" *Al-Qatra*, Sept. 6, 2018, http://www.the-drop.net/en/al42.

[30] See, for example, Alex Vatanka, "The Islamic Republic's Cross-Sectarian Outreach," *Current Trends in Islamist Ideology* (April 2011): 25–39; Frederic Wehrey et al., "Saudi–Iranian Relations since the Fall of Saddam: Rivalry, Cooperation and Implications for US Policy," RAND Corporation, 2009, chapter 2, https://www.rand.org/content/dam/rand/pubs/monographs/2009/RAND_MG840.pdf.

machinations – of which Wahhabism is often portrayed as a tool.[31] As is widely noted, Iran recognizes that the more it is seen as a Shi'a power the less the potential appeal and soft-power utility of its revolutionary Islamic ideology. Hence it has traditionally sought to downplay its Shi'a identity on the international stage while its rivals have sought to overplay it. Events since 2003 and the aggressive role that Iran has played in Iraq and Syria have of course undermined Iran's claims to sect-blind ecumenism. Nevertheless, it is important to note that Iranian activity, and even aggressive Iranian attempts at extending strategic advantage, are not the same as anti-Sunnism even if they are readily perceived as such. In other words, while Iran has at times instrumentalized Shi'a identity, it has done so without encouraging overt anti-Sunnism for the simple reason that doing so would work against its own interests.[32] Equally important, encouraging anti-Sunnism not only works against Iranian interests but ideologically goes against their pan-Islamist inclinations (again demographics are key: a Shi'a-led pan-Islamism *needs* Sunnis, while a Sunni-led pan-Islamism can do without Shi'as). As Sadeghi-Boroujerdi has argued, "The Islamic Republic's pan-Islamist commitments ... and the minority status of Shi'a in the broader region [...] mitigate its overt resort to and exploitation of sectarian rhetoric and symbols ... [A] negation of Sunni Islam is not integral to Iran's self-image and ideological projection."[33] This stands in stark contrast to the openness and ease with which anti-Shi'ism is expressed in parts of Saudi Arabia where "some [Saudi] Sunni Muslims ... consider their [i.e., Shi'a] mere existence, and any political claims by Saudi Shi'a, to

---

[31] For an overview of Iranian discourse on this subject, see Maghen, "Unity or Hegemony?" in *The Sunna and Shi'a in History*, ed. Bengio and Litvak; Akbarzadeh, "Iran and Daesh."

[32] See chapter 3. The utility of sectarian categories is further influenced by national-level demographic variances. As Christopher Phillips argues, Iran's regional messaging notwithstanding, playing 'the sectarian card' is more of an option for Iran within Iraq than it is within Syria given the demographic realities in the two countries. "SEPAD Pod: Chris Phillips," *Sectarianism, Proxies and De-sectarianization*, Dec. 4, 2018, https://www.sepad.org.uk/announcement/sepadpod-chris-phillips.

[33] Sadeghi-Boroujerdi, "Strategic Depth, Counterinsurgency, and the Logic of Sectarianization," in *Sectarianization*, ed. Hashemi and Postel, p. 177.

be anathema."[34] The reason for the discrepancy is, again, the different costs and benefits that encouraging such sentiment will have from minoritarian and majoritarian standpoints and, consequently, the different ideological leanings that this can potentially engender.

It is easy to regard Iran's cross-sectarian proclamations as a cynical smokescreen, but the ideological element and the fact that anti-Sunnism is not integral to it should not be dismissed. This is not because Shi'ism, let alone the Iranian state, is inherently tolerant – as attested to by minorities living in Shi'a-majority contexts – rather, it is a function of the fact that most variants of Shi'ism regard themselves as part of a larger Sunni-dominated Islamic world. Hence, even a highly critical study of Iranian textbooks found that while school curricula privileged male, Shi'a Persians and were strongly anti-Western, anti-Semitic and xenophobic, nowhere did they express anti-Sunni sentiment.[35] Rather, where Sunni–Shi'a relations were touched upon it was in the context of the imperatives of Islamic unity and the dangers of sectarian division. For example, textbooks designed for the Sunni majority province of Sistan and Baluchistan included an introduction written by the Supreme Leader of Iran, Ali Khamenei, in which he warns: "be aware that the enemies of Islam will not destroy this coexistence and brotherhood between Shiites and Sunnis."[36] Again, this is not a function of Iranian or Shi'a tolerance and is as much a function of demographics as it is of ideological commitment to pan-Islamism: the same study of Iranian textbooks notes the exceptionally harsh tone reserved for Iran's Baha'i minority. Indeed, the way that Baha'is are framed is strikingly similar to how Shi'as are framed in extreme anti-Shi'a texts: as a plot to undermine Islam, a tool of imperial or otherwise hostile foreign machinations, a cabalistic scheme aimed at dividing Muslims, and so forth.[37] This is part of broader systemic discrimination against

---

[34] Matthiesen, *The Other Saudis*, p. 1.

[35] Eldad J. Pardo, "Iranian Education: The Continuous Revolution," IMPACT-se, 2016, http://www.impact-se.org/wp-content/uploads/Iranian-Education_The-Continuous-Revolution-2016.pdf.

[36] Ibid., p. 54.

[37] Ibid., pp. 55–56. Tellingly, Baha'ism is treated under the subtitle "Colonialism's Cult Fabrication."

and criminalization of Baha'ism in Iran.[38] As for Iranian Sunnis, while explicit anti-Sunnism is mitigated by the state's pan-Islamic aspirations and by Shi'ism's minority position in the broader Islamic world, Sunnis in Iran are nevertheless securitized and excluded in ways similar to Shi'a Arabs in the Arab world – as will be seen below. Textbooks may not attack or disparage Sunnis or Sunnism, but both are excluded through the promotion of an Iranian identity that is inescapably intertwined with Shi'ism.[39] The state may not be intrinsically anti-Sunni in an ideological sense but there is much structural discrimination arising out of the securitization of Iranian Sunnis and the intertwinement of sectarian discrimination, ethnic discrimination, the securitization of minorities, and the superimposition of regional geopolitical rivalry onto communal diversity.[40] The point to stress here is that highlighting the greater likelihood that Shi'ism will adopt an ecumenical stance or profess acceptance of Sunnism is less a reflection of a progressive mentality or a greater tendency towards tolerance and more a function of demographics and power relations in a modern context that places a premium on Islamic unity in a normatively Sunni-inflected global Islam.

The same factors (demographics and the relations of power) distinguish anti-Shi'ism from anti-Sunnism in at least two ways: firstly, the frankness of anti-Shi'ism and, secondly, the threatening way in which Shi'ism is framed in anti-Shi'a polemics – not just as aberrant or

---

[38] See, for example, "Inciting Hatred: Iran's Media Campaign to Demonize Baha'is," *Baha'i International Community*, 2011, https://www.bic.org/sites/default/files/pdf/inciting-hatred-book_0.pdf.

[39] Shervin Malekzadeh, "What Iran's textbooks can teach us about sectarianism and ancient hatreds," *Washington Post*, Monkey Cage Blog, Jan. 25, 2016, https://www.washingtonpost.com/news/monkey-cage/wp/2016/01/25/how-irans-view-of-sectarianism-has-evolved-since-its-revolution/?noredirect=on&utm_term=.2ba309025744.

[40] Scheherezade Faramarzi, "Iran's Sunnis Resist Extremism, but for How Long?" Atlantic Council, South Asia Center, April 2018, https://www.atlanticcouncil.org/images/Iran_s_Sunnis_WEB.pdf; Sabahi, "Iran, Iranian Media and Sunnite Islam," in *The Dynamics of Sunni–Shia Relationships*, ed. Marechal and Zemni; Stephane A. Dudoignon, "Sunnis and Shiites in Iran since 1979: Confrontations, Exchanges, Convergences," in *The Dynamics of Sunni–Shia Relationships*, ed. Marechal and Zemni; Dudoignon, *The Baluch, Sunnism and the State in Iran*, chapter 6.

heretical but as an insidious threat corroding Islam from within. While the opportunity cost of explicitly standing against Sunnism is simply too high for most Shi'a clerics and Shi'a political figures, the exclusion of Shi'ism holds far lower costs for Sunnis outside Shi'a-majority contexts. The matter is inflated in the case of Saudi Arabia where anti-Shi'ism receives official blessing in a manner that has few parallels. For example, at the opening ceremony of the 37th Summer Festival of al-Kharj province in Saudi Arabia in 2016, a children's operetta was performed to celebrate the Festival and the Eid al-Fitr marking the end of Ramadhan. The theme of the operetta was a militarized celebration of Saudi nationalism in which the armed forces, national pride and the war in Yemen served as the central props. In one segment, the children's troupe performed the following poem:

> All who hear the call, rise and defeat the enemy
> Oh sons of Abu Bakr and Omar
> Before all unfolds
> Unite against the enemy
> Arabs, *ajam* [non-Arabs], *hadhar* [townsfolk], *bedu* [Bedouins]
> This is our Yemen and dying at its walls is an honour
> The *rafidha* [Shi'as] are the army of the Maji [Iranians][41]
> They revived all manner of filth
> From Karbala and Bushehr, they are its agents in the middle of Yemen
> We drink from the red blood
> They are prey for our choosing[42]

---

[41] *Rafidha* (meaning rejectionists) is a derogatory word for Shi'as. It is a reference to the Shi'a rejection of the first three caliphs. Referring to Iranians as Maji (*majus*) is a common way of casting doubt on their Islamic credentials by emphasizing the ancient Iranian link to Zoroastrianism.

[42] The operetta has the ironic title of "Love and Peace" and was performed by the stars of Saudi satellite channel *Atfal wa-Mawahib* (Children and Talents). The original poem was written by Islamic preacher Muhammad al-Shimmari to celebrate Operation Decisive Storm of 2015 – the Saudi Arabian-led intervention in the Yemeni conflict. The poem was a modified version of an earlier poem written in support of the Syrian uprising. Full footage of the opening ceremony of the Summer Festival and the operetta is available on "Iftitahiyyat ihtifalat Eid wa-sayf al-Kharj 1437h (al-yawm al-awal) al-juz' al-awal" (The opening of Eid and summer celebrations, al-Kharj 1437h (day 1) part 1), uploaded Aug. 12, 2016, https://www.youtube.com/watch?v=6zazKrM4y0M.

That such a poem can be so uncontroversially recited by children at an official public event speaks volumes as to how normalized anti-Shi'ism has become in Saudi Arabian public discourse.[43] Nor is this an entirely Saudi Arabian phenomenon. There is an explicitness in extreme anti-Shi'ism that is not as readily found in anti-Sunnism. Demographic facts and the facts of political power make the wholesale exclusion of Shi'ism an option for Sunni extremists who, for the same reasons, are able to be more direct in their identification of Shi'as and Shi'ism in their polemics without feeling the need to adopt a suggestive or coded stance. This is reflected in the literature and also in the basic vocabulary of sectarian othering: the term *nawasib* has an elasticity that the more clear-cut *rawafidh* or *rafidha* does not. In turn, and for the same reasons, the former is far more theorized than the more straightforward *rawafidh*.[44]

The other distinguishing feature between anti-Sunnism and anti-Shi'ism is the matter of threat perception. A common theme in anti-Shi'a polemics is that which frames Shi'ism not just as heretical or as a form of apostasy but as a *danger*, a cancer to be expunged and an insidious threat against which Islam is to defend and define itself.[45] In this genre of anti-Shi'ism, Islam becomes the target of a timeless

---

[43] Structural anti-Shi'ism in Saudi Arabia and the prevalence of anti-Shi'ism in Saudi Arabian public discourse are well documented. See, for example, "'They Are Not Our Brothers': Hate Speech by Saudi Officials," Human Rights Watch, Sept. 26, 2017, https://www.hrw.org/report/2017/09/26/they-are-not-our-brothers/hate-speech-saudi-officials#; "Saudi Arabia: Religion Textbooks Promote Intolerance," Human Rights Watch, Sept. 13, 2017, https://www.hrw.org/news/2017/09/13/saudi-arabia-religion-textbooks-promote-intolerance.

[44] Tarabishi, *Hartaqat II*, p. 63. For exceptions, see pp. 85–87. For overviews of anti-Shi'a discourse, see Shiraz Maher, *Salafi-Jihadism: The History of an Idea* (London: Penguin, 2017), pp. 102–110; Raihan Ismail, "The Saudi Ulema and the Shi'a of Saudi Arabia," *Journal of Shi'a Islamic Studies*, 5:4 (Autumn 2012): 403–422; Guido Steinberg, "Jihadi-Salafism and the Shi'is: Remarks about the Intellectual Roots of Anti-Shi'ism," in *Global Salafism: Islam's New Religious Movement*, ed. Roel Meijer (New York: Columbia University Press, 2009). For an extensive collection of anti-Shi'a works, see *Al-Maktaba al-Takhasusiyya fi-l-Red ala al-Shi'a al-Rawafidh* (The Specialist Library on Responding to the Rawafidh Shi'a), http://azahera.net/showthread.php?p=69901.

[45] See Barzegar, "The Persistence of Heresy," pp. 222–223.

Shi'a plot transcending all sense of context. One of the more famous iterations of this theme is that relating to the Shi'a Abbasid minister Muhammad Ibn al-Alqami's alleged role in facilitating the Mongol sacking of Baghdad in 1258. The episode was revived in anti-Shi'a polemics following the Iraqi invasion in 2003, whereby a parallel was drawn between Iraqi Shi'a figures facilitating the invasion of Iraq and al-Alqami facilitating the sack of Baghdad in order to frame Shi'as as the eternal and eternally treacherous enemy within.[46] Of course the similarity to anti-Semitic tropes regarding global conspiracies, insidious influence and cabalistic takeovers is obvious enough. In some cases this similarity seems to be consciously pursued: strongly echoing the infamous *Protocols of the Elders of Zion*, some anti-Shi'a polemicists allege a fifty-year plan for a Shi'a takeover of the Middle East through a process of infiltration and the spreading of chaos.[47] Some conspiracy theories are even more fantastical. Salafi thinker Muhib al-Din al-Khatib argued that Sufism is a Shi'a invention designed as a Trojan horse to infiltrate and undermine Sunni society.[48] The same paranoia about secret Shi'a infiltration sees efforts at doctrinal rapprochement being rejected on the grounds that they are in fact a subversive tool with which to implement a secret plan to turn Sunnis into Shi'as.[49] At a more banal level, Shi'a tourists and Shi'a religious tourism have

---

[46] See Nibras Kazimi, "Zarqawi's Anti-Shi'a Legacy: Original or Borrowed?" *Current Trends in Islamist Ideology*, 1 (2006): 53–72, https://www.hudson.org/content/researchattachments/attachment/1351/kizimi_vol4.pdf.

[47] For example, see Hadif al-Shimmari, *Al-Khutta al-Khamsiniyya al-Sirriyya li-Ayat Qom wa-In'ikasatiha ala Waqi' Mamlakat al-Bahrain* (The Secret Fifty Year Plan of the Ayat[ollas] of Qom and Its Reflection on the Reality of the Kingdom of Bahrain), 2nd edn (self-published, 2008). For discussions of the '*khuttat al-khamsin*' or '*al-khutta al-khamsiniyya*' (the 50-year plan), see http://www.dd-sunnah.net/forum/showthread.php?t=143371.

[48] Quoted in Abd al-Satir al-Hussain, *Tahthir al-Bariyya min Nashat al-Shi'a fi Syria* (Warning Creation of Shi'a Activity in Syria) (Cairo: Dar al-Muhadithin, 2007), p. 6.

[49] Ibid., pp. 97–98. Less fantastical are the commonly heard fears of Shi'a proselytization in Sunni majority countries. For example, see Pierret, "Karbala in the Umayyad Mosque," in *The Dynamics of Sunni–Shia Relationships*, ed. Marechal and Zemni; Abd al-Rahman al-Haj, *Al-Ba'th al-Shi'i fi-Syria* (The Shi'a Ba'th in Syria) (London: International Institute for Syrian Studies, 2008); Khalid Sindawi, "The Shiite Turn in Syria," *Current Trends in Islamist Ideology*, 8 (2009): 82–107.

been viewed by polemicists with suspicion as yet another Shi'a Trojan horse. We already encountered this in chapter 3 in the context of Iranian tourists in Egypt. A similar example comes from Jordan where Muhammad Nuh – religious preacher and former Minister of Youth and of Islamic Endowments – warned of the dangers of Shi'a religious tourism: "this will be our death if such visits are allowed to happen … On the surface, the term religious tourism is about [visiting] the Imams … But the reality of the matter is the search for a [Shi'a] foothold."[50] In such ways a combination of fear and disdain sustains the myth of perpetually pernicious Shi'a motives, thereby facilitating a wholesale demonization and exclusion of Shi'as and Shi'ism in a way that is rarely mirrored in anti-Sunni polemics. As already mentioned, Shi'ism's minority mindset is in less of a position to jettison Sunnism and is more likely to try to secure mainstream legitimacy in global Islamic terms by gaining a measure of Sunni acceptability.

The same dynamics and the same manifestations of how the sectarian divide is viewed from minority and majority perspectives are evident not just in sectarian bigotry but in its inverse, in sectarian ecumenism or *taqrib*. Again we see in the Shi'a approach to *taqrib* an effort to secure acceptance – this is apparent at both the doctrinal and the transnational levels: be it clerical efforts at doctrinal rapprochement or Iranian use of *taqrib* as a foreign policy tool with which to project soft power and reduce its international isolation through greater normalization with other Muslim states.[51] On the other hand, Sunni approaches to *taqrib* often seek the dilution of certain aspects of Shi'ism deemed offensive or blasphemous. This points to a structural imbalance that is evident in *taqrib* initiatives, historical and modern, whereby "the Shi'is needed to get the stamp of approval from the Sunnis that they were not

---

[50] See, "Bina' al-hussainiyyat fi-l-Urdun red muwjaz" (The Building of Hussainiyyat [Shi'a congregation halls] in Jordan Summarized Response), uploaded Oct. 24, 2016, https://www.youtube.com/watch?v=hh3KKooXKGQ.

[51] On Iran's use of ecumenism as a foreign policy tool, see Wilfred Buchta, "Tehran's Ecumenical Society (*Majma' Al-Taqrib*): A Veritable Ecumenical Revival or a Trojan Horse of Iran?" in *The Twelver Shia in Modern Times: Religious Culture and Political History*, ed. Rainer Brunner and Werner Ende (Leiden: Brill, 2001); Ende, "Sunni Polemical Writings," in *The Iranian Revolution and the Muslim World*, ed. Menashri, p. 224.

disbelievers …"[52] Elvire Corboz reached a similar conclusion in an insightful study that examined different strategies towards *taqrib*. In the case of Islamic unity discourse among Shi'a institutions in London, Corboz found that they ultimately aimed at securing Sunni acceptance, thereby reflecting the fact that they lacked the power to define Sunnis and include or exclude them from conceptions of Islamic unity.[53]

As noted at the outset, not every binary is balanced and not every relation is symmetrical. J.M. Berger's treatment of white nationalism in 1970s America offers an interesting illustration. Berger analyses *The Turner Diaries* (1978) – the American white nationalist's novel of choice – and contrasts its depiction of black people with how white people are depicted in a near-contemporaneous and similarly racially charged novel written by an African American – *The Spook Who Sat by the Door* (1969). Berger notes that while hatred for whites can be found in the latter in ample supply, and while the chief protagonist is incapable of interacting with whites "without an expression of hostility and a critical racial commentary," he "never expresses or acts on genocidal intentions." This stands in marked contrast to the theme of *The Turner Diaries* in which the protagonists actively pursue

---

[52] Litvak's description of Sunni–Shi'a relations in Ottoman Iraq. Litvak, "Encounters between Shi'i and Sunni Ulama," in *The Sunna and Shi'a in History*, ed. Bengio and Litvak, pp. 71–72. See also pp. 74–77 for a similar imbalance and similar dynamics in the correspondence between Najafi clerics and Abd al-Aziz bin Saud in 1795. An earlier example of this sentiment can be seen in Nadir Shah's pursuit of ecumenical rapprochement with the Ottomans; see Tucker, *Nadir Shah's Quest for Legitimacy*, chapters 4 and 7. For similar dynamics in *taqrib* initiatives in the twentieth century, see Brunner, "Sunnis and Shiites in Modern Islam," in *The Dynamics of Sunni–Shia Relationships*, ed. Marechal and Zemni, pp. 31–38.

[53] Elvire Corboz, "Islamisk enhedsdiskurs. Et studie af Sunni–Shiarelationer fra britiske shiamuslimers perspektiv" (Islamic Unity Discourse: A Study of Sunni–Shi'i Relations from the Perspective of British Shi'i Muslims), *Tidsskrift for Islamforskning*, 13:1 (2019): 62–86. The study identified four strategies: highlighting traditions that emphasize Shi'ism's commitment to Islamic unity; highlighting commonalities between Sunnis and Shi'as; highlighting internal divisions within Sunni Islam, thereby reducing the distinctiveness of Shi'ism and framing it as just one part of a diverse Islamic landscape; and, finally, arguing for a new way of framing minorities and majorities, ingroups and outgroups: a diverse mainstream Islam (which includes Shi'ism) against Salafis, Wahhabis, *takfiris*.

a genocidal cleansing of America.[54] This neatly sums up how power relations can shape the manner in which extremism, hatred, conflict and competition are imagined, enunciated and pursued. Pointing this out and examining imbalances in power relations and how they shape Sunni–Shi'a interactions and framing strategies is not a commentary on virtue or morality nor is it ground for value judgements. The fact that most variants of Shi'ism profess an acceptance of Sunni Islam is not proof of a more progressive or more tolerant stance; rather, it is a reflection of the framing strategies and demographic awareness of a minority group trying to normalize its place in a broader Islamic landscape that is informed by the broad spectrum that forms Sunni Islam. It is important to be aware of these imbalances to better understand how sect-centric actors position themselves and to what ends. This section has mainly focused on these dynamics at the transnational and doctrinal levels and on the extremes of sectarian polemics and proactive sectarian ecumenism – as argued earlier, banal coexistence is far closer to the norm. The next section will look at the national dimension and the role of the modern state in the twentieth-century Arab world. Here the matter of sectarian demographics is made all the more problematic as it is refracted through the prism of the nation-state and is mediated through an additional paradigm of inclusion and exclusion.

State–Sect Relations: Minoritization, Majoritization, Securitization

The role of the state is key in formulating demographic parameters. Likewise it has been key in mediating the evolution of modern sectarian relations and the relations of power between Sunnis and Shi'as at the national level. As we have seen in the previous chapter, this is especially pronounced given the degree to which the nation-state intrudes upon individual lives, the role it plays or is expected to play in the distribution of economic, social and political goods, and the sense of entitlement to, and ownership of, the state that

---

[54] J.M. Berger, "The Turner Legacy: The Storied Origins and Enduring Impact of White Nationalism's Deadly Bible," International Centre for Counter-Terrorism, The Hague, Sept. 2016.

the principle of national identity engenders. Added to that is the role the state can potentially play in the inclusion or exclusion of differentiated sectarian identities in formulations of citizenship, national identity and political community. This of course differs from one national context to another, with ideology and state capacity playing a deciding role. Lebanon, for example, always lacked the strong central state that might attempt to govern and shape sectarian relations in the way that regimes in the Iraqi and Syrian states did. Arab nationalist ideology played a role in how sectarian relations were framed in the latter two cases, just as puritanical strains of Islam played a role in how sectarian relations were framed in Saudi Arabia. One generalization that can be made here is that modern state–sect relations in the age of the nation-state, despite significant variations from one national context to another, are ultimately a question of politics, representation and control.

Here the subject's vocabulary again does us a disservice in that it misdirects analytical focus and implants faulty assumptions. Terms like Sunni–Shi'a competition, Sunni–Shi'a sectarian dynamics – to say nothing of Sunni–Shi'a 'sectarianism' – in addition to lending themselves to being imagined as describing a dynamic between two roughly balanced halves of a whole, also conjure images of broad-based, horizontal contestation between Sunni and Shi'a communities. In reality, however, if we leave doctrinal competition to one side, a given country's sectarian issue is far more likely to be a state–outgroup issue (and a state–state issue where Iran and the transnational dimension are concerned) rather than a Sunni–Shi'a issue in any communal sense of the term. Again, Lebanon's historically weak state sets it apart somewhat in that regard, but Lebanon aside, and exceptional episodes notwithstanding, the reality is that horizontal conflict between Sunnis and Shi'as has been less common than vertical sect-coded contestation of power between political authorities and individual sectarian outgroups (and more specifically their activists and representatives). In other words, Sunni–Shi'a conflict at the local, communal level has been relatively unusual; certainly less common than, say, the history of mass-led anti-Semitic pogroms in Europe or modern Hindu–Muslim communal violence in India, where the popular element is more pronounced than has ordinarily been the case with Sunni–Shi'a conflict

191

in the Arab world.[55] Olivier Roy makes a similar point, arguing that modern Sunni–Shi'a tensions are more likely to be state-led rather than mass-led. This does not mean that Sunni–Shi'a relations are immune to bottom-up drivers nor that the matter is entirely and exclusively one of state policy – as is amply demonstrated in instances of sect-coded civil war (Lebanon 1975–90, post-2003 Iraq, post-2011 Syria) and, in Roy's analysis, by the Pakistani case where, beginning in the 1980s, radical Sunni movements emerged almost exclusively to fight Shi'as.[56] Nevertheless, horizontal Sunni–Shi'a conflict in a communal sense remains the exception. Likewise, sect-coded contestation at the transnational level may see the instrumentalization of the doctrinal dimension with an eye towards legitimating political postures by sect-coding geopolitics and deepening prejudices at the subnational level. Few examples better illustrate this than the popularization and accelerated dissemination of anti-Shi'a tracts from Saudi Arabia across the Arab world in response to the Iranian Revolution of 1979.[57] However, as profound an impact as this propaganda effort had, it nevertheless had to contend with conflicting norms and narratives of national or Islamic unity. Hence, tensions may have been temporarily heightened, episodic clashes may have occurred but, by and large, the sectarian issue, particularly at the national and subnational levels, continued to be experienced primarily as an issue of state–outgroup contestation rather than as one of horizontal Sunni–Shi'a contestation at the communal level.

---

[55] Obviously this is not to deny the well-documented role of political leaders and identity entrepreneurs in communal conflict in India. See Sudhir Kakar, *The Colors of Violence: Cultural Identities, Religion and Conflict* (Chicago: University of Chicago Press, 1996); Christophe Jaffrelot, *Religion, Caste and Politics in India* (London: Hurst & Co., 2011), especially chapters 16 and 17.

[56] Olivier Roy, "The Impact of the Iranian Revolution on the Middle East," in *The Shi'a Worlds and Iran*, ed. Sabrina Mervin (London: Saqi, 2010), pp. 31–32. See also Zaman, "Sectarianism in Pakistan: The Radicalization of Shi'a and Sunni Identities"; Nasr, "International Politics, Domestic Imperatives."

[57] See Ibrahim, "Al-Su'udiyya: al-Hiwar al-Masmum," in *Nawasib wa Rawafidh*, ed. Saghiya, pp. 168–171; Ali al-Mu'min, *Min al-Mathhabiyya ila al-Ta'ifiyya: Al-Mas'ala al-Ta'ifiyya fi-l-Waqi' al-Islami* (From Schools of Thought to Sectarianism: The Sectarian Question in Islamic Reality) (Beirut: Dar al-Kawakib, 2007), p. 128.

Given historical legacies, power relations and the minority status of Shi'ism in both pan-Islamic and pan-Arab terms, Shi'as were the weaker party – the outgroup – in Sunni–Shi'a relations in the twentieth-century Arab world, and this was often mirrored in state–Shi'a relations.[58] While regimes across the region have ferociously suppressed politicized Islamist movements regardless of sectarian identity, organized Shi'ism was susceptible to a securitized approach by political authorities, regardless of whether or not it spawned political opposition, because of the relative autonomy and transnational aspect of Shi'a religious structures. The same cannot be said about Sunni identity and the modern Arab state. This is not just a function of demographics but of political ideology, historical legacy and the normativity of Sunnism in the way a post-Ottoman, pan-Arab socio-political sphere came to be imagined. This does not mean that the twentieth-century Arab world was composed of 'Sunni regimes' oppressing Shi'a minorities nor does it mean that state–Shi'a relations were a Manichaean zero-sum struggle for hegemony. Rather, a recurring theme saw modernizing states adopting a problematic approach to unity, diversity and the subject of communal plurality that at times strained state–sect – or state–sectarian outgroup – relations. The following sections will look at some of the most important aspects of this as they relate to Sunni–Shi'a relations: firstly, the normativity of Sunni Islam and, by extension, the sectarian othering of Shi'ism; secondly, the taboo that surrounded sectarian identity and – precisely because of the normativity of Sunni Islam – how this often manifested itself as Sunni majoritarianism; and, finally, the securitization of sectarian plurality and how, owing to the preceding factors, this often turned into the securitization of Shi'as. To better understand the process, it is important to examine the role of authoritarianism and of Arab–Iranian rivalry in how Arab Shi'as came to be seen by state and society in the Arab world. Needless to say, Syria is an ill fit on all three counts: while Sunni Islam was adopted as the basis for normative, state-sanctioned Islam, there was no othering of Shi'ism; while the taboo surrounding sectarian identities

---

[58] Weiss, *In the Shadow of Sectarianism*, p. 10: "Perhaps the most significant and contentious dimension of the history of Shi'a communities in the Arab world during the modern period relates to their encounters and engagements with the state."

was rigorously enforced, it did not amount to Sunni majoritarianism outside specific fields – education, for example; finally, Damascus's relations with revolutionary Iran, Syria's minuscule Shi'a population, and the attempts to endow Alawism with Islamic legitimacy by framing it as part of Shi'ism meant that Shi'ism was never specifically targeted in Syria.[59] Nevertheless, what is being described is relevant to the way transnational norms regarding sectarian relations were formulated, and to several national and subnational contexts such as Iraq, Bahrain and Saudi Arabia.

Sunni Muslim, Normal Muslim?

Though not absolute, the centrality of Sunnism (in its vastly differing orientations) in the way Islam and the Arab world are imagined, while perfectly understandable given demographic, historical and cultural realities, has proven problematic where sectarian plurality is concerned. For one thing, it has imposed a trans-Arab or trans-Islamic lens that assumes the centrality of Sunnism and sect-codes, minoritizes and often securitizes other identities regardless of local or national variations, such as where Sunnis or Arabs may be in a minority. This has reinforced the normative role of Sunni identity and Sunni Islam in the way notions of community, majority and minority are constructed, with profound consequences for how sectarian relations are imagined and practised. This is as relevant to the transnational and doctrinal dimensions as it is to the national and subnational dimensions in that it has engendered a problematic awkwardness in how plurality within Islam is viewed in some circles: as deviant and threatening – something that has been mirrored in the securitization of plurality within the nation-state in the case of the Arab world. One is reminded of British historian Conrad Russell's quip: "It can be said of the English in Britain, as wags say of the Catholics in Heaven, that they think they are the only ones here."[60] A similar logic can be extended to Sunni Arabs in the Arab

---

[59] The effort to recast the Alawis as part of the Shi'a fold goes back to the early twentieth century. See Farouk-Alli, "The Genesis of Syria's Alawi Community," in *The Alawis of Syria*, ed. Kerr and Larkin, pp. 39–40; Leon T. Goldsmith, *Cycle of Fear: Syria's Alawites in War and Peace* (London: Hurst & Co., 2015), pp. 88–93.

[60] Quoted in Kumar, *The Making of English Identity*, p. xv.

world. Indeed, as will be argued in the following chapter, the manner in which 2003 disturbed that sense of identity security and challenged the dominance of Sunni identity in Arab national and transnational public spheres is an important factor in the regional sectarianization that followed. The normativity of Sunni Islam and the demographic weight of Sunni Muslims in the Arab and Islamic worlds have meant that Sunnis have traditionally not thought of themselves as a sect, and there remains considerable resistance to applying the language of sects to Sunnis – a language often reserved for minorities and outgroups. For example, Azmi Bishara rejects the idea that Sunnis can form a sect at all, let alone a minority sect, cautioning that "the sectarian mentality turns the majority into a minority."[61] Such a view obviously becomes problematic in national contexts where Sunni Muslims are numerical minorities. Furthermore, exempting Sunnis from the vocabulary of sect may not be so problematic were it not for the fact that it is an often securitized vocabulary that has been used by authoritarian regimes for purposes of regime maintenance, social engineering, inclusion and exclusion (see chapter 1).

Bishara's resistance to the sect-coding of Sunnis is far from unusual;[62] rather, its prevalence reflects demographic realities and the reification of a concomitant set of hierarchies that centre Sunni and Arab identities at the heart of national, religious and transnational abstractions of self and other in the Arab Middle East. It also reflects historical and political legacies predating the modern Arab nation-state. From the outset, post-Ottoman national regimes were resistant to granting non-Sunni Muslims recognition as communal groups.

---

[61] "Azmi Bishara: al-Sunna laisu ta'ifa – al-ta'ifiyya suluk aqaliyya" (Azmi Bishara: Sunnis are not a sect – sectarianism is the behaviour of minorities), uploaded June 2, 2015, https://www.youtube.com/watch?v=X3fPlDhFxl4.

[62] For example, Abd al-Razaq Eid, "Al-Sunna laisu ta'ifa ... al-Sunna umma" (Sunnis are not a sect, they are a nation), *Al-Hewar al-Mutamadin*, Sept. 23, 2013, http://www.m.ahewar.org/s.asp?aid=379241&r=0; Hussam Tammam, "Ahl al-Sunna wa-l-Jama'ah laisu ta'ifa min al-Muslimin, bal hum al-umma al-Islamiyya" (Sunnis are not an Islamic sect, rather they are the Islamic nation), *Al-Rased*, March 20, 2007, http://www.alrased.net/main/articles.aspx?selected_article_no=5031; Muhammad al-Rabbani, "Ahl al-Sunna laisu ta'ifa" (Sunnis are not a sect), *Atlantic Media*, Oct. 21, 2015, http://atlanticmedia.info/?q=node/11918.

There are several reasons for this: firstly, given that minority interests had long been used as a pretence for Western imperialist interference in the Ottoman Empire, there was understandable reluctance to create yet more minority categories which could potentially give imperial powers yet more inroads with which to interfere in and dominate the post-Ottoman landscape. Secondly, expanding the concept of minorities could potentially erode the cohesion of the national whole and particularly its imagined core (Muslim Arabs). Finally, in addition to whatever political calculations were at play – such as resisting imperial machinations and the like – the reluctance to grant recognition to Shi'as and other Muslim groups was a reflection of the historical legacy of the way the Ottomans imagined society as being composed of Muslims and non-Muslim communities: no matter how othered Shi'as and Shi'ism were, they were never a separate *millet*.[63] This created a double-edged legacy that was bequeathed to the modern Middle East: on the one hand, a premium was placed on Sunni–Shi'a unity, sectarian differences were downplayed, and intra-Muslim diversity was not a bar to a transcendent Muslim identity; on the other hand, for demographic, historical and political reasons, the category of Muslim was inevitably Sunni-inflected in the Ottoman Empire and its successor states, thereby making a differentiated non-Sunni Muslim identity problematic within them.[64]

The case of Syria may again seem exceptional at first glance: an authoritarian regime whose hierarchies of power are topped by networks of loyalty and patronage linked to the Alawi minority from which the Assad dynasty hails. As mentioned in chapter 1, the 'Alawi regime' label is as problematic for Syria as are 'Shi'a regime' and 'Sunni regime' for post- and pre-2003 Iraq. Nevertheless, in all three cases – and others besides them – the relations of power underpinning the

---

[63] For a broader discussion of these themes, see Ceren Belge and Ekrem Karakoc, "Minorities in the Middle East: Ethnicity, Religion and Support for Authoritarianism," *Political Research Quarterly*, 68:2 (2015): 280–292; White, *The Emergence of Minorities*, pp. 57–58.

[64] This goes beyond Sunni–Shi'a relations and has intra-Sunni implications. For example, Syrian nationalists resisted granting special recognition to Circassians on the grounds that they are Sunni Muslims and should be categorized as such. White, *The Emergence of Minorities*, p. 139.

state favoured, and were more associated with, one sectarian group (more precisely a tribally, regionally and personally inflected subset thereof) than others. In the case of Syria, the centre of power revolves around an Alawi core. This has added a sectarian dimension – not unwarranted but easily exaggerated – to how the authoritarianism and economic failures and injustices of the Assads' regime are perceived. This builds on and amplifies pre-existing prejudices and sectarian stereotypes, with the regime being regarded by some of its opponents as a perversion of the natural ordering of Syria's urban–rural divide and of the Sunni–minority divide.[65] For example, as early as 1965, a disillusioned former Ba'thist authored a book that framed the Ba'th – or what it had become – as part of a conspiracy to elevate minorities and supplant the traditional order in which Sunnis (or urban, wealthy and educated Sunnis to be more precise) dominated.[66] Likewise the 1980 programme of the Muslim Brotherhood refers to Alawi dominance in Syria as "against the logic of things," and defined their conflict with Syria's rulers as one between Sunnis and Alawis.[67] In short, unlike other instances of state–sect turbulence such as in Iraq, Bahrain or Saudi Arabia, in Ba'thist Syria Sunnis and Sunni-centricity are driven by resentment at a state that is widely regarded as 'sectarian' and as one that victimizes Sunnis. Despite that, Sunnis in Ba'thist Syria are not a perfect inverse of Shi'as in Ba'thist Iraq, Bahrain or Saudi Arabia. Sunnism retained its normative role and, Sunni identity, provided it lacked political expression, was never othered in Syria in the same way that Shi'a identity has at times been in the other cases. In Syria as in Iraq, Bahrain and Saudi Arabia, the modern state's homogenizing

---

[65] Nikolaos van Dam, *Destroying a Nation: The Civil War in Syria* (London: I.B. Tauris, 2017), chapter 1; Hanna Batatu, "Some Observations on the Social Roots of Syria's Ruling Military Group and the Causes for Its Dominance," *Middle East Journal*, 35:3 (Summer 1981): 331–344; Christa Salamandra, *A New Old Damascus: Authenticity and Distinction in Urban Syria* (Bloomington: Indiana University Press, 2004), pp. 85–88.

[66] Van Dam, *Destroying a Nation*, pp. 28–30. For more recent examples of similar views, see Kazimi, *Syria through Jihadist Eyes*, pp. 2–3, 63–69.

[67] Hanna Batatu, "Syria's Muslim Brethren," *MERIP*, 12:110 (Nov.–Dec. 1982), http://www.merip.org/mer/mer110/syrias-muslim-brethren#4. At the time Syria was in the midst of an insurgency that was dominated by the Muslim Brotherhood. The conflict accentuated sectarian divisions.

and authoritarian attempts at nation-building have had a symbolic proximity to (state-sanctioned) Sunni frames of identity, to the relative exclusion of others. Hence, though many Syrian Sunnis have cause to feel politically marginalized, Sunnism retained its normative function in how Islam was imagined and propagated by state and society, as can be seen in the way the subject is covered in school curricula, where a Sunni-informed conception of Islam is taught. As Joshua Landis has argued in his examination of the subject, Islamic education in Syria was entirely informed by Sunni conceptions of Islam with no allowance made for other creeds, with the exception of Christianity. This fits into the broader pattern of the securitization of plurality; however, in Syria the policy is somewhat inverted in that a privileged non-Sunni minority seeks to blend into a regime-sanctioned version of Sunni identity. As Landis argued, the Syrian Ba'th's attempts at integrative nation-building involved "the Assads [becoming] good Sunnis," rather than Sunnis turning away from or diluting their sectarian identity.[68] This stance is dictated by demographic and cultural realities at the national, transnational and doctrinal levels. Domestically, the regime can scarcely afford to turn its back against a majority demographic by suppressing Sunni Islam or forcefully asserting non-Sunni variants. Likewise, regionally speaking, the regime is better served by cloaking itself in Sunni garb to avoid being ostracized as an 'Alawi regime' – something the Assads' rivals have periodically done.[69] This is all the more important given the Syrian regime's pan-Arab pretensions: rather than the sectarian Esperanto that should theoretically emerge from a nominally or aspirationally secular Ba'thist regime, the Assads' professions of Arab nationalism have been better served, both domestically and regionally, by being Sunni-inflected. While pan-Arabists are loath to admit this, the reality is that, despite its commitment to some form of secularism, the dream of Arab unity

---

[68] Joshua Landis, "Islamic Education in Syria: Undoing Secularism," *Insania*, 13:3 (Sept.–Dec. 2008): 534–549. Intentionally or not, the original quote problematically frames liberalism and being Sunni as mutually exclusive: "The Assads have struggled to be good Sunnis, not to make Sunnis into good liberals."

[69] For example, Egyptian President Anwar al-Sadat referred to the Syrian regime as the 'Alawi Ba'th' and even went as far as using terms such as 'dirty Alawis'. See van Dam, *The Struggle for Power in Syria*, pp. 93–94.

would be even more fantastical were it to be imagined as being led by a non-Muslim or a non-Sunni. Hence, though Syrian state–Sunni relations are readily susceptible to securitization and discrimination, demographics and the normative role of Sunni identity meant that state–Sunni relations under the Syrian Ba'th were the inverse of state–Shi'a relations under the Iraqi Ba'th where identity and symbolism were concerned. As Christopher Phillips argues: "Unlike in Saddam's Iraq, where the majority Shi'a had their culture repressed, Hafez al-Assad prioritized Sunni culture. Rather than dominate, he sought to have the Alawis, long rejected by Sunnis as heterodox, integrated."[70] In other words, where other regimes demanded outgroups dilute their identities in state-sanctioned formulae of national unity, in Syria the regime itself sought to dilute the distinctiveness of its sectarian identity behind a unifying facade that drew on Sunni symbols and frames of reference.[71] Rather than Syria, Lebanon may be the real exception in that the historical weakness of the Lebanese state, combined with its far greater demographic dilution, prevented any single group from establishing a cultural hegemony, not to mention the ability to assert state-sponsored sectarian biases.[72]

A Counterproductive Taboo

Though somewhat weakened since 2003, there has been a long-standing taboo in the Arab world, with the exception of Lebanon, surrounding discussions of sectarian identity and sectarian dynamics – a taboo that was further accentuated by the negativity of the term 'sectarianism'. This fostered a general awkwardness and aversion to sectarian issues and was reflected in the twentieth century in state-

---

[70] Christopher Phillips, "Sectarianism and Conflict in Syria," *Third World Quarterly*, 36:2 (2015): 365.

[71] Farouk-Alli, "The Genesis of Syria's Alawi Community," in *The Alawis of Syria*, ed. Kerr and Larkin, pp. 44; in the same volume see, Kerr, "Introduction," p. 4 and Hinnebusch, "Syria's Alawis and the Ba'ath Party," in *The Alawis of Syria*, ed. Kerr and Larkin, pp. 117–118; Kazimi, *Syria through Jihadist Eyes*, pp. 22–23, 68–69.

[72] For more on this point and particularly as it contrasts with other cases in the region, see Bahout, "The Unravelling of Lebanon's Taif Agreement"; see also Farha, "Global Gradations," pp. 376, 382.

enforced and socially upheld restrictions and forms of political correctness which imposed a contrived sect-blindness on public discourse. The pervasiveness and strength of the taboo surrounding sectarian identities can be glimpsed in Kazimi's fascinating account of his attempt to visit the tombs of the founder of the Umayyad state, Mu'awiya ibn Abi Sufyan, and that of Hussain bin Hamdan al-Khasibi, one of the founders of the Alawi sect. That the memory of the two figures is so highly sect-coded meant that the location of their tombs was not publicized and access was tightly restricted.[73] This allergy to sectarian difference and to expressions of sectarian identity ultimately proved counterproductive: the attempt to obscure or weaken sectarian categories by hiding them beneath a state-imposed sect-neutral and supposedly unifying terminology did not make people less aware of sectarian identities, even if it deepened the taboo surrounding their discussion. If anything, this policy exacerbated the problem it was supposed to address.[74]

Contrary to conventional wisdom, and precisely because of the asymmetries discussed in the previous sections, sect-blindness and sect-neutrality are not as straightforwardly benign as is often assumed. If structural inequities or systemic discrimination remain unaddressed, then sect-blindness, far from guaranteeing neutrality and balance, ends up reproducing and shielding from scrutiny the (real and perceived) structural injustices and hierarchies of power that underpin sectarian divisions. This is as true in the Middle East as it is anywhere else and has also been noted with regard to gender-blindness and race-blindness: as Young and others have argued, it is impossible to think of oppression or discrimination as a "systematic, structured, institutional process" if we cannot conceptualize both dominant and subordinate groups.[75] Such hierarchies are inevitable and must be factored into supposedly identity-neutral mechanisms. For example, owing to the attendant relations of power in the two countries, Ba'thist secularism in Iraq

---

[73] Kazimi, *Syria through Jihadist Eyes*, pp. 56–61.

[74] Van Dam, *Destroying a Nation*, p. 8; Robin Yassin-Kassab and Leila al-Shami, *Burning Country: Syrians in Revolution and War* (London: Pluto Press, 2016), p. 117.

[75] Iris Marion Young, "Gender as Seriality: Thinking about Women as a Social Collective," *Signs*, 19:3 (1994): 718, quoted in Lewis, "'What Group?'", p. 636.

and Syria was often resented by conservative, religiously minded Shi'as in the former and conservative, religiously minded Sunnis in the latter, who often saw it not as a sect-neutral mechanism of national integration but as a cover for sectarian oppression.[76] The contradictory relationship between structural imbalances in the relations of power on the one hand and the efficacy of supposedly identity-neutral mechanisms on the other is no less evident in less extreme cases. To illustrate: while French secularism theoretically maintains an equal distance from all religions, this is not straightforwardly so in practice. As Gat argues, this is only to be expected in that, whatever the intention and assumption, *la laïcité* is naturally more aligned with the "modern secularized version of Christian (or post-Christian) culture than with that of many of France's citizens who originated in Muslim countries. The reality ... is that some religions (as contemporary social phenomena, to be sure, and not in any essentialist sense) are more secular than others."[77]

Like secularism, civic nationalism is often proposed as a neutral and unifying mechanism that can mitigate the ills of 'sectarianism'; however, the presumed benefits of sect-blindness (or identity-blindness) can prove misplaced. While civic nationalism theoretically does not differentiate between citizens, in practice it is often constructed in terms that reflect the culture and historical consciousness of a dominant group. This recalls the structural proximity of Sunni frames of reference and narratives of Islam to sect-blind and secular Arab nationalism – in this way (to paraphrase Gat's argument) some sects become more Arab nationalist than others depending on the context.[78] Whether it is in France or in the Arab world, the point is that the notion that an ideology, nationalism or state can actually maintain an equal distance from all subnational groups is more of a theoretical ideal than an attainable reality. Nor should this necessarily be problematic: following on from Modood's

---

[76] Van Dam, *Destroying a Nation*, pp. 48–49. Of course, conservative religiously minded Sunni Iraqis were no less opposed to Ba'thist secularism. The difference with their Shi'a Iraqi counterparts is they had no reason to feel that it targeted them *as Sunnis* even if it was resented as anti-Islamic.

[77] Gat, *Nations*, p. 338.

[78] For the synergy between pan-Arabism and Sunni-centric readings of the history and societies of the region, see Haddad, *Sectarianism in Iraq*, pp. 38–45.

critique of the widespread assumption that Western multiculturalism precludes liberal democracies from promoting a national culture, it can likewise be argued that a multisectarian or a multicultural polity need not pretend to be culturally neutral in order to adequately embrace diversity.[79] The problem arises when a dominant culture (invariably presented as a national – 'normal' – culture) is asserted in a way that turns inclusion into cultural majoritarianism or cultural oppression, whereby minorities and outgroups must dilute their identities in order to fit into the secular civic nationalism that is presented by those it benefits – or at least by those upon whose lives it does not intrude – as the most inclusive, neutral formula and the best bulwark against the corrosive factionalism of identity politics.[80] Therefore, the existence of a dominant culture is not necessarily problematic; the extent to which it becomes so depends on how it interacts with outgroups or minorities and how the broader issue of plurality is framed and governed.[81] Interestingly in that regard, Theodor Hanf argues that, rather than mobilized communities facing one another, intergroup conflict is more commonly the result of a clash between a Jacobinistic, culturally blind view of society and a communal, group-specific ideology.[82]

---

[79] See Tariq Modood, "Majorities, Minorities and Multiculturalism," *Discover Society*, Dec. 4, 2018, https://discoversociety.org/2018/12/04/majorities-minorities-and-multiculturalism/.

[80] To give an extreme example from Iraq, official Arab nationalist discourse reached bizarre levels when in 1978 the Iraqi Ministry of Education published a study that argued that the Kurds were of Arab (specifically Yemeni) descent: "The Kurds trace their lineage to Kurd bin Murad bin Amro bin Sa'sa'ah bin Mu'awiya bin Bakr bin Hawazin." Quoted in Salim Muttar, *Al-Dhat al-Jariha: Ishkalat al-Hawiyya fi-l-Iraq wa-l-Alam al-Arabi 'al-Sharqmutawasiti'* (The Wounded Self: The Problems of Identity in Iraq and in the 'Middle Eastern' Arab World) (Beirut: Al-Mu'asasa al-Arabiyya li-l-Dirasat wa-l-Nashr, 1997), p. 100.

[81] For a discussion of these themes, see Gat, *Nations*, pp. 341–343.

[82] Theodore Hanf, *Coexistence in Wartime Lebanon: Decline of a State and Rise of a Nation* (London: I.B. Tauris, 2015), p. 31. Hanf argues that the various approaches to multicommunalism can be condensed into three broad positions: a Jacobinistic approach that seeks to level communal differences, an approach that explicitly seeks to mobilize communal identities, and a third approach that he terms syncretistic nationalism, which seeks to use communal groups as the building blocks of a transcendent nation. See pp. 26–32.

Official sect-blindness raised similar problems in the twentieth-century Arab world in that it was too simplistic a stance for the layered complexities of sectarian dynamics. Even well-intentioned policies aimed at levelling sectarian identities in the name of national or regional unity proved problematic owing to the fact that sectarian identity was more pronounced, more keenly felt and more relevant to definitions of self and other among sectarian outgroups. Accordingly, attempts at sectarian levelling (through state-enforced sect-blindness, for example) required self-censorship and dilution of group-specificity among sectarian outgroups while requiring little of ingroups given that, generally speaking, theirs was not a sect-coded identity. The demographic and political realities of the Arab world meant that this was more commonly seen in state–Shi'a relations. Needless to say, not all Shi'as were equally invested in their sectarian identities and it is important to note that Arab regimes were not anti-Shi'a per se. Rather, it would be more accurate to argue that official sect-blindness was problematic for those Shi'as whose lives and identities were embedded in Shi'a social and religious structures that had a degree of autonomy and that provided parallel truths which diverged from official narratives of community, state, faith and nation. As a result, social and political mobility was more readily available to Shi'as whose sectarian identity was as invisible as state-sanctioned forms of sect-blind religious identity. It is important to note that the autonomy of religious structures has historically been more a feature of Shi'a Islam, with their Sunni counterparts being more directly intertwined with the state.

These dynamics continue to distort sectarian relations and the way the subject of 'sectarianism' is viewed. For example, when asked how trust between Sunnis and the Iraqi state should be rebuilt, Sunni-centric Iraqi politician Khamis al-Khanjar's suggestions included urging Iraqi state television to "Get rid of the Shi'a call to prayer, make it a national TV station."[83] The obvious point to make, one that al-Khanjar, his interviewer and countless others routinely overlook, is that a non-Shi'a call to prayer is not automatically a sect-neutral — and hence

---

[83] Quoted in Michael Weiss, "Fallujah and the Failed Iraqi State," *Daily Beast*, June 6, 2016, https://www.thedailybeast.com/fallujah-and-the-failed-iraqi-state.

ostensibly national – one any more than a non-Sunni call to prayer is.[84] This example again recalls the supposition that what is Sunni is 'normal' and that this can become problematic in contexts of high sectarian heterogeneity. Indeed, it can be argued that one of the chief aims of the Shi'a-centric state-building (chapter 7) that has marked post-2003 Iraq is to turn this supposition on its head and place Shi'a identity at the heart of what is normatively assumed by 'Iraq' and 'Iraqi'. This entails reformulating the hierarchies of power underpinning cultural norms, social capital, and economic and political power in a manner that privileges Shi'a identities. Unfortunately for post-2003 Iraq, this has meant a reversal of roles in sect-coded hierarchies of power rather than their elimination.

None of this is unique to Iraq nor is it the preserve of Sunni–Shi'a relations. For example, in 2004 some Lebanese public schools were allowed to close on Friday and Saturday rather than the traditional Saturday and Sunday. This proved controversial and was deplored in some quarters where it was condemned as evidence that 'sectarianism' was eroding Lebanon's national identity.[85] Such a stance, besides again highlighting the shape-shifting and ultimately meaningless nature of the term 'sectarianism', was an expression of despair at the further decline of Maronite-informed cultural norms – long before 2004, Muslim activists had campaigned against the Saturday–Sunday weekend, as it was seen as a sign of Christian dominance. The point to note is that the change in regulation allowing some schools to close on Friday and Saturday was viewed by critics as an affront against what they held as a non-sectarian *national* norm rather than an expression of Christian dominance or Christian mores. In this way, the demands of others are more readily sect-coded while one's own norms – more so, if they are those of a dominant group – are framed as "part of a natural, civil, and secular order, not as a form of dominance, while any activity directed against this dominance is viewed as sectarianism, which harms national

---

[84] The basic difference between the Sunni and Shi'a calls to prayer is that the latter includes an invocation of Ali ibn Abi Talib and his love of God (*Ash-hadu anna Ali wali-u-Allah*) in addition to a call for good deeds (*hay ala khayr al-amal*). A call to prayer without these invocations can be perceived as a Sunni call to prayer and not a sect-neutral one.

[85] Shaery-Eisenlohr, *Shi'ite Lebanon*, pp. 1–2.

unity."[86] Again, these dynamics recur beyond the Middle East and beyond the prism of Sunni–Shi'a relations: similar views regarding the 'natural order' and reflecting traditional hierarchies of power animated the backlash against mass migration in Europe and the American 'whitelash' that followed the Obama presidency.[87]

Whether it is white identity in Europe and North America or Sunni identity in the twentieth-century Arab world, it is important to note that the centrality and empowerment being described are not necessarily a reflection of tangible material, economic or political power – after all, how much of that is extended to the working classes or those lacking the right connections? It is more a sense of identity empowerment or identity security that derives from a conviction that 'we' are the *staatsvolk* whose identity is validated in the daily reproduction of power relations. That identity security can blind a dominant group to the facts of its own identity empowerment and the realities of the other's marginalization. Conversely, the weaker actor in these power relations is likely to form an accentuated sense of the very identity that they feel is targeted and a better understanding of the conditions of their exclusion. Just as women are more likely to be aware of gender dynamics and racial minorities are more likely to be aware of racial dynamics, so too are sectarian outgroups more aware of sectarian dynamics. The point to be made is that the allergic reaction to 'sectarianism' and the taboo surrounding sectarian identity are experienced differently by sectarian ingroups and outgroups. In the absence of structural reforms, sect-blindness has served to shield sectarian dynamics from critique, thereby maintaining the status quo and perpetuating the imbalances underpinning sectarian relations in the Arab world.

---

[86] Ibid., p. 2. Similarly, I have often encountered Shi'a Baghdadis defending the display of images of the first Shi'a Imam, Ali ibn Abi Talib, and his son and third Shi'a Imam, Hussain ibn Ali, on the grounds that both figures are also revered by Sunnis – whether my informants were feigning ignorance or were actually blind to the difference between an Islamic symbol and a Shi'a-specific depiction of an Islamic symbol is open to debate.

[87] John Blake, "This is what 'whitelash' looks like," CNN, Nov. 30, 2016, https://edition.cnn.com/2016/11/11/us/obama-trump-white-backlash/index.html.

The Securitization of Sectarian Plurality

As discussed in chapters 3 and 4, the modern official and social resistance to expressions of sectarian plurality were partly rooted in Western-inflected conceptions of modernity and nation-building that framed differentiated sectarian identities as the antithesis of progressive modernity.[88] They were also a function of weakness and insecurity: in the early twentieth century, sectarian plurality, and more so the assertion of differentiated sectarian identities, came to be feared as a potential threat to the unity that nationalists prioritized in the struggle against colonialism. This had an all-too-common post-colonial afterlife in the form of problematic conceptions of unity and nation-building that imposed a somewhat Jacobin approach to the matter of sectarian plurality, whereby sectarian differentiation is concealed to the greatest extent possible the better to strengthen unity and the homogenization of the citizenry.[89] This was aptly captured by Egyptian psychoanalyst Moustapha Safouan in his critique of 'servitude' in the Arab world where he noted "an unconditional attachment to 'unity' … to the point of refusing difference as being a threat to life …"[90] Needless to say this has easily translated into the securitization of minorities and outgroups or what one scholar described as a state–minority relationship "locked in a loop of exclusionary

---

[88] As noted by Max Weiss, this has been a recurring theme across the post-colonial world, most notably in South Asia where communalism was seen as antithetical to modernizing state-building and nation-building projects. Weiss, *In the Shadow of Sectarianism*, pp. 14–15.

[89] This was most pronounced in contexts where authoritarian states embarked on top-down secular nation-building projects; Belge and Ekrem Karakoc, "Minorities in the Middle East," p. 285. This is relevant to the broader issue of minority rights in the Middle East, which goes far beyond the relatively narrow prism of Sunni–Shi'a relations. See Elizabeth Picard, "Conclusion: Nation-Building and Minority Rights in the Middle East," in *Religious Minorities in the Middle East: Domination, Self-Empowerment, Accommodation*, ed. Anne Sofie Roald and Anh Nga Longva (Leiden: Brill, 2012).

[90] Moustapha Safouan, *Why Are the Arabs Not Free? The Politics of Writing* (Oxford: Wiley-Blackwell, 2007), p. 8. Likewise Bozarslan notes the "redefinition of ethnic, religious and political 'otherness' as potential expressions of enmity, betrayal and 'vital threats' to the nation." Bozarslan, "Rethinking the Ba'thist Period," in *Writing the Modern History of Iraq*, ed. Jordi Tejel et al., p. 145.

politics and securitization."[91] In highly diverse settings such as Syria and Iraq, the state's adoption of an ethnically based political ideology (Arab nationalism) under increasingly authoritarian regimes made the securitization of diversity all the more pronounced.[92] This often took the paradoxical form of officially celebrating communal diversity while at the same time securitizing it as a potential threat to national unity.[93] In such circumstances, it becomes easy for the assertion of minority or outgroup identities to be viewed with suspicion. As a result, the much-celebrated language of the 'communal mosaic' requires that all but a dominant, state-sanctioned constellation of identities remains private. This inclusion through dilution was perhaps most succinctly reflected in Egyptian Coptic leader Makram Ebeid's oft-quoted statement that he was "a Muslim by country and a Christian by religion."[94] The matter goes beyond political representation and legal rights and extends to the expression and visibility of outgroup identities and access to national public space.[95] As this chapter has made clear, whether by fault

---

[91] Buyuksarac, "Unheard Voices," p. 2560. Likewise, see Sami Zubaida, "Contested Nations: Iraq and the Assyrians," *Nations and Nationalism*, 6:3 (2000): 363–382.

[92] This is especially evident in the case of the Kurds in both Iraq and Syria (with Turkey offering a non-Arab parallel). Jordi Tejel, *Syria's Kurds: History, Politics and Society* (New York: Routledge, 2009), pp. 60–68; Peter Fragiskatos, "The Stateless Kurds in Syria: Problems and Prospects for the Ajanib and Maktumin Kurds," *International Journal of Kurdish Studies*, 21:1 (2007): 109–122; Muhammad Ihsan, "Arabization as Genocide: The Case of the Disputed Territories of Iraq," in *The Kurdish Question Revisited*, ed. Gareth Stansfield and Muhammad Shareef (London: Hurst & Co., 2017).

[93] Marwan Muasher, *The Second Arab Awakening – and the Battle for Pluralism* (New Haven: Yale University Press, 2014); Gabriel Ben-Dor and Ofra Bengio, "The State and Minorities toward the Twenty-First Century: An Overview," in *Minorities and the State in the Arab World*, ed. Ofra Bengio and Gabriel Ben-Dor (London: Lynne Rienner, 1999); David Bond, "Tunisia's Minority Mosaic: Constructing a National Narrative," in *Minorities in the Modern Arab World*, ed. Robson; Samuel Liebhaber, "From Minority to Majority: Inscribing the Mahra and Touareg into the Arab Nation," in *Minorities and the Modern Arab World*, ed. Robson.

[94] Quoted in Mahmood, *Religious Difference in a Secular Age*, p. 12.

[95] Elizabeth Iskander, *Sectarian Conflict in Egypt: Coptic Media, Identity and Representation* (London: Routledge, 2012), pp. 20–21. To illustrate, the depiction of Coptic families in Egyptian television dramas in 2000 was alleged to have caused some controversy in the Egyptian press. See Selim Muttar, *Jadal al-Hawiyat: Arab,*

or design, there is an intra-Islamic Arab parallel to Ebeid's dictum that sees the relegation of Shi'a identity beneath normative Sunni-inflected conceptions of Islam and Muslims.

When considering the securitization of plurality, a key variable is authoritarianism – ultimately the potential extent of the former is dependent on that of the latter. One of the reasons that authoritarianism viewed plurality with suspicion is that differentiated communal identities (such as sectarian outgroups) are often not under the same degree of control or as integrated into state structures – they are not as legible to the state – as ingroups; the more authoritarian the state, the more relevant this becomes.[96] Few examples are more illustrative in this regard than the economic and institutional autonomy of the *marji'iyya* in Iraq.[97] Ultimately, therefore, rather than a religious issue or a matter of doctrinal divergence, the sectarian issue at the national and subnational levels is a political one driven in large part by the degree of distance from or proximity to the state and the degree of governmentality over sectarian outgroups.[98] In a sense this reflects the concern with which authoritarian regimes

---

Akrad, Turkuman, Siryan, Yezidiyya – Sira' al-Intima'at fi-l-Iraq wa-l-Sharq al-Awsat (The Identity Debate: Arabs, Kurds, Turkmens, Syriacs, Yezidis: The Struggle of Belonging in Iraq and the Middle East) (Beirut: Arab Institute for Research and Publishing, 2003), pp. 25–26.

[96] For state–outgroup relations and the link between legibility, securitization, repression and identity formation, see Lisa Blaydes, *State of Repression: Iraq under Saddam Hussein* (Princeton: Princeton University Press, 2018).

[97] The *marji'iyya* is a term referring to the sources of emulation (*maraji'*, singular *marji'*) both in terms of their personal religious authority and the organizational infrastructure built around them. Traditionally the *marji'iyya* have maintained financial autonomy from the state, depending instead on their followers and on charitable foundations or endowments. See Faleh A. Jabar, *The Shi'ite Movement in Iraq* (London: Saqi, 2003), chapter 7; Nakash, *The Shi'is of Iraq*, chapter 8.

[98] This borrows from Gellner's analysis of the Arab–Berber divide. Ernest Gellner, *Saints of the Atlas* (London: Weidenfeld and Nicolson, 1969), chapter 1. It also recalls James C. Scott's reading of identity in what until recently were the ungoverned border regions of Southeast Asia ('Zomia'): "The ethnic zone was feared and stigmatized by state rhetoric precisely because it was beyond its grasp and therefore an example of defiance and an ever-present temptation to those who might wish to evade the state." Scott, *The Art of Not Being Governed*, p. 39.

generally view organized religion and its potential for oppositional politics regardless of sectarian categories. However, when it comes to sectarian outgroups this is augmented by the factors described in this chapter – the way sectarian outgroups are othered, the way they are ascribed ownership of or proximity to 'sectarianism', and so forth – so that they come to be seen as inherently problematic regardless of whether or not they form oppositional movements. For example, the Iraqi Ba'th perceived organized Shi'ism as structurally problematic, regardless of political orientation. This much was unambiguously stated by Saddam Hussain's former minister of the interior Sa'dun Shakir, who remarked that "the *hawza* [Shi'a religious seminary] was essentially established to distribute money and separate the people from the state."[99] For a variety of reasons, differentiated outgroups often develop social structures that enjoy a degree of social autonomy and some distance from the state.[100] This distance is precisely what is feared and securitized by authoritarian regimes in that, if for no other reason, such (semi)autonomous structures can act as sources of parallel and competing formulations of religious and national truths. Typically the state will try to penetrate these structures, attempting to co-opt some elements and suppressing others. Yet such efforts to subsume minorities and outgroups into a broader state-sanctioned whole often, though not always, spur the very identity entrenchment that the state seeks to control.[101] As Alexander Yakobson has argued, rather than demanding state neutrality, outgroups are often more concerned with attaining official recognition of their own communal

---

[99] Comments made at a Ba'th Party committee meeting in August 1987. Quoted in Amatzia Baram, *Saddam Husayn and Islam, 1968–2003: Ba'thi Iraq from Secularism to Faith* (Baltimore: Johns Hopkins University Press, 2014), p. 166.

[100] For a discussion of how such mechanisms of distinction are a prerequisite for the existence of minority groups and how this factors into state security and societal security, see Paul Roe, "Securitization and Minority Rights: Conditions of Desecuritization," *Security Dialogue*, 35:3 (Sept. 2004): 279–294.

[101] Blaydes, *State of Repression*, chapters 1–2. This is not without exceptions. Some voices actively try to resist identity entrenchment. A good example is that of Lebanese Shi'a cleric Muhammad Mahdi Shams al-Din who urged Lebanese Shi'as to resist sect-centricity and not to think of themselves as a minority in any Arab land even if they are subject to injustices. Shaery-Eisenlohr, *Shi'ite Lebanon*, pp. 35–36.

specificity, thereby accentuating their minority or outgroup status while securing it through legal protections.[102]

Securitized state–sect relations have seen sectarian plurality framed as a potential conduit for an undefined 'sectarianism' – be it as a potentially destabilizing force domestically or as a potential entry point for foreign interference and subterfuge. This was, and continues to be, instrumentalized in regime maintenance strategies: authoritarian regimes routinely frame their continued survival as the only safeguard against these sect-coded domestic and foreign threats – in other words, as a firewall against a conveniently amorphous 'sectarianism'. Likewise, the fear of sectarian strife and 'sectarianism' has been used by regimes to silence, isolate and criminalize opponents who belong to sectarian outgroups, especially if there is any sect-centricity to their activism (drawing attention to sect-coded structural discrimination, for example), by framing them as agents of foreign interests guilty of spreading 'sectarianism'.[103] A most common manifestation of this sees Shi'a Arabs (or targeted subsets) stigmatized as potential Iranian fifth columnists. This is as much ethnic as it is religious othering. While anti-Shi'a religious polemics frame Shi'ism as the hidden enemy that corrodes Islam from within, a common trope of Arab nationalist and pan-Arab polemics frames Shi'a Arabs (or subsets thereof) as potential Iranian fifth columnists threatening Arab unity and cohesion.[104] This

---

[102] Alexander Yakobson, "State, National Identity, Ethnicity: Normative and Constitutional Aspects," in Gat, *Nations*, p. 377. The example he uses is linguistic minorities who, rather than suggesting Esperanto, seek to upgrade the official status of their language.

[103] Laurence Louer, "Sectarianism and Coup-Proofing Strategies in Bahrain," *Journal of Strategic Studies*, 36:2 (2013): 245–260; Justin Gengler, "The Political Economy of Sectarianism: How Gulf Regimes Exploit Identity Politics as a Survival Strategy," in *Beyond Sunni and Shia*, ed. Wehrey; Matthiesen, "Sectarianization as Securitization," in *Sectarianization*, ed. Hashemi and Postel; in the same volume see Pinto, "The Shattered Nation," and al-Rasheed, "Sectarianism as Counter-Revolution." For older examples of the same dynamics, see Ofra Bengio, "Shi'is and Politics in Ba'thi Iraq," *Middle Eastern Studies*, 21:1 (Jan. 1985): 1–14.

[104] For example, in the brief hysteria that ensued after an alleged Hizbullah cell was discovered in Egypt in 2009, the Egyptian press first framed Shi'ism as a sectarian threat to Sunnism and then framed Hizbullah as a non-Arab threat to the stability of the Arab world. Elizabeth Monier, "Egypt, Iran and the Hizbullah Cell:

creates a dangerous overlap and ambiguity between anti-Iranian xenophobia and anti-Shi'ism, which has been instrumentalized at various times to cast aspersion on Arab Shi'a individuals, groups and communities that fall foul of ruling regimes. These dynamics were perhaps most pronounced in state–Shi'a relations in Ba'thist Iraq – a function of the regime's authoritarian paranoia, the extent of state capacity there, its Jacobin ambitions, the size of Iraq's Shi'a population, and the fact that it bordered on Iran. This often took the form of casting doubts on the Iraqi or Arab or Islamic credentials of targeted Shi'a Arabs.[105] Such tactics were episodically used in Iraq as early as the 1920s to delegitimize political opposition emanating from Shi'a quarters, but it was to become more systemic, more ruthless and more divisive with the consolidation of Ba'th power after 1968.[106] Nor was this discourse restricted to Iraq: in fact, if anything, Iraq's

---

Using Sectarianism to 'De-Arabize' and Regionalize Threats to National Interests," *Middle East Journal*, 69:3 (Summer 2015): 341–357. Likewise, Nibras Kazimi notes that anti-Alawi literature can be divided into two strands: one that others Alawis along ethnic lines by highlighting their supposedly non-Arab and specifically Persian origins, while another strand others them along doctrinal lines by framing their heterodoxy as fundamentally un-Islamic. Kazimi, *Syria through Jihadist Eyes*, p. 16.

[105] For the conflation of ethnic and sectarian identities in the way Iraqi Shi'as were othered, see Haddad, *Sectarianism in Iraq*, pp. 40–51. For an overview of anti-Iranianism in Arab nationalist discourse and how it overlapped with anti-Shi'ism, see Osman, *Sectarianism in Iraq*, pp. 219–230.

[106] For state–Shi'a relations in pre-2003 republican Iraq, see Jabar, *The Shi'ite Movement in Iraq*; Abbas Kadhim, "The Hawza under Siege: A Study in the Ba'th Party Archive," Institute for Iraqi Studies, Boston University, IISBU Occasional Paper, 1, June 2013; Baram, *Saddam Husayn and Islam*; al-Alawi, *Al-Shi'a wa-l-Dawla al-Qawmiyya*; Kanaan Makiya, *Cruelty and Silence* (New York: W.W. Norton & Co., 1993); Sa'id al-Samarra'i, *Saddam wa-Shi'at al-Iraq* (Saddam and the Shi'a of Iraq) (London: Mu'asasat al-Fajr, 1991); Sa'id al-Samarra'i, *Al-Ta'ifiyya fi-l-Iraq: Al-Waqi' wa-l-Hal* (Sectarianism in Iraq: The Reality and the Solution) (London: Mu'asasat al-Fajr, 1993); Adil Ra'uf, *Al-Amal al-Islami fi-l-Iraq: Bayn al-Marji'iyya wa-l-Hizbiyya, Dirasa Naqdiyya li-Masirat Nisf Qirin (1950–2000)* (Islamic Activism in Iraq: Between the Marji'iyya and Party Affiliation; a Critical Study of a Half-Century Journey (1950–2000)) (Damascus: Al-Markaz al-Iraqi li-l-I'lam wa-l-Dirasat, 2000); Bengio, "Shi'as and Politics in Ba'thi Iraq"; Faleh A. Jabar, "The Genesis and Development of *Marja'ism* versus the State," in *Ayatollahs, Sufis and Ideologues*, ed. Jabar. For Shi'a clerical opposition in the early years of the monarchy and the deportation of Persian clerics, see Nakash, *The Shi'is of Iraq*, pp. 75–88.

demographic make-up meant that there were limits to how far the association between Shi'ism and Iran could be overtly pushed. Further afield, Shi'a populations were insignificant enough and Shi'ism was obscure enough for unambiguous anti-Shi'ism to be openly expressed. For example, a Libyan publication from 1992 described Shi'ism in the following terms: "It is one of the Iranians' old beliefs ... and is a sanctuary in which all those that seek to destroy Islam take shelter."[107]

The authoritarian tendency to securitize plurality was significantly amplified in the case of Arab Shi'a minorities and outgroups as a result of the Iranian factor. Though this was magnified after 1979, it had a longer history and Iran's connections with Arab Shi'as were potentially susceptible to securitization if and when deemed necessary by the authorities (national or pre-national) or whenever relations with Iran soured. However, this was not a constant and it was always shaped by the regional political climate. Prior to 1979, relations with Iran lacked the toxicity that was to follow; hence, even if Saudi Arabia viewed pre-1979 Iran as a regional rival, the two could still make common cause when their interests aligned, as they did in the 1960s with regard to the Communist threat, Arab nationalism, the coups in Iraq and Syria, and the Yemeni conflict.[108] Most importantly for our purposes, whatever rivalry existed between Iran and various Arab regimes prior to 1979, the Shah's Iran did not pose a sect-coded ideological challenge. This underlines the fact that the transnational dimension of sectarian relations is not auto-configured by sectarian identity alone; rather, it is contingent upon a broader array of factors that variously shape sectarian identities and their socio-political salience.

The relation between Arab Shi'as and Iran is one that is routinely misunderstood or wilfully misrepresented. Arab regimes and less charitable Arab voices tend to overstate the commonalities between Arab Shi'as and Iran and to exaggerate their potential to act as a vehicle for Iranian penetration of the Arab world. This was especially pronounced after 1979: in response to the ideological and strategic challenge of the Iranian Revolution, Arab nationalist discourse amplified its anti-Iranian rhetoric, framing Iran as the Arab world's

---

[107] Quoted in Muttar, *Al-Dhat al-Jariha*, p. 125.
[108] Keynoush, *Saudi Arabia and Iran*, pp. 71–79.

immutable enemy across the ages. Likewise, Wahhabi anti-Shi'ism was actively disseminated across the region in order to neutralize the Iranian Revolution's potential appeal by questioning Shi'ism's Islamic bona fides.[109] In this way, anti-Iranian polemics framed Iranian Shi'ism as a nefarious tool in the hands of the enemies of Islam or the Arabs.[110] Conversely, some Arab Shi'a responses to this discourse have gone too far in denying any and all connection or link with Iran. The reality is that Arab Shi'ism and Iran undoubtedly do have shared links underpinned by a nexus of connections – religious, commercial, institutional, familial, ethnic and so forth. As a minority group in Islamic terms, and often an outgroup in national terms, international Shi'ism affords Iran a role that is not readily replicated in Sunni Islam. Despite efforts to cast al-Azhar or Saudi Arabia as an Islamic equivalent of the Vatican, there is no real Sunni parallel to the gravitational role played by Iran (and Iraq) in international Shi'ism – a peculiarity that is fundamentally shaped by demographics, the normativity of Sunni Islam, and modern Shi'ism's (and, more so, political Shi'ism's) internal tension between pan-Islamism and Shi'a specificity.[111] As mentioned in chapter 3, this makes the transnational dimension of sectarian identity inherently problematic: firstly, it presents non-Iranian Shi'a-centric actors with a potential foreign Shi'a sponsor; secondly, it gives Iran a potential avenue through which to advance its strategic interests abroad; thirdly, and as a result, it blurs the line between sectarian identity and geopolitics, in turn complicating relations between non-Shi'a political authorities and Shi'a minorities or outgroups. In the process the transnational and the national or subnational dimensions of sectarian identity are further intertwined, with the possibility of the doctrinal dimension being tapped for legitimation and mobilizational support.

The linkages between non-Iranian Shi'as and Iran should not be seen as synonyms for loyalty or dependence. As Sabrina Mervin

---

[109] See Ibrahim, "Al-Su'udiyya: al-Hiwar al-Masmum," in *Nawasib wa Rawafidh*, ed. Saghiya, pp. 168–171; Al-Mu'min, *Min al-Mathhabiyya ila al-Ta'ifiyya*, p. 128.

[110] Osman, *Sectarianism in Iraq*, pp. 223–224.

[111] The centrality of Iran and Iraq in transnational Shi'ism is evident in several studies. See, for example, Chibli Mallat, *The Renewal of Islamic Law: Muhammad Baqir as-Sadr, Najaf and the Shi'i International* (Cambridge: Cambridge University Press, 1993); *The Shi'a Worlds and Iran*, ed. Mervin; Louer, *Transnational Shia Politics*.

has noted, the 'Shi'a world' is in fact an ecosystem of multiple Shi'a worlds which are connected through tenuous relations that are constantly being renegotiated.[112] Crucially, and contrary to popular perception, the transnational networks that underpin these Shi'a worlds do not create a contradiction between national Shi'a identities and Shi'a transnationalism.[113] More to the point, Iran may have links to Shi'a Arab communities that it will try to instrumentalize for its own strategic ends, but these efforts do not automatically meet with success. Iranian strategic goals and non-Iranian Shi'as' domestic considerations are sometimes incompatible, and non-Iranian Shi'as are not devoid of agency in the relationship. Further, not all Shi'as are equally proximate or sympathetic to Iran: for example, while the Iranian Revolution served to galvanize and mobilize Shi'a activists (and Sunni ones too in the early aftermath), the revolution and revolutionary Iran's role in international Shi'ism ultimately proved divisive among Shi'as.[114] Likewise, the terror that Arab regimes felt towards Iran's potential to mobilize Arab Shi'as often proved unfounded: as Louer and others have pointed out, whatever domino effect the Iranian Revolution had was ultimately restricted to Shi'a populations that were already involved in conflictual relations with ruling powers.[115] In other words, the causal variable behind post-1979 Shi'a activism in the Arab world was less sectarian identity or Iranian linkages and more the pre-existence of conflictual state–sect relations in places like Iraq, Bahrain or Saudi Arabia.

The fears and passions and mistakes that followed 1979 were repeated on a larger scale after 2003. The arguments outlined in this chapter – from demographics to securitization – are crucial to understanding sectarian relations in the wake of 2003 and the 'sectarian wave' that swept the region. At heart, the fire that consumed sectarian relations after the invasion of Iraq was fundamentally a product of the

---

[112] Sabrina Mervin, "Introduction," in *The Shi'a Worlds and Iran*, ed. Mervin.

[113] Ibid., p. 21.

[114] Roy, "The Impact of the Iranian Revolution," in *The Shi'a Worlds and Iran*, ed. Mervin, pp. 36–41.

[115] Laurence Louer, "The Rise and Fall of Revolutionary Utopias in the Gulf Monarchies," in *The Shi'a Worlds and Iran*, ed. Mervin. The point is most vividly illustrated by contrasting Kuwait and Bahrain.

fact that regime change disturbed the balance of power between sect-centric actors – firstly in Iraq and then in the region – in a way that 1979 did not. In other words, 2003 saw the realization of many of the fears that failed to materialize following 1979. What began in Iraq reverberated throughout the region and was accelerated by several dynamics that altered sectarian relations beyond recognition. The next two chapters will examine the rise and retreat of these processes.

6

2003 AND THE 'SECTARIAN WAVE'

Prior to 2003, a book such as this – to say nothing of the burgeoning literature on 'sectarianism' in which it sits – would have been relatively unusual. The concept of 'sectarianism', particularly as it relates to the Sunni–Shi'a divide, had neither the policy relevance nor the public resonance that it has today. Where the Middle East was concerned, the term was inordinately associated with Lebanon, where it was understood as a referent to that country's political system and to both inter- and intra-religious dynamics – though, for the most part, the Sunni–Shi'a divide was not especially salient in the literature on twentieth-century Lebanese 'sectarianism'. More broadly, there was little conceptualization of the term and little thought given to what it could mean beyond the confines of a specific national context or a particular historical episode. Moreover, while there has long existed a venerable body of literature on various aspects of Shi'ism and Shi'a identity, there was next to nothing on Sunni identity or Sunni–Shi'a relations (a reflection of the general perception that regarded Sunnis as 'sect-less').

All of this was to change after 2003. The political transformations of that year and the processes unleashed by them have proven pivotal to the modern history of Sunni–Shi'a relations in fairly unparalleled ways. While the next chapter will look at the evolution of sectarian dynamics within the specific context of post-2003 Iraq, this chapter will describe the region-wide, transformative fallout of 2003 and how the events of that year triggered what Daniel Byman aptly labelled a sectarian wave that swept across the region after the invasion of 2003, later intensifying with the civil war in Iraq, the Arab uprisings of 2010–11 and the Syrian civil war.[1] Debunking the ancient hatreds theme and 'sectarianism' as useful frameworks for understanding sectarian relations and the post-2003 sectarian wave is something that has been discussed in the previous chapters and that other scholars have examined at length. Accordingly, rather than offering a history of events since 2003, I am more concerned here with identifying and explaining the dynamics and variables that might help us answer the basic question of why sectarian identities gained such unprecedented social and political relevance in the Middle East and beyond after 2003. Fundamentally, two interrelated factors are at the heart of the various forces that generated and powered the sectarian wave: firstly, the challenge that 2003 and subsequent events presented to the relations of power that had governed sectarian relations (as outlined in the previous chapter) and, by extension, the way that 2003 disturbed the balance of power between sect-centric actors at the national and transnational levels; and, secondly, state collapse and regime fragility and the openings, fears and incentives that these provided and created for sect-centric actors to assert their vision of state and society and to project their fears and ambitions upon the region.

Before continuing, it is important to note that the fallout from 2003 did not traverse a unidirectional or uninterrupted trajectory. Indeed, the post-2003 era offers us a fascinating, if grim, illustration of the fluidity of sectarian identity's salience. This underlines a fundamental point about sectarian identity – or any group identity for that matter – namely, the context-dependent volatility not just of its relevance but of its content and meaning as well. Whether we are looking at individual countries or regional trends, sectarian dynamics waxed and waned throughout the post-2003 era in a way that is easily missed when using euphemisms like sectarian wave. Indeed, at the time of writing the political relevance of sectarian categories had significantly

---

[1] Daniel Byman, "Sectarianism Afflicts the New Middle East," *Survival*, 56:1 (2014): 80.

receded from the highs of recent years when power was still being ferociously contested between sect-centric actors across the region in Iraq, Syria, Bahrain and elsewhere. Of course, the point about fluidity and fluctuating salience should be kept in mind here as well. As will be seen in the next chapter, sectarian relations have passed through several phases since 2003 and the fact that sectarian entrenchment is in retreat at the time of writing should not be taken as an end point; rather, it is part of the longer and endless process that is intergroup, in this case sectarian, relations.

Framing the Sectarian Wave

Byman called it a sectarian wave, another study described it as the geopolitical equivalent of an asteroid (driving some identities to extinction and creating new ones),[2] and I once framed it as a 'Copernican moment'.[3] Other euphemisms like tsunami and seismic shift are routinely used to try to capture the degree to which 2003 was an epochal turning point and to convey the scale and profundity of the processes and dynamics that were unleashed. The reverberations of 2003 of course went far beyond sectarian identity; however, the environment that emerged was one in which sectarian categories had gained unprecedented relevance and an outsized ability to colour social and political perceptions. As a result, an ever-increasing number of issues came to be seen through a sect-centric prism (and thereby sect-coded) – not just issues relating to sectarian dogma or sect-specific symbolism but social relations, political movements, political interests, regional conflict, and so forth.[4] And this has been driven as much by foreign actors as by local protagonists, by victims as by perpetrators, by

---

[2] Cyrus Malik, "Washington's Sunni Myth and the Middle East Undone," Aug. 23, 2016, https://warontherocks.com/2016/08/washingtons-sunni-myth-and-the-middle-east-undone/.

[3] Haddad, "Sectarian Relations before 'Sectarianization'," in *Sectarianization*, ed. Hashemi and Postel, p. 101. 'Copernican' in the sense that 2003 created a political landscape that did not revolve around Arab Sunnis.

[4] For a discussion of sect-coding, see Fanar Haddad, "'Shia Forces', 'Iraqi Army' and the Perils of Sect-Coding," *Jadaliyya*, Sept. 8, 2016, http://www.jadaliyya.com/pages/index/25064/shia-forces-iraqi-army-and-the-perils-of-sect-codi.

elite instrumentalization as by popular fear and prejudice, and as much from above as from below. What emerged was a regional narrative of sectarian conflict and sectarian victimhood in which sectarian dynamics in a given national or subnational setting were seen as part of a larger transnational contest. In this way sectarian solidarities were actively strengthened and enlisted to rally support for protagonists in foreign sect-coded conflict, often in pursuit of domestic political agendas.[5] This blurring of national boundaries and the perception that what was unfolding was part of a grand, epochal and existential sectarian struggle sweeping the region, if not the globe, recall previous cases of highly emotive internationalized conflicts. As one account of the Spanish civil war puts it, the conflict "raised the collective consciousness in other countries ... The war in Spain contributed to the Manichean beliefs of the time when people thought, as Piers Brendon notes, 'that the World was the scene of a cosmic duel between good and evil'."[6] The impact that the sectarian wave, and particularly the Iraqi and Syrian conflicts, had on the early twenty-first-century Middle East, can be described in near-identical terms.

How is the post-2003 sectarian wave best contextualized in the broader history of Sunni–Shi'a relations or even in the far narrower history of Sunni–Shi'a conflict? Is it unique? Is it a stand-alone event birthing a new form of Sunni–Shi'a relations? Or is it just the latest episode in a longer, 1400-year history of sectarian conflict? Needless to say, the rigid binary that such questions suppose – either a unique moment of genesis or just another episode in a longer conflict – is unrealistic. Some aspects of the sectarian wave are indeed unique but these are mostly a reflection of its time and the unique set of circumstances that define it. For instance, the role that social media played in sustaining and deepening the sectarian wave is one such element that clearly differentiates 2003 from previous episodes.

---

[5] For example, Shi'a political actors taking up the cause of Bahraini protesters or Sunni political actors doing the same with Syrian protesters. See, for example, Tim Arango, "Shiites in Iraq support Bahrain's protestors," *New York Times*, April 1, 2011; Mona Alami, "The Impact of the Syria Conflict on Salafis and Jihadis in Lebanon," Middle East Institute, April 18, 2014.

[6] Julian Casanova, *A Short History of the Spanish Civil War* (London: I.B. Tauris, 2013), p. 81.

Likewise, the greater popular role fostered by both the communications revolution and the construct of the nation-state engendered a different set of drivers and a different enabling environment from what would have been the case in earlier times. When it comes to the broader stretch of history, 2003 is by no means the first instance, nor will it be the last, in which sectarian identity gains political relevance or in which sectarian relations are soured through intensified competition of one sort or another. As we have seen, the Mongol sack of Baghdad, instances of Ottoman–Iranian conflict, and other such episodes accentuated, for a time, the political relevance of sectarian identities and served to sharpen sectarian boundaries. However, the fact that these episodes, along with 2003 and what followed, can be sect-coded does not turn them into signposts along a singular conflict culminating in the twenty-first century. More to the point, whatever episode we choose to examine, including the post-2003 sectarian wave, the drivers of sectarianization are always found in relatively proximate causes relating to socio-political grievances, legacy issues and points of contestation from recent living memory which may then be cloaked in the language of religious doctrine or age-old animosity. Consequently, it is almost always recent, local, material and political factors that are at the heart of sectarian conflict – the national and subnational rather than the doctrinal dimension.[7]

Portraying 2003 as the latest in millennia-old sectarian conflict (as is the wont of Orientalists and post-2003 sectarian jihadists alike) would be as silly as trying to understand a future conflict between France and the United Kingdom through the prism of the Hundred Years War. While the historical background is essential to an ability to comprehend the symbolic content of sectarian conflict today (or Anglo-French conflict tomorrow), it is not a *causal* factor nor can it act as an explanatory one on its own. Antagonistic, even aggressive, historical sect-specific myths, symbols, grievances and the like may be

---

[7] This does not preclude exceptions, and the *takfiri* violence seen in Iraq, Syria and sporadically elsewhere in the region since 2003 is clearly framed in doctrinal terms. It would be short-sighted to dismiss this as mere rhetorical cover but it is also important to be mindful of the broader struggle for political power in Iraq, Syria and elsewhere within which much of this violence takes place.

resuscitated and used for legitimation, mobilization and the creation of a sense of solidarity and continuity in service of contemporary conflicts and socio-political aims; however, these neither cause nor do they explain sectarian dynamics today: whatever is unearthed from a sect's symbolic reservoir, whatever is pulled out of its historical closet, is invariably repackaged and repurposed for the needs of the moment.[8] This is as applicable to Shi'a militants invoking the Battle of Karbala in the bloody turf wars of twenty-first-century Iraq or Syria as it would be to British militants invoking Poitiers or Agincourt in a hypothetical future conflict with the French. Of course, the parallel is an imperfect one, not least given the salience of Karbala in contemporary Shi'a identity formation. Nevertheless, the point stands regarding narrative construction and the modern drivers of what are instrumentally framed as timeless conflicts. What is being suggested here is not that such evocation is a form of false consciousness or cynical narrative construction or emplotment.[9] Rather, it is to question what can be inferred from such examples and how they fit into contemporary sectarian competition. Sunnis and Shi'as have more recent, and less abstract, group-defining myths and symbols related to their experiences at the national and transnational levels that often have a more tangible impact on people in the here and now – consider any of the innumerable atrocities, genocidal acts and historical injustices that fall within living memory. At times of sectarian entrenchment or

---

[8] On the modern use of deeply rooted symbols, see Kakar, *The Colors of Violence*, p. 42; Marilynn B. Brewer, *Intergroup Relations*, 2nd edn (Maidenhead: Open University Press, 2003), pp. 23–24; Kinnvall, "Globalisation and Religious Nationalism," p. 760; Stuart J. Kaufman, *Modern Hatreds: The Symbolic Politics of Ethnic War* (New York: Cornell University Press, 2001), pp. 4–11; Bayart, *The Illusions of Cultural Identity*, p. 110. For an example from China, see Chen's fascinating look at the use of burial sites in China's relations with Western imperial powers: Song-Chuan Chen, "The Power of Ancestors: Tombs and Death Practices in Late Qing China's Foreign Relations, 1845–1914," *Past and Present*, 239:1 (2018): 112–142.

[9] The use of the term 'emplotment' to understand sectarian dynamics comes to us courtesy of Adam Gaiser, who used a narrative identity approach to frame sectarian divisions as "participatory discourses in which individuals ultimately choose to locate themselves in a plot ('emplot' themselves) – or not to do so." Gaiser, "A Narrative Identity Approach to Islamic Sectarianism," in *Sectarianization*, ed. Hashemi and Postel, pp. 61–62.

episodes of acute sectarian competition, sect-centric actors – elite or otherwise – may draw a link between these and older episodes, myths and symbols in order to weave a narrative of timelessness, authenticity and a feeling that the group-defining struggles of old continue today complete with reincarnated versions of historical foes. That way, older, foundational group-defining myths, symbols and narratives are drawn upon to lend weight to the causes of today. The point is, however, that such linkages do not *cause* modern sectarian conflict nor do they explain modern sectarian dynamics. Viewing contemporary episodes of sectarian antagonism as extensions of previous episodes spanning the breadth of Islamic history lends them an unfounded air of inevitability. Further, such an approach risks blinding us to more recent and often more proximate political and material drivers by misleadingly reducing modern sectarian dynamics to a question of conflicting doctrines.

Being mindful of the multidimensionality of sectarian identity is especially important when considering the post-2003 sectarian wave. Like 1979 before it, what makes 2003 stand out is the importance of the transnational dimension in blurring the lines between the national, the transnational, the doctrinal and the geopolitical, and the way it superimposed geopolitics onto sectarian identity – sect-coding geopolitics and geopolitically coding sectarian identities.[10] There are any number of sect-coded episodes from the twentieth century that were too short-lived or too localized to have had a regional and long-lasting impact even if they were pivotal to particular national or subnational contexts. Some of these are extremely localized and rather fleeting – a momentary sect-coded controversy at the subnational level in this country or that.[11] Other episodes were far more consequential,

---

[10] On regional powers and their reinforcement of the sectarian divide for geopolitical purposes, see, among many others, Luomi, "Sectarian Identities or Geopolitics?" pp. 5, 16, 47–48; *The Politics of Sectarianism*, POMEPS Briefing 21; Salloukh, "The Sectarianization of Geopolitics in the Middle East," in *Sectarianization*, ed. Hashemi and Postel.

[11] For example, the publication in 1927 of what was regarded by many Iraqi Shi'as as an attack against the House of the Prophet – the so-called 'Nusuli affair'. It was controversial while it lasted, but the episode had no discernible long-term impact nor did it have any consequences beyond Iraq. For details, see Abd al-Razzaq al-Hasani, *Tarikh al-Wizarat al-Iraqiyya* (The History of the Iraqi Cabinets) (Baghdad: Dar al-Shu'un al-Thaqafiyya al-Ama, 1988), vol. 2, pp. 88–89.

yet even the most serious of these – the 1976–82 uprising in Syria, the 1991 uprising in southern Iraq or the uprising in Bahrain in the early 1990s – while having a transformative effect on the course of sectarian relations in the countries concerned, did not have a long-lasting regional echo.[12] Of course, these events provide the backdrop to 2003 and form part of the cumulative, sect-coded detritus and legacy issues with which sect-centric actors formulated their positions, fears, ambitions and messaging, but in and of themselves they did not have a regionally transformative impact in their time nor were they accompanied by anything resembling the twenty-first-century sectarian wave. By contrast, 2003 was a sect-coded affair with transformative regional ramifications from the start. It employed the language of sectarian victimhood and entitlement, it consciously empowered sect-centric actors, and it disturbed the balance of power between Iraqi sect-centric actors and between Iran and its regional rivals. The ensuing security dilemmas and the attendant regional threat and opportunity perceptions incentivized elites – local, regional and international – to perpetuate and deepen this sect-coding. This in turn was further augmented by the enabling environment of the time, which allowed for a no less robust process of sectarianization from below as a result (not always intentional) of social media and other less regulated forms of communication and information creation. These are some of the factors that distinguish 2003 in the history of modern sectarian relations: it was a game changer of regional and even global magnitude on a par with, if not surpassing, the impact of 1979.

A final cautionary note on how best to frame the sectarian wave relates to the importance of regional and national variations. Put simply, the sectarian wave was not uniformly felt, experienced, perceived or utilized across the region, and the reality was more

---

[12] For the uprising in Syria in the late 1970s and early 1980s, see Raphael Lefevre, *Ashes of Hama: The Muslim Brotherhood in Syria* (London: Hurst & Co., 2013), chapter 6. For the 1994–9 uprising in Bahrain, see Louay Bahry, "The Opposition in Bahrain: A Bellwether for the Gulf?" *Middle East Policy*, 5:2 (May 1997): 42–57; Falah al-Mdaires, "Shi'ism and Political Protest in Bahrain," *DOMES: Digest of Middle East Studies*, 1 (Spring 2002): 20–44. For the uprisings in southern Iraq in 1991, see Dina Rizk Khoury, "The 1991 *Intifada* in Three Keys: Writing the History of Violence," in *Writing the Modern History of Iraq*, ed. Tejel et al.

complex than instrumentalist or essentialist accounts would allow. Again, we need to be mindful of multidimensionality and to employ a suitably multidimensional framework such as that introduced in chapters 3 and 4 to better account for variations in what might otherwise be mistaken for an undifferentiated sectarian wave evenly and uniformly washing over the Middle East. In some instances (Iraq, Syria, Bahrain) there were legacy issues and an element of cumulative sect-coded grievances and lines of contestation that exploded with the openings that emerged after 2003, providing ample fodder for regional intervention. This was not the case in other contexts which nevertheless felt the reverberations of the sectarian wave (Kuwait and Saudi Arabia, for example). This was either due to a more benign history of sectarian relations at the national level or to greater regime success in harnessing the sectarian wave and denying or suppressing openings through which (potentially) sect-coded grievances could be aired. The demographic make-up of a given national or subnational setting, the history of sectarian relations in a given context, and the cohesiveness and integrative capacity of state institutions and hierarchies of power went a long way towards determining how the heightened relevance of sectarian categories would be reflected in individual national settings. A history of contested sectarian relations at the national level (Iraq, Syria, Bahrain, Saudi Arabia) creates added incentives and opportunities for elites to play the sectarian card just as it creates a more receptive constituency below. This was grimly demonstrated in the relentless and successful way the regimes of Syria, Bahrain and Saudi Arabia played the sectarian card to neutralize the 'Arab Spring' when it reached their shores.[13] In other contexts, rather than pent-up grievances or contested relations of power between Sunnis and Shi'as at the national or subnational levels, it was the transnational and doctrinal dimensions that dominated people's perceptions of sectarian

---

[13] The regimes played on long-standing and long-propagated stereotypes and prejudices to vilify and discredit the protests in their respective countries. Where Shi'a protesters were concerned, the pro forma accusation was being agents of Iranian machinations; in the case of Syria, the pro forma accusation against Sunni protesters was religious intolerance, terrorism and serving foreign agendas. In both cases the protests were accused of being 'sectarian' and in both cases there was a significant constituency that was inclined to believe the charge.

dynamics as they came to see themselves as part of a regional sect-coded struggle. In such cases the threat was not framed as an internal one and hence did not have a divisive national impact. In this way, despite variations, the ripple effects of 2003 extended across the entire region even to unlikely places where sectarian outgroups are not demographically competitive, such as Jordan or North Africa.[14] In short, the prism of sectarian identity gradually became part of a shared regional narrative of self and other, and its idiom was to spread beyond Iraq and the Middle East.

2003: A Historical Disruption

Rather than the metaphors and euphemisms that we have been accustomed to using to try to capture the impact of 2003, we may be better served and gain greater clarity by thinking about 2003 in terms of what it actually was: a historical disruption. Taking her lead from William Sewell's argument that historical disruptions are an important theoretical category, Staci Strobl uses this approach in her analysis of British colonialism and its impact on the sect-coded evolution of the criminal justice system in Bahrain.[15] The same framing is useful for understanding the impact of 2003 in that such disruptions are transformative of broader social structures in ways that cannot be contained through reference to the previous social order. In Sewell's conception, a historical disruption is something of a big-bang event in that it creates a new socio-political reality by redrawing the relations of power and altering the 'rules of the game' that had previously governed power and society. Such disruptions can create a vacuum or an opening through which various actors emerge to compete in creating a new

---

[14] For anti-Shi'ism in Jordan, see Wagemaker, "Anti-Shi'ism without the Shi'a." For North Africa, see Monier, "Egypt, Iran and the Hizbullah Cell," and Saleh and Kraetzschmar, "Politicized Identities, Securitized Politics." For a general look at anti-Shi'ism in North Africa, see Jonathan Laurence, "In Sunni North Africa, Fears of Iran's Shia Shadow," *Middle East Monitor*, Oct. 27, 2017, https://www.middleeastmonitor.com/20171027-in-sunni-north-africa-fears-of-irans-shiite-shadow/.

[15] Staci Strobl, "The Roots of Sectarian Law and Order in the Gulf: Bahrain, the Eastern Province of Saudi Arabia and the Two Historical Disruptions," in *Beyond Sunni and Shia*, ed. Wehrey.

normative order. In Strobl's words: "Disruptive events are moments when competing conceptions clash, many outcomes are possible, and the result of the competition sets the stage for authority, legitimacy and security going forward."[16] In such situations there is enough uncertainty to create the perception that everything is politically up for grabs and open to fundamental contestation; social and political norms are momentarily suspended and what was inconceivable, ridiculous or fantastical suddenly enters the realm of the possible. Needless to say, such an environment easily inflames fears and ambitions.

Yet the question remains: Why was this historical disruption so easily sect-coded? Why was 2003 and the landscape that emerged from it so easily framed in terms of the Sunni–Shi'a divide, and why did the sect-coding of Iraq extend to the region and to subsequent upheavals? An essentialist understanding of the subject would regard sect-coding as an inescapable result of any vacuum in the Arab world. After all, if one believes these categories are the perennially relevant basic organizing principles of the Middle East, then it stands to reason that they are forever poised to fill whatever opening emerges. This is plainly not the case, however. That so many observers nevertheless accept this mistaken logic is all the more remarkable given that there is no shortage of disruptions in modern Iraqi and regional history that were not sect-coded.[17] Rather than wrongly presuming the inevitability of sect-coding, the answers to post-2003 sectarianization are found in relatively recent Iraqi and regional history; the policies of the occupation authorities in Iraq; the timing of the invasion (coinciding with the new media revolution); and the way in which these processes disturbed the balance of power between sect-centric actors and challenged the relations of power that were described in the previous chapter.

---

[16] Ibid., p. 208.

[17] For example, any of Iraq's long list of military coups from 1937 to 1968 and, in particular, the instability that followed the coups of 1958, 1963 and 1968. The same can be said of the Syrian coup of 1963 and, more broadly, the ideological struggles between Arab nationalists and communists throughout much of the twentieth century. Another example is the Yemeni conflict of the 1990s and more so that of the 1960s, where sectarian categories were all but irrelevant in what was an internationalized conflict.

A lot of the regional consternation surrounding the invasion of Iraq reflected not just the concerns at the precedent that was being set, the imperial aggression that it embodied, or the upheaval that was being unleashed, but it was also a reflection of concerns that regime change and the empowerment of Shi'a-centric Iraqi actors, many of them with Iranian ties, were very likely to end up benefiting Iran and its clients and allies. The most famous iteration of this was the fear, voiced by Jordanian King Abdullah as early as 2004, that the post-2003 Middle East was witnessing the emergence of a 'Shi'a crescent' emanating from Iran and stretching from the Persian Gulf to the Mediterranean.[18] This built on and rejuvenated the fears that had followed 1979: a predatory and revolutionary Iran using Shi'ism as cover to spread its influence and networks throughout the Middle East in an effort to undermine the regional order and overturn long-standing regimes to its own strategic advantage.[19] In invading Iraq and in empowering the Iraqi opposition, several factions of whom were intensely Shi'a-centric with varying degrees of proximity to Iran, American policy seemed to be guaranteeing the realization of these fears. By extension, the regional backlash against the political change in Iraq, at least where sectarian relations were concerned, was not just a reaction to the political empowerment of Shi'as per se (though this was always likely to be controversial), but it was a backlash that was amplified by the sort of Shi'as that were being empowered: not just politicians who happened to be Shi'a but, in some of the more prominent cases, Shi'a-centric Islamist politicians whose political outlook and political history revolved around the politics of sect and who enjoyed varying degrees of proximity to and ideological congruence with Iran. That is not to deny that both the Iraqi opposition in exile and the post-2003 Iraqi political elite formed a spectrum. However, the reality is that, at least since the 1990s, the dominant factions within the Iraqi opposition, and certainly those best placed to benefit from regime change, were Shi'a-centric actors (alongside Kurdish nationalists) who, to one

---

[18] Wright and Baker, "Iraq, Jordan See Threat to Election from Iran."

[19] The threat was most acutely felt in Iraq and the Gulf. See Jabar, *The Shi'ite Movement in Iraq*, chapters 13–14; Louer, "The Rise and Fall of Revolutionary Utopias," in *The Shi'a Worlds and Iran*, ed. Mervin; Matthiesen, *The Other Saudis*, chapters 3–4.

degree or another, championed the cause of Shi'a victimhood and Shi'a empowerment.[20] Not for nothing did Muqtada al-Sadr emerge as the only indigenous political actor with a genuine popular base after 2003 nor was it a coincidence that the only returning political exile to gain a notable reception was Shi'a cleric Muhammad Baqir al-Hakim (head of the Supreme Council for the Islamic Revolution in Iraq, as it was then known) when he returned from his long exile in Iran.[21] The Iraqi case will be discussed in greater detail in the following chapter. Suffice it to say here that one of the main reasons that the historical disruption of 2003 was so immediately sect-coded was the Iraq-specific historical backdrop (including the growth of a political culture of Shi'a sect-centricity over the course of the twentieth century) and the fact that regime change disrupted and threatened the balance of power between sect-centric actors in both Iraq and the region. The ensuing chaos only served to deepen and incentivize the reliance on sectarian categories.

At a popular level, the invasion of Iraq inflamed passions throughout the Middle East and confirmed the worst assumptions about American power in the region. An attack against Muslims, an attack against Arabs, an attack against the Global South, the invasion incensed public opinion on any number of levels and turned Iraq into a cause célèbre across much of the political spectrum. Yet there was also a sect-coded element that, with hindsight, may have been inevitable: the fact that the invasion's most visible Iraqi supporters and beneficiaries were Shi'as – alongside Kurdish nationalists – meant that hostility towards the American invasion of Iraq all too easily extended

---

[20] For the opposition in exile during the 1990s, see Tareq Y. Ismael and Jacqueline S. Ismael, *Iraq in the Twenty-First Century: Regime Change and the Making of a Failed State*, Durham Modern Middle East and Islamic World Series 34 (Oxford: Routledge, 2015), pp. 84–89.

[21] See Juan Cole, "Shiite Religious Parties Fill Vacuum in Southern Iraq," Middle East Research and Information Project, April 22, 2003, http://www.merip.org/mero/mero042203. On Hakim's return to Iraq, see Joel Roberts, "Triumphant Return of Shiite Leader," CBS News, May 11, 2003, http://www.cbsnews.com/news/triumphant-return-of-shiite-leader/; Associated Press, "Iraqi Opposition Leader Returns Home," *USA Today*, May 10, 2003, http://usatoday30.usatoday.com/news/world/iraq/2003-05-10-shiite-leader_x.htm; "Prominent Iraqi Shi'ite Leader Returns from Exile," *Irish Times*, May 10, 2003, http://www.irishtimes.com/news/prominent-iraqi-shi-ite-leader-returns-from-exile-1.476266.

to hostility towards Shi'as and, of course, towards the nascent post-2003 Iraqi state.[22] This very easily dovetailed with long-standing anti-Shi'a polemics that frame them as an insidious internal threat forever trying to corrode Islam from within. Further, as we saw in the previous chapter, sect-centricity and the public assertion of outgroup identity had long been regarded as distasteful, if not dangerous, by conventional forms of Arab political correctness. This further added to, and sect-coded, the outrage that accompanied regime change: this most blatant act of American imperialist aggression was supported by Iraqi Shi'a political and intellectual elites in exile and was set to empower them and a previously reviled culture of Shi'a sect-centricity. More than just opposing the tyranny of the Ba'th regime as Iraqis who happened to be Shi'a, such actors were also concerned with highlighting what they regarded as the unique victimization of Shi'a Iraqis under the Ba'th. Thus, in this view, if 2003 was a moment to right historical wrongs, many of these were framed in distinctly communitarian terms. As we will see, this was as much a feature of US rhetoric as it was of the Iraqi opposition in exile which was soon to be handed power in Iraq: the narrative of communal victimhood and of oppressive Sunnis victimizing Shi'as and Kurds was one around which US interests, Shi'a-centric actors and Kurdish nationalists could coalesce for the purposes of regime change. This further blurred the line between hostility towards America and hostility towards Iraqi Shi'as in the region and deepened the perceived complicity between them. Nor was the language of communal victimhood the preserve of Shi'a-centric political elites and American officials: far from being a simple top-down process, there was a significant Shi'a-centric Iraqi constituency that, in 2003, prioritized the twin pillars of political Shi'a sect-centricity: victimhood and entitlement. Indeed, for Arab publics, a shocking element of 2003 was the explosion of popular Iraqi Shi'a

---

[22] On Arab public opinion towards the new Iraq, see Marc Lynch, "New Iraq, New Arab Public," *Voices of the New Arab Public: Iraq, Al Jazeera, and Middle East Politics Today* (New York: Columbia University Press, 2006); Daoud Kuttab, "The Media and Iraq: A Blood Bath for and Gross Dehumanization of Iraqis," *International Review of the Red Cross*, 89:868 (Dec. 2007): 879–891 (esp. 889–890). For an overview of contentious Iraqi perceptions of Arab media coverage, see Osman, *Sectarianism in Iraq*, pp. 237–239.

expression which immediately followed the fall of the regime and which signalled the end of the socio-political norms and hierarchies of power that had governed sectarian relations.

From Apologetic to Assertive: Sect-Centricity Unveiled

Regime change allowed for the full, unfettered assertion of previously circumscribed subnational identities and previously unmentionable grievances. In doing so, 2003 highlighted the uncomfortable fact that there were multiple, indeed contradictory, visions of what it meant to be an Iraqi and, by extension, what it meant to be part of the Arab world. This was later to be repeated with the fragmentation of authoritarian regimes elsewhere in the region following the Arab uprisings.[23] It applied as much to how the past was imagined as to how the present was perceived. As one analyst described it, 2003 was the moment in which the grand narratives of the Iraqi nation-state crumbled and the depth of division in historical memory was revealed particularly through the fact that "a large section of Iraqi society accepted the old colonizer as a saviour from national dictatorship."[24] While it is important to be mindful of the obvious fact that this does not apply to *all* Shi'as or *all* Sunnis, it is nevertheless true that there was a basic divergence between how significant sections of Shi'a and Sunni public opinion regarded regime change. For the former, it was a historic opportunity and a moment of salvation no matter how bitter the taste of invasion and occupation; for the latter, a national calamity and an existential threat that saw the removal of a despotic but nevertheless Iraqi order and its replacement by an alien regime that represented all that they had long been told to fear: Shi'a Islamism, Kurdish separatism, foreign machinations, Iranian aggression and so

---

[23] Byman, "Sectarianism Afflicts the New Middle East," p. 83; Bahout, "The Unravelling of Lebanon's Taif Agreement," p. 3.

[24] Haider Saeed, *Siyasat al-Ramz: 'An Nihayat Thaqafat al-Dawla al-Wataniyya fi-l-Iraq* (The Politics of the Symbol: On the End of the Culture of the National State in Iraq) (Beirut: Al-Mu'asasa al-Arabiyya, 2009), p. 103. See also Osman, *Sectarianism in Iraq*, pp. 172–173; Haddad, *Sectarianism in Iraq*, pp. 151–178; "The Next Iraqi War? Sectarianism and Civil Conflict," International Crisis Group, Middle East Report no. 52, Feb. 27, 2006, pp. 6–22.

forth.[25] For most Sunni Arabs, Iraqi or otherwise, the unveiling of these divergences was part of the broader shock of encountering the full gamut of Shi'a identity. As we discussed in the previous chapter, Arab Shi'ism is numerically weak and geographically concentrated in a few places and, in any case, the expression of sectarian identity was generally muted if not stigmatized for much of the twentieth century. In other words, the full otherness of Arab Shi'ism (from alternative formulations of national consciousness to the vast pantheon of Shi'a-specific rituals and symbols to differing historical memories and differing beliefs) was not something that most Arabs in the twenty-first century had encountered or even been aware of beyond the vaguest of terms. The sect-centricity of the emergent post-2003 Iraqi political order and the loud assertion of Shi'a ownership of Iraq therefore came as something of a shock to many Arabs.

A few days after the fall of the Iraqi regime, the magnitude of the shift in political norms and sectarian relations was on full display in the annual *arba'in* commemorations – the 40th day after the Battle of Karbala in which the third Shi'a Imam, Hussain ibn Ali, was killed and which in 2003 took place less than a fortnight after the fall of the regime. Since the 1970s, and with only slight openings in the 1990s, Shi'a mass rituals had been banned. The first post-Saddam *arba'in*, coming so soon after his demise, was therefore as much religious ceremony as it was an assertion of Shi'a identity, Shi'a strength and the Shi'as' place in the emergent 'new Iraq'.[26] The dynamics described in the previous chapter – the securitization and suppression of expressions of Shi'a identity, the normativity of Sunni frames of reference, the enforcement of sect-blindness – meant that many Iraqi Sunnis (to say nothing of Sunnis beyond Iraq) were somewhat oblivious to the facts of Shi'a sect-centricity and also to Iraqi Shi'ism's demographic weight. The *arba'in* commemorations of 2003, and the expression of sectarian

---

[25] As Harith al-Qarawee put it: "In 2003, Sunni Arabs woke up and saw these three enemies – the occupiers, the Kurdish nationalists, and the Shi'a Islamists – sitting together and setting the rules for the new Iraq." Available at "National Reconciliation and Negotiation: The Path Forward in Iraq and Syria: Panel 1," uploaded Dec. 16, 2014, https://www.youtube.com/watch?v=Na5tfjOiB3M.

[26] Patrick Cockburn, *Muqtada al-Sadr and the Fall of Iraq* (London: Faber and Faber, 2008), p. 21.

identity on such an enormous scale and so soon after the shock of regime change, were therefore viewed with much consternation by many Sunnis.

All of which brings us back to the divergence in how 2003 was perceived in Arab Iraq – a divergence that considerably reflected Iraq's sectarian divide. What Iraqi Shi'as welcomed as the freedom to express their identity and assert their presence, many Sunni Iraqis and even some anti-Islamist Shi'a Iraqis saw as confirmation that Iraq was being taken over by forces that were altogether alien and threatening – whether in relation to conceptions of what constitutes 'normal Islam' or to conceptions of a modern, secular, ostensibly sect-blind Iraq.[27] For Iraqi opponents of regime change, the assertion of Shi'a identity was seen as an existential challenge at the national and subnational levels: as a threat to the definition and nature of Iraqi state and society and as an appropriation of Iraqi public space in the name of Shi'a sect-centricity – the 'Shi'ification' of Iraq, as it was often framed. For others the shock at what was happening, at least where sectarian dynamics were concerned, was linked more to the doctrinal dimension and what was regarded as the enabling and empowering of heretical practice. This is how Vali Nasr recalls his Pakistani hosts (the Sunni fundamentalist group Jamaat-e Islami) reacting to footage of the 2003 *arba'in* ("aghast at what they were seeing").[28] This of course stands to reason: Pakistani fundamentalists cannot but see Sunni–Shi'a competition in Iraq at the doctrinal (and perhaps the transnational) level, for what concern of theirs is the Iraq-specific national or subnational dimension? In any case, Nasr's anecdote is a useful reminder of the multidimensionality of sectarian identity, the multilayered complexity of what was happening in 2003, and the way different audiences view sectarian issues according to different dimensions.

The emergence of a more assertive Shi'a identity – soon to be paralleled by an emergent and no less assertive Iraqi and regional Sunni

---

[27] Put simply and to the point by Rayburn, "When the long-contained Shi'a population began to emerge in 2003, many Sunnis simply could not believe their eyes." Rayburn, *Iraq after America*, p. 130.

[28] Vali Nasr, *The Shia Revival: How Conflicts within Islam Will Shape the Future* (New York: W.W. Norton & Co., 2006), pp. 18–20.

identity – highlights several important points about sectarian dynamics. Firstly, and most obviously, is the importance of context: ideology alone, doctrinal differences in and of themselves, the existence of antagonistic myths and so forth, explain very little about sectarian relations. How an identity is constructed, imagined, performed and expressed is anything but static and it is especially vulnerable to the transformative impact of conflict and violence.[29] Even the content and meaning of an identity – seemingly timeless symbols or eternally sacred myths – are prone to change and fluctuate. In his examination of Jewish identity and Holocaust remembrance in the United States, Peter Novick gives us a lucid illustration of the fluidity of identity even where seemingly sacrosanct myths are concerned. According to Novick's research, until the 1970s American Jewry was far more interested in downplaying Jewish identity (including the Jewish specificity of the Holocaust) as part of the broader priority of securing social and political acceptance in every area of American society. This integrationist impulse was reflected in an apologetic Jewish-American identity, itself a response to perceived hostility and fears of encirclement. Interestingly, Novick argues that the success of this integrationist push eventually led to the re-emergence of fears of group extinction but not as a result of hostility, but rather, due to its absence, which prompted concerns that successful integration could lead to identity dilution or extinction through assimilation. This, Novick argues, along with developments relating to the Arab–Israeli conflict and the need to secure American support for Israel, precipitated a shift in the 1970s from 'integration' to 'survival' as the driving force of Jewish activism in the United States and, with it, a shift from an apologetic to a more assertive posture for Jewish-American activism.[30] This underlines the fluidity of identity not just in terms of its salience but also in how it is perceived and framed – in this case, from a more apologetic stance that shies from and even fears the consequences of differentiation to a more assertive one that

---

[29] This has been vividly demonstrated in several contexts since 2003 and particularly in Iraq and Syria. For example, Christopher Phillips notes the previously unheard-of proliferation of sect-specific symbolism in Syria as a result of the war. Phillips, "Sectarianism and Conflict in Syria," p. 369.

[30] Peter Novick, *The Holocaust in American Life* (New York: First Mariner Books, 2000), pp. 184–185.

seeks to accentuate difference and assert specificity.[31] Such shifts affect not just enunciation and framing but content as well. For example, the siege of Masada in which a thousand or so besieged Jews chose death through suicide over capture by the Romans was, according to Novick, "absent from Jewish memory for almost two thousand years," because traditional Judaism was more focused on survival than military resistance or martial valour.[32] However, come the twentieth century, Masada acquired new meaning and has been actively propagated and mythologized in a context of militarized Zionist state-building.[33]

Needless to say, this kind of fluidity, flexibility and ambiguity is no less a feature of sectarian (or any other) identities. Being mindful of this can help us better understand the previously mentioned oscillations between the contradictory pulls of sectarian division and sectarian harmony (see chapters 2 and 3). The sectarian wave occasioned a shift in how sectarian identity was imagined as political contestation in Iraq came to be seen through an increasingly sectarian lens. In this way, Iraq became the centre of what was regarded as a regional Sunni–Shi'a or Arab–Iranian contest – a perception that was amplified after 2011 during the Syrian conflict. There is an interesting but imperfect parallel here between the impact that the emergence of the state of Israel had on Arab–Jewish relations in the Arab world and how post-2003 Iraq complicated sectarian relations across the region. In both cases we see the transposing of regional politics onto communal relations and the redefinition of how certain identities are perceived: whether it is mid-century Arabs and Jews or Sunnis and Shi'as after 2003, the other came to be seen less as a neighbour and more as a potential extension of region-wide geopolitical and ideological struggles. Thankfully the parallel only goes so far in that the souring of Sunni–Shi'a relations after 2003 did not have the permanent effect that the emergence of the state of Israel had on Arab–Jewish relations.

---

[31] The interesting thing about this example is that it also indicates that such shifts happen and the salience of identity is reinforced not only through adversity, as is more broadly recognized, but also through the reverse.

[32] Novick, *The Holocaust in American Life*, p. 4.

[33] For the memory of the Masada in Israeli narratives of state, see Idith Zertal, *Israel's Holocaust and the Politics of Nationhood* (Cambridge: Cambridge University Press, 2005), pp. 23–25, 29–33.

The dynamics and relations of power described in the previous chapter had often encouraged an apologetic Shi'a sectarian identity throughout much of the twentieth century; however, with the transformation of power relations after 2003 we see a shift towards a more assertive (in some cases aggressive) Shi'a sectarian identity, one that was soon met with a Sunni parallel as a region-wide backlash gained steam. There are historical precedents in such shifts: as we saw in chapter 4, some accounts of the tenth century – the so-called 'Shi'a century' – including later medieval chronicles, portray a shift in Shi'a identity from an apologetic stance (for fear of antagonizing the Sunni majority) to a more assertive one following the rise of the Buwayhids and other Shi'a and pseudo-Shi'a powers. Predictably, this more assertive, more visible and more expressive Shi'a identity was met with a backlash that resulted in a rise in sectarian violence in the form of rioting between the various quarters of Baghdad.[34] One cannot help drawing parallels with how the heightened relevance of sectarian identity after 2003 gave sectarian polemicists a limelight and an audience that they would scarcely have dreamed of in earlier years – it is hardly a coincidence that, for a while, people like Yasser al-Habib, whom we met in the previous chapter, or Salafi preachers like Taha al-Dulaimi or Adnan al-Ar'ur became near-household names among Sunnis and Shi'as in the years following 2003. The sense of sectarian entrenchment that Iraq and then Syria engendered, and the perception that region-wide political conflict was becoming increasingly synonymous with the Sunni–Shi'a divide, temporarily broadened the appeal and relevance of the politically incorrect and relatively unusual discourse of division and outright rejection of unity for which such preachers are known. Of course, over a thousand years

---

[34] Kohlberg, "From Imamiyya to Ithna-Ashariyya," pp. 524, 533. For an example of displays of Shi'a identity leading to Sunni–Shi'a violence in Buwayhid Baghdad (1042), see al-Kirami (ed.), *Al-Kamil fi Tarikh Ibn al-Athir*, pp. 1441–1442. The incident was triggered by the Shi'a quarter of Karkh raising columns with "Muhammad and Ali are the best of mankind" written on them. In what seems like a case of Chinese whispers in medieval Baghdad, violence ensued when some Sunnis became convinced that the columns read, "Muhammad and Ali are the best of mankind. Whoever accepts this, gives thanks; whoever refuses, commits apostasy." After that the conflict developed a momentum of its own for several days.

separate tenth-century Baghdad from 2003, and whatever similarities and parallels exist have less to do with essentialist aspects of sectarian identity or ageless animosities and more to do with similar socio-political pressures and power dynamics.

Sect-Coding and Social Media

Following 2003, what began in Iraq spread across the region with the idiom of sect increasingly colouring political interests, political messaging and threat perceptions far beyond the Iraqi centre. The heightened awareness and salience of sectarian identity quickly turned into an obsession, with the maximalist approach (see chapter 2) dominating commentary on all manner of subjects relating to Iraq and to identity in the Middle East. Not only was this framing used to characterize the present but it was also projected onto the past the better to validate an ahistorical view of a Middle East or Iraq forever torn and animated by 'sectarianism'.[35] This was not just a feature of Western commentary nor was it the preserve of tabloid journalism. Even some scholarly works promoted the maximalist tendency, and the obsession with sects was nowhere more keenly felt or expressed than within the region and in Arabic-language sources. This was of course partly a reflection of the emergence of a salient sense of Sunni identity (in a doctrinal, national and transnational sense) driven by the dislocation of 2003 and ensuing perceptions of victimization and encirclement by what appeared to be an ascendant Iranian-led Shi'ism. This was a novel development in that, outside the partial exception of modern Syria, Arab Sunnis rarely felt the need to identify along sectarian lines: more often than not, prior to 2003 they were seen and self-identified as 'normal' Muslims without the sectarian hyphenation

---

[35] To give two examples from the recent literature on Iraq, one Iraqi writer argued that "if Karl Marx argued that human history is the result of class struggle then I believe that modern Iraqi history is the result of sectarian struggle more than any other." Hussain, *Al-Ta'ifiyya al-Siyasiyya*, p. 7. A more specific example is an account that frames the Iraqi coup of 1958 as one led by a Shi'a Kurd (Abd al-Karim Qasim) against a 'Sunni monarchy'. In this reading 'Sunni supremacy' was restored by a succession of Ba'thist coups. Nicolas Pelham, *A New Muslim Order: The Shia and the Middle East Sectarian Crisis* (London: I.B. Tauris, 2008), p. xiii.

commonly associated with minorities and outgroups. Hence the dearth of specifically Sunni causes or explicitly Sunni organizations in the twentieth-century Arab world. This was to change after 2003; as Fred Wehrey and others have noted, the post-2003 environment saw the conflation of the norms of Arabism and Islam with a specifically Sunni frame of reference juxtaposed with Shi'ism.[36] This process was driven both from above and from below, endogenously and exogenously.[37] Moreover, the transformation of 'Muslims' into 'Sunni Muslims' primarily contrasted with the Shi'a other was something that was eventually echoed beyond the Middle East and as far afield as Southeast Asia, where Shi'as constitute less than 1 per cent of any national population.[38] In this way, events in Iraq triggered a regional and even

---

[36] Wehrey, *Sectarian Politics in the Gulf*, pp. 211–212.

[37] An interesting expression of this is presented in Sahar Bazzaz's examination of the term 'Sunni triangle' – a reference to the supposed Sunni heartland of Iraq. Here was a sect-coded geographical reference that was being used by Western media and commentary to describe an area that was at the heart of a spiralling insurgency. According to Bazzaz, this Western media-friendly phrase was picked up by Arabic-language media and reified as part of the sectarian mapping of Iraq. Sahar Bazzaz, "The Discursive Mapping of Sectarianism in Iraq: The 'Sunni Triangle' in the Pages of the *New York Times*," in *Imperial Geographies in Byzantine and Ottoman Space*, ed. Sahar Bazzaz et al. (Cambridge: Harvard University Press, 2013).

[38] For example, in 2013 the Universiti Sains Malaysia held a seminar entitled 'Confronting the Shi'a Virus'. See Rahat Husain, "Malaysian 'Confronting the Shia Virus' Seminar was Precursor to Anti-Shia Alliance Meeting," *Communities Digital News*, May 2, 2014, http://www.commdiginews.com/world-news/middle-east/malaysian-confronting-the-shia-virus-seminar-was-precursor-to-anti-shia-alliance-meeting-16310/#HDE78HVBvde5Uerw.99. Later that year, an anti-Shi'a public rally was held in Indonesia where a call for an anti-Shi'a jihad was made. This was a function of populist electioneering; however, it speaks volumes about the salience of Sunni identity at the time that anti-Shi'ism passed as a populist message in a country where Shi'as form less than 1% of the population. See Yuli Krisna, "Calls for Jihad, Purges Emerge at Hate-Filled Anti-Shiite Gathering in Indonesia," *Jakarta Globe*, April 20, 2014, http://www.thejakartaglobe.com/news/calls-jihad-purges-emerge-hate-filled-anti-shiite-gathering/. For recent Sunni–Shi'a dynamics in Southeast Asia and particularly on the rise of anti-Shi'a discourse, see Formichi, "Violence, Sectarianism and the Politics of Religion"; Rachmah Ida, "Cyberculture and Sectarianism in Indonesia: The Rise of Shia Media and Anti-Shia Online Movements," *Jurnal Komunikasi Islam*, 6:2 (2016): 194–215; Kamaruzzaman Bustamam-Ahmad, "From Power to Cultural Landscapes: Rewriting History of Shi'ah in Aceh," *Journal*

a global Sunni identity awakening of sorts that aligned with the policy prerogatives of regional powers; in the process, a newly salient Sunni sense of self at the societal level and the utility of sectarian identity at the state level have acted in mutually reinforcing and circular ways.[39]

The emergence of new media, social networking, and the revolutionary changes in the way information is generated, disseminated, censored and regulated were key variables in the sectarian contagion that followed 2003. User-generated platforms, privately owned satellite channels and social media enabled expression and connectivity in unprecedented ways, giving even the most local events a potentially transnational echo and thereby further facilitating the sect-coding of the region. Of utmost significance here is timing: the convergence and coincidence of the new Iraq's tortuous birth with the emergence of new media is an often overlooked but fundamental accelerant in the region-wide relevance that sectarian identity acquired after the Iraq war. The invasion of Iraq was followed by the cascading roll-out of the main social media platforms: after regime change in 2003 Facebook was launched in 2004, YouTube came online in 2005, and Twitter appeared in 2006. In other words, just as events in Iraq were kindling an unprecedented interest in sectarian dynamics and making people scrutinize sectarian relations as never before, the information landscape was altered beyond recognition in ways that amplified once marginal voices, accelerated the spread of information, and afforded all and sundry a new platform whose ramifications and workings are still being debated today. As a result, by the simple virtue of timing, sectarian polemicists, sectarian vitriol and sectarian violence were

---

of Indonesian Islam, 11:2 (Dec. 2017): 509–530. For recent Sunni–Shi'a dynamics in contemporary Europe, see Linge, "Sunnite-Shiite Polemics in Norway."

[39] For a broader discussion of Sunni identity after 2003, see Bernard Rougier, *The Sunni Tragedy in the Middle East: Northern Lebanon from al-Qaeda to ISIS* (Princeton: Princeton University Press, 2015), pp. 233–238; "Invention or Rediscovery? The Emergence of Sunni Identity in the 21st Century," Middle East Institute, NUS, Feb. 2017, https://www.youtube.com/watch?v=qSQPQxSCQro&list=PLMKn9 JnbU2xCLbUTwtpvFht-Wha4aUB93; Haddad, "A Sectarian Awakening"; Yassir al-Za'atra, "Tahwil al-Sunna ila Tai'fa" (Turning Sunnis into a sect), Al Jazeera, June 16, 2015, https://www.aljazeera.net/knowledgegate/opinions/2015/6/16/ تحويل-السنة-إلى-طائفة .

among the pioneering genres in social networking and user-generated media in the Arab world. This worked from above and from below, at a national level in individual countries and at a regional level. With the help of new media and the new information environment, and given that the sectarianization of the post-2003 landscape tied in with regional powers' interests in pushing back against Iran's advantage in Iraq, the sect-coding that began in Iraq cast an ever-expanding shadow over the region and beyond, as a result of which sectarian categories gained more relevance in colouring social and political horizons.

These innovations intensified the shock of sudden acquaintance with the sectarian other by eroding the censorship, long-standing taboos and conventions of political correctness that had obscured the full extent and political significance of sectarian heterogeneity, and by unshrouding what had previously been visible to group members alone. Previously, hearsay and polemics regarding egregious sect-specific practices or beliefs could be deflected with denials by the more ecumenical or less puritanical. Now, accusations often came complete with footage of what had previously been the preserve of group members or a subset of them. In no time, YouTube was filled with clips showcasing the worst of the sectarian other – be it with regard to doctrine, ritual, political views, or the endless stream of atrocities from Iraq's and, later on, Syria's sect-coded conflicts. This helped to further weaken the taboo surrounding discussions of sectarian categories, but it also deepened sectarian division and strengthened attachment to sectarian identity and sectarian solidarity. In the process, sectarian polemics acquired mainstream relevance. However, an important point to make about causality is that it was not a proliferation of hate preachers that sect-coded the post-2003 Arab world; rather, 2003 set in train a series of processes that served to increasingly sect-code or sectarianize regional developments and popular perception, thereby affording hate preachers – who have always existed – an unprecedented (albeit temporary) appeal and relevance. This further underlines the fact that sectarian entrenchment, today more than ever before given the information and communications revolution, is just as likely to be driven from below as from above. As we saw in chapter 2, the above–below binary should in any case be treated with caution given the circular interdependence of the two frames and the difficulty of disentangling them. By extension, in trying to understand the impact of social media, it should not come down to a question of the extent to which social media activity contributed to the sectarianization of the landscape versus the extent to which it was a reflection of processes already under way. Rather than two separate variables, these are circularly linked, interdependent sides of the same process. A further point about the impact of social media is the role that novelty and acculturation play: it takes time for people to understand new platforms, learn their flaws and perhaps take things with a pinch of salt. Novelty is also important when considering the shock value of the other's 'otherness'. What is controversial today can lose shock value as it becomes normalized over time and ceases to be a point of contestation. This will be explored in more detail in the following chapter, but suffice it to say here that much of what enraged public opinion after 2003 has been normalized – from sect-centric politics to public assertions of sectarian identity to variations in sect-specific beliefs and rituals.

Social media and user-generated platforms also played a role in facilitating the pervasive sect-coding that followed the sectarian wave after 2003. The matter of sect-coding – when is a corpse a Shi'a or Sunni victim, when is a demonstration a Sunni or Shi'a one, and so forth – is more than just a question of semantics and accuracy. Far more problematic is that it can distort dynamics by imposing upon them an otherwise unwarranted sectarian logic that, with time and in a climate as inflamed as that which followed the invasion of Iraq in 2003, is easily internalized and taken as fact. This does not mean that sect-coding is inherently problematic: at times, the vocabulary of sects and sectarian relations is inescapable. As argued in chapter 1, in some instances it would be misleading to avoid mentioning sectarian identity when describing or analysing a certain context. Contriving a sect-blind framing for 2003 and subsequent Iraqi developments, for example, would be counterfactual to the point of fantasy. The issue is therefore not whether we avoid or adopt the vocabulary of sects; rather, it is one of exercising caution and questioning assumptions – being allergic to the vocabulary of sects is as counterproductive as being obsessed by it. For instance, there is no denying that sectarian identity was a major part of the political contestation that followed regime change in Iraq. Yet not everything about post-2003 Iraq should be automatically assumed to warrant sect-coding. By the same token, Iraq's civil wars were undoubtedly sect-coded, but that does not mean that all violence in Iraq can be categorized a priori as 'sectarian violence' nor does it mean that one's sectarian identity governs all interactions. An illustrative example, one among many, is the November 2007 bombing of the Ghazil animal market in Baghdad: being a bombing of a popular civilian area, it was naturally blamed on the Islamic State in Iraq. That the Ghazil market is in a mixed but predominantly Shi'a area only served to reinforce this perception. However, there was speculation at the time that Shi'a militants were in fact behind the attack or that the bombing was the result of a dispute between criminal groups involved in the animal trade (of course these two possibilities are by no means mutually exclusive).[40] Similarly, a Shi'a government employee was assassinated in his home in early 2008; while his sectarian identity and his occupation made it easy to assume that this was a case of sectarian violence, it was later alleged that he was the victim of Shi'a militants who were punishing him for refusing to cooperate in granting their patrons lucrative government contracts. What these two examples, and countless others like them, illustrate is the ambiguity of violence and identity, and the caution that is needed when it comes to sect-coding and conventional wisdom.[41]

---

[40] This was not the only time the market had been bombed. The allegation that the attack was the result of competition between criminal groups over the animal trade was one that was widely discussed among Iraqis at the time – and one that shouldn't readily be dismissed. For reporting suggesting that it was the work of Sunni militants and another suggesting that it was Shi'a militants, see Stephen Farrell, "Bomb at a market shatters lull for Baghdad," *New York Times*, Nov. 24, 2007, https://www.nytimes.com/2007/11/24/world/middleeast/24iraq.html; "'Shia militia' behind Iraq blast," BBC News, Nov. 24, 2007, http://news.bbc.co.uk/2/hi/middle_east/7110988.stm.

[41] In that context it is interesting to note the case of the massacres of the Algerian civil war: it was widely assumed at the time that the perpetrators were Islamic militants and any suggestion that government forces bore responsibility for the massacres was often dismissed as an indulgence of baseless conspiracy theories. Since then, there has been considerable research into the subject that suggests pro-government forces being responsible for at least some massacres as part of their counterinsurgency campaign. See Youcef Bedjaoui, "On the Politics of Massacres," in *An Inquiry into the Algerian Massacres*, ed. Youcef Bedjaoui et al. (Geneva: Hoggar, 1999), pp. 312–320.

There are other problems with sect-coding beyond issues of accuracy. Firstly, the negativity associated with the vocabulary means that sect-coding is sometimes little more than an attempt to discredit and delegitimize opponents (see chapter 1). This can be seen where state forces are sect-coded ('Shi'a army', 'Sunni forces') and thereby denied the legitimacy that comes with being an arm of a recognized state.[42] More common, perhaps, is the sect-coding of political opposition the better to marginalize and discredit it – the cases of Bahrain and Syria being paradigmatic in that regard. Secondly, as has been far too commonly seen in coverage of the Middle East since 2003 and more so since 2011, once sect-coded, anything related to the subject is assumed to be 'sectarian'. Hence, in a sect-coded environment all interactions between Sunnis and Shi'as come to be framed as necessarily 'sectarian'.[43] Yet even at the height of a sect-coded civil war, we have to allow for the fact that individual Sunnis and Shi'as can interact with reference to other interests and other frames of identity. This applies to violence as well: there is a difference between Sunni–Shi'a violence and violence between people who happen to be Sunni and Shi'a; in the sect-coded conflicts of recent years violence was never entirely one or the other. This recalls the already mentioned tendency of speaking of sectarian harmony or coexistence, sectarian hate or conflict, while overlooking the more common setting of sectarian irrelevance.

Thirdly, a sect-coded environment disincentivizes political moderation. Rather, particularly when combined with insecurity and political uncertainty, a sect-coded environment is a recipe for zero-sum, alarmist politics revolving around artificially simplified and hardened categories that in normal times would have more ambiguity and permeability. The fact that after 2003 this was happening alongside the emergence of novel media sources and platforms further accentuated the issue, but social media and new technologies were not the cause of the region's sectarianization, even if they facilitated it. After all,

---

[42] Few examples are more illustrative in that regard than the delegitimization through sect-coding witnessed in Arabic media coverage of post-2003 Iraq. See Marc Lynch, "Sectarianism and the Campaign to Retake Fallujah," *Diwan*, Carnegie Middle East Center, June 17, 2016, https://carnegie-mec.org/diwan/63834?lang=en.

[43] This borrows from and mirrors the problems with race-coding as identified by Karen and Barbara Fields. Fields and Fields, *Racecraft*, pp. 115–117.

the impact of uncertainty and insecurity on communal relations is hardly a product of the Internet age. Yasmin Khan notes near-identical dynamics in the confusion and polarization that preceded Partition in South Asia: long-standing, layered and overlapping ideas about identity and intergroup relations are stripped back to more simplistic badges of allegiance – be it Hindu and Muslim in the run-up to 1947 or Sunni and Shi'a in the aftermath of 2003.[44] It is worth mentioning that, given its fundamentally relational nature, the process of sect-coding is as much about intra-group competition as it is about intergroup dynamics – a point well made by Byman in his treatment of the sectarian wave that followed 2003. The "competition in demonization," as he puts it, seeks to exclude the sectarian other and thicken sectarian boundaries and group cohesion, but at the same time this competition works internally among aspiring representatives of the sect who will seek to outflank their competitors in hawkishness.[45] Needless to say, while this is in evidence at times of heightened fear and division, the norms of unity and sectarian coexistence render such tactics ineffective in less charged times. The impact of violence can scarcely be overstated here: it inflames passions, deepens feelings of encirclement, and provides further disincentive for compromise. Again, social media played an outsized role in this regard. Reports of atrocities and other outrages often made it politically difficult to push for moderation at a time when the crowd was more likely to be baying for blood.[46]

Finally, sect-coding runs a high risk of being divisive in that it risks tying entitlement and political, social and economic goods to sectarian identity. Once institutionalized, such linkages become self-perpetuating and reify sectarian boundaries to the point of making

---

[44] Yasmin Khan, *The Great Partition: The Making of India and Pakistan* (New Haven: Yale University Press, 2008), p. 68. Of course, a major difference between the two cases is that this crisis-born deepening of communal divides resulted in a final break in South Asia.

[45] Byman, "Sectarianism Afflicts the New Middle East," p. 85.

[46] Again, social media may provide an accelerant but the role that violence plays in hardening positions is fairly obvious and long predates the Internet. To pick another parallel from Yasmin Khan's treatment of Partition, she argues that trust between the parties had largely collapsed by 1946 under the weight of graphic news of communal violence from northern India. Khan, *The Great Partition*, p. 62.

them relevant to most aspects of public life.[47] Another manifestation of the linkage between sectarian identity and political goods, one that has been particularly evident in the post-2003 era, is the pernicious dynamic of competing sectarian victimhoods.[48] Of course this is a common feature of conflict and identity politics generally, but it has been accentuated by the political and social capital that has come to be associated with a group being recognized as a victim in recent times.[49] Here 2003 is as good an illustration as any in that communal grievances (and particularly Shi'a and Kurdish victimhood) formed some of the foundational building blocks of the new order, with very divisive consequences. While victimhood had long been a defining pillar of Shi'a identity, it was only in the twenty-first century that a Sunni identity defined by victimhood was to emerge.[50] This

---

[47] The clearest expression of this is Lebanon where the linkage between sectarian identity and political goods is formally institutionalized. Indeed, in Lebanon, legally and administratively, one cannot be a citizen independently of sect or without a sectarian identity – a category that the Lebanese state applies to both intra- and inter-religious categories.

[48] Fanar Haddad, "Competing Victimhoods in a Sectarian Landscape," *Jadaliyya*, Nov. 1, 2016, http://www.jadaliyya.com/Details/33690/Competing-Victimhoods-in-a-Sectarian-Landscape.

[49] This is very well captured in the prolonged controversy over who was to be commemorated in the United States Holocaust Memorial Museum: 6 million Jews or a broader spectrum of 11 million victims. See Novick, *The Holocaust in American Life*, pp. 216–220. For a broader discussion of the politics of victimhood, see Ian Buruma, "The Joys and Perils of Victimhood," *New York Review of Books*, April 8, 1999; Pascal Bruckner, *The Tyranny of Guilt: An Essay on Western Masochism* (Princeton: Princeton University Press, 2010), pp. 114–115; Bradley Campell and Jason Manning, "Hate Crime Hoaxes Are More Common than You Think," *Quillette*, Feb. 22, 2019, https://quillette.com/2019/02/22/hate-crime-hoaxes-are-more-common-than-you-think/?fbclid=IwAR3iDzhs2F-0qozZatNoiziGLEITxo6xl2Co4y4V0qStED3y-Q1qgMgaoXs.

[50] There are exceptions, such as earlier Syrian Islamist polemics lamenting the plight of Sunnis in Syria. However, this discourse did not have the mainstream and regional salience that it was to acquire after 2003. For pre-2003 examples regarding Sunni victimization in Syria, see the tract written by Abu Mus'ab al-Suri in 2000, "Ahl al-Sunna fi-l-Sham fi Muwajahat al-Nusayriyya wa-l-Salibiyya wa-l-Yahud" (The Sunnis in Syria in Confronting the Nusayriyya, the Crusaders and the Jews), pp. 32–33. Available at https://www.cia.gov/library/abbottabad-compound/1D/1D8 B8465CBFC9E8BA7CB1DE89DCB8B25_ANUSIREA.pdf. Interestingly, Shi'as are

turned what was largely a one-sided and insular dynamic – Shi'ism's obsession with its own sense of victimhood – into a competition between sectarian victimhoods. Turning group victimhood into the coinage with which to claim a greater portion of shared social and political goods is inherently offensive and divisive. To quote Novick once again: "The assertion that the Holocaust is unique – like the claim that it is singularly incomprehensible or unrepresentable – is, in practice, deeply offensive. What else can all of this mean except 'your catastrophe, unlike ours, is ordinary; unlike ours is comprehensible; unlike ours is representable'."[51] This same tension underlay the way that Sunnis and Shi'as perceived the mounting costs of post-2003 sect-coded violence: each claiming to be the primary victim, each claiming the moral high ground, and each outraged that their sense of being uniquely victimized was not adequately recognized and validated. Needless to say, such a competition of communal, in this case sectarian, victimhood and the framing of justice and injustice in terms of Sunni–Shi'a identity cannot but perpetuate the salience of sectarian categories. To paraphrase Fields and Fields' critique of the champions of race-coded affirmative action, the obsession with sectarian victimhood, as with any group-specific victimhood, often means that those seeking closure or solutions are often unable to promote or even define justice except by enhancing the authority and prestige of sectarian identity: intentionally or otherwise, such forms of advocacy often end up pushing for the reallocation of injustice rather than its abolition.[52] This insight from critical race theorists working in an entirely different context perfectly encapsulates the problematic stance adopted by Iraqi Shi'a-centric actors after 2003, in which the legacy of 'sectarianism' was to be remedied through Shi'a ascendancy rather than through cross-sectarian (or indeed asectarian) conceptions of justice.

---

hardly mentioned at all. Where they do come up, it is in near-neutral terms even if they are clearly distinguished and separated from Sunnis (pp. 15–16 for example). The worst that is said about Shi'as in this tract is that they have masterminded a systematic proselytization campaign in Syria.

[51] Novick, *The Holocaust in American Life*, p. 9.

[52] Fields and Fields, *Racecraft*, p. 147.

Sectarian Identity and the 'Arab Spring'

The Iraq effect discussed thus far is necessary for understanding the environment in which the upheavals of the so-called 'Arab Spring' would unfold, particularly in contexts of long-standing sect-coded legacy issues and pre-existing tension between ruling regimes and sectarian outgroups. In far too many accounts, one encounters a rather strange conflation of the Arab uprisings with 'sectarianism': the latter is a characteristic feature of the former or the former plays an explanatory role in trying to understand the latter or some other supposedly organic link between the two. This grossly mischaracterizes the nature of the Arab uprisings and vastly inflates the role of sectarian identity in them and in the Middle East. After all, far from just a matter of sectarian competition or seeking redress for sect-coded grievances and righting sect-coded historical wrongs, the Arab uprisings represented a far broader struggle for political rights and a challenge to what had been considered immovable authoritarian regimes. In fact, the only places where sectarian identity played a central role in the narratives and counter-narratives of the uprisings were in countries with pre-existing sect-coded legacy issues, such as Bahrain and Syria. There are several dimensions to this: from below, protesters may be seeking redress for sect-specific grievances (discriminatory distribution of economic and political goods for example). Shi'as in Saudi Arabia, for instance, have a set of sect-specific, and perfectly legitimate, grievances such as state-sanctioned doctrinal anti-Shi'ism, in addition to more universal or sect-blind demands such as the call for a constitutional monarchy. Likewise, a cross-section of Bahrainis may rally in calling for political reform, but Bahraini Shi'as may also seek to redress sect-specific grievances such as discriminatory hiring practices in state institutions, particularly in the security establishment. Again, it should be perfectly legitimate to protest against discrimination, but the unjust reality is that sect-coding spells doom to the perceived national legitimacy of the activism of sectarian outgroups. None of this means that oppositional politics, even in sect-coded settings, are the preserve of sectarian outgroups. However, an important distinction is that sect-centricity is not central to the opposition of sectarian ingroups – after all, they do not feel their sectarian identity to be targeted by the state (to illustrate, Islamists

247

in Egypt may see the state as anti-Islamic or ungodly but will not see it as anti-Sunni). A common problem that emerges from this is the expectation or even demand that sectarian identity should hold similar irrelevance in the oppositional politics of sectarian outgroups. This is simply impractical in places with a sectarian issue like twenty-first-century Bahrain or Syria: after all, sectarian outgroups may pursue any number of civic, sect-blind political demands but they will also seek redress for sect-specific grievances and what they regard as sectarian discrimination – indeed, for sect-centric actors, the former is indistinguishable from (but does not obscure) the latter. An obvious parallel here is the difference between Black Lives Matter and All Lives Matter: the former is resistant to race-blindness (indeed, regards it as part of the problem) and insists on highlighting the racial element of police brutality while the latter seeks to underplay or dismiss the relevance of racial identity because of a dislike either of racial cleavages or of black activism.

This points to another dimension: from above, regimes will immediately reach for the tried and tested method of isolating and containing political threats emanating from sectarian outgroups by employing the vilifying and delegitimizing language of 'sectarianism' and foreign collusion, thereby portraying the political mobilization of sectarian outgroups as a threat not just to the regime but to the rest of the citizenry and to the nation as well. Notably, this narrative has a receptive constituency from below as a result of repeated exposure and popular, even if latent, prejudice. There is also the matter of historical memory: the 1976–82 Islamist uprising in Syria, transnational Shi'a militancy in the Gulf in the early 1980s, the uprising in Bahrain in the 1990s, to say nothing of the broader region since 1979 and more so since 2003, were divisive in sectarian terms and fed into a perception that the sectarian other (or at least significant elements among them) was capable of the malicious intent of which regimes were accusing them. There *was* an element of Islamist extremism and even a violent, explicitly anti-Alawi fringe in the Syrian uprising of the 1970s and 1980s; Shi'a activists and militants *had* sought to violently overthrow Gulf regimes in the 1980s in the cause of the Iranian Revolution. Unfortunately, these historical memories, regardless of their distance or their relevance, are successfully used by regimes to isolate, discredit and vilify any activism or political threat emanating from sectarian outgroups, and they also lend these regime maintenance strategies their efficacy and resonance with segments of popular opinion. Hence, in Bahrain, the Shi'a-majority composition of the protesters and the pre-existence of state–Shi'a tensions and sect-coded legacy issues were enough for the regime to frame the demonstrations of 2011 as an Iranian plot seeking to undermine Bahrain and the region and threatening sectarian war — a charge that was readily accepted by broad swathes of public opinion in Bahrain and in the wider Arab world.[53] In Saudi Arabia the protests in the Eastern Province were effectively isolated from the rest of the Saudi population and successfully framed as a nefarious movement by Shi'as and Iranians.[54] In Syria, the Sunni-majority composition of the protesters likewise allowed the regime to paint the demonstrators as terrorists and sectarian Islamist extremists.[55] Domestically and across

[53] "Al-Qaradhawi: thawrat al-Bahrain mathhabiyya tastahdif al-Sunna" (Al-Qaradhawi: Bahrain's revolution is sectarian and targets Sunnis), CNN, Feb. 7, 2013,http://archive.arabic.cnn.com/2011/bahrain.2011/3/19/qaradawi. bahrain/index.html; "Bahrain: Manama recalls ambassador to Iran, alleging 'blatant interference'," Los Angeles Times, March 15, 2011, https://latimesblogs. latimes.com/babylonbeyond/2011/03/bahrain-iran-diplomacy-ambassador-recall-.html; "Dawr Iran fi ahdath al-Bahrain" (Iran's role in Bahrain's events), Al Jazeera, Oct. 6, 2011, https://www.aljazeera.net/news/presstour/2011/10/6/ دور-إيران-في-أحداث-البحرين; "Al-Bahrain takhsha inshiqaqan ta'ifiyyan" (Bahrain fears a sectarian schism), Al Jazeera, Feb. 19, 2011, https://www.aljazeera.net/news/ arabic/2011/2/19/البحرين-تخشى-انشقاقا-طائفيا.

[54] Toby Matthiesen, "A 'Saudi Spring'? The Saudi Protest Movement in the Eastern Province 2011–2012," Middle East Journal, 66:4 (Autumn 2012): 628–659; Patrick Cockburn, "Saudi police 'open fire on civilians' as protests gain momentum," The Independent, Oct. 5, 2011, https://www.independent.co.uk/news/world/middle-east/saudi-police-open-fire-on-civilians-as-protests-gain-momentum-2365614. html; Ian Black, "Saudis crush dissent and point finger at Iran for trouble in Eastern Province," The Guardian, Oct. 6, 2011, https://www.theguardian.com/ world/2011/oct/06/saudi-crush-protests-iran.

[55] Oliver Holmes, "Assad's Devious, Cruel Plan to Stay in Power by Dividing Syria — and Why It's Working," New Republic, Aug. 15, 2011, https://newrepublic. com/article/93286/syria-assad-shabbiha-sectarianism; CNN, "June: Assad calls protestors terrorists," uploaded June 20, 2011, https://www.youtube.com/ watch?v=9BC-UHDBa34; Nour Ali, "Syrian regime steps up propaganda war amid bloody crackdown on protests," The Guardian, July 20, 2011, https://www. theguardian.com/world/2011/jul/20/syria-propaganda-protests-assad.

the region, these strategies met with significant success in contexts where there was a pre-existing sectarian issue in the form of sect-coded lines of political contestation.

Even then, however, it is important to recognize that sectarian identity was but one of an array of factors. Rather than framing the 'Arab Spring' and 'sectarianism' as somehow synonymous or organically linked, it would be more accurate to view the uprisings as another historical disruption; one that created the space for legacy issues – sect-coded or otherwise – to be openly contested within individual countries, leading to a region-wide sense of insecurity as the zones of conflict, vacuum and instability increased. Regimes across the region feared both domestic dissent and regional rivals (acting directly or through proxy) as potentially linked and existential threats. In terms of why this environment was sect-coded on a region-wide scale, again 2003 is a key causal factor in that it provided the backdrop for the intensification of the sectarian wave after 2011 and particularly after the uprisings in Bahrain and Syria ignited the sectarian tensions, fears and ambitions that had been accumulating since 2003.[56] In that sense, the sect-coded conflicts that followed the uprisings in Bahrain and Syria fitted into a pre-existing regional narrative of Sunni victimization and Sunni–Shi'a competition synonymized with Arab–Iranian rivalry, thereby further blurring the lines between geopolitics and sectarian identity, and between national and transnational distinctions. This narrative did not emerge in 2010/11 but rather it had already been set by events in and related to Iraq over the preceding eight years.[57] In this way, the reverberations of 2003 set the stage for what was to come after 2011. One can only wonder whether the sect-coding of the Syrian civil war would have been as locally and

---

[56] Christopher Phillips, *The Battle for Syria: International Rivalry in the New Middle East* (New Haven: Yale University Press, 2016), pp. 20–21, 130; Byman, "Sectarianism Afflicts the New Middle East," pp. 87–88.

[57] Of course, 2003 built on the pre-existing securitization of the sectarian divide following the Iranian Revolution of 1979. However, the narrative of regional Sunni victimhood only emerged after 2003. Beyond narrative construction, there are other factors relating to the Iraq debacle that enabled the sectarianization of the region after 2003 and 2011: for example, the militant networks and infrastructure created by the jihadi mobilization in Iraq, the reduced American footprint in the region, and the emergence of a multipolar and more anarchic order.

internationally successful without the backdrop of post-2003 Iraq; equally one wonders whether 2003 would have been sect-coded to the same extent without the Iranian Revolution.

The Arab uprisings were far too momentous an event to be restricted to the narrow frame of sectarian identity, which in any case was hardly a relevant factor, let alone a driving one, in North Africa. However, east of the Sinai, the Arab uprisings took on a rather different character, with one of the chief divergences between the 'Arab Spring' in the *maghrib* and the *mashriq* being the inflated role of sectarian identity in the latter.[58] Three factors account for this: firstly, the reverberations of Iraq over the preceding eight years were more keenly felt in the *mashriq* because of proximity, the existence of sizeable Shi'a populations and sect-coded political contestation in several countries in the *mashriq*, and the outsized place of Iran in regional threat perception. Under the long shadow of 2003, these factors inflamed the salience of sectarian categories and the relevance of Sunni and Shi'a identities in regional threat perception, popular and populist prejudice, and regime maintenance strategy. Secondly, the Arab countries that have a Sunni–Shi'a 'sectarian issue' – those with sect-coded legacy issues and sect-coded political contestation at the national level – are all in the *mashriq*. Finally regimes in the *mashriq* had a strong interest in augmenting – if not creating – the sectarian dimension of the uprisings once they reached their shores.[59] This was most starkly illustrated in the cases of Bahrain, Syria and Saudi Arabia, and in the divisive impact of the uprisings in the former two on sectarian relations throughout the region.

The first protests began in Tunisia in December 2010, resulting in the downfall of the Ben Ali regime the following month. Over the

---

[58] This point was made early on by Cockburn, who noted that what at the time was seen as the success of the democratic uprisings in Tunisia, Egypt and Libya was faltering east of Egypt. Patrick Cockburn, "Muslim sectarianism will halt democracy in its tracks," *The Independent*, Oct 2, 2011, http://www.independent. co.uk/opinion/commentators/patrick-cockburn-muslim-sectarianism-will-halt-democracy-in-its-tracks-2364259.html.

[59] On regional powers and their reinforcement of the sectarian divide for geopolitical purposes, see Luomi, "Sectarian Identities or Geopolitics?" pp. 5, 16, 47–48.

course of the next six months, almost every country in the Arab world had an 'Arab Spring' moment. The wave of uprisings quickly spread east of the Sinai with protests breaking out in Yemen in late January 2011 followed by Lebanon, Palestine and Jordan in the same month. However, in some cases these were sporadic displays of political and economic dissatisfaction rather than sustained protests on a par with what had taken place in Egypt and Tunisia over the course of the preceding six weeks. In February the 'Arab Spring' began its accelerated sectarianization when the wave of protests reached Bahrain, followed by Saudi Arabia and Syria in March.[60] While sectarian identity had played little or no role in the 'Arab Spring' dynamics of any other country, these three cases fed into an already burgeoning sense of securitized sectarian competition at a domestic level and also in a transnational sense in the form of rivalry with Iran and fear of Iranian designs on the region following 2003. By 2011 the idiom of 'sectarianism' had already gained region-wide currency, which could be easily appropriated in pursuit of domestic and regional political goals far removed from any direct relation with sectarian identity itself. The already mentioned example of anti-Shi'ism in post-2011 Egypt is a case in point. More than just a doctrinal issue, it was as much about regional rivalries as it was about domestic politics: the anti-Shi'a rhetoric of Saudi-backed Egyptian Salafis after 2011 sought to derail improved bilateral relations between Cairo and Tehran; and, on the domestic front, it was also a tactic aimed at outflanking the Muslim Brotherhood and presenting Salafis as a viable and more Islamically legitimate alternative.[61]

Where possible, the heightened relevance of sectarian identity was exploited by various regimes as they tried to navigate the turmoil of the 'Arab Spring'. As was only to be expected, regimes across the region scrambled to discredit domestic mass protest by issuing proclamations of national or religious or ethnic excommunication: the protests are composed of foreign infiltrators, they are terrorists, they are Islamic

---

[60] For an interactive timeline of the uprisings in 2010 and 2011, see Garry Blight, Sheila Pulham and Paul Torpey, "Arab Spring: An interactive timeline of Middle East protests," *The Guardian*, Jan. 5, 2012, https://www.theguardian.com/world/interactive/2011/mar/22/middle-east-protest-interactive-timeline.

[61] Saleh and Kraetzschmar, "Politicized Identities, Securitized Politics," pp. 548, 556.

extremists, they are a prelude to chaos, and so forth. In addition to this, some regimes had the demographic or political backdrop that enabled them to use the vocabulary of sects to isolate, discredit and neutralize domestic opposition by casting it as 'sectarian'. Though Ben Ali could hardly discredit Tunisian protesters by labelling them 'sectarian',[62] it was an effective tactic against sectarian outgroups in places like Syria, Bahrain, Saudi Arabia or Iraq where discrediting the activism of sectarian outgroups has long been common practice.[63]

The effectiveness of the sectarian card is largely dependent on the pre-existence of a national-level 'sectarian issue' that, even if dormant or out of fashion, can be reawakened and repurposed to meet the political needs of the moment or that can be conflated with the transnational dimension of sectarian dynamics in the form of Arab–Iranian rivalry. In this way sectarian identity can be used to divide loyalties by tapping into divergent historical memories and sect-specific narratives of national history and political community. Given the region-wide and unfocused consternation at 'sectarianism' after 2003, this proved to be a most effective way for regimes to counter the threat of popular unrest: accusing protesters in Benghazi of being al-Qaeda extremists and foreigners – as former Libyan leader Mu'ammar al-Qaddafi did – did not have the same resonance or salience as, for example, accusing Syrian protesters of being Sunni fundamentalist

---

[62] For a hilarious demonstration of how ill-fitting such a tactic would be in North Africa, see Egyptian satirist Bassem Youssef's lampooning of a ridiculously choreographed attempt at constructing a narrative of Iranian penetration (with the help of "Hizbullah, Qatar, Palestine and some Shi'a Iraqis") during the Egyptian demonstrations of 2011. "Al-Barnamaj? Ma'a Bassem Youssef ... al-Sharifa Majida wa-l-Sharif Mubarak" (Al-Barnamaj? With Bassem Youssef ... Sharifa Majida and Sharif Mubarak), uploaded Oct. 7, 2011, https://www.youtube.com/watch?v=-4CUdoTgGys.

[63] Amira Muhammad, "Al-Su'udiyya tal'ab bi-l-waraqa al-Shi'iyya ... wa-l-Islamiyyun fazza'at al-hukkam" (Saudi Arabia plays the Shi'a card and the Islamists are the rulers' scarecrow), *Deutsche Welle*, March 11, 2011, https://www.dw.com/ar/السعودية-تلعب-بالورقة-الشيعية-والإسلاميون-فزاعة-الحكام/a-14906452; Matthiesen, "Sectarianization as Securitization," in *Sectarianization*, ed. Hashemi and Postel; in the same volume, see Pinto, "The Shattered Nation," and al-Rasheed, "Sectarianism as Counter-Revolution." See also Jones, "Contesting the Iranian Revolution," in *Gulfization*, ed. Jones et al.

extremists. The latter case ties into a long history of divisive identity politics and a more recent history of sect-coded political opposition and sect-coded militancy (including explicitly anti-Alawi splinters) which was ferociously put down by the regime.[64] This recent history cast a long, radicalizing, divisive and sectarianizing shadow on all sides, driven by the shock and memory of episodes of targeted sectarian violence, such as the 1979 Aleppo Artillery Academy massacre in which anti-regime militants from the Muslim Brotherhood splinter group 'the Fighting Vanguards' singled out Alawi cadets for execution or the later levelling of the city of Hama by regime forces in 1982. Not for nothing have some scholars cast these episodes as irreversible turning points separating two irreconcilable eras in the history of sectarian relations in Syria.[65] The point here is that in such cases, 'sectarianism' as a regime maintenance tool becomes a viable and potent option given that it taps into popular fears and prejudices relating to recent and very divisive episodes of national history. Hence its successful usage by the Bahraini, Saudi Arabian and Syrian regimes in 2011: all three regimes inflated the relevance of the sectarian identity of the protesters (or a majority of them) and linked it with the associated prejudices that had long been perpetuated by state and society – be it the conflation of Sunni activism and Sunni Islamists with violent extremists in Syria or the conflation of Shi'a activism and Shi'a Islamists with Iran.[66]

---

[64] For the uprising in Syria in the late 1970s and early 1980s, see Lefevre, *Ashes of Hama*, chapter 6; Seale, *Asad*, pp. 320–338; Van Dam, *The Struggle for Power in Syria*, chapters 7–8.

[65] Yassin al-Haj Salih described the Artillery Academy massacre as separating two stages of Syrian history where "sectarian problems" are concerned. Al-Haj Salih, "al-Ta'ifiyya wa-l-Siyasa fi Syria," in *Nawasib wa Rawafidh*, ed. Saghiya, p. 64. Likewise, Van Dam writes of it leaving an "ineffaceable mark on the relations between Alawis and Islamist Sunnis." Van Dam, *Destroying a Nation*, p. 50. Ende argues that events in the 1980s had an important transnational dimension in that many Syrians saw a 'Shi'a regime' suppressing a Sunni majority with the support of an Iranian theocracy. Ende, "Sunni Polemical Writings on the Shi'a," in *The Iranian Revolution*, ed. Menashri, p. 226.

[66] For example, Cockburn, "Saudi police 'open fire on civilians'"; Bill Law, "Police brutality turns Bahrain into 'island of fear'," BBC News, April 7, 2011, https://www.bbc.co.uk/news/world-middle-east-12975832; Patrick Cockburn, "Bahrain: The divided kingdom," *The Independent*, Aug. 8, 2011; Holmes, "Assad's Devious, Cruel Plan to Stay in Power by Dividing Syria"; CNN, "June: Assad calls protesters terrorists."

This very quickly developed a logic of its own, which was used to frame internal political contestation, overseas interventions and transnational solidarities. The Gulf Cooperation Council's deployment of its military arm, Peninsula Shield Force, to quell the Bahraini uprising in 2011 is one such example.[67] However, nowhere was the language of sectarian solidarities more evident than in Syria, where the war strengthened perceptions of a Sunni–Shi'a regional conflict. Regional powers facilitated the flooding of foreign militants into Syria to fight the regime and lent their support to anti-regime insurgents while Iran's and particularly Lebanese Hizbullah's involvement in the conflict went a long way towards further sect-coding the Syrian civil war and validating the narrative of a regional Sunni–Shi'a struggle.[68]

The recent political history of Syria and Bahrain had lent sectarian identity a measure of political relevance and rendered the 'Arab Spring' susceptible to sect-coding in these settings. While this does not mean that all Syrians and Bahrainis viewed politics through the prism of sectarian identity, it does mean that, in the early twenty-first century, a critical mass of at least one sectarian group within these national settings viewed sectarian identity as intertwined with questions of political power and regime legitimacy. This has a profound impact on perceptions towards sect-coded oppositional activism. While sectarian ingroups in such environments will not necessarily feel advantaged by their sectarian identity, enough of them might accord the regime some measure of legitimacy which, no matter how residual, ties them to its continuation and makes them view its overthrow with trepidation, particularly if political change is linked to sectarian outgroups.[69]

---

[67] On 14 March 2011, Saudi-led Peninsula Shield Force units crossed the King Fahad Causeway to put down the Bahraini uprising under the guise of countering Iranian intervention – for which scant evidence was ever presented. See Louer, "Sectarianism and Coup-Proofing Strategies in Bahrain"; Wehrey, *Sectarian Politics in the Gulf*, pp. 81–94; Ethan Bronner and Michael Slackman, "Saudi troops enter Bahrain to put down unrest," *New York Times*, March 14, 2011, https://www.nytimes.com/2011/03/15/world/middleeast/15bahrain.html.

[68] On the impact of Hizbullah's role in the Syrian conflict on sectarian relations and the sect-coding of the Syrian civil war, see Phillips, *The Battle for Syria*, pp. 157–159.

[69] For example, on Alawi solidarity with the regime in Syria, see Nir Rosen, "Assad's Alawites: The guardians of the throne," Al Jazeera, Oct. 11, 2011; Goldsmith,

This divergence in views about regime legitimacy and its linkage (albeit imperfect) with sectarian identity was a particularly vivid and destructive avatar of the sectarian wave in Iraq, Syria, Bahrain and Saudi Arabia, to greatly divisive effect. In such cases, people who have had little sympathy towards imperfect, failing and authoritarian regimes may, in times of sect-coded crisis, come to accept them, despite their shortcomings, as the guarantors not just of national welfare but of communal welfare as well. A particularly virulent strain of this stance is that which frames Bashar al-Assad and the Syrian Ba'th as defenders of secularism, guarantors of the safety of minority groups, and the surest defence against 'sectarianism' (as embodied, in this discourse, in Sunni extremism). This argument plays on communal fears, vilifies all Sunni activism, and also serves several distinct agendas, not least of which is that of the Syrian regime's own survival.[70] Whether in Syria or elsewhere, the intertwinement (albeit imperfect) of sectarian identity with divergent views of regime legitimacy transforms views of regime survival in the face of a sect-coded challenge into a zero-sum issue whereby one sect is approximated with the state and the other with the opposition, and everyone is expected to play these simplified roles or risk being accused of national and communal treason. Support or opposition to the regime becomes synonymous with loyalty to the group and to the nation-state, regardless of whether a given regime has any genuine grassroots popularity. Hence, sectarian ingroup support for a regime in the face of a sect-coded challenge is as much a reflection of their fear of outgroup activism as a defence of institutional privilege. Of course, from the regime's point of view this is precisely the point of

"Alawi Diversity and Solidarity," in *The Alawis of Syria*, ed. Kerr and Larkin. For the Bahraini example, see Gengler, "The Political Economy of Sectarianism," in *Beyond Sunni and Shia*, ed. Wehrey, p. 201. For Sunni Iraqi views towards the uprisings of 1991, see Haddad, *Sectarianism in Iraq*, pp. 127–132. By the same token, Shi'a Iraqis in post-2003 Iraq have been inclined to believe that Sunni political opposition is cover for Ba'thist revanchists or sectarian jihadists.

[70] See Christopher Phillips, "The World Abetted Assad's Victory in Syria," *The Atlantic*, Aug. 4, 2018; Goldsmith, "Alawi Diversity and Solidarity," in *The Alawis of Syria*, ed. Kerr and Larkin; Majid Rafizadeh, "For Syria's minorities, Assad is security," Al Jazeera, Sept. 16, 2011; Abed L. Azab, "Anti-Assad? You are supporting the murder of Christians," *Haaretz*, April 16, 2017.

the sectarian card. Few cases are more bluntly illustrative than Bahrain in that regard, where Sunni mobilization against the Bahraini regime has become increasingly difficult in the wake of the uprising of 2011 owing not just to rentier calculations but also to the fact that dissent is increasingly associated with Shi'a mobilization.[71]

Does the preceding mean that the sectarianization of the Arab uprisings – from below or from above – was an inevitability? In a way, it does but not for the reasons imagined by primordialists or Orientalists or maximalists. Rather than innate antagonisms, ancient hatreds or doctrinal incompatibility, the reason that the sectarianization of the upheavals of 2011, at least where Bahrain, Saudi Arabia and Syria were concerned, was something of an inevitability was due to very recent history spanning less than half a century and accentuated by the post-2003 environment.[72] In other words, rather than age-old historical animosities or intractable doctrinal conflicts, the high risk of sect-coding in the early twenty-first century was the result of the particular enabling environment of the time and recent national and regional history. To take the Syrian example again, domestic power relations (state and opposition) were sect-coded to a significant extent given the role of Alawi solidarity in a personalized, under-institutionalized system based on patronage and informal procedures, on the one hand, and the prominence of Sunni Islamism in the Syrian opposition, on the other.[73] Events in Iraq had already laid the groundwork for accelerated sectarian entrenchment and jihadi mobilization and had nurtured sect-coded fears and ambitions related to Iranian expansion (itself a variable of fluctuating salience since 1979). Along comes a historical disruption – the 'Arab Spring' – that heightens the perceived possibility of the regime's overthrow and, by extension, sharpens the regime's threat perception. Given the pre-existence of sect-centric actors and

---

[71] Gengler, "The Political Economy of Sectarianism," in *Beyond Sunni and Shia*, ed. Wehrey, p. 201; Courtney Freer, "Challenges to Sunni Islamism in Bahrain since 2011," Carnegie Middle East Center, March 6, 2019, https://carnegie-mec.org/2019/03/06/challenges-to-sunni-islamism-in-bahrain-since-2011-pub-78510.

[72] Byman, "Sectarianism Afflicts the New Middle East," p. 88; Van Dam, *Destroying a Nation*, pp. 68–74.

[73] Hinnebusch, "Syria's Alawis and the Ba'ath Party," in *The Alawis of Syria*, ed. Kerr and Larkin.

the recent history of sect-coded contestation of power, it was certainly inevitable that such actors would use the openings afforded by 2011 to assert a sect-centric frame of anti-regime activism. Of course, sect-centric actors were not the only ones rising against the regime, but the trepidation that such actors caused in some sections of society meant that their presence easily overshadowed less extreme voices – at least in the perception of those who felt threatened by sect-centric opposition movements. In any case, and for the same reason, the regime would inevitably have tried to create the impression that the protests were not a legitimate Syrian challenge to an odious authoritarian regime but a Sunni-centric, extremist, Islamist, anti-Syrian plot orchestrated by foreign powers. There was also a regional dimension to the likelihood of conflict in Syria being quickly sect-coded: events in Iraq, a rising fear of Shi'a proselytization in Syria throughout the early 2000s, fears of Iranian expansionism, a growing regional narrative of Sunni victimization and sectarian division, the Syrian regime's ties with Iran and Hizbullah (and the role the latter two would play in supporting the Syrian regime), and the regional utility of framing the Syrian conflict as a subsidiary of a broader conflict between Arab Sunnis and Shi'ism/Iran. Combined with deeper legacy issues specific to Syria, this made any major upheaval in 2011 highly prone to sect-coding. Writing in 2010, Nibras Kazimi described Syria's propensity for sect-coded division at that stage (and not in any primordialist or essentialist sense) in remarkably prescient terms:

> These samplings of embittered [sect-coded] sentiments do not mean that any of these people will pick up arms sometime soon. They do, however, capture an increasingly dominant narrative of sectarianism among Syria's population that could signify that those expressing such sectarian frustrations and fears would not stand in the way of either jihadists fighting against the regime, or the regime fighting back.[74]

It should be emphasized that the focus here on the national dimension should not blind us to the transnational dimension: indeed, it is precisely the contours of the national dimension that facilitated

---

[74] Kazimi, *Syria through Jihadist Eyes*, p. 75. One gets a similar sense of rising sect-coded fears in Syria from Pierret's 2012 essay, "Karbala in the Umayyad Mosque."

the internationalization of these conflicts and the transnationalization of the sect-coded contestation of national politics in places like Iraq, Bahrain and Syria. Further, the instrumentalization of sectarian identity on the home front was mirrored in foreign policy and the transnational dimension: even though the Arab uprisings were not just or even primarily about sectarian identity, they did create instability, uncertainty and vacuums that regional actors tried to turn to their advantage. Where possible, this was pursued by playing the sectarian card – for example, where Iran emerges as a strong contender or where a given setting is seen as vulnerable to Iranian penetration. In addition, there can be no separating different national contexts given how the narrative of sectarian victimhood and sectarian competition had been internationalized so that each national context became an act in a broader Sunni–Shi'a conflict. Nowhere was this clearer than in the destructive way in which the Syrian conflict came to be seen by sect-centric actors across the region as either a threat or an opportunity for their political struggles at home. To illustrate, when the Syrian regime seemed most imperilled, regional Shi'a-centric actors accelerated their support while their Sunni-centric counterparts felt confident that post-2003 Iranian gains and the gains of Shi'a-centric actors in the region could be rolled back. This much was clear in the reflections of a Sunni-centric Iraqi politician in 2012, in which he connected the Syrian conflict with sectarian dynamics in Iraq and broader transnational trends:

> once the change happens in Syria [i.e. the fall of the Assad regime] and when Iran is cornered through sanctions – and Sunnis are relying on this scenario a lot; they are hoping for a change in the regional map. This Iranian expansion will end soon at which point [Iraqi] Shi'a politicians will realize that the [Iranian] support they used to get and their feeling empowered will decrease. At that point they will be more reasonable.[75]

The Perils of Sect-Coding

One commonly hears retrospective cynicism towards, or rejection of, the uprisings in Bahrain and Syria on the grounds that they were

---

[75] Interview, Iraqi politician (who requested anonymity), Baghdad, Feb. 2012.

'sectarian'. Indeed, in many cases this was not even retrospective and was rather a knee-jerk reaction to the uprisings as they emerged: I recall hearing a senior Shi'a Iraqi lawmaker publicly referring to the 'Arab Spring' – and particularly in relation to Syria – as the Salafi Spring (*al-rabi' al-Salafi*) as early as February 2012. Likewise, Arab media (and especially social media) coverage of the protests in Bahrain was, from the outset, adamant in framing them as products of Iranian machinations far removed from the otherwise positively portrayed 'Arab Spring'. These are symptoms of a broader environment that was obsessed with sect-coding, whereby political contestation must necessarily be 'sectarian' unless the protagonists share the same sectarian affiliation. While the post-2003 environment, the sectarian wave and the 'Arab Spring' vastly accelerated this unhelpful propensity, it was hardly new: as we have seen, it is standard practice to use the negatively charged vocabulary of 'sectarianism' to discredit the activism of sectarian outgroups: their sectarian otherness suffices to cast them as 'sectarian' and hence prevent them from attaining national acceptance. This is as good an example as any of how the false dichotomization of 'national' and 'sectarian' that was discussed in chapter 4 is routinely weaponized for political purposes. A pressing question to ask in that regard is what Sunnis in Syria, Shi'as in Bahrain, Sunnis in post-2003 Iraq, Shi'as in pre-2003 Iraq, and so forth must do to avoid their political activism and their political dissent being sect-coded and hence doomed to stigmatization. The notion that for political expression to be legitimate the sectarian identity of its proponents must be invisible is patently unworkable. This shibboleth of Arab political correctness has exacted a heavy toll on the political freedom of the region and, given that the mere sight of what are often unavoidable displays of sectarian affiliation can be enough to spell doom for budding political movements, it has stood in the way of national political mobilization in contexts of high sectarian heterogeneity. In his study of sectarian dynamics in the 'Arab Spring', Heiko Wimmen makes a similar argument, pointing out that religious space or religious symbolism is sometimes unavoidable (the role of Friday prayers in offering an otherwise impossible space for mass gatherings, for example). This, he argues, meant that even original and creative forms of public action "were always accompanied by protest repertoires steeped in religious imagery ... But since religiously inspired repertoires and places of worship revealed sectarian affiliations, they also identified the movements with sectarian groups, again raising doubts about the sincerity of their inclusive discourse."[76] Again we see the deleterious impact of the widespread allergy to expressions of sectarian identity and sectarian difference — be it in the name of unity, modernity, secularism, regime maintenance or plain old sectarian bigotry.

Similarly, in his examination of the 'Arab Spring' in Bahrain, Toby Matthiesen wonders why the protests of 2011 were so quickly sect-coded as 'Shi'a protests'. As he points out, given that most Bahrainis are Shi'a, it should not be surprising — let alone grounds for presuming a transnational conspiracy — that most of the protesters were Shi'a.[77] In their earlier phases the protests even had cross-sectarian participation and the demands were consistently focused on universal political rights rather than any sect-specific agenda. Matthiesen notes that as the protests progressed "some of the imagery became related to the history of Shi'a political mobilization in Bahrain."[78] Yet this raises the same question: if the demographic realities of Bahrain make the mostly Shi'a composition of the protesters unsurprising, does it not follow that their drawing on the symbols of previous mobilizations should likewise be neither surprising nor controversial? This speaks directly to Wimmen's point regarding the consequences of revealing or displaying sectarian affiliation — something that is all but inevitable without an absurd level of social, political and historical amnesia. Unfortunately for reformists in Bahrain, the term 'Shi'a protests' created an instant cognitive separation between what was happening in Bahrain and what had taken place earlier in North Africa and facilitated their conflation among significant sections of Arab public opinion with Iranian plotting and the dreaded 'sectarianism'.[79] Something similar happened when

---

[76] Heiko Wimmen, "Divisive Rule: Sectarianism and Power Maintenance in the Arab Spring: Bahrain, Iraq, Lebanon and Syria," German Institute for International and Security Affairs, Research Paper no. 4, March 2014, p. 26.

[77] Matthiesen, *Sectarian Gulf*, p. 12.

[78] Ibid., p. 13.

[79] An illustrative example is Salafi preacher Adnan al Ar'ur's comments made soon after the start of the protests in Bahrain. In a talk show on Salafi satellite channel Safa he was asked whether the protests in Bahrain were an example of

protests erupted in Syria: the majority of the protesters were Sunni but so is the demographic make-up of Syrians. That Islamists formed a part of the spectrum of political activism was likewise all but inevitable given the history of Islamist activism against the Assads' regime. The protests were quickly sect-coded both by their detractors and by the more extreme elements of the Syrian opposition, thereby facilitating the wholesale conflation of the anti-regime uprising with religious extremism and identity politics, and drawing the light away from other issues at play and the broader spectrum of actors involved beyond Islamist extremists.

Interestingly, defenders of the Bahraini and Syrian protesters sometimes end up formulating their position according to the same flawed logic that looks upon expressions of sectarian identity or of sect-centricity with fatal suspicion; the difference is that defenders deny sectarian identity any place whatsoever in the protests of 2011 whereas detractors deny that anything but sectarian identity was at issue. Here we are taken back to the problems discussed in chapters 1 and 2: why is sect-centricity viewed as inherently problematic or incriminating, and why is it seen as such a damning accusation (usually formulated ambiguously as "the protests were 'sectarian'"). Indeed, given the undisputed existence of structural sectarian discrimination in places like Bahrain or Syria – be it through formal institutions or through patronage networks and their linkages to the apparatus of the state – can sect-centricity be completely divorced from civic, nationalist political activism? Indeed, *should* it be divorced? Why should members of disadvantaged sectarian outgroups be expected to refrain from raising a sect-specific issue (government neglect of sectarian outgroups or discriminatory employment practices aimed at them, for example) while engaging in broader civic activism in pursuit of political rights within a national framework? Why should seeking redress for sectarian discrimination completely and fatally sect-

---

people demanding their rights or evidence of a foreign plot. Naturally he insisted that they were the latter, calling the protests barbaric, seditious and anarchic, and explicitly distinguishing what was happening in Bahrain from what was happening in the rest of the Arab world. "Mudhaharat al-Bahrain wa-ta'liq al-Shaikh Adnan al-Ar'ur" (Bahrain's demonstrations and Shaikh Adnan al-Ar'ur's comments), uploaded Feb. 23, 2011, https://www.youtube.com/watch?v=8E4AhZ4KdD8.

code an otherwise civic political protest and turn it into a 'sectarian protest'? Rather than surrendering to the same flawed logic that places an impractical tax on sectarian identity and its expression, defenders of Syrian and Bahraini protesters would do better to push back and question why seeking redress for structural sectarian discrimination should be equated with 'sectarianism' and why it is we should accept that such demands are different from the demands of national, secular, civic, political or any other positively charged description of people demanding political rights.

7

IRAQ, 2003–2018
SECTARIAN IDENTITY AND THE CONTESTATION OF
THE STATE

Post-2003 Iraq is a perfect case study with which to demonstrate many of the themes and concepts discussed throughout this book. Firstly, Iraqi sectarian relations between 2003 and 2018 reveal the redundancy of the term 'sectarianism' and its inability to fully encapsulate Sunni–Shi'a dynamics, let alone explain them. Applying an unchanging 'sectarianism' – however defined – to nearly two decades of social and political history cannot but fail to grasp the considerable volatility inherent in sectarian dynamics and the shifting social salience, political relevance, meaning, content and utility of sectarian categories over the course of fifteen years of upheaval. By extension, secondly, the case of Iraq underlines the complexity of sectarian identity and sectarian relations and the fact that they are beyond the analytic and explanatory capacity not just of the term 'sectarianism' but of any framing that reduces sectarian dynamics to monochrome conceptions along the lines surveyed in chapter 2. Accordingly, the example of post-2003 Iraq highlights the importance of adopting a multidimensional approach that can capture and convey the layered nature of sectarian identities along the lines discussed in chapters 3 and 4. After all, post-2003 Iraqi sectarian dynamics were not just a product of top-down elite manipulation any more than they were solely a product of pent-up legacy issues. The relevance of sectarian identity was driven by a broad spectrum of actors, drivers and dynamics: top-down as well as bottom-up factors, Iraqi as much as regional and international actors. Rather than just being a matter of religious beliefs or political contestation or any other singular frame, sectarian identity operates at the multiple, overlapping and mutually reinforcing levels identified in this book: doctrinal, subnational, national and transnational. It is impossible to understand the role of sectarian identity in post-2003 Iraq on the basis of a single dimension to the exclusion of all others. Finally, post-2003 Iraq is an excellent case study with which to demonstrate the fluidity and variable salience of sectarian identity. Importantly, sectarian dynamics did not travel in a singular direction: alongside episodes of entrenchment and polarization, a less scrutinized feature of this period is the instances where sectarian identity lost political relevance and where sectarian entrenchment waned. Indeed, at the time of writing sectarian identity seems less relevant than at any time since 2003.

This chapter will explore the shifting relevance of sectarian identity in Iraq since 2003. In doing so it will chart the various phases that Iraqi sectarian relations have gone through between 2003 and 2018. What emerges are ebbs and flows in the intensity and salience of sectarian competition in post-2003 Iraq; or, put another way, the oscillations in what can be termed the tension between Shi'a-centric state-building and Sunni rejection.[1] Briefly, the former involves ensuring that the central levers of the state are in Shi'a-centric hands and that Shi'a identities are represented and empowered. What is referred to here as Shi'a-centric state-building encompasses a spectrum of positions that, at heart, aim at reifying the primacy and seniority of Shi'as in Iraq's multicommunal framework. Sunni rejection, on the other hand, is the spectrum encompassing the Sunni-centric pushback against this – from begrudging accommodation all the way to anti-state violence. To give an example from the non-violent end of the spectrum, speaking in 2011 Sunni-centric politician Adnan al-Dulaimi described the shift in the official position of many Sunni-centric actors towards federalism – from opponents to advocates – as a reflection of the desire to "weaken

---

[1] For a broader discussion, see Haddad, "Shi'a-Centric State-Building and Sunni Rejection."

the central government which is dominated by the Shi'ite parties since strengthening the government is not in the interests of the Sunnis."[2] The structural flaws in Iraqi parliamentary politics, in this case the absence of a formal opposition, make such a stance problematic.

As will be seen, the contours and relevance of the interplay between Shi'a-centric state-building and Sunni rejection have changed considerably over the course of the post-2003 era. Importantly, the waxing and waning of this interplay over the years are as much a function of the evolution of the broader enabling environment (domestically and regionally) as they are a result of anything particularly unique to or inherent in sectarian identity. The uncertainty, the violence and the vacuum that followed the invasion of Iraq in 2003 created an environment in which even the most basic parameters of social and political life were contested and renegotiated and where what would ordinarily be considered fantastical – say, setting up an 'Islamic state' – suddenly appeared possible. For reasons that were discussed in the previous chapter and that will be expanded upon below, coming as it did in 2003, recent Iraqi and regional history made such a moment of upheaval – such a historical disruption – highly liable to sect-coding. Here, it is important to consider the difference between, on the one hand, what is a reflection of broad-based pent-up popular sentiment or organic political trends and, on the other, what is an example of fringe elements taking advantage of a peculiarly enabling environment to assert their otherwise unusual and aberrant views and visions. This is not always an easy task but it is an important one, for it can help us avoid the pitfall of making unfounded social and political generalizations and normative deductions based on the extremes that flourish in unusual times. Complicating matters further is the fact that in a climate of fear and uncertainty, the extremist fringe can tap into the darker corners of popular sentiment, ultimately normalizing what would ordinarily be unacceptable to the mainstream. In a nutshell: pre-existing sect-coded political contestation, the existence of contradictory if not antagonistic sect-coded narratives of state, faith and society, and long-standing sect-coded prejudices and stereotypes are clearly not a bar to sectarian coexistence (and, more importantly, sectarian irrelevance) on their

---

[2] Quoted in Osman, *Sectarianism in Iraq*, p. 249.

own nor are they enough to empower sectarian fringe movements.[3] However, combined with the appropriate enabling environment, they can become more relevant in governing intergroup relations and perceptions of self and other, thereby bridging, even if temporarily, the gap between fringe and mainstream – something the former is likely to pursue by evoking the fear and uncertainty that broaden their appeal and utility to the latter thereby reinforcing the idea that competing groups (Sunnis and Shi'as, black and white, etc.) are fatally incompatible.[4] Again the enabling environment is key: in 2003 and for many years thereafter, Iraq suffered from state collapse and a profound uncertainty within which sect-centric actors fought to redraw the parameters of state and society in conditions of extreme violence and insecurity, ultimately leading to sect-coded civil war.[5] In the process, sectarian categories – 'Sunni', 'Shi'a' – gained an unusual emotional currency that turned them into slogans whose meaning was intertwined with an array of vague and poorly defined hopes and dreams, fears and fantasies that flourished in a climate of fear, uncertainty and insecurity where everything seemed to be up for grabs and open to contestation.[6] As will

---

[3] Guido Steinberg argues that anti-Shi'a violence for example is very rare and only happens when certain extreme conditions concur: (1) Radical Sunnis believe that 'true Islam' is in existential danger (usually by a foreign threat) and that Shi'as form part of this threat. (2) Radical groups need able and ruthless leaders as well as the opportunity to build an infrastructure in order to turn into a force to be reckoned with. (3) For major conflict to break out, Shi'a militants have to retaliate. Steinberg, "Jihadi-Salafism and the Shi'is," p. 108.

[4] Perhaps the starkest example of this is jihadi leader Abu Mus'ab al-Zarqawi's explicit pursuit of a Sunni–Shi'a war in post-2003 Iraq. See Kazimi, "Zarqawi's Anti-Shi'a Legacy." The same dynamic was noted by Khan in her study of Partition where violence served as a way for Muslim- and Hindu-centric actors to demonstrate to British policy-makers, to Indian elites, and to Hindus and Muslims generally the supposed incompatibility of the two communities. Khan, *The Great Partition*, p. 66.

[5] For a similar argument emphasizing the role of the broader enabling environment caused by the political and security vacuum, see Toby Dodge, "State Collapse and the Rise of Identity Politics," in *Iraq: Preventing Another Generation of Conflict*, ed. Markus Bouillon et al. (Boulder: Lynne Rienner Publishers, 2007).

[6] This borrows from and echoes other historical disruptions – particularly Khan's description of how the terms 'Partition' and 'Pakistan' came to signify a host of symbolic and emotive issues that made the matter unbridgeable. Khan, *The Great Partition*, pp. 67–68. A similar example from our own times is Brexit.

be seen, the easing of these conditions along with the normalization and stabilization of the post-2003 order (domestically and regionally) was accompanied by an easing of violence and sectarian entrenchment and the commensurately diminished political relevance of sectarian identity. Just as the enabling environment was crucial to the outbreak of sectarian conflict after 2003, so too was it crucial to the first retreat of sectarian violence in 2007–8. In Rayburn's words: "The Shi'a sectarians ... stopped short not because there were no Sunnis left to displace, but because they could no longer roam freely through the city killing and threatening the populace with police assistance, the same applies to the Sunni sectarian cleansers ...".[7]

To illustrate the importance of the broader enabling environment with a hypothetical scenario from a far less extreme setting: the London riots of August 2011. These lasted for just under a week with only one night of what felt like true lawlessness;[8] yet even this ultimately fleeting sense of anarchy saw fringe extremists trying to mainstream their views and turn them into action. Watching London's rioting from the coastal city of Grimsby about 200 miles away in north-east England, one man tried to take advantage of the unfolding – though, in retrospect, momentary – mayhem to mobilize racial and anti-Muslim violence. More than just encouraging his fellow Grimbarians to riot, he urged them to target Muslims: "Let's do our riot different," he wrote on Facebook. "Let's burn all the Paki shops and takeaways ... And the Islamic Centre, we can't forget that."[9] Given the brevity of the vacuum and the relatively quick reassertion of police authority, nothing came of this and the episode itself proved as inconsequential

---

[7] Rayburn, *Iraq after America*, p. 93.

[8] Though it seems ridiculous in hindsight, there was even talk of deploying the army to bring the riots under control. See, for example, Robert Verkaik, "Police fury at Downing Street plan to bring in Army to stop rioting," *Daily Mail*, Aug. 14, 2011, https://www.dailymail.co.uk/news/article-2025787/UK-riots-Police-fury-Downing-Street-plan-bring-Army-stop-rioting.html; Emily Fox, "UK riots: 92 per cent say bring in the Army," *Daily Express*, Aug. 9, 2011, https://www.express.co.uk/news/uk/263973/UK-riots-92-per-cent-say-bring-in-the-Army.

[9] "Grimsby man jailed over Facebook race-hate posts," BBC News, Nov. 4, 2011, http://www.bbc.co.uk/news/uk-england-humber-15600667. In the UK, 'Paki' is a racially charged, derogatory term for Pakistanis and South Asians.

as its hate-filled author. Yet one can only wonder whether it would have been as forgettable had the unrest lasted longer. Sustained periods of lawlessness, especially when combined with broader enabling factors (legacy issues, economic downturn, political polarization, and so forth) can make it possible for such actors to successfully coalesce with like-minded people, gain greater public resonance, and trigger a spiral of communal, tit-for-tat violence. That vacuums can empower society's demons, be they criminal or ideological, is as applicable to Baghdad as it is to London or elsewhere.[10] In the case of Iraq, the vacuum lasted years, in conditions of violence and a degree of pressure that few societies have had to endure, and the situation was compounded by deeply divisive legacy issues and the fact that domestic, regional and international actors were at times invested in the perpetuation of the dynamics of violence and sectarian entrenchment in Iraq. These, rather than whatever 'sectarianism' is supposed to mean, are the conditions that plunged Iraq into a sect-coded civil war. This chapter will try to shed light on how this vicious cycle emerged and, more importantly, how it receded as it was replaced by a somewhat more virtuous cycle.

The Pre-2003 Roots of Shi'a Political Sect-Centricity

Vacuums, upheavals and historical disruptions are not sect-coded by default, neither in Iraq nor anywhere else. That the fall of Saddam Hussain's regime in 2003 was followed by an unprecedented inflammation of sectarian categories should not be grounds for assuming that sectarian categories are perennially primed to fill all political vacuums or that the politics of sect must inevitably gain relevance during historical disruptions. In 2003, there was a recent history that made sectarian identity the more likely, though not inevitable, prism through which post-Ba'th politics would be contested. Much of this was rooted in Shi'a political sect-centricity and the feeling among many Shi'as – at both an elite and a popular

---

[10] The vacuum that followed Hurricane Katrina in New Orleans saw shocking incidents of targeted racial violence. A.C. Thompson, "Katrina's hidden race war," *The Nation*, Dec. 17, 2008, https://www.thenation.com/article/katrinas-hidden-race-war/.

level – that 2003 represented an opportunity to right the historical wrongs that afflicted Iraq and Iraqi Shi'as. This sect-coded political aspiration – and not doctrinal differences – provided the basic raw material with which a sect-coded political order was inaugurated and with which an array of actors – from American neoconservatives to the Bush administration to the occupation authorities to Iraq's newly elevated political elites – instrumentalized sectarian identity in pursuit of their own ends. Understanding the history of Iraqi Shi'a political sect-centricity is therefore a key part of understanding Iraqi sectarian dynamics after 2003.

Many an account of the politics of sect in post-2003 Iraq hesitates to accept that, by the twenty-first century, Shi'a sect-centricity (and there was very little in terms of a coherent Sunni equivalent) was not restricted to Shi'a-centric politicians but was also echoed in the sentiments of significant sections of Iraq's Shi'a population. The idea that Iraqi Shi'as were uniquely victimized and that they were the long-denied majority whose demographic weight ought to be reflected in political empowerment is a long-standing one going back to the earliest days of the modern Iraqi state. For much of the twentieth century political Shi'a sect-centricity was of limited political significance and was readily subsumed or overshadowed by other political currents such as Arab nationalism or communism, but it nevertheless existed. Likewise, the oil-fuelled state-building and development programmes of the Ba'th in the 1970s and the regime's expanded integrative and distributive capacities may have prevented political Shi'a sect-centricity from attaining mainstream appeal, but it could not eliminate it – on the contrary, the decade was to prove pivotal in the evolution of Shi'a-centric oppositional politics.[11] Unlike their Sunni counterparts, Iraqi Shi'as always had the paraphernalia of political sect-centricity – Shi'a leaders, Shi'a issues, Shi'a organizations and the like. This was chiefly aimed at redressing Shi'a political and institutional under-representation but it was also concerned with the institutional extent of organized Shi'ism, the role of Islam in state and society (and of Shi'a Islam within that), and the limits of Shi'a identity in the public

---

[11] For the state's success in co-opting Shi'as in the 1970s, see Blaydes, *State of Repression*, chapter 3 and pp. 242–252.

sphere. In that sense, pre-2003 Iraq's 'sectarian issue' was in fact a state–Shi'a issue rather than a Sunni–Shi'a one. Again, lest I arouse the chagrin of Iraqi nationalists and minimalists (see chapter 2), none of this contradicts the facts of sectarian coexistence in Iraq nor does it preclude other political currents. It is simply to point out the pre-2003 roots of what was institutionalized and reified after 2003 and the bottom-up and top-down drivers of sect-centricity. Expressions of Shi'a political sect-centricity – which in and of itself is not necessarily problematic nor inherently antithetical to sectarian coexistence or nationalist sentiment (see chapter 4) – can be found throughout the twentieth century and into the twenty-first in the form of repeated calls for greater Shi'a representation and recognition. For example, pioneering Iraqi nationalist and statesman Muhammad Ridha al-Shibibi lamented what he saw as anti-Shi'a sectarian discrimination in Ottoman and post-Ottoman Iraq in the following verses:

> To secure power you eliminated [*qadhaytum*] a sect,
> Not for whom is power nor ancestry nor states.
> [We are] A people from among the Arabs for whom the bees' sting is their lot,
> While the lot of others besides us is nectar and honey.
> When it comes to spoils you forget about us,
> While we are loaded with the unbearable burden of defeat.[12]

Likewise, in his rejection of the British Mandate and in calling for an independent Iraqi state in 1922, Shi'a cleric Mahdi al-Khalisi also insisted that half of cabinet and official positions be set aside for Shi'as.[13] Similarly the 1920s saw the emergence of the short-lived but unabashedly sect-centric al-Nahdha Party, which championed the cause of Shi'a rights and Shi'a representation.[14] Along the same lines, in an article entitled "The Majority in Iraq," published in 1925, noted

---

[12] Quoted in al-Khayyun, "al-Iraq: Tawdhif al-Ta'ifiyya Siyasiyyan," in *Al-Ta'ifiyya*, ed. al-Mesbar, p. 37. Al-Shibibi, himself a Shi'a, was an early nationalist activist who later served in parliament throughout the monarchy and was Minister of Education in several cabinets. He died in 1975.

[13] Sluglett, *Britain in Iraq*, p. 224.

[14] Ibid., pp. 103–105; Batatu, *The Old Social Classes*, pp. 327–328.

historian Abd al-Razzaq al-Hasani (himself a Shi'a) spoke out against what he regarded as structural anti-Shi'a discrimination – or in his words "the monopolization of [government] employment in one sect to the exclusion of another ..."[15] A slightly later example is the People's Pact (also known as the Najaf Pact) of 1935, which raised similar issues; so too did the 1965 memo submitted by Muhammad Ridha al-Shibibi to Prime Minister Abd al-Rahman al-Bazzaz and the 2002 *Declaration of the Shi'a*, authored by exiled Shi'a opposition figures and Shi'a activists.[16] All these examples revolve around the twin pillars of Shi'a sect-centricity, namely victimhood and entitlement, and their message was echoed by any number of Iraqi public figures, from the likes of al-Shibibi to Iraqi nationalist figure and statesman Muhsin Abu-Tbikh in the 1930s, to the cleric Muhammad Sadiq al-Sadr in the 1960s, to former minister Abd al-Karim al-Uzri in the 1990s, and so on.[17] This reflects the fact that, long before 2003 and far beyond the post-2003 political elite, there was a conviction among significant sections of Iraqi Shi'as that they were victimized on the basis of their sectarian identity, thereby adding a national Iraqi narrative of suffering and exclusion to long-standing mythologies of victimhood inherent to Shi'ism at the doctrinal level. Shi'a resentment against what many of them regarded as the Iraqi state's structural sectarian discrimination was even noted by Iraq's first monarch, Faisal I, who, writing in 1932, argued that whatever disadvantage existed among Iraqi Shi'as was the result of structural and historical factors rather than anti-Shi'a sentiment, but that this had nevertheless "led this majority [the Shi'a] ... to claim that

---

[15] "Al-Akthariyya fi-l-Iraq," *Al-Irfan*, 1925. Quoted in al-Khayyun, "al-Iraq: Tawdhif al-Ta'ifiyya Siyasiyyan," in *Al-Ta'ifiyya*, ed. al-Mesbar, p. 32.

[16] For the People's Pact see al-Hasani, *Tarikh al-Wizarat al-Iraqiyya*, vol. 4, pp. 92–94. For al-Shibibi's memo and broader Shi'a consternation at government policy in the 1960s, see Osman, *Sectarianism in Iraq*, pp. 76–78. For the *Declaration of the Shi'a* see "Declaration of the Shi'a of Iraq," AL-BAB, https://al-bab.com/documents-section/declaration-Shi'a-iraq.

[17] Muhsin Abu Tbikh, *Al-Mabadi' wa-l-Rijal: Bawadir al-Inhiyar al-Siyasi fi-l-Iraq* (Principles and Men: Signs of Political Collapse in Iraq) (Beirut: Al-Mu'asasa al-Arabiyya li-l-Dirasat wa-l-Nashr, 1983), pp. 282–284; Abd al-Kareem al-Uzri, *Mushkilat al Hukum fi-l-Iraq* (The Problem of Governance in Iraq) (London: self-published, 1991); al-Sadr, *Al-Ta'ifiyya fi Nadhar al-Islam*.

they continue to be oppressed simply by being Shi'a."[18] It is this belief that forms the bedrock of sect-centric Shi'a political movements and, in 2003, of Shi'a-centric state-building.

Sect-centricity is not inherently problematic; however, in practice it became so in the Iraqi context of authoritarian state-led attempts at nation-building and social engineering, social and official deafness to legitimate political sect-centricity, and a tense regional context that deepened the securitization of sectarian plurality. From about the 1960s several processes lent Shi'a sect-centricity a gradually increasing political relevance. By the 1970s, Shi'a political activism was becoming more outspoken and more brazen in a context of growing authoritarianism, resulting in several violent confrontations.[19] This escalation was partly shaped by the regional environment and deteriorating relations with Iran – naturally, this downward spiral only accelerated after the Iranian Revolution of 1979, which had a considerably radicalizing impact on Iraqi Shi'a activism.[20] The demise of Arab nationalism and communism as popular mobilizers and the emergence of the Islamic Republic (and regional Islamist movements in general) further explain the growing relevance of Shi'a-centric movements in the opposition to the regime within Iraq and beyond. The climax was the uprisings of 1991 and their brutal suppression. In many ways this signalled an irreparable break between the regime and significant sections of Shi'a Iraq.[21] Beginning in the 1980s, but particularly in the 1990s, the opposition in exile was undeniably dominated by Kurdish ethno-centric and Shi'a sect-

---

[18] Memorandum written by Faisal in March 1932 addressing Iraq's political elite in which he gave his personal assessment of the state of the country. Full text available in Abd al-Razzaq, *Masharee' Izalat al-Tamyiz al-Ta'ifi fi-l-Iraq*, pp. 16–27.

[19] On the disturbances of 1979, see Jabar, *The Shi'ite Movement in Iraq*, pp. 228–231. On the disturbances of 1977, see ibid., pp. 208–215; Marion F. Sluglett and Peter Sluglett, *Iraq since 1958: From Revolution to Dictatorship* (London: I.B. Tauris, 2001), pp. 198–199.

[20] Baram, *Saddam Husayn and Islam*, chapter 3; Jabar, *The Shi'ite Movement in Iraq*, pp. 225–263.

[21] For more on the impact of the 1991 uprisings on sectarian relations, see Haddad, *Sectarianism in Iraq*, chapters 4–6; Khoury, "The 1991 *Intifada* in Three Keys," in *Writing the Modern History of Iraq*, ed. Tejel et al.; Dina Rizk Khoury, *Iraq in Wartime: Soldiering, Martyrdom and Remembrance* (Cambridge: Cambridge University Press, 2013), chapter 5.

centric actors. Their growing role in the opposition in exile, the fact that they were among the United States' key Iraqi interlocutors, and the hollowing out of political life within Iraq meant that the US-led invasion was always likely to empower these forces. More importantly for our purposes, this brief overview of the growing relevance of Shi'a sect-centricity in the years leading up to 2003 explains why Iraqis were primed to differ in their views towards 2003 and regime change and why this divergence was likely to fall largely (though imperfectly) along ethno-sectarian lines. This has nothing to do with immutable antagonisms and everything to do with incompatible political visions of Iraq and how the country's and the region's recent political history had differently shaped sectarian identities at the national level. By 2003 there was a salient sect-coded, group-defining, political grievance in the form of the victimhood and entitlement that characterized Iraqi Shi'a sect-centricity. Short of either very long-term and gradual change or extraordinarily far-sighted and sagacious leadership, it was almost impossible for these issues to be redressed in a sect-blind way or without eliciting a sectarian backlash.

2003 and the Empowerment of Shi'a-Centricity

The year 2003 provided a set of conditions, almost impossible to reproduce, and an enabling environment that allowed for Iraqi sect-centric actors and an array of regional and international actors to rewrite the nature of Iraqi politics and sectarian relations. More specifically, where sectarian relations were concerned, the American-led invasion empowered Shi'a sect-centric actors who sought to overturn the relations of power governing sectarian relations and to normalize social and political sect-centricity. Needless to say, this was of consequence not just to domestic Iraqi politics but to regional rivalries as well given the networks linking many of Iraq's Shi'a-centric political classes and Iran. In Iraq, the political changes of 2003 elevated sectarian identity into the primary characteristic and chief organizing principle of politics in Arab Iraq and saw the long-standing taboo surrounding 'sectarianism' that had led to an apologetic sectarian identity or a contrived sect-blindness quickly becoming an anachronism. The chief authors of these transformations were the US administration, the policies of the

US occupation, and what was to become the post-2003 Iraqi political elite. Regional powers also played a key part in this sectarian spiral by doubling down on the sectarianization of post-2003 Iraq in an attempt to forestall its normalization and, in the case of some, to push back against Iranian gains – with Tehran, of course, in turn seeking to extend its advantage through its sect-centric allies and clients in Iraq.

The sect-centricity of many of the US administration's Shi'a Iraqi interlocutors in exile (alongside the ethno-centricity of their Kurdish partners) fitted in with American thinking on pre-2003 Iraq, which tended to simplify the country into a three-way conflictual ethno-sectarian stew: oppressive Sunnis alongside victimized Shi'as and Kurds. The convergence between much of the opposition's sect- or ethno-centricity and US views towards and interests in Iraq is most succinctly encapsulated in the genesis of the *muhasasa* system that they instituted and that sought to establish a form of ethno-sectarian proportional representation through the apportionment of political office according to the assumed demographic make-up of Iraq. Rather than an American imposition – as is often claimed and assumed – *muhasasa* reflected not just American interests but those of their Iraqi partners as well. Specifically, it was an expression of the sect- or ethno-centricity of much of the exiled Iraqi opposition and their long-standing faith in the efficacy of ethno-sectarian quotas as a fair arbiter of political representation and entitlement.[22] The principle of *muhasasa*

---

[22] As early as 1992 the principle was adopted at the Iraqi opposition conferences of Vienna in June and Salah al-Din, Iraq, in October. See Ibrahim Nawar, "Untying the Knot," *Al-Ahram Weekly*, Feb. 19, 2003; Ali A. Allawi, *The Occupation of Iraq: Winning the War, Losing the Peace* (New Haven: Yale University Press, 2008), p. 50; Ismael and Ismael, *Iraq in the Twenty-First Century*, pp. 86, 88; Salim al-Hasani, *Islamiyu al-Iraq: Min al-Mu'aradha ila al-Hukum* (Iraq's Islamists: From Opposition to Power) (unpublished, n.d.), pp. 17, 19–20, www.almalaf-press.net. Hayder al-Khoei has argued that the idea of ethno-sectarian quotas was floated earlier in an opposition conference held in Tehran in 1987; Hayder al-Khoei, "The Construction of Ethno-Sectarian Politics in Post-War Iraq: 2003–05," Master's thesis, International Studies and Diplomacy, School of Oriental and African Studies, 2012, p. 12. It should be mentioned that some of those within the Iraqi opposition in exile, including some Shi'a-centric actors, did warn of the dangers of ethno-sectarian quotas. For example, article 6 of *The Declaration of the Shi'as* directly warned that "the division of powers on the basis of overt sectarian percentages ... cannot be workable in the context of

was enshrined in post-2003 Iraq's earliest institution, namely the Iraqi Governing Council (IGC), which was appointed by the occupation authorities in July 2003 and whose 25-member composition was explicitly based on the assumed demographic weight of Iraq's main ethno-religious or sectarian communities.[23] The entire exercise was a farce that recalls other episodes of imperial powers inflating the political relevance of communal categories and reifying them as the basic currency of political contestation. This is as true of the American-sponsored IGC as it was of the British-sponsored Manama Council of 1919, the British Raj's 1909 decision to split the Indian electorate according to religious communities, or European diplomats and missionaries in the nineteenth-century Ottoman Levant.[24] From the vantage point of the incoming Iraqi political classes, the IGC was also a vehicle for the advancement of ethno-centric and sect-centric political actors and the implementation of their vision for Iraq. That Sunnis, generally speaking, lacked a culture of political sect-centricity put them at an immediate disadvantage, one that was amplified by the simplistic narrative that regarded them (implicitly at least) as beneficiaries of, if

---

Iraq." For full text, see "Declaration of the Shi'a of Iraq," AL-BAB, https://al-bab. com/documents-section/declaration-Shi'a-iraq.

[23] On the divisiveness of the IGC, see "The Next Iraqi War?", International Crisis Group, p. 11; Andrew Arato, *Constitution Making under Occupation: The Politics of Imposed Revolution on Iraq* (New York: Columbia University Press, 2009), pp. 20–24; Qasim Hussain Salih, *Al-Mujtama' al-Iraqi: Tahlil Sikosociology lima Hadath wa Yahduth* (Iraqi Society: A Psycho-Sociological Analysis of What Happened and Is Happening) (Beirut: Arab Scientific Publishers: 2008), pp. 13–14. Salih points out that, more than just a sectarian issue, the IGC also embodied other divisive dualities; namely, insiders versus outsiders (meaning the returning exiles) and victims versus oppressors. For more on the split between insiders and outsiders in 2003–6, see Phebe Marr, "Iraq's New Political Map," United States Institute for Peace, Special Report 179, Jan. 2007.

[24] For the case of the Ottoman Levant, see Bruce Masters, *Christians and Jews in the Ottoman Arab World: The Roots of Sectarianism* (Cambridge: Cambridge University Press, 2001); also see Makdisi, *The Culture of Sectarianism*. For the Manama Council and the British role in the institutionalization of sectarian identity in Bahraini politics, see Omar H. AlShehabi, "Contested Modernity: Divided Rule and the Birth of Sectarianism, Nationalism and Absolutism in Bahrain," *British Journal of Middle Eastern Studies*, 44:3 (2016): 333–355. For the communalization of electoral policy under the British Raj, see Sumit Sarkar, *Modern India: 1885–1947* (New Delhi: Macmillan, 1983), pp. 418–423.

not complicit in, the previous regime. This was but one of the ways in which views of the post-2003 environment were quickly sect-coded from an early stage. This had a corrosive effect on Iraqi society in that an ever-expanding orbit of dynamics, events, issues, debates and points of contention relating to the 'new Iraq' was being similarly sect-coded: from the constitution to federalism, the insurgencies, Iraq's international relations, and so on. It seemed that everything had the capacity to become an unbridgeable symbolic and existential issue seemingly threatening to forever determine the fate of 'Sunnis' and 'Shi'as'. This was a reflection of the cascading fallout of the basic sect-coded divergence in views towards 2003: in the immediate aftermath, political opinion was similarly distilled through sectarian filters with a 'Shi'a position' and a 'Sunni position' on a bewildering array of subjects. An incisive and remarkably early recognition of this was made by Raad Alkadiri and Chris Toensing in their analysis of Iraqi opinion of the IGC just two months after its establishment. They noted a 'sectarian hue' to how Iraqis viewed the IGC, with Shi'as more willing to give it the benefit of the doubt than Sunnis.[25] This reflected the basic divergence in how 2003 was viewed by significant bodies of Sunnis and Shi'as: a calamity for the former, an opportunity for the latter. This divergence was to persist in the way political horizons were viewed for some years to come and was rooted in different perceptions of the past. The Shi'a sect-centricity of the incoming order, and the feeling among Sunnis that the political change of 2003 was one that, at best, came at their expense and, at worst, targeted them, ultimately gave birth to the struggle between Shi'a-centric state-building and Sunni rejection. This dialectic was to go through several stages – including civil war – and was fundamental in shaping the evolution of post-2003 Arab Iraq.

The Diminishing Relevance of the Sunni–Shi'a Divide

There is a wealth of analysis of Iraqi political development and political violence since 2003, and what remains of this chapter does

---

[25] Raad Alkadiri and Chris Toensing, "The Iraqi Governing Council's Sectarian Hue," The Middle East Research and Information Project, Aug. 20, 2003, http://www.merip.org/mero/mero082003.

not allow for a detailed chronicling of fifteen years of unusually turbulent politics.[26] Rather, the remainder will focus on what at the time of writing appears to be the diminishing political relevance of sectarian categories. As will be seen, sectarian relations in Iraq went through several stages after 2003 and, beginning around 2015, Iraqi and broader regional dynamics entered a new stage, one marked by a retreat in the political relevance and political utility of sectarian identity. Even if this proves to be temporary, it is still worth examining in order to better understand how sectarian tensions ease and how sectarian identities lose relevance. However, in the case of Iraq, even if sectarian dynamics were to take a turn for the worse or if there were renewed instability or civil war, it is unlikely that Iraq would revert to what it went through in 2003 or 2014 given the unique set of enabling conditions (nationally and regionally) fuelling events in those years and the difficulty, if not impossibility, of re-creating them.

Around 2017–18, with the territorial collapse of the Islamic State, the dramatic reduction of violence in Iraq, the de-escalation of the civil war in Syria, and the Iraqi elections of 2018, there were a number of headlines and much commentary heralding the 'end of sectarianism' in Iraq and the region, and the dawning of a supposedly 'post-sectarian' era.[27] Understandably, this stretched credulity in some quarters,

---

[26] For overviews of politics in post-2003 Iraq, see Toby Dodge, *Iraq: From War to a New Authoritarianism* (London: International Institute for Strategic Studies, 2012); Toby Dodge, "Seeking to Explain the Rise of Sectarianism in the Middle East: The Case Study of Iraq," POMEPS, March 9, 2014, https://pomeps.org/2014/03/19/seeking-to-explain-the-rise-of-sectarianism-in-the-middle-east-the-case-study-of-iraq/; "Iraq between Maliki and the Islamic State," Project on Middle East Political Science, July 9, 2014, https://pomeps.org/wp-content/uploads/2014/07/POMEPS_BriefBooklet24_Iraq_Web.pdf; Zaid al-Ali, *The Struggle for Iraq's Future: How Corruption, Incompetence and Sectarianism Have Undermined Democracy* (New Haven: Yale University Press, 2014); Allawi, *The Occupation of Iraq*.

[27] For example: Salam Khoder, "Iraq: The end of sectarian politics?", Al Jazeera English, May 2, 2016, https://www.aljazeera.com/news/2016/05/iraq-sectarian-politics-160502093754018.html; Borzou Daragahi, "Welcome to Iraq's First Post-Sectarian Election," *Foreign Policy*, May 10, 2018, https://foreignpolicy.com/2018/05/10/welcome-to-iraqs-first-post-sectarian-election/; Matthew Schweitzer, "Interview with Fanar Haddad: After Sectarianism," *EPIC*, Nov. 20, 2017, https://www.epic-usa.org/after-sectarianism/.

and with good reason: such phrases are simply too unwieldy and all-encompassing to hold analytic water.[28] This again brings us back to the problematic nature and questionable utility of the term 'sectarianism': it has been used to refer to so much, that any proclamation of its definitive end would be as implausible as announcing the end of politics or indeed the end of history. As should be clear by now, the problem here is not the permanency of 'sectarianism' but the maddening fluidity of the term, encompassing so much that it ends up meaning nothing. As argued in chapter 1, it is a term best discarded.

If we leave the circuitous debates regarding 'sectarianism' aside and focus instead on sectarian identities and sectarian relations and their constantly evolving meaning, utility, social salience and political relevance, it becomes clear that Iraq and the region saw significant change on this front between 2003 and 2018. To take the Iraqi case, at the time of writing the country still suffered from chronic instability and continued to wrestle with serious security threats; however, while this is likely to persist into the foreseeable future, the sources and drivers of these problems have shifted somewhat. Specifically, where once the sectarian divide and issues relating to sectarian identity and sectarian relations were the chief drivers of political violence, instability and political competition, other factors have since taken over. Beyond Iraq, this has also been reflected in recent regional developments. These include the regional normalization of Iraq and its thawing relations with Saudi Arabia.[29] Another example is regional powers' reframing of their approach to the Syrian conflict, and the

---

[28] For example, Zmkan A. Saleem, "The Myth of Rising above Sectarianism in Iraq," Washington Institute for Near East Policy, April 20, 2018, https://www.washingtoninstitute.org/fikraforum/view/the-myth-of-rising-above-sectarianism-in-iraq; Toby Dodge, "Iraq: A Year of Living Dangerously," *Survival*, 60:5 (Sept. 18, 2018), https://www.tandfonline.com/doi/full/10.1080/00396338.2018.1518368.

[29] Mehiyar Kathem, "A New Era Beckons for Iraqi–Saudi Relations," *War on the Rocks*, Feb. 2, 2018, https://warontherocks.com/2018/02/a-new-era-beckons-for-iraqi-saudi-relations/; "Saudi Arabia: Back to Baghdad," International Crisis Group, Middle East Report no. 186, May 22, 2018; Renad Mansour, "Saudi Arabia's New Approach in Iraq," Center for Strategic and International Studies, Nov. 2018, https://csis-prod.s3.amazonaws.com/s3fs-public/publication/181105_RM_Gulf_analysis.pdf?AWXv0HPipY0ev0TR2M08l_PbRCQQSY99.

demise of the contrived illusion of a 'Sunni crusade' against the regime of Bashar al-Assad in Damascus: in early 2019, several tentative steps were taken toward the reintegration of Syria into regional politics.[30] None of this signalled the end of regional instability, conflict or Arab–Iranian rivalry, but it did point to the diminishing political relevance of sectarian categories. Instead of cynically conflating anti-Iranianism and anti-Shi'ism, for example, regional actors seem to have shifted their strategy towards creating greater distance between the two. There is less stoking of fears of a 'Shi'a crescent' and regional powers are no longer passively tolerating sect-coded jihadist mobilization, as happened with both the Iraqi and Syrian conflicts. The reasons for this shift included concerns about jihadist blowback, and the risks of it feeding domestic sectarian violence.[31] More importantly, the shift also had the aim of better isolating Iran and its Shi'a Arab clients and allies from the broader spectrum of Arab Shi'ism. Where once a Shi'a-centric Iraq was rejected and isolated the better to deny Iran a strategic advantage, Arab powers changed tack and sought to make inroads into Iraqi political Shi'ism. In this they sought to compete with Iran in Iraq by trying to outperform and outflank them rather than by trying to undermine Iran by acting as spoilers in Iraq. This approach may serve

---

[30] In an interview with *Time*, Saudi Arabian Crown Prince Muhammad bin Salman bluntly stated that "Bashar is staying." See W.J. Hennigan, "Saudi Crown Prince says US troops should stay in Syria," *Time*, March 30, 2018, http://time.com/5222746/saudi-crown-prince-donald-trump-syria/. See also Kamal Alam and David Lesch, "The road to Damascus: The Arabs march back to befriend Assad," *War on the Rocks*, Dec. 7, 2018, https://warontherocks.com/2018/12/the-road-to-damascus-the-arabs-march-back-to-befriend-assad/.

On Syria's reintegration, see Hashem Osseiran, "UAE reopens embassy in Damascus after six years," *The National*, Dec. 27, 2018, https://www.thenational.ae/world/mena/uae-reopens-embassy-in-damascus-after-six-years-1.806947; Bethan McKernan and Martin Chulov, "Arab League set to readmit Syria eight years after expulsion," *The National*, Dec. 26, 2018, https://www.theguardian.com/world/2018/dec/26/arab-league-set-to-readmit-syria-eight-years-after-expulsion; Jeyhun Aliyev, "Bahrain reopens embassy in Syria," *Anadolu Agency*, Dec. 28, 2018, https://www.aa.com.tr/en/middle-east/bahrain-reopens-embassy-in-syria/1350510.

[31] These fears proved well founded in 2015, when the Islamic State claimed several suicide bombings of Shi'a mosques in Saudi Arabia and one in Kuwait.

to de-securitize sectarian boundaries both domestically and regionally, even while traditional rivalries between the likes of Saudi Arabia and Iran persist and deepen.[32]

These developments occasioned a shift in the vocabulary of conflict and contestation away from sectarian categories, and helped diminish (though not eliminate) the emotive force and ready utility of sectarian identities from what they were a few years previously. What had been transformed into artificially simplified categories of 'Sunni' and 'Shi'a' eventually lost the ersatz veneer of monolithic homogeneity that was created by and for the sect-coded conflicts that followed 2003, giving way to a more familiar intersectionality and intra-sectarian heterogeneity and lines of contestation. An indicative example of this was the life imprisonment of Bahraini opposition figure Ali Salman in late 2018 for collusion – not with Iran, but with Qatar.[33] The point is not to suggest that these shifts are irreversible or that sectarian identity has been reduced to irrelevance but to note that the landscape changed significantly between 2003 and 2018 and that the political relevance of the Sunni–Shi'a divide considerably diminished in the latter years of that period. Accounting for these changes tells us much about the nature of sectarian identity and sectarian relations in the region. Accordingly, rather than proclaiming the 'end of sectarianism', the following will highlight, firstly, that sectarian relations went through several phases after 2003, and, secondly, that, beginning around 2016, sectarian dynamics were no longer the chief driver of political instability – neither in Iraq nor the region. More broadly, this fluidity highlights

---

[32] The example of Saudi Arabia is instructive. In addition to the improvement of bilateral ties with Iraq, some analysts noted tentative improvements in regime–Shi'a relations domestically as part of the reorientation of the state's strategies towards social and religious affairs following the Islamic State crisis of 2014 and the rise of Crown Prince Muhammad bin Salman in 2017. See Smith Diwan, "Saudi Nationalism Raises Hopes of Greater Shi'a Inclusion."

[33] "Bahraini opposition leader sentenced to life in prison," BBC News, Nov. 4, 2018, https://www.bbc.com/news/world-middle-east-46088430. At the time of writing Bahrain was part of the quartet (led by Saudi Arabia and the United Arab Emirates and also including Egypt) spearheading the boycott of Qatar that began in 2017 ostensibly for its support of terrorism and Islamist groups and its regional interventions.

the analytical limits of viewing Iraqi or regional politics solely through the prism of communal identity, and the necessity of appreciating the multidimensionality of sectarian identity. Sunni–Shi'a dynamics unfold in national and regional settings that shape the meaning of sectarian identity and the parameters of sectarian competition. Thus, sectarian identity in post-2003 Iraq was not a stand-alone factor but was part of a broader set of variables operating in the context of the nation-state and the broader regional state system.

The Shifting Politics of Sect in Post-2003 Iraq

As central as sectarian identities were to the very foundation of the post-2003 Iraqi political order, and as pivotal as Sunni–Shi'a cleavages have been in Iraqi political contestation and political violence, the role, utility and political relevance of sectarian identity have not stood static over the years. The inflamed salience of sectarian identities at various junctures since 2003 should not blind us to the ebbs and flows of sectarian dynamics between 2003 and 2018. The politics of sect in post-2003 Iraq are best understood as having gone through several stages that can be loosely divided into two cycles:

- First cycle
  - 2003–2005: Entrenchment
  - 2005–2007: Civil war
  - 2008–2010: Retreat
- Second cycle
  - 2011–2012: Entrenchment
  - 2013–2015: Civil war
  - 2016–2018: Retreat

It is important to note the fundamental differences between the two cycles. For instance, the drivers of entrenchment and the broader political climate in 2003–5 differ in many respects from those of 2011–12. The impact of the American occupation in the former and that of the Arab uprisings and the Syrian civil war in the latter fundamentally shaped perceptions of sectarian identity and sectarian relations. Likewise, internal Iraqi dynamics and the positive regional shifts mentioned above differentiate retreat in 2016–18 from the earlier stage of retreat in 2008–10. Again, the broader enabling environment is crucial.

By taking these changes into account we can better grasp the shifting sands of Iraqi politics and the fluctuating political relevance of sectarian categories. Failing to do so leads to the all-too-common mistake of anchoring one's understanding of sectarian relations in too narrow a context – by considering, for example, sectarian identity to be as relevant in 2018 as it was in 2005 with no recognition of the profound changes that unfolded in the intervening period. To illustrate, one of the defining features of the Iraqi elections of 2018 was the intensification of intra-sectarian competition and the proliferation of cross-sectarian alliances. Yet despite this, and despite the fact that post-election lines of contestation were primarily intra-Shi'a and intra-Sunni, many post-election headlines framed the delay in government formation as a function of "sectarian agendas" or as the result of "Sunni–Shi'ite dispute."[34] To take an example from April 2019, an op-ed by political scientist Robert Pape saw Iraq's problems entirely through the prism of sectarian identity and Sunni grievances, striking a tone more suitable for 2013 than 2019.[35]

The stages of sectarian dynamics listed above are a reflection of the shifting political stakes of sectarian competition. They are also a reflection of the gradual stabilization of the post-2003 order and the consequent restriction of what was politically up for grabs. More broadly, the stages outlined above chart the evolution of the tension between Shi'a-centric state-building and Sunni rejection: its ebbs and flows, from inflammation and civil war to retreat and diminished relevance. By extension, the shifts from one stage to another are also indicative of the shifts in the way sectarian identity and sectarian relations

---

[34] For example, "Iraq: Political Alliances Hindered by Sectarian Agendas, Foreign Influence," Asharq Al-Awsat, July 3, 2018, https://aawsat.com/english/home/article/1319166/iraq-political-alliances-hindered-sectarian-agendas-foreign-influence; "Sunni–Shi'ite Dispute to Delay Appointment of Iraq Ministers," Rudaw, Nov. 6, 2018, http://www.rudaw.net/english/middleeast/iraq/051120184.

[35] Robert A. Pape, "The Path Forward in Iraq: What Robert A. Pape Thinks," National Interest, April 13, 2019, https://nationalinterest.org/feature/path-forward-iraq-what-robert-pape-thinks-52017.

have been perceived and experienced since the US invasion. Political contestation in the earlier stages was more zero-sum and more identity-based, with the very nature of the Iraqi state and the foundational rules of political life seemingly at stake. This is where the most basic and crudest level of Shi'a-centric state-building (the empowerment of Shi'a-centric political actors and the institutionalization of a vision for Iraq in which Shi'as are the senior partners) was still being contested. In these early years, sect-centric and ethno-centric actors believed they were in an existential struggle to ensure their place and survival in an Iraq whose contours had yet to be solidified. Since then, the prism of sectarian or ethnic identity eventually lost the capacity it once had to dominate political perceptions and calculations as the relations of power between sect-centric actors waxed and became less open to contestation – thereby leaving greater room for intra-sect, or indeed trans-sect, dynamics. Ultimately, the progression of sectarian politics across these various stages reflects the waning of the tension between Shi'a-centric state-building and Sunni rejection, with the ascendance of the former and the weakening of the latter. At the time of writing, the most visible consequence of this was the diminished appeal and relevance of political sect-centricity.

The Normalization of the Post-2003 Order

The shifting stages of the politics of sect in Iraq also underline the slow normalization of the post-2003 order and the structures underpinning post-2003 sectarian relations. What was contentious or shocking in 2005 is often no longer so today. For example, the assertion of Shi'a identity, something so zealously and provocatively exhibited after 2003, was at one time a contentious issue that reflected the disputed claims of ownership of public space and of the national narrative.[36] At the time of writing, however, many aspects of Shi'a symbolism have by and large become an everyday banality. At the height of the war against the Islamic State, international journalism made much of the divisive potential of Shi'a flags and symbols that were displayed by the

---

[36] See Haddad, "Sectarian Relations and Sunni Identity," pp. 67–115.

Iraqi military and allied paramilitary units.[37] The reality, however, was that by that point these symbols had been a part of daily life for well over a decade, and had been normalized. That is not to say that the issue of symbolism had been resolved or that it had completely lost its divisive potential.[38] Rather, it is only to point out that the parameters of the matter had shifted, and what was once regarded as controversial or threatening in Iraqi sectarian dynamics had changed. Perhaps the most straightforward illustration of this normalization process is the changing attitudes, in Iraq and beyond, to the empowerment of Shi'a-centric political actors, including those aligned with Iran. Initially, in 2003 this was controversial enough to cause regional consternation and ultimately led to an internationalized civil war. Today, for good or ill, the political ascendance of Iraqi Shi'a-centric actors is accepted by domestic, regional and international policy-makers and political actors as a fact of the political landscape.

A key indicator of these shifts is changing threat perceptions – both elite and popular. A large part of normalization is the waning of fear. Fears of group extinction and of group encirclement were heavily sect-coded in the early years after the US invasion. This had a divisive social impact, as spiralling violence led people to seek safety in their own sectarian communities and to frame the sectarian other as a threat.[39] By 2015 or thereabouts this was no longer the case. The

---

[37] Tamer El-Ghobashy and Ben Kesling, "Iraqi troops fly Shi'ite flags, stoking tensions," *Wall Street Journal*, Oct. 21, 2016, https://www.wsj.com/articles/iraqi-troops-stoke-sectarian-tensions-in-mosul-fight-1477042201.

[38] As recently as Dec. 2018, the potential for symbolism to cause controversy was evidenced by reactions to the display of portraits of Saddam Hussain at a celebration at the University of Anbar. See for example, "Badr al-Niyabiyya: kan al-awla raf' suwar al-shuhada' min abna' al-Anbar wa-baqi al-muhafadhat badalan min mujrimin" (Badr Parliamentary Bloc: It would have been better to display pictures of martyrs from Anbar and other governorates instead of criminals), Buratha News Agency, Dec. 24, 2018, http://burathanews.com/arabic/news/342879.

[39] On the central role of fear in shaping action in conflict, see Lina Haddad Kreidie and Kristen Renwick Monroe, "Psychological Boundaries and Ethnic Conflict: How Identity Constrained Choice and Worked to Turn Ordinary People into Perpetrators of Ethnic Violence during the Lebanese Civil War," *International Journal of Politics, Culture and Society*, 16:1 (2002): 5–36; Michael J. Boyle, "Bargaining, Fear and Denial: Explaining Violence against Civilians in Iraq 2004–2007," *Terrorism and Political Violence*, 21 (2009): 261–287.

rise of the Islamic State weakened Sunni–Shi'a division in Iraq by presenting Iraqis with a more serious threat that transcended sectarian boundaries. Despite the Islamic State's unambiguously genocidal stance towards Shi'as, post-2003 Iraq's second phase of civil war was not sect-coded in the same way that the first was – not least because of the diversity of forces that fought against the Islamic State. Again, normalization and, by extension, the waning of fear are key elements to this: at the time of writing in 2019, the sectarian other may be loved, hated or viewed with indifference, but is no longer regarded as an existential threat. One manifestation of this is a greater ability to distinguish between the individual and the group and between the sectarian other and the militants claiming to represent the sectarian other. The intra-Sunni divisiveness of the Islamic State, the diminished relevance of sectarian categories, and the normalization of the politics of sect mean that unlike in 2005–7, Iraqis after 2014 might fear Sunni or Shi'a militants without viewing Sunnis or Shi'as in general as a threat. Put another way, views of the sectarian other have shifted from a 'high generality of difference', where the other is viewed negatively as an undifferentiated mass, to a 'lower generality of difference' that allows for nuance and variation in line with the easing of existential threat and the relative normalization of power relations and of the political order.[40] To illustrate, in July 2016 Baghdad experienced its deadliest attack to date, when more than three hundred civilians were killed in an Islamic State suicide truck-bombing in the mostly Shi'a area of Karrada.[41] Yet despite the backdrop of wartime mobilization against the Islamic State, popular outrage at the atrocity was aimed not at Sunnis or at Sunni neighbourhoods but at the Iraqi government for its failure to protect civilians.[42] This differs starkly from the grim

---

[40] This shift away from a zero-sum negative framing to a more spectral one was noted by Neta Oren in how Arab entities have been framed in Israeli political discourse: the easing of tensions and fear encourages a lower generality of difference. Oren, "Israeli Identity Formation," p. 198.

[41] Ahmed Rasheed, "Death toll in Baghdad bombing rises to 324: Ministry," Reuters, Aug. 1, 2016, https://www.reuters.com/article/us-mideast-crisis-iraq-toll-idUSKCN10B0VK?il=0.

[42] "Ghadhab muwatinin athna' ziyarat al-Abadi li-mawqi' tafjir al-Karrada" (Citizens' anger during al-Abadi's visit to the site of the Karrada bombing), BBC Arabic,

patterns of 2005–7, when such an incident would have stoked fear of and anger toward 'the Sunnis', further fuelling the tit-for-tat atrocities between Sunni and Shi'a armed camps that so marked the first stage of civil war.

A corollary of the process of normalization relates to the perceived reversibility of the post-2003 order. In the first stage of civil war in 2005–7, the political order was young, insecure, internationally isolated, and directly linked to and dependent on the American occupation. In other words, its situation was precarious enough for its longevity to be doubted by its opponents – and in some cases even by some of its supporters, hence the abortive calls for an abandonment of insurgent areas of Iraq in times of extreme crisis.[43] Today, over a decade later, memories and experiences of pre-2003 Iraq are dimming, and powerful interests spanning sectarian, ethnic and even international boundaries are firmly entrenched in Iraq and are vested in the survival of the state. This is a product of the two stages of civil war and the ascendance of the state and its allied forces: whereas 2005–7 signalled the irreversibility of the post-2003 order in the capital, 2013–15 did so on an Iraq-wide scale. Insurgency will undoubtedly persist and is likely to be a feature of the Iraqi landscape for years to come, but the idea of reversing the changes of 2003 or of overthrowing the political order in a sect-coded revolution is one entertained by a group that gets smaller and more extreme by the year.[44] Again, this is reflected regionally: in 2018 Iraq

---

July 3, 2016, http://www.bbc.com/arabic/multimedia/2016/07/160628_iraqi_haider_abadi.

[43] An extreme example is Basim al-Awadi – affiliated with what was then known as the Supreme Council for the Islamic Revolution in Iraq – calling for an independent Shi'a state in September 2004. See Basim al-Awadi, "Alaysa al-istiqlal ashraf li-l-Shi'a min ma yahsul al-an?" (Isn't independence more honourable for the Shi'a than what is happening now?), *Shabakat al-Iraq al-Thaqafiyya*, Sept. 20, 2004, http://www.iraqcenter.net/vb/showthread.php?t=9079. Likewise, the same logic explains why the fall of Mosul in 2014 saw the emergence of the abortive 'Sumerian project'. This was a marginal, mostly online, call for a new independent state based on what are purportedly the boundaries of ancient Sumeria – conveniently portrayed as encompassing Shi'a majority areas of modern Iraq.

[44] As is widely noted, after losing their territorial 'caliphate', Islamic State militants have been staging a resurgence in rural parts of Iraq. While a repeat of

enjoyed positive relations with all of its neighbours, regional interests were increasingly invested in Iraqi stability, and would-be spoilers had fewer potential regional patrons than ever before; all of which underlines the contingent and multidimensional nature of sectarian dynamics. None of this means that in 2018 Iraqi political instability had become a thing of the past. Rather, it signalled that the parameters of instability had changed in line with the increasing complexity of the Iraqi state and of Iraqi political contestation, which, fifteen years after regime change, had moved beyond broad-stroke foundational issues relating to the politics of sect and the balance of power between sect-centric political actors. These changing parameters were evidenced in political messaging, electoral behaviour, public opinion and patterns of violence.

The *Muhasasa* System

A common refrain holds the *muhasasa* system (the apportionment of political office) as the epitome and cause of all that is wrong with post-2003 Iraq. The resilience of the *muhasasa* system and its persistence are often taken as evidence of the persistence of 'sectarianism'. There are several misconceptions in discussions of *muhasasa*. These include the belief that it was created and imposed upon Iraq by the American occupation in addition to the belief that it *causes* systemic corruption. Needless to say, *muhasasa* is hardly a prerequisite for corruption, and indeed it is somewhat incidental when compared to institutional weakness or the absence of the rule of law as causal factors. The networks of patronage that dominate Iraqi economic and political activity are not a product of *muhasasa* even if they are shaped

---

2014 will remain unlikely, the Islamic State and insurgency in general will continue to threaten Iraqi stability for some time. For analysis of post-caliphate Islamic State fortunes and strategies in 2018, see Michael Knights, "The Islamic State Inside Iraq: Losing Power or Preserving Strength?" *CTC Sentinel*, 11:11 (Dec. 2018): 1–10, https://ctc.usma.edu/app/uploads/2018/12/CTC-SENTINEL-122018. pdf; Hisham al-Hashimi, "Tandhim Da'ish fi 'am 2018: al-Iraq Namuthaj" (The Islamic State in 2018: The Case of Iraq," Center of Making Policies for International and Strategic Studies, Oct. 2018, https://www.makingpolicies.org/ar/posts/isisin2018.php.

by it. After all, patron–client relations do not have to be predicated on *muhasasa* – indeed, they were no less significant prior to 2003, except that the patterns of patronage were more centralized. In any case, more important for our purposes is the tendency of analysis to restrict *muhasasa* to its sectarian dimension.

The *muhasasa* system was never just a *muhasasa ta'ifiyya* (sectarian apportionment); it was always also a *muhasasa hizbiyya* (party apportionment). These two overlapping components of the *muhasasa* system serve as important drivers of inter- and intra-sectarian political competition respectively. The former was more prominent in the earlier stages of the post-2003 era when the basic balance of power between sect-centric actors was being contested – in other words, when the contours of sectarian apportionment were being established. Between 2003 and 2018, however, contestation within the *muhasasa* system shifted increasingly toward party apportionment as a function of the political classes' acceptance of the rules governing the relations of power between sect-coded camps. As one politician put it to me in a private conversation in 2018: "Today it is all about the parties. They [the political classes] have moved beyond *muhasasa ta'ifiyya* because, especially after 2014, everyone knows their size and place." Put another way, at the level of political elites, ethno-sectarian *muhasasa* and the political shares accorded to 'Sunnis', 'Shi'as' and 'Kurds' are, for the moment, reified and minimally contested. Even at a popular level, opposition is less animated by how political office is apportioned or how much is given to a particular sect, and is instead driven by wholesale rejection of the *muhasasa* system itself.

The tilt of the lines of contestation animating the *muhasasa* system from sectarian to party apportionment has several implications for how we think about sectarian dynamics. Most obviously, it again reflects the importance of normalization as sectarian relations of power become more formalized and less contested: moving away from inter-sect divisions in a contested *muhasasa ta'ifiyya* and more towards intra-sect divisions in a contested *muhasasa hizbiyya*. One effect of this is an even greater distance between the *muhasasa* system and broader society. A sectarian *muhasasa* is an elite bargain ostensibly aimed at governing sectarian relations by, among other things, ensuring an agreeable political share for the various sects and ethnicities that make up the polity.[45] In this way, sectarian apportionment shapes horizontal relations among both elites and people, thereby lending it a socially divisive element, as seen in the earlier stages of Sunni–Shi'a division after 2003. By contrast, party *muhasasa* is more directly concerned with horizontal relations among elites. Short of these elites having genuine political constituencies, this party *muhasasa* has less of a social echo in that it is far more nakedly about the division of spoils among unrepresentative political actors. The increasing tilt towards a party *muhasasa* is a function of the normalization of the post-2003 order and of the culmination of the tension between Shi'a-centric state-building and Sunni rejection. This in turn has driven a shift from identity politics to issue politics, and is at the heart of the emergence of what is increasingly becoming Iraq's main political fault line, namely that between the people and the ruling classes.[46] Importantly, this anti-elite feeling has existed from the very beginning of the post-2003 era, as illustrated by the consistent abundance of anti-elite poetry and motifs championing the downtrodden (something the Sadrists have always excelled at); however, it was often overshadowed and subsumed by the perceived need for sectarian solidarity at times of heightened sectarian conflict. The greater the normalization and stability of sectarian power relations, the less relevant sectarian competition and, hence, the less necessary sectarian solidarity becomes. To illustrate, the retreat of sectarian competition in 2008–10, for example, created greater room for focus to be placed on long-simmering anti-elite sentiment and intra-sectarian resentments. A fairly well-known example from 2008

---

[45] For an interesting discussion of elite bargains in conflict situations and the role that such bargains played in the period immediately after 2003, see Dodge, *Iraq: From War to a New Authoritarianism*, pp. 40–48, 148–157. More generally, see Stefan Lindemann, "Do Inclusive Elite Bargains Matter? A Research Framework for Understanding the Causes of Civil War in Sub-Saharan Africa," Development Studies Institute (LSE), Crisis States Discussion Papers, no. 15, Feb. 2008.

[46] Faleh A. Jabar, "The Iraqi Protest Movement: From Identity Politics to Issue Politics," LSE Middle East Centre Paper Series no. 25, 2018, http://eprints.lse.ac.uk/88294/1/Faleh_Iraqi%20Protest%20Movement_Published_English.pdf; Renad Mansour, "Protests Reveal Iraq's New Fault Line: The People vs. the Ruling Class," World Politics Review, July 20, 2018, https://www.worldpoliticsreview.com/articles/25161/protests-reveal-iraq-s-new-fault-line-the-people-vs-the-ruling-class.

is Na'il Mudhaffar's poem informally referred to by one of its more controversial verses: 'We [Sunni and Shi'a Iraqis] are brothers, one slaughters the other.' After expounding on Shi'a victimhood (pre- and post-2003) and giving a Shi'a-centric rendering of the preceding five years, he turns to the common man and laments the state of the poor and the callous disregard of the political classes:

> Because the rulers are Shi'a, you [Sunnis] want me to pay a tax?
> And what did I receive? And what did the Shi'a [politician] give me?
> He was heartbroken by my shack; he said, "I will demolish it today,
> And build you a palace for you to live in, just wait."
> Just wait, just wait, and I have been waiting for five years,
> And you [the politician] haven't built one brick of the palace.
> I will not vote anymore, no by al-Abbas [Hussain ibn Ali's stepbrother],
> Even if they wrote their names in Qur'anic verse.
> The mud hut shivers [in the cold] while they [politicians] are sweating.
> Their slogans on a length of cloth nailed to my house,
> And I don't have anything to swaddle my infants with.
> Go back to your hotel and take what you brought with you.
> I don't want the palace, give me back the shack.[47]

After fifteen years of sect-coded political contestation, Iraqi politics ceased being about managing the coexistence of communities nor were they any longer about establishing or tearing down a state. Rather, elite bargains evolved into an exercise in managing the coexistence and working arrangements of complicit elites. This reflects the reality that the political classes have long made common cause through their mutual interests and collusion in an exclusionary system that has given them all a stake in its continuation. The political classes also share a common threat perception with regard to the burgeoning social pressure from a public that has grown ever more distant from the political elites as the politics of sect have lost relevance.[48]

---

[47] Available on "Shi'ir sha'bi … musibat al-Iraq al-yom" (Popular poetry … Iraq's calamity today), uploaded Feb. 1, 2008, https://www.youtube.com/watch?v=bv7thKQylA4.

[48] The scale of the near-annual summer protests across southern Iraq and Baghdad in 2018 is a case in point. See Harith Hasan al-Qarawee, "The Basra Exception," *Diwan*, Carnegie Middle East Center, Sept. 19, 2018, http://carnegie-mec.org/

Electoral Politics

Nowhere have these changes and the diminishing political relevance and utility of sectarian identities been more clearly visible than in the evolution of electoral politics. In addition to provincial elections, Iraq held five legislative elections between 2003 and 2018: twice in 2005 and then again in 2010, 2014 and 2018. If we survey the political evolution of these elections, one of the most visible patterns that emerge is the shift from inter- to intra-sectarian competition. This is chiefly represented in the fragmentation of the grand ethnic and sectarian political blocs of 2005. In the earlier elections the contest was about the fundamental political norms that would govern the post-2003 order: establishing the *muhasasa* system and determining the practical extent of communal representation and particularly of the respective shares of Sunnis, Shi'as and Kurds. The more these broad and foundational issues were settled, the less contested inter-sect and inter-ethnic political competition became. By extension, this diminished the perceived need for sectarian solidarity and allowed for greater intra-sectarian and intra-ethnic competition, thereby intensifying the fragmentation of electoral politics with every electoral cycle. The formalization and normalization of the ethno-sectarian division of office were bluntly described by former Speaker of Parliament Mahmud al-Mashhadani in a television appearance soon after the elections of 2018: "Our share [i.e. Sunnis'] is known: six ministries, nine commissions, and more than sixty other positions – special grades. So, what do we care who comes and who is the largest bloc and who is Prime Minister? What do I care? Whoever comes, we will say: this is our share, give it to us. He cannot say no, because this is agreed upon."[49] This perspective, of course, is a stark departure from

---

diwan/77284?lang=en. The protests of 2019 posed a far greater challenge for the governing order. In both cases, as well as those preceding them, the politics of sect were marginal: protests were concentrated in Baghdad and other Shi'a majority areas, driven by issue politics rather than identity politics, and in the case of 2019, these protests were an expression of rage towards the political system in its entirety.

[49] "Sa'et Mukashafa 'ra'is majlis al-nuwab al-asbaq al-Mashhadani'" (Sa'et Mukashafa 'former head of the Council of Representatives al-Mashhadani'), uploaded Nov. 7, 2018, https://www.youtube.com/watch?v=ioeMo2uJmeo. In the same interview Mashhadani emphasizes the fact that, beyond sectarian identity, *muhasasa* today is a function of family links, tribal connections and party affiliation.

the hotly contested debates surrounding demographics and political entitlement that proliferated in the early years following 2003.[50]

The elections of 2005 were the most zero-sum and most bluntly sect-coded: in January of that year the vote was dominated by three lists – Sunni, Shi'a, Kurdish – who between them secured more than 87 per cent of the vote. The Shi'a list alone secured more than 48 per cent of the vote. In December, 90 per cent of the vote went to just five ethno- or sect-coded lists, with the largest share again going to the grand Shi'a coalition, which received more than 41 per cent of the vote.[51] Though fundamentally differing in stakes and lines of contestation, the 2010 election was also a tightly knit affair with just four lists sharing more than 81 per cent of the vote.[52] Thereafter,

---

[50] In particular, a fairly common view among Sunni Arab politicians in the early post-2003 years rejected the notion that Sunni Arab Iraqis were a minority. This position was voiced by mainstream Sunni politicians as well as more extreme voices; from religious leaders such as Harith al-Dhari (former general secretary of the Association of Muslim Scholars), to politicians such as Khalaf al-Ulayyan, Mohsen Abdel Hamid (former head of the Iraqi Islamic Party) and Osama al-Nujaifi, to extremists such as Salafi jihadist preacher Taha al-Dulaimi. In fact, as early as August 2003 Dulaimi was describing the idea that Sunnis are a minority as a lie. See Taha al-Dulaimi, "Hathihi Hiya al-Haqiqa: al-A'dad wa-l-Nisab al-Sukaniyya li-Ahl al-Sunna wa-l-Shi'a fi-l-Iraq" (This Is the Truth: Population Numbers and Percentages of Sunnis and Shi'as in Iraq), published online, Aug. 2003, re-published in 2009, https://ia601608.us.archive.org/19/items/adel-0044/Aqidah05778.pdf. For a less extreme iteration, see comments of Vice President Tariq al-Hashemi in which he claimed that the notion of a Shi'a majority in Iraq is a lie. "Media bias 'threat' to Iraq," Al Jazeera, Jan. 3, 2007, https://www.aljazeera.com/news/middleeast/2007/01/2008525184921434756.html.

[51] For the elections of 2005, see the relevant pages of the Iraqi Independent High Electoral Commission: http://www.ihec.iq/page6/page18.aspx and http://www.ihec.iq/page6/page16.aspx; Adam Carr's election archive, http://psephos.adam-carr.net/countries/i/iraq/; Dodge, *Iraq: From War to a New Authoritarianism*, pp. 44–48.

[52] In theory, the elections of 2010 saw the *muhasasa* system challenged by the top two contenders. On the one hand, incumbent prime minister Nouri al-Maliki's State of Law Coalition attempted to break with *muhasasa* and the politics of sect, and run independently on a strongman, security-first platform. On the other hand, the Iraqi National Movement (also known as the al-Iraqiyya List), headed by former prime minister Ayad Allawi, sought to do the same but on an anti-Shi'a-Islamist platform. Following a contested outcome, Maliki secured a second term with the aid

former prime minister Nouri al-Maliki's second term proved divisive not just in terms of Sunni–Shi'a relations but also in terms of intra-sect dynamics as well.[53] This was reflected in the unprecedented fragmentation of the 2014 elections. While there was hardly any overlap between Sunni, Shi'a and Kurdish constituencies in 2014, the three were internally fragmented, with the Shi'a vote dominated by three lists, and the Sunni vote split mostly among four lists, in addition to smaller lists across the spectrum. In that sense, where 2005 was an inter-sect and inter-ethnic contest for position in the new order, 2014 was more akin to three separate intra-sect or intra-ethnic elections. Underlining the degree of fragmentation and the intensity of intra-sect or intra-ethnic competition, in 2014 the highest share of the vote stood at 24 per cent (compared to 48 per cent in 2005), beyond which no other list or entity received more than 7.5 per cent of the vote.[54]

---

of an Iran-brokered reconstitution of the Shi'a alliance, and all concerned, including Allawi, reverted to form in a 'consensus government' that apportioned political office among the key political actors – in other words, back to *muhasasa*. For the elections of 2010, see the relevant pages of the Iraqi Independent High Electoral Commission's website, including http://www.ihec.iq/page6/page13.aspx; Carr's election archive, http://psephos.adam-carr.net/countries/i/iraq/; Kenneth Katzman, "Iraq: Politics, Elections and Benchmarks," *Congressional Research Service*, March 1, 2011, pp. 9–19, 25, https://www.everycrsreport.com/files/20110301_RS21968_755bf620139afe0896cb6b2d4d5a6fd6bc7d65a8.pdf; "Iraq's Uncertain Future: Elections and Beyond," International Crisis Group, Middle East Report no. 94, 2010.

[53] Maliki's second term had the double effect of increasing internal division within Sunni and Shi'a political coalitions while at the same time fostering cross-sectarian and cross-ethnic efforts to weaken Maliki. The most notable example of this was the failed attempt in 2012 to unseat Maliki through a vote of no confidence. The effort was spearheaded by the Sadrists, Ayad Allawi's al-Iraqiyya, and the Democratic Patriotic Alliance of Kurdistan. See Faleh A. Jabar, Renad Mansour and Abir Khaddaj, "Maliki and the Rest: A Crisis within a Crisis," Iraq Institute for Strategic Studies, June 2012, http://iraqstudies.com/books/featured3.pdf. For the fragmentation of the Iraqiyya List in this period, see Stephen Wicken, "Iraq's Sunnis in Crisis," Institute for the Study of War, May 2013, pp. 9–23; "Iraq's Secular Opposition: The Rise and Decline of al-Iraqiyya," International Crisis Group, Middle East Report no. 127, July 31, 2012.

[54] For the elections of 2014, see the relevant pages of the Iraqi Independent High Electoral Commission's website, http://www.ihec.iq/page6/page10.aspx; and Adam Carr's election archive http://psephos.adam-carr.net/countries/i/iraq/.

The fragmentation and diminishing relevance of sectarian categories were even more evident in the elections of 2018. Whereas in January 2005, more than 87 per cent of the vote was split among three lists, with the top list netting 48 per cent of the vote, in 2018 the top nine lists shared 80 per cent of the vote, with the top performer, Sadrist-led Sa'irun, netting only 14 per cent. Furthermore, in another departure from prior practice, many of the major lists campaigned across ethnic and sectarian lines. Sa'irun ran in all governorates except for Kirkuk and Kurdistan. The Nasr alliance, headed by the incumbent prime minister Haider al-Abadi, ran in all governorates and even won in Sunni-majority Nineveh. The Fatah Alliance, led by the more powerful and Iran-leaning elements of the Popular Mobilization Units (PMUs), campaigned in all governorates of Arab Iraq.[55] And some lists, such as Ayad Allawi's National Coalition and Ammar al-Hakim's National Wisdom Movement, even campaigned in the Kurdish governorates.[56] These dynamics were subsequently reflected in the government formation process, which defied ethno-sectarian compartmentalization. For example, the trademark backroom

---

[55] PMU is an umbrella term for the mostly Shi'a (and certainly Shi'a-dominated) paramilitary groups that were mobilized in the war against the Islamic State and that have since been formally institutionalized as part of Iraq's security structures. The formations of the PMU vary in their ideological leanings, the date and manner of their formation, and their proximity to Iran. For details, see Inna Rudolf, "From Battlefield to Ballot Box: Contextualising the Rise and Evolution of Iraq's Popular Mobilisation Units," International Centre for the Study of Radicalisation and Political Violence, May 2018, https://icsr.info/wp-content/uploads/2018/05/ICSR-Report-From-Battlefield-to-Ballot-Box-Contextualising-the-Rise-and-Evolution-of-Iraq%E2%80%99s-Popular-Mobilisation-Units.pdf; Fanar Haddad, "Understanding Iraq's Hashd al-Sha'bi," Century Foundation, March 5, 2018, https://tcf.org/content/report/understanding-iraqs-hashd-al-shabi/; Renad Mansour and Faleh A. Jabar, "The Popular Mobilization Forces and Iraq's Future," Carnegie Middle East Center, April 2017, http://carnegie-mec.org/2017/04/28/popular-mobilization-forces-and-iraq-s-future-pub-68810.

[56] For the elections of 2018, see the relevant pages of the Iraqi Independent High Electoral Commission's website, http://www.ihec.iq/HOME/IconFiles/pageC3; Adam Carr's election archive http://psephos.adam-carr.net/countries/i/iraq/; and Renad Mansour and Christine van den Toorn, "The 2018 Iraqi Federal Elections: A Population in Transition?" LSE Middle East Centre, July 2018, http://eprints.lse.ac.uk/89698/7/MEC_Iraqi-elections_Report_2018.pdf.

jockeying for ministerial positions that follows every Iraqi election yielded unexpected bedfellows in the form of Shi'a-centric and Sunni-centric political actors more accustomed to hurling accusations of treason and complicity with Iran or the Islamic State at each other.[57]

This cross-sectarian collusion between what had been regarded as implacable enemies is another marker of the development of a more transactional Iraqi politics, shaped by political interests and pragmatism.[58] This echoes the literature on the evolution of political marketing in post-authoritarian or post-conflict settings, in which an initially more blunt and narrowly focused messaging gives way to more politically flexible and professional strategies.[59] Furthermore, with time the increasing complexity of the electoral system alters incentive structures away from zero-sum calculations and shapes electoral behaviour accordingly: from intergroup competition to increased intra-group competition.[60] Indicative of this is the banality

---

[57] Perhaps the starkest example was the umbrella 'Construction Bloc'. This political alliance linked the (Sunni-centric) National Axis, former prime minister Maliki's State of Law, and the PMU-led Fatah Alliance. This combined two sect-centric camps that had long framed each other as the sect-coded hate figures par excellence embodying the heart of sectarian narratives of victimhood.

[58] Needless to say, political interests and pragmatism are often regarded as a euphemism for political cynicism. Iraqi public opinion was taken aback by the unexpected alignment of political actors who had previously expended much energy demonizing each other as Islamic State supporters or nefarious Iranian militiamen. This fed into the wider popular alienation from the political classes. See Helene Sallon, "In Iraq, the Revolt of Generation 2018," *Worldcrunch* (originally in French in *Le Monde*), Oct. 13, 2018, https://www.worldcrunch.com/world-affairs/in-iraq-the-revolt-of-generation-2018.

[59] For a discussion of these themes, see Adam Harmes, "Political Marketing in Post-Conflict Elections: The Case of Iraq," *Journal of Political Marketing* (2016), DOI: 10.1080/15377857.2016.1193834. Harmes applies the Lees-Marshment model of political marketing that categorizes political parties along three ideal types: product-oriented, sales-oriented and market-oriented parties. Post-conflict electoral evolution goes through these stages from the least sophisticated (product-oriented) to the more layered, nuanced and practical market-oriented model – be it in inter- or intra-group dynamics.

[60] Ibid. To give an example of the evolution of incentive structures away from zero-sum identity politics, referencing Dodge and Benraad, Harmes argues that legislative and procedural changes in the voting system aided in the reduction of

of the once-controversial and contested apportionment of the highest political positions among Shi'a, Sunni and Kurdish representatives – a banality that was evidenced in the cross-sectarian and cross-ethnic collaboration that underpinned the nominations for these positions after the elections of 2018. For example, the nomination of the new parliamentary speaker in September 2018 (a position reserved for Sunnis), Muhammad al-Halbusi, was supported by the Iran-leaning head of the PMU and of the Fatah Alliance, Hadi al-Amiri, a figure long demonized in Sunni-centric discourse as the embodiment of Shi'a-centric militias and of Iranian interference in Iraq.[61] However, contrary to what some observers assumed, this was not proof that Halbusi was pro-Iranian, nor did it mean that he was a Shi'a lackey.[62] On the contrary, Halbusi's reliance on Amiri reflected a pragmatic strategy to outflank his Sunni rivals and secure

---

sectarian mobilization. For example, Benraad points to the controversial decision following the elections of 2010, allowing the head of the largest coalition created *after* the elections to form a government. This, she argues, incentivized parties to run individually rather than in a broad list in future elections. Quoting Myriam Benraad, "Al-Maliki Looks at a Third Term in Iraq," Al Jazeera Center for Studies, April 22, 2014, p. 3. Also see Dodge, *Iraq: From War to a New Authoritarianism*, pp. 147–180.

[61] Hadi al-Amiri has had a long career in Shi'a-centric politics with significant ideological and personal proximity to Iran. In the 1980s al-Amiri fought alongside the Iranians against Iraq as part of the Badr Brigade (the military wing of the then Iran-based Supreme Council for the Islamic Revolution in Iraq – the two parted ways in 2012, by which time they had rebranded as the Islamic Supreme Council of Iraq and the Badr Organization). Badr was embedded in the Ministry of the Interior as early as 2005 and has been accused of gross human rights violations and complicity in the sectarian violence of 2005–7. Al-Amiri, who at one point was minister of transportation, is the head of the Badr Organization and is one of the most prominent leaders in the PMU. In the elections of 2018 he headed the Fatah coalition, which represented the more powerful, politicized and Iran-leaning elements of the PMU. Fatah came second after Sadrist-led Sa'irun. He has strong ties with the upper echelons of Iran's security and political establishment.

[62] For example, "Iraq Elects Pro-Iran Sunni Parliament Speaker," Radio Free Europe/Radio Liberty, Sept. 16, 2018, https://www.rferl.org/a/iraq-elects-pro-iran-sunni-as-parliament-speaker/29492394.html; and "Iraq Parliament Elects Pro-Iran Candidates," France24, Sept. 15, 2018, https://www.france24.com/en/20180915-iraq-parliament-elects-pro-iran-candidates.

the parliamentary speakership.[63] This situation echoed the broader dynamics of government formation in 2018 where, rather than Sunni and Shi'a politicians disagreeing over a position or how it was to be apportioned, there were rival cross-sectarian alignments pushing their respective Shi'a and Sunni nominees.

Some observers were resistant to the idea that sectarian categories in Iraq had lost political relevance by 2018, viewing it as an unrealistically optimistic proposition. Yet such scepticism rests on reducing Iraqi political dysfunction to, and synonymizing it with, its sectarian component. The fact that the relevance of sectarian categories had diminished in Iraqi politics did not mean that Iraq's political problems were over. That the prism of sectarian identity was not what it once was did not mean that Iraq was any closer to addressing the structural drivers of political dysfunction. Likewise, if sectarian dynamics lose their capacity to drive conflict and instability, it does not follow that other drivers will not persist or that new ones will not emerge. From *muhasasa* to corruption, political violence, weak rule of law and shortcomings in governance, these and many more structural issues continue to plague Iraq at the time of writing, even if they are less sect-coded today.[64] Thus, what is being described here is more the evolution than the resolution of instability and dysfunction between 2003 and 2018.

Political Behaviour and the Parameters of Populism

Another way to gauge the shifting politics of sect is by charting the evolution of what passes for a populist message in the different stages of entrenchment, retreat and conflict listed above. Here, elections are again a useful indicator. In 2014, Sunni politicians campaigned on little besides the theme of Sunni victimhood, whereas in 2018 there was very little in terms of sect-coded campaigning. Further, those who

---

[63] Ibrahim al-Marashi, "Iraq's New Leaders Can't Be Reduced to a US vs Iran Binary," *Middle East Eye*, Oct. 31, 2018, https://www.middleeasteye.net/columns/iraq-s-new-triumvirate-navigating-exile-power-and-iran-796203352.

[64] For a concise overview of the challenges and internal contradictions that faced the incoming government of 2018 (none of which were particularly sect-coded), see Kirk H. Sowell, "A Fractured Iraqi Cabinet," Sada, Carnegie Endowment for International Peace, Nov. 8, 2018, https://carnegieendowment.org/sada/77674.

did try to play the sectarian card – former prime minister Maliki and former Vice President Osama al-Nujaifi, for example – were poorly rewarded at the polls.[65] Likewise, the perceived exigencies of Shi'a-centric state-building in 2005 propelled the coalescence of a unified Shi'a alliance and a high Shi'a voter turnout.[66] However, by the time of the elections of 2014 and much more so those of 2018, things had changed: Shi'a empowerment no longer had to contend with a serious existential threat, security had improved, and sect-coded existential fear had waned. Consequently, the *raison d'être* of political Shi'a sect-centricity had diminished. Rather than sect-coded appeals to solidarity, entitlement or victimhood, the language of populism in 2018 was the language of reform and anti-elite anger. While it was always unlikely for this to be translated into an actionable reform agenda in the short term, it did indicate the shifting parameters of populism.

These shifts in public opinion were, in turn, reflected in public discourse. A cartoonishly blunt demonstration of this can be found in the tonal changes of Shi'a cleric and public figure Shaikh Salah al-Tufaili's sermons. Shortly before the provincial elections of 2013, Tufaili attracted much attention and controversy when he urged his listeners to vote for the benefit of Shi'as and Shi'ism – in a national sense. Noting the widespread popular alienation from electoral politics and the systemic failures of the political classes, Tufaili warned his congregation against the dangers of voter apathy by making reference to the previous regime's suppression of Shi'a rituals and by frankly urging his listeners to defend Shi'a gains since 2003:

> Who do you want us to give [political power] to? To [senior Ba'athist and Saddam Hussain's deputy] Izzat al-Duri so that Umayyad rule returns?[67] … Go out [and vote] in support of the *mathhab* [Shi'ism] …

---

[65] For an overview of Sunni campaigning in the elections of 2014, see *Inside Iraqi Politics*, no. 84 (April 30, 2014). For the 2018 campaign, see *Inside Iraqi Politics*, nos. 174, 176, and 177.

[66] In the words of an International Crisis Group report, voters sought to ensure "the realisation of the Shi'ite majority's dream of ruling Iraq," and to take advantage of "a historical opportunity for the Shi'ites." See "The Next Iraqi War?" International Crisis Group, p. 29.

[67] Reference to the seventh- and eighth-century Umayyad dynasty, which in Shi'a lore is regarded as the epitome of injustice, oppression and anti-Shi'ism.

Despite all the government's faults … despite that, may God reward them: at least [the government] is one that calls for *Ali wali-u-Allah* [the Shi'a call to prayer] – even if not truthfully … Did you ever dream that in Iraq you would have live-feed and [broadcasts of] mourning rituals?[68]

That was in December 2012, in a context of rising security challenges and increasing instability.[69] Regionally, the uprising in Bahrain and, more so, the Syrian civil war created a sense of sectarian crisis across the Middle East, further incentivizing sectarian entrenchment. Domestically, violence was again rising in the context of a poisonous political atmosphere that was dominated by Prime Minister Maliki's increasing authoritarianism, and especially his increasingly fraught relations with the Sunni political classes.[70] Indeed, Tufaili's sermon was delivered on the eve of mass protests in Sunni-majority areas that would continue for a year and lead to the re-emergence of sustained insurgency.[71] In short, there was enough uncertainty, violence, fear

---

[68] The sermon was delivered in Dec. 2012. See "Laylat 25 Muharram 1434 – al-Shaikh Salah al-Tufaili" (The Night of 25 Muharram 1434 – Shaikh Salah al-Tufaili), uploaded Dec. 20, 2012, https://www.youtube.com/watch?v=xIrFXJzGdYQ.

[69] For a snapshot of the security situation in that month, see Joel Wing, "Iraq's Insurgency Tries to End November 2012 with a Bang," *Musings on Iraq*, Dec. 3, 2012, http://musingsoniraq.blogspot.com/2012/12/iraqs-insurgency-tries-to-end-november.html. That same month, Maliki ordered the arrest of Minister of Finance Rafi' al-Issawi's security detail and the raiding of Issawi's offices, setting off a chain reaction of instability that would lead to the emergence of widespread protests in Sunni-majority areas of Iraq, and ultimately to the renewal of full-scale insurgency in the spring of 2013. This in turn paved the way for the Islamic State takeover of 2014.

[70] For Maliki's second term in office, see "Iraq between Maliki and the Islamic State," Project on Middle East Political Science, July 9, 2014, https://pomeps.org/wp-content/uploads/2014/07/POMEPS_BriefBooklet24_Iraq_Web.pdf.

[71] For the Sunni protest movement of 2012–13 and the state of Sunni politics generally at the time, including the re-emergence of widespread insurgency in the spring of 2013, see Joel Wing, "Understanding Iraq's Protest Movements: An Interview with Kirk H. Sowell, Editor of Inside Iraqi Politics," May 7, 2013, *Musings on Iraq*, http://musingsoniraq.blogspot.sg/2013/05/understanding-iraqs-protest-movements.html; Stephen Wicken and Jessica Lewis, "From Protest Movement to Armed Resistance: 2013 Iraq Update #24," June 14, 2013, Institute for the Study of War, http://iswiraq.blogspot.sg; Yahya al-Kubaisi, "Iraq: Recent Protests and the Crisis of a Political System," Arab Centre for Research and Policy Studies, Feb.

and sectarian entrenchment in Iraq and beyond for the language of Shi'a empowerment and the imperatives of its defence to resonate with sections of the Shi'a electorate – hence the alleged Ba'thist coups that some Shi'a voices had warned of in every prior election.[72] Hence, also, a Shi'a-centric populism heavily coloured with insecurity. For example, a poem from 2014 entitled "If we don't vote"[73] echoes Tufaili's narrative, in which the listener is warned that voter apathy will bring back the Ba'th and see the banning of Shi'a rituals; the same message is repeated in a 2013 anthem with the self-explanatory title "Our government is Shi'a";[74] and, also in 2013, "Till death we will not hand it [power] over"[75] was the chorus to a mass recitation at the shrine of Hussain ibn Ali in Karbala.[76] In that sense, Tufaili's sermon was a reflection of the broader context and the popular mood among some sections of Shi'a Iraq.

After 2014 and the war against the Islamic State, there was a shift in the parameters of populism. There emerged a belief that Iraq's security challenges, serious though they might be, were no longer an existential threat. This new belief was a result of the way the challenge of the Islamic State was met after 2014: the rise of the PMUs against the

---

2013; Wicken, "Iraq's Sunnis in Crisis"; "Make or Break: Iraq's Sunnis and the State," International Crisis Group, Middle East Report no. 144, Aug. 14, 2013.

[72] Maliki's messaging in 2013 and 2014 (both election years) was heavily invested in the theme of defending Shi'a interests. Pro-Maliki social media accounts would even refer to him as "Mukhtar al-'Asr" (the Mukhtar of our age) – a reference to Mukhtar al-Thaqafi, a seventh-century figure who led a rebellion ostensibly to claim vengeance for the killing of the Prophet's grandson and third Shi'a Imam, Hussain ibn Ali, at the Battle of Karbala.

[73] Author's personal collection.

[74] "Shi'iyya hukumatna Yusuf al-Subaihawi" (Our government is Shi'a Yusuf al-Subaihawi), uploaded Feb. 8, 2013, https://www.youtube.com/watch?v=1bdoY7BUEz8.

[75] "Li-l-mawt ma ninteeha min dakhil marqad al-Imam al-Hussain" (Till death we will not hand it over from inside the shrine of Imam Hussain), uploaded March 25, 2013, https://www.youtube.com/watch?v=Z9fxF5uQXpA.

[76] Needless to say, in all three cases there were countervailing messages of national unity and ecumenism, but the imperative to protect Shi'a gains in the face of what was a deteriorating security situation and a growing feeling of domestic and regional threat and deepening sectarian division was palpable and made calls for Shi'a solidarity more resonant.

Islamic State and the resulting sense (part real, part myth) of popular agency in the war and in Iraqi security; the popularity, legitimacy and eventually the successes of the war against the insurgent group; and the renewed regional and international investment in Iraq's survival. This had a direct effect on the relevance of Shi'a political sect-centricity and on the resonance of the language of Shi'a empowerment. To illustrate, in a sermon from March 2016, the same Tufaili struck a very different tone – one that was in step with recent shifts in popular discourse. After expounding on the theft, corruption and failures of governance that abound in Iraq, Tufaili addressed the political classes: "You made us yearn for that man [Saddam Hussain]. Despite all the sorrow, prisons, fear and death [in Saddam Hussain's time], let him come back – we've had enough! Let him come back." Then, addressing the congregation: "Perhaps half of you would vote for Saddam if he returned!"[77] He even went on to praise the public distribution system of food rationing in Saddam's time, contrasting it with the shortcomings of the system in 2016.

This nostalgia for Saddam Hussain (an increasingly common phenomenon) need not be taken literally, but it does highlight the shifting parameters of populism and of political Shi'a sect-centricity.[78] In the early years after the American invasion of 2003, such longing for the Saddam Hussain era, even if plainly hyperbolic, was generally too politically incorrect for Shi'a actors and audiences, particularly in a public setting. Yet as the above example shows, by 2016 this was clearly no longer so. In most cases the figurative yearning for a resurrection of Saddam Hussain can be read as an act of protest and performative irreverence through which people could express their profound and widespread disillusionment with the political classes. This had been a feature of Sunni protest repertoires since 2003 (with varying degrees of ideological conviction), but by 2016 Shi'as had

---

[77] "Al-Shaikh Salah al-Tufaili laylat 21 Jumadi al-Akhira 1437h al-Kut" (Shaikh Salah al-Tufaili the night of 21 Jumadi al-Akhira 1437h Kut), uploaded March 31, 2016, https://www.youtube.com/watch?v=Uu78_6JrlDw.

[78] See Marsin Alshamary, "Authoritarian Nostalgia among Iraqi Youth: Roots and Repercussions," *War on the Rocks*, July 25, 2018, https://warontherocks.com/2018/07/authoritarian-nostalgia-among-iraqi-youth-roots-and-repercussions/.

adopted the practice too.[79] The perceived security and irreversibility of the post-2003 political order, and of Shi'a dominance within it, facilitated the normalization of such behaviour in Shi'a quarters. The easing of existential threat (or perceptions thereof), and particularly of sect-coded challenges to the existing political order, weakened the relevance of political sect-centricity, and lessened the perceived need to defend sectarian boundaries or uphold sectarian solidarity.[80] All of which further underlines the diminished political relevance of sectarian identities and the evolution of political contestation (and political instability) beyond zero-sum sectarian competition.

The Politics of Sect after 2014

Events between 2014 and 2018 – the fall of Mosul, the subsequent war against the Islamic State, the change of leadership in Iraq, the deceleration of the Syrian civil war, and the reorientation of Iraq's regional politics in a more benign direction – had a pivotal effect on sectarian relations in Iraq and the region. Again, this did not signal the end of insurgency or political violence, but it rendered sect-coded civil war of the sort witnessed prior to 2014 unlikely. The first phase of Iraq's civil war in 2005–7 was sect-coded in a way that 2013–15 was not. This was primarily due to the intra-Sunni divisiveness of the phenomenon of the Islamic State, and the broad cross-sectarian, cross-ethnic and even international cooperation (rivalries and strategic contradictions notwithstanding) that went into the war against the group. This blurring of sectarian boundaries reflected the

---

[79] From the earliest days of the post-2003 order, the image and memory of Saddam have been used as symbols of protest against the new order. At one point, Saddam's burial site was turned into a shrine and something of a pilgrimage site. See Saad Salloum, "Ziyara ila Qabr Saddam Hussain" (A Visit to Saddam Hussain's Grave), *Niqash*, Aug. 2009, http://www.niqash.org/articles/?id=2501&lang=ar.

[80] Similar examples can be found from 2006–9, where the climate of 2006 created the space for an aggressive and highly sect-coded populism while the relative stabilization of 2009 encouraged a more pan-Iraqi civic and ecumenical populism. For a stark illustration of Sadrist cleric Hazim al-A'raji calling for the murder of 'Wahhabis' in 2006 while striking a far more ecumenical tone in late 2008, see Haddad, *Sectarianism in Iraq*, pp. 188–189, 202.

normalization and relative stabilization of the post-2003 order (for the meantime at least) and the diminished political relevance of the Sunni–Shi'a divide. Consequently, if Iraq were to go through another bout of civil war, it is unlikely to be significantly sect-coded, owing to the intensified intersection of shared interests and cross-sectarian political alignments. Evidence of this can be glimpsed in power relations and patterns of violence since 2014. Despite the stubborn assumptions of many an observer, it was inaccurate to frame the campaign in Iraq against the Islamic State as a 'Sunni–Shi'a' or 'sectarian' conflict. Rather than a Sunni–Shi'a war, it was a war between the Islamic State and its allies and the state and its allies, with the latter being far too layered and heterogeneous for clear-cut sect-specific labelling, despite being obviously Shi'a-led. As early as 2014, and even prior to the fall of Mosul, there were warnings that the rise of the Islamic State was threatening to turn intra-Sunni violence into a long-term problem.[81] And, indeed, in areas liberated from the Islamic State, intra-Sunni violence and tribal vengeance have been a more persistent issue than sectarian violence.[82] The grim human rights situation in liberated areas and the primacy of vengeance over justice have been too systemic and have implicated too broad an array of actors to be reduced solely to a form of sectarian violence.[83]

---

[81] Wa'il Ni'ma, "Al-Anbar takhsha 'harb tharat' wa-rijaluha musta'idun li-tard Dai'sh itha taghayar ra'is al-hukuma" (Anbar fears 'a war of vendettas' and its men are ready to expel Da'ish if there is a change in head of government), *Al-Mada Newspaper*, June 4, 2014, https://almadapaper.net/Details/106910.

[82] See, for example, Kamal al-Ayash, "Anbar Tribes Exact Revenge upon Iraqis Who Worked with Extremists," *Niqash*, Oct. 13, 2016, http://www.niqash.org/en/articles/security/5378/; Kamal al-Ayash, "Anbar's New Anti-Extremist Militias Get Bigger, Cause New Problems," *Niqash*, Nov. 2016, http://www.niqash.org/en/articles/security/5417/.

[83] For an excellent report on the human rights situation in liberated areas of Iraq and the fatal challenges facing those accused of Islamic State affiliation or of being related to anyone with such affiliation, see Ben Taub, "Iraq's Post-ISIS Campaign of Revenge," *New Yorker*, Dec. 24, 2018, https://www.newyorker.com/magazine/2018/12/24/iraqs-post-isis-campaign-of-revenge. The report's occasional portrayals of a campaign of revenge aimed at Sunnis are contradicted by the many examples it gives of locally perpetrated predation and locally driven targeting of suspected Islamic State members and their families.

Ultimately, the war against the Islamic State served to move Iraq beyond Shi'a-centric state-building and Sunni rejection, by elevating the former and weakening the latter. The cataclysmic scale of the phenomenon of the Islamic State left Sunni-centric political actors, who had long held ambivalent views toward the post-2003 Iraqi state, with little option: they had to accept the political order and to secure their interests by working with the relevant state-aligned power-brokers. This stands in stark contrast to the incentive structures and enabling environment of the first few years after 2003: the insurgency was strong enough and the state's survival precarious enough that Sunni-centric political actors felt it prudent to have one foot in each camp and often acted as a conduit between the two. For example, in 2005, Sunni-centric politicians convinced insurgents to allow the December elections to take place unhindered in Sunni areas by persuading them that real Sunni political influence would follow a robust Sunni turnout.[84] Later on, some Sunni-centric politicians maintained relations with insurgent groups, including the Islamic State's former incarnation, the Islamic State in Iraq.[85] In some ways this is only to be expected in contexts of civil war, corruption and weak institutions. Indeed, collusion with the Islamic State and its fellow travellers, and corruption in general, are hardly the preserve of Sunni-centric actors.[86] However, particularly

---

[84] This created a post-election problem as Sunni-centric actors – politicians and insurgents alike – had vastly overestimated Sunni demographics. As reported by ICG: "Adnan Dulaimi [the head of the Sunni electoral coalition Tawafuq] publicly cried out: 'What should I tell the resistance now? How can I deliver on my promise?'" See "The Next Iraqi War?", International Crisis Group, p. 32. This echoes the findings of Foster et al., who argue that, contrary to common assumptions, electoral participation in fractionalized societies actually increases the likelihood of militancy: "In such circumstances, proportionalism institutionalizes extreme groups' political impotence." See Dennis M. Foster et al., "There Can Be No Compromise: Institutional Inclusiveness, Fractionalization and Domestic Terrorism," *British Journal of Political Science*, 43:3 (July 2013): 541–557.

[85] Benjamin Bahney, Patrick B. Johnston and Patrick Ryan, "The Enemy You Know and the Ally You Don't," *Foreign Policy*, June 23, 2015, https://foreignpolicy.com/2015/06/23/the-enemy-you-know-and-the-ally-you-dont-arm-sunni-militias-iraq/.

[86] For example, corrupt Iraqi officials are known to accept bribes from the Islamic State to free imprisoned militants, as was recently proven in Islamic State

in the earlier years after the American invasion, the ambivalence of Sunni-centric political actors toward the post-2003 state meant that their insurgent links involved more than transactional greed. Rather, for some, it was more a case of having a foot in insurgency and a foot in government, and leaning between the two according to the perceived balance of power and the perceived room for political progress. Hence, Maliki's disastrous second term (2010–14) and the profound sense of Sunni victimhood and resentment that it engendered saw several mainstream Sunni-centric politicians voicing support for insurgency in 2013 and 2014, and even positively couching the fall of Mosul in terms of revolution and liberation.[87] However, reflecting the transformed incentive structures and enabling environment, events after 2014 altered political calculations in a manner more aligned with the political order and the relations of power underlining the Iraqi state.

Khamis al-Khanjar, a Sunni-centric politician from Anbar governorate, provides a stark illustration. In the immediate aftermath of the fall of Mosul, when the political order briefly looked precarious enough to conceivably collapse, Khanjar declared an openly anti-state position: "Our aim is not just the overthrow of [Prime Minister] Maliki. We want to overthrow this oppressive, sectarian order … The revolutionaries control half of Iraq and they are at the gates of Baghdad."[88] However, the territorial defeat of the Islamic State, the

---

documentation. See Hisham al-Hashimi's tweet: @hushamalhashimi, Oct. 29, 2018, https://twitter.com/hushamalhashimi/status/1056904129170288641. Also see Patrick Cockburn, "More than just revenge: Why ISIS fighters are being thrown off buildings in Mosul," *The Independent*, July 17, 2017, https://www.independent. co.uk/news/world/middle-east/isis-mosul-iraq-fighters-killed-thrown-off-buildings-reasons-corruption-revenge-patrick-cockburn-a7845846.html.

[87] A month after the fall of Mosul, Osama al-Nujaifi – at the time one of the most prominent Sunni-centric politicians – continued to describe what was happening as a revolution, while accepting that terrorists were taking advantage of it. Abigail Hauslohner, "Iraq's crisis won't be resolved by fighting, Sunni leader says," *Washington Post*, July 12, 2014, https://www.washingtonpost.com/news/worldviews/wp/2014/07/12/iraqs-crisis-wont-be-resolved-by-fighting-sunni-leader-says/?utm_term=.02df7906e956.

[88] "Al-muqabala al-kamila li-l-Shaikh Khamis al-Khanjar ma'a qanat Al-Hadath" (The full interview of Khamis al-Khanjar with al-Hadath Channel), uploaded June 28, 2014, https://www.youtube.com/watch?v=47kuL0VnOC8&t=752s.

survival of the political order, and the practicalities of Iraqi politics quickly saw Khanjar returning to the political fold. In 2018 he was politically aligned with none other than Maliki, the former prime minister, as part of the Construction Bloc.[89] This political constellation was sponsored by the Fatah Alliance, the coalition representing the more Iran-leaning and more prominent factions of the PMUs, which until recently had featured heavily and very negatively in the political rhetoric of Khanjar and others.[90] All of this underlines the importance of not assuming the causal effects of ideology, identity, grievance or injustice independently of the broader enabling environment and the incentive structures it creates at any given time.

The End of Shi'a-Centric State-Building and Sunni Rejection?

That such U-turns in political positioning are a reflection of political opportunism is obvious enough. More importantly, however, they are also a reflection of the limits both of Sunni rejection and of Shi'a-centric state-building. This ties in with the themes of normalization, state stabilization, the shifting parameters of populism, and the shifting relevance of sectarian identities and, ultimately, of the contingent, multidimensional nature of sectarian dynamics. As sect-coded existential contestation of the state subsided, and as serious contestation of the balance of power between sect-centric actors waned (regionally and domestically), so too did political sect-centricity and, by extension, the political utility and relevance of the sectarian divide. For example, prior to 2014 mainstream Sunni-centric political discourse in Iraq

---

[89] See note 57.

[90] At one point al-Khanjar and other Sunni leaders viewed the PMUs as an existential threat and promised to fight them. See, for example (from 2015), "Khamis al-Khanjar sanuqatil al-Hashd wa bi-quwa wa mahma kanat al-tadhhiyat itha dakhal al-Hashd al-Anbar" (Khamis al-Khanjar we will strongly fight the Hashd and whatever the sacrifices if the Hashd enters Anbar), uploaded May 9, 2015, https://www.youtube.com/watch?v=8tjgwsoFJcE. Regarding the post-election convergence of political interests between Khanjar and Hadi al-Amiri, the head of the Fatah Alliance, see "Nuwab yakshifun safqat tahaluf al-Khanjar ma'a al-Amiri" (MPs reveal coalition deal between al-Khanjar and al-Amiri), NRT Digital Media, Oct. 2, 2018, http://www.nrttv.com/ar/News.aspx?id=4993&MapID=2.

used phrases such as 'Maliki's army' and the 'Safavid army' to frame the Iraqi security forces as illegitimate, anti-Sunni and anti-Iraqi. But after the fall of Mosul in 2014 and the ensuing war against the Islamic State, the parameters of populism and of political correctness shifted in a way that forbade such a stance. To illustrate, when the operation to liberate Mosul from the Islamic State was being debated in parliament in 2016–17, the consensus position was to praise the army, while voicing concerns regarding the intense destruction that accompanied the operations. To borrow from cultural framing theory, this signalled a shift in the degree of 'legal cynicism' (the disconnect between a population and law enforcement) in mainstream Sunni political discourse – much of which had previously regarded law enforcement and security services as illegitimate, anti-Sunni and anti-Iraqi.[91] The regional and domestic environment, and especially events since 2014, changed such perceptions, with legal cynicism giving way under the weight of experience, normalization and integration.

Like their Sunni-centric counterparts, Shi'a-centric politicians have also had to adapt to the diminished political utility of sectarian identity in Iraqi politics. With Shi'a political ascendance seemingly secured in Iraq and accepted regionally, intra-Shi'a politics and issue politics could better come to the fore, as evidenced by the escalating yearly protests in Baghdad and the southern governorates since 2015. Gone were the days when Shi'a-centric political actors could stoke fears of recalcitrant Sunnis, murderous *takfiris* or closeted Ba'thists. Hence, despite broad support for the war against the Islamic State, no amount of wartime jingoism was capable of preventing the emergence of a robust protest movement against perceived government failings in Baghdad and other Shi'a-majority cities in 2015.[92] In the years

---

[91] The concept was previously used to account for neighbourhood variations in Chicago homicides. One study applied it to the Iraqi case – though the analysis does not extend into the post-2014 period. See Johan Hagan et al., "The Theory of Legal Cynicism and Sunni Insurgent Violence in Post-Invasion Iraq," *American Sociological Review*, 81:2 (2016): 316–346.

[92] Harith Hasan al-Qarawee, "Ab'ad al-ihtijajat al-ijtima'iyya bi-l-Iraq wa mu'tayat al-khilaf al-Shi'i" (The Parameters of Social Protests in Iraq and the Nature of Shi'a Division), Al Jazeera Center for Studies, Aug. 17, 2015, http://studies.aljazeera.net/mritems/Documents/2015/8/17/201581712140930734Iraq-Shi'ite.pdf; Ali

following the cataclysm of 2014, political leaders were no longer able to distract attention from their failures by pointing to the security situation or by blaming the sectarian other. Today, Shi'a-centric actors have as much reason to fear a disgruntled Shi'a public as they do the re-emergence of insurgency in Sunni areas. As this book goes out to print, Iraq is witnessing the largest mass mobilization in its history, with millions of young men and women, mainly in Baghdad and the southern governorates, holding mass rallies calling for the downfall of the political system. It is too soon to draw firm conclusions about the socio-political impact and meaning of the protests of 2019 and, in any case, it is beyond the scope of this book. For our purposes, the most pertinent aspects of the protests have been the irrelevance of sectarian identity and the limits of Shi'a-centric state-building and its appeal in 2019. Where once a contested Shi'a sense of state ownership was rallied to uphold and defend the nascent order against a sect-coded challenge, today the same Shi'a motifs, symbols and rituals that were enlisted in the service of Shi'a-centric state-building are being directed against the state for its failure to offer much beyond the prism of identity politics. 'Shi'a rule' is no longer an emotive issue for a younger Shi'a public that has grown up knowing no other reality. This generation is less concerned with Shi'a victimhood and entitlement, instead they are more animated by rage at the systemic failures, dysfunction and criminality that have marked the post-2003 order. Rather than identity issues, Iraqi popular mobilization in 2019 is animated by the demand for a peace dividend, political representation, economic opportunity, functioning services and the elusive promise of a better life.

Does this signal the end of sect-centricity? Not at all; rather, it underlined its evolution. Further, and particularly at the level of political elites, it signals the normalization of the balance of power between sect-centric actors and, by extension, the normalization of the main contours of Shi'a-centric state-building: ensuring that the central levers of power are in Shi'a hands (and, more so, Shi'a-

---

Taher, "Harakat al-ihtijajat al-madani fi-l-Iraq ba'd 31 July 2015: aliyat al-tashakul wa ma'alat al-mustaqbal" (The Social Protest Movement in Iraq after 31 July 2015: Mechanisms of Formation and Future Implications), King Faisal Center for Research and Islamic Studies, Oct. 2015; Jabar, "The Iraqi Protest Movement."

centric hands), and institutionalizing a vision of Iraq that sees Iraqi Shi'as as the big brother or senior partner in Iraq's multicommunal framework. This insistence on Shi'a seniority is sometimes framed arrogantly, or condescendingly, as a sense of entitlement: "The junior partner [Sunnis] must recognize the Shi'a as the senior partner," as one Iraqi member of parliament put it in 2016.[93] Alternatively, it is framed paternalistically or patronizingly as a burden or a sense of duty: "The clear majority in Iraq are the Shi'a," Muqtada al-Sadr wrote in 2013, "this requires Shi'as to be the big brother [al-akh al-akbar] to all, and it falls to them to ensure unity and to show kindness."[94] In either guise, arrogant or patronizing, the idea of the Shi'a as the senior partner in Iraq's multicommunal framework enjoys considerable currency among many Iraqi Shi'as and reflects the long-standing culture of Shi'a political sect-centricity going back to the early twentieth century. In the immediate aftermath of the war against the Islamic State, the concept of Shi'a seniority has become less open to contestation even if it continues to be a source of resentment.

Unfortunately, at the time of writing, there was little indication of any move towards a sect-blind framework that fully divorces the relations of power from sectarian identity. This feeds a latent Sunni resentment against the state that is not unlike that which characterized Shi'a perceptions prior to 2003. In both cases, feelings of sectarian victimization are magnified with the result that even universally felt hardships, poor services for example, are seen through the prism of sectarian victimhood by those who feel targeted by structural sectarian discrimination. This again recalls Fields and Fields' warning that identity

---

[93] Iraqi member of parliament and television personality Wagih Abbas, interview, Baghdad, Dec. 2016. The extreme of this is an aggressively condescending narrative that revolves around incendiary accusations of cowardice and stained honour. For example, a poem recited by a PMU fighter attacks the men of the Sunni regions of Iraq, accusing them of cowardice, low morals and selling their daughters to foreign Islamic State fighters: "She got pregnant and gave birth to a bastard, have you no shame?" Available on "Istami' ma yaqul ahad abna' al-Hashd al Sha'bi" (Listen to what one of the sons of the PMU says), uploaded Sept. 18, 2016, https://www.youtube.com/watch?v=e-cFmMpRB8c.

[94] Muqtada al-Sadr writing in Muhammad Sadiq al-Sadr (with commentary by Muqtada al-Sadr), Al-Ta'ifiyya fi Nadhar al-Islam, p. 58.

politics are likely to result in the reallocation of injustice rather than its abolition.[95] Even when couched in the most benign terms, there is no escaping the fact that the actualization of Shi'a political sect-centricity inevitably relegates Sunni political actors to the status of dependants and pushes Sunni identity to the margins of official narratives of Iraqi state and people. The latent resentment this causes does not necessarily equate to a resurgence of violence. However, it lays the groundwork for sect-coded conflict if and when an enabling environment emerges that allows for the open contestation of the relations of power. Again, in this we have an inverse of sectarian dynamics prior to 2003.[95]

The broader acceptance (even if begrudging) and normalization of Shi'a-centricity are reflected in the evolution of its expression. In that regard, it is instructive to compare the cultural output and messaging of the Mahdi Army in 2005–7 and that of the PMUs following 2014. In 2005–7, the anthems, songs and poetry associated with the Mahdi Army were often an assertion of either Shi'a pride or of Sadrist pride.[96] By contrast, PMU anthems and poetry are far more likely to emphasize Iraqi pride. Despite its unmistakable Shi'a-centricity, the vocabulary used in PMU messaging is very much focused on identifying with the Iraqi polity and asserting a core narrative of Iraqi patriotism defined by a cross-confessional, but unambiguously and uncompromisingly Shi'a-led, fight against the Islamic State.[97] By contrast, in 2005–7, Sadrist and, more so, Mahdi Army messaging was often irreverent, taboo-busting, Shi'a-centric, and intentionally controversial. In that sense Mahdi Army messaging often displayed more of a similarity to 'gangsta rap' than to a would-be arm of the state – they even released 'dis tracks' against detractors.[98] Between 2014 and 2019, one of the main

---

[95] Fields and Fields, Racecraft, p. 147.

[96] These were not the only themes; a Shi'a-centric Iraqi nationalism was also a common theme (as it is today). See Fanar Haddad, "Sectarian Relations in Arab Iraq: Contextualizing the Civil War of 2006–2007," *British Journal of Middle Eastern Studies*, 40:2 (2013): 115–138.

[97] James Garrison, "Popular Mobilization Messaging," International Centre for Counter-Terrorism, The Hague, April 2017, https://icct.nl/wp-content/uploads/2017/04/ICCT-Garrison-Popular-Mobilization-Messaging-April-2017-1.pdf.

[98] For example, when Prime Minister Nouri al-Maliki turned against the Mahdi Army in 2008 there were a number of anthems released aimed at him. Another

objectives of PMU messaging was the instrumental construction of an image of mainstream respectability. To that end, the PMUs' narrative was one of national salvation: they framed themselves as a legitimate military, political and sociocultural force that aimed to shape Iraq's future far beyond the fight against the Islamic State.[99] Mahdi Army messaging, by contrast, seemed to revel in its outcast status and in the Sadrist ability to project power and strike fear into people. For example, an anthem from about 2008 declared:

I'm a Sadrist and I light big fires,
As big as my enemy gets, I am as big as him.
To the guy who makes the car-trunk: make it bigger,
So it can carry every ten [people] together.
[chorus] We're the ones nobody messes with.[100]

Unlike the PMUs, the Mahdi Army never cared much for normalization, institutionalization or mainstream respectability, nor was it aimed at playing a non-military role in any significant way prior to its "freeze" in 2007, when Sadr ordered the Mahdi Army to suspend military activity. By contrast, the PMUs have more far-reaching ambitions and have expended considerable effort highlighting and normalizing their non-military role – from medical services, to one PMU faction's abortive plan to establish a university,

---

example is a 'dis anthem' from about the same time aimed at politician Mish'an al-Jiburi (at the time a Sunni-centric, pro-insurgency figure). The chorus is telling: "We're the ones nobody messes with." Available on "Qasida Sadriyya qadima hamasiyya itkhabul dhid Mish'an al-Jiburi" (Old, exciting, amazing, Sadrist poem against Mish'an al-Jiburi), uploaded Jan. 23, 2016, https://www.youtube.com/watch?v=MjYNaLKX-LY.

[99] For an example of how the PMUs and their supporters view themselves, see Majid Hamid Abbas al-Hadrawi, "Dawr al-Marji'iyya al-Diniyya fi-l-Difa' 'an al-Iraq: Khutab al-Jum'ah al-Siyasiyya li-'Am 2014 Namuthaj" (The Role of the Religious *Marji'iyya* in the Defence of Iraq: The Case of the Political Friday Sermons of 2014), *Al-Ameed Journal*, 7:1 (2018): 22–83. Further underlining the mainstreaming of the PMUs, the author is an assistant professor at the University of Kufa and the journal is published by the Shi'a Endowments.

[100] From the 'dis track' aimed at politician Mish'an al-Jiburi (see note 98). The reference to car trunks is in particularly bad taste given their association with the epidemic of kidnappings and assassinations taking place at the time.

to the opening of a Hashd martyrs' museum in central Baghdad, and so forth.[101]

Charting this evolution of Shi'a militancy and Shi'a-centricity highlights the shifting parameters of sectarian identity, the normalization of once-controversial issues, and the evolution of political contestation and threat perceptions. By extension, it illustrates the shift from a more insecure Shi'a-centricity concerned with survival in a zero-sum, sect-coded civil war to a more secure and confident stance that seeks to assert and further normalize the role of senior partner at a national level beyond the relatively narrow confines of a securitized sectarian divide. Ultimately this was a product of the post-2014 landscape and of the cumulative effect of the war against the Islamic State. In what is undoubtedly a gross overstatement, Wagih Abbas (member of parliament, TV presenter and one of the most unabashedly Shi'a-centric public figures in Iraq) described 2014 as a pivotal moment of empowerment and finality: "In 2014, the question of Iraqi history was resolved ... 2014 is the moment that [Iraqi] Shi'as emerged out of *taqiyya*."[102] Iraqi Shi'ism, in this view, has moved from an apologetic stance to a more assertive one.

This degree of certainty is never advisable when thinking about Iraq's future or about the vicissitudes of sectarian relations. The trigger for the accelerated elevation of the political relevance of sectarian identities was ultimately the manner in which the American invasion of 2003 disturbed the balance of power between sect-centric actors both in Iraq and in the broader region. The political and military contestation that followed and the sect-coded fears and ambitions they

---

[101] See general coverage in www.al-hashed.net. For the Hashd martyrs' museum see, "Fi awwal iftitah lahu – tawafud al-za'irin ila mathaf shuhada' al-Hashd fi shari' al-Mutanabi bi-Baghdad" (In its first opening – the arrival of visitors in the Hashd martyrs' museum in Mutanabi Street in Baghdad), Sept. 14, 2018, http://al-hashed. net/2018/09/14 في-أول-افتتاح-له-توافد-الزائرين-إلى-مت/. A most bizarre example that nevertheless further highlights the extent of the PMUs' normalization is the reported idea of setting up an official PMU soccer team. See Mustafa Saadoun, "Iraq's PMU Militia Wants Its Own Soccer Club," *Al-Monitor*, Oct. 18, 2018, https:// www.al-monitor.com/pulse/originals/2018/10/iraq-sport-football-popular-mobilization-units.html.

[102] Interview, Wagih Abbas, Baghdad, Dec. 2016. *Taqiyya* is a reference to the practice of dissimulation that is adopted for fear of persecution.

engendered had considerably receded by 2018 with the normalization of post-2003 hierarchies of power. Iraqi and regional developments seem to be veering away from the prism of sectarian identity: at the time of writing, the sectarian wave of chapter 6 seems to have crested. However, another black swan event that once again allows for the contestation and renegotiation of relations of power between sect-centric actors could nevertheless reinvigorate the political relevance of sectarian identity. For example, at the time of writing, tensions in the Gulf appear to be nearing breaking point as a result of American bullishness on Iran, to say nothing of the barely restrained hawkishness currently ascendant in several Middle Eastern capitals, threatening to spark yet another major war.[103] Such a conflict would likely reignite sectarian tensions as sect-centric actors across the region try to defend gains or reverse losses incurred since 2003 and as sectarian identities come to be intertwined yet again with regional hostilities.

Changes since 2014, including the relative stabilization of the Iraqi state, may ultimately be squandered, as were the gains made in Iraq's brief moment of optimism in 2008–10.[104] The changes being described here are not necessarily permanent. Indeed, permanence is a problematic concept where identity is concerned: the politics of sect have gone through several stages and will continue to evolve in line with broader sociocultural and political conditions. Nevertheless, even if sectarian dynamics take a turn for the worse, it is almost impossible for them to revert to what they were in the early post-2003 years. The entrenchment and civil war of 2003–7 were caused by a set of

---

[103] For example, Ishaan Tharoor, "The White House builds a path to war with Iran," *Washington Post*, May 15, 2019; Eric Schmitt and Julian E. Barnes, "White House reviews military plans against Iran, in echoes of Iraq War," *New York Times*, May 13, 2019; Bob Dreyfuss, "Trump and Bolton are putting war with Iran on a hair trigger," *The Nation*, May 7, 2019.

[104] There were great improvements in these years: violence continued declining, the politics of sect were in very clear retreat, militia and insurgent networks had been crippled, and many were optimistic that post-2003 Iraqi politics had come of age – unfortunately this proved illusory and was derailed by the controversies surrounding the elections of 2010 (see note 52). Writing in 2009, Visser provides an overview of the reasons for optimism and also why optimism needed to be cautious. See Reidar Visser, "Post-Sectarian Strategies for Iraq," Historiae.org, March 2009, http://historiae.org/post-sectarian.asp.

extraordinary circumstances and an enabling environment that cannot readily be re-created: foreign invasion and occupation, state collapse, a backdrop of decades-long isolation and sect-coded legacy issues. The Iraqi state eventually grew more complex after its destruction in 2003 and, by 2018, political alignments and political contestation reflected a complexity that could no longer be contained in the framework of 'sectarianism' – however defined. This was even more glaring at the level of regional politics, where the illusion of Sunni and Shi'a camps had long been unsustainable.[105] In Iraq, the war against the Islamic State created an exceedingly complex landscape marked by fragmented and layered security and governance structures. While certain Shi'a-centric actors retained outsized leverage in these hierarchies of power, they remained nevertheless part of a larger picture marked by bargaining, cooperation and competition between a range of actors whose alignments and calculations were governed by far more than their communal identities.[106] Regionally too, policy towards Iraq was no longer framed (cynically or otherwise) in sectarian terms and, at the time of writing, Iraq's neighbours were invested in Iraqi stability and unlikely to support spoilers or act as spoilers themselves. This feeds into a virtuous cycle – domestic and regional – which has seen the political relevance of sectarian identity in Iraq in clear retreat and which is the inverse of the vicious cycle – domestic and regional – that followed after 2003. In this way, Iraq demonstrates the way

---

[105] On the transformation of regional politics between 2011 and 2018, see Marc Lynch, "The New Arab Order: Power and Violence in Today's Middle East," *Foreign Affairs*, Sept.–Oct. 2018, https://www.foreignaffairs.com/articles/middle-east/2018-08-13/new-arab-order.

[106] These dynamics are captured well in a 2018 report that provides a granular look at security and governance in northern Diyala governorate. See Zmkan Ali Saleem, Mac Skelton and Christine van den Toorn, "Security and Governance in the Disputed Territories under a Fractured GoI: The Case of Northern Diyala," *LSE Middle East Centre Blog*, Nov. 14, 2018, http://blogs.lse.ac.uk/mec/2018/11/14/security-and-governance-in-the-disputed-territories-under-a-fractured-goi-the-case-of-northern-diyala/. Likewise, see Erica Gaston and Andras Derzsi-Horvath, "It's Too Early to Pop the Champagne: The Micro-Politics of Territorial Control in Iraq," *War on the Rocks*, Oct. 24, 2017, https://warontherocks.com/2017/10/its-too-early-to-pop-champagne-in-baghdad-the-micro-politics-of-territorial-control-in-iraq/.

that sectarian relations and sectarian identities evolve according to a multidimensional context and respond to ever-changing incentive structures and enabling environments rather than being driven solely by ideology or having an ancient logic of their own transcending time, space, reason and comprehension. One Iraqi politician offered a simple summation: "Like pan-Arabism before it, sectarianism is a trend [*moda*] and one day it will pass."[107]

---

[107] Interview, Dhafir al-Ani, Baghdad, Jan. 2012. Again, it is worth cautioning against viewing such shifts with finality or permanence.

CONCLUSION

A chief motivation behind the writing of this book has been the urgent need to demystify and de-exoticize the study of sectarian identity. One of the primary agents of that mystification is the term 'sectarianism': a term that is open to a dizzying variety of interpretations and that is irredeemably mired in negativity and political toxicity – precisely the characteristics that lend it its shape-shifting and distorting qualities. Moreover, in addition to being fatally flawed in an analytical sense, the term 'sectarianism' is one that is easily and regularly weaponized to isolate, stigmatize and criminalize political opponents and political activism particularly when it emanates from sectarian outgroups – as the examples of 2011 Bahrain and Syria demonstrate. It is ironic that so many scholars accept a loose definition of 'sectarianism' as the instrumentalization of sectarian categories for political purposes where, practically speaking, one of the primary facilitators of this instrumentalization is the undefined, nebulous and morally charged nature of the term itself. Instrumentalizing sectarian identity by, for example, accusing political opponents of 'sectarianism' would be that much harder were the term constrained by anything resembling a coherent definition. As a result of that lack of meaning and the absence of any demarcation as to the contours of the term, the negativity of 'sectarianism' has often unduly stigmatized sectarian identity itself. Further, the term 'sectarianism' deepens the mystification, exoticization and presumed exceptionalism of sectarian relations in the Middle East and, in doing so, places Sunni–Shi'a dynamics beyond the broader literature on intergroup relations. Indeed, the term increases the distance between students of sectarian relations and the broader social sciences in that what is elsewhere labelled 'populism' or 'clientelism', for example, is given the opaque title of 'sectarianism' where Sunnis and Shi'as are concerned. In the process, we unwittingly perpetuate the mystification and fetishization that have so often featured in commentary on sectarian relations in the Middle East by framing sectarian dynamics as somehow different from more familiar concepts. In doing so we also deny ourselves the analytical depth that comes from a comparative perspective that can draw upon several rich bodies of literature dealing with phenomena relevant to and, in some cases, reflective of modern sectarian identities: nationalism, identity theory, ethnic conflict, critical race theory, state formation, and so forth.

Rather than just admiring the problem, this book has attempted to put forth a solution that might help advance the study of sectarian dynamics and move the debate on sectarian relations in the Middle East forward without the confusion that accompanies the term 'sectarianism'. The framework suggested here is simple enough and begins with a shift in analytic focus, one that discards the undefinable ism and focuses instead on the root, namely sectarian identity. After all, however one chooses to define 'sectarianism', it is ultimately a referent to one or more facets or dynamics associated with sectarian identity. By finally abandoning 'sectarianism' we can start thinking about the innumerable phenomena to which the term refers and begin theorizing sectarian identity. To date, almost all theoretical attention has been devoted to 'sectarianism' with hardly any theorization of sectarian identity. It is hoped that this book will have made some progress towards filling that gap.

The model presented here aims to grasp the multidimensionality and inherent fluidity of sectarian identity. The first step, therefore, is recognizing the inadequacy of viewing sectarian identity as having any one meaning. With that starting point, the model I have proposed frames sectarian identity as something that is formed, imagined, perceived and practised at four overlapping, interdependent and mutually dialogical levels: doctrinal, subnational, national and transnational. There is no need to repeat how these dimensions relate to each other and how the model works (see chapters 3-4), but it is worth outlining the benefits of adopting an explicitly multilayered model such as this one. Firstly, it allows for a sharper focus in that it alerts us to the multifaceted nature of sectarian identity and enables us to identify which of its aspects are more relevant to a given context. This can help us avoid analytical misdirection as in, for example, assuming that sectarian dynamics in a given context are driven solely by regional geopolitics where they are in fact driven by contested claims to political and economic goods at the national level; or, to give another example, assuming that a given sectarian issue can be solved by a doctrinal solution – an act of clerical ecumenism, for example – when what is needed is a political solution. Secondly, by switching our focus from 'sectarianism' to sectarian identity and by recognizing sectarian identity's inherent multidimensionality, we are better able to move beyond the stultifying binaries that have dominated discussion of 'sectarianism' (see chapter 2). This is essential to understanding how sectarian identity actually works and how it relates to recent sect-coded events in the Middle East. To take the region-wide aftermath of the US-led invasion of Iraq in 2003, our understanding of the sectarian wave that followed (see chapter 6) cannot be restricted solely to international relations and Arab–Iranian rivalry any more than it can be limited exclusively to pent-up grievances at the national level. Likewise, we cannot ignore local issues and competing sect-specific claims while focusing on elite instrumentalization nor vice versa – particularly given that, to be effective, the two need and rely on each other. Further, while doctrinal issues and religious narratives may be used to justify violence, mobilize sectarian solidarities, and formulate parameters of inclusion, exclusion and political community, these cannot be taken as causal factors in isolation of the national, subnational and transnational lines of contestation with which they interact; all of this underlines the need for a multidimensional model such as the one proposed in this book. Finally, I believe that this framework is naturally conducive to an interdisciplinary methodology. This allows us to sharpen our analytical approach by enabling us to better identify which analytical tools and bodies of literature are most relevant to a given context. For example, the doctrinal dimension of sectarian identity requires us to tap into sectarian polemics, theological and jurisprudential exegeses, religious traditions and narrations, and the like; however, these are of no practical use in understanding the transnational dimension of sectarian identity, which is better explained by, for instance, international relations theory. In my own case, beyond identity theory I have heavily relied in this book on theories of nationalism and critical race theory. The former is an obvious tool with which to understand the national dimension of sectarian identity while I have found the latter to be invaluable in deciphering sectarian dynamics at the subnational dimension. This is more than mere theoretical self-indulgence; rather, I would argue that this kind of interdisciplinarity is indispensable: given the multidimensional nature of sectarian identity, no single body of literature is sufficient to understanding sectarian dynamics *in toto*. This can also illuminate linkages between sectarian dynamics and other processes and frames of identity, as in the intersection of sectarian prejudice with class prejudice or the way sectarian dynamics overlap with tribal categories, patronage, corruption and the like. This has the added benefit of further demystifying sectarian identity by shedding light on the many ways in which it operates, much like other mass-group identities. Viewing sectarian identity in a rigid monochrome way obscures such linkages and parallels from view.

Like any identity, the relevance, meaning and even content of sectarian identity are in constant flux and constantly responding to and reflecting the broader, ever-shifting socio-political and economic environment. At the time of writing, the political relevance of the Sunni–Shi'a divide had considerably diminished. This does not necessarily mean a more stable Middle East, but it does alleviate the internecine tensions that surrounded sectarian categories in the years following 2003. At one point it seemed that nothing involving Sunnis and Shi'as could escape being sect-coded. The consequences of this were often tragic. It raised and hardened inter-sect boundaries and it even engendered a cruelty in how some viewed the sectarian other during times of heightened escalation – as in the sect-coding of victimhood and solidarity whereby sympathy is only extended to 'our' victims. At other times the ubiquity of sect-coding was such as to be downright ridiculous. As part of my research into what at the time was an increasingly salient sense of Sunni victimhood, I travelled to Baghdad in 2012 to conduct fieldwork where I contacted a source at the Iraqi Sunni Endowments to arrange a meeting. Naturally, in explaining what my research was about, I used the Arabic word for victimhood, *madhlumiyya*, at which point my source interrupted me: "No! That [*madhlumiyya*] is the Shi'as' thing. What we [Sunnis] have is exclusion and marginalization [*al-iqsa' wa-l-tahmish*]." He was being neither funny nor ironic, but was reinforcing sectarian boundaries even in the way sect-coded victimhoods were to be labelled. This level of absurdity was reflective of a broader environment where sectarian categories had acquired an inordinate capacity to colour social and political perceptions. Thankfully, at the time of writing, that capacity had significantly receded. The artificially clear-cut and impossibly distilled conceptions of 'Sunni' and 'Shi'a' that gained currency after 2003 have given way to a less binary picture as feelings of sectarian encirclement wane, as several once-contested issues become normalized, and as the post-2003 balance of power between sect-centric actors settles. The permanence of this shift should not be assumed. Like any set of relations, sectarian relations are liable to go through periods of tension, harmony and irrelevance. This was discussed in chapter 7, and the all-important paradoxical dialectic of unity and division that lies at the heart of sectarian relations has been discussed at several points in this book. What is worth pointing out in this concluding section is that rather than using the waning of sectarian tensions to make unfounded normative claims about unity or division, future research would do better by thinking about what could shift the trajectory in the other direction and halt this de-escalation. Surveying the rise and retreat – for now at least – of sectarian conflict in the twenty-first-century Middle East, we can shed light on the multilayered drivers of escalation and de-escalation. This was touched upon in chapter 7 in the context of Iraq, but the coming years may be opportune for the formulation of a theoretical framework that can account for the escalation and de-escalation of sectarian tensions beyond rigid and simplistic top-down instrumentalist explanations. Any such model would have to be mindful of the multidimensionality of the subject: as seen in the example of Iraq in chapter 7, the drivers will inevitably be local and regional, national and transnational, endogenous and exogenous, top-down and bottom-up. The model must also be mindful of the fluidity of sectarian categories and the volatility of their salience. All intergroup relations are given to periods of harmony and tension; however, one may tentatively suggest that the sectarian divide – which in this book has specifically and strictly been a referent to the Sunni–Shi'a divide – is unusually elastic and is unusually capable of sustaining pressure. This may primarily be due to the fact that, leaving the extremes aside, the vast majority of Sunnis and Shi'as view their sectarian identities as subsidiaries of larger Islamic and national identities. This is an important driver of the unity–division dialectic, one that also stands in the way of a complete break in sectarian relations, be it in doctrinal terms in the form of an irreversible and final break between Sunnism and Shi'ism, or in national terms along the lines of the break-up of Yugoslavia or the Partition of India. It also explains why we have yet to see a sectarian (as opposed to ethnic) separatist movement.

To end on a forward-looking note: the future of sectarian relations is likely to be messy – a condition that is the natural concomitant of the inherent ambiguity of intergroup relations. Whether looking at the medieval period, the early-modern or the modern period, narratives framing Sunni–Shi'a relations as characterized by perpetual hate or unbreakable unity, or as driven by either sectarian conflict or ecumenical love, are all equally absurd. Rather, Sunni–Shi'a relations are characterized by a seemingly unbreakable inner tension between the ideals of unity and the facts of sect-specificity. The normative value that is vested in the concepts of Islamic and national unity should not be underestimated. These do not preclude future bouts of conflict or tension but they do stand in the way of a final break between Sunnis and Shi'as absent a major redefinition of what passes for mainstream Islam and, where relevant, a major redefinition of what passes for acceptable forms of nationalism. By the same token, these drivers of unity have their limits given the inscription of difference and exclusionary specificity into the very concept of sects. True unity would mean the elimination of sect-specificity and, by extension, an elimination of the concept of Shi'as or Sunnis. However, difference does not make conflict or hatred likely; rather, the implications of difference are dictated by the context-dependent ways in which it is framed and perceived. To illustrate, the future of Sunni–Shi'a relations in the Arab world will evolve under the shadow of the upheaval that followed 2003. The early twenty-first century has produced a wealth of contested historical memory that will undoubtedly feature in Sunni–Shi'a dynamics in the future. Depending on the context, this can be imagined positively or negatively: as a symbol of how even the worst of times and the most demonic of conspiracies could not divide an ecumenical Islamic or national 'us', or as a reminder of the crimes and injustices committed by the sectarian other against a more distilled sect-specific 'us' and why the sectarian other can never be trusted. When thinking about the fluctuations in sectarian relations, a crucial factor is the multidimensionality of sectarian identity, which in turn means a multidimensionality of potential sources of escalation and de-escalation: doctrinal, subnational, national and transnational, working in mutually dialogical tandem to create either virtuous or vicious cycles, as seen in the case of Iraq. Therein lies the messiness, or the ambiguity, of sectarian relations. We would do better by trying to understand the dynamics of that messiness rather than trying to wish it away with simplistic binaries, monochrome analyses and futile hopes for finality or closure to the endless and endlessly evolving story of sectarian relations.

BIBLIOGRAPHY

Abd al-Razzaq, Salah, *Masharee' Izalat al-Tamyiz al-Ta'ifi fi-l-Iraq: Min Muthakarat Faisal ila Majlis al-Hukum, 1932–2003* (Projects to Remove Sectarian Discrimination in Iraq: From Faisal's Memorandum to the Governing Council, 1932–2003) (Beirut: Ma'aref Forum, 2010).

Abdelal, Rawi et al., "Identity as Variable," *Perspectives on Politics*, 4:4 (Dec. 2006): 695–711.

Abdo, Geneive, "The New Sectarianism: The Arab Uprisings and the Rebirth of the Shi'a-Sunni Divide," The Saban Center for Middle East Policy at Brookings, Analysis Paper, no. 29, April 2013.

Abu Tbikh, Muhsin, *Al-Mabadi' wa-l-Rijal: Bawadir al-Inhiyar al-Siyasi fi-l-Iraq* (Principles and Men: Signs of Political Collapse in Iraq) (Beirut: Al-Mu'asasa al-Arabiyya li-l-Dirasat wa-l-Nashr, 1983).

Akbarzadeh, Shahram, "Iran and Daesh: The Case of a Reluctant Shia Power," *Middle East Policy*, 22:3 (Fall 2015): 44–54.

Alami, Mona, "The Impact of the Syria Conflict on Salafis and Jihadis in Lebanon," Middle East Institute, Apr. 18, 2014.

Alaoudh, Abdullah, "State-Sponsored Fatwas in Saudi Arabia," Carnegie Endowment for International Peace – Sada, Apr. 3, 2018, http://carnegieendowment.org/sada/75971.

al-Alawi, Hasan, *Al-Ta'thirat al-Turkiyya fi-l-Mashru' al-Qawmi al-Arabi fi-l-Iraq* (Turkish Influences on the Arab Nationalist Project in Iraq) (London: Dar al-Zawra', 1988).

al-Alawi, Hasan, *Al-Shi'a wa-l-Dawla al-Qawmiyya fi-l-Iraq, 1914–1990* (The Shi'a and the National State in Iraq, 1914–1990) (Qom: Dar al-Thaqafa, 1991).

al-Ali, Zaid, *The Struggle for Iraq's Future: How Corruption, Incompetence and Sectarianism Have Undermined Democracy* (New Haven: Yale University Press, 2014).

Alkadiri, Raad and Toensing, Chris, "The Iraqi Governing Council's Sectarian Hue," The Middle East Research and Information Project, Aug. 20, 2003, http://www.merip.org/mero/mero082003.

Allawi, Ali A., *The Occupation of Iraq: Winning the War, Losing the Peace* (New Haven: Yale University Press, 2008).

Allen, Matthew, "Sectarianism, Respectability and Cultural Identity: The St Patrick's Total Abstinence Society and Irish Catholic Temperance in Mid-Nineteenth Century Sydney," *Journal of Religious History*, 35:3 (Sept. 2011): 374–392.

Alshamary, Marsin, "Authoritarian Nostalgia among Iraqi Youth: Roots and Repercussions," *War on the Rocks*, July 25, 2018, https://warontherocks.com/2018/07/authoritarian-nostalgia-among-iraqi-youth-roots-and-repercussions/.

AlShehabi, Omar H., "Contested Modernity: Divided Rule and the Birth of Sectarianism, Nationalism and Absolutism in Bahrain," *British Journal of Middle Eastern Studies*, 44:3 (2016): 333–355.

Amarilyo, Eli, "History, Memory and Commemoration: The Iraqi Revolution of 1920 and the Process of Nation Building in Iraq," *Middle Eastern Studies*, 51:1 (2015): 72–92.

Anderson, Benedict, *Imagined Communities: Reflections on the Origins and Spread of Nationalism* (London: Verso, 1983).

Arato, Andrew, *Constitution Making under Occupation: The Politics of Imposed Revolution on Iraq* (New York: Columbia University Press, 2009).

Armstrong, John, *Nations before Nationalism* (Chapel Hill: University of North Carolina Press, 1982).

Babakhan, Ali, "The Deportation of Shi'as during the Iran-Iraq War: Causes and Consequences," in *Ayatollahs, Sufis and Ideologues: State, Religion and Social Movements in Iraq*, ed. Faleh A. Jabar (London: Saqi, 2002).

Back, Les and Solomos, John (eds), *Theories of Race and Racism: A Reader* (London: Routledge, 2000).

Baha'i International Community, "Inciting Hatred: Iran's Media Campaign to Demonize Baha'is," 2011, https://www.bic.org/sites/default/files/pdf/inciting-hatred-book_0.pdf.

Bahney, Benjamin et al., "The Enemy You Know and the Ally You Don't," *Foreign Policy*, June 23, 2015, https://foreignpolicy.com/2015/06/23/the-enemy-you-know-and-the-ally-you-dont-arm-sunni-militias-iraq/.

Bahout, Joseph, "The Unravelling of Lebanon's Taif Agreement: Limits of Sect-Based Power Sharing," Carnegie Endowment for International Peace, May 2016.

Bahry, Louay, "The Opposition in Bahrain: A Bellwether for the Gulf?" *Middle East Policy*, 5:2 (May 1997): 42–57.

Baker, Christine D., *Medieval Islamic Sectarianism* (Leeds: Arc Humanities Press, 2019).

Baram, Amatzia, *Saddam Husayn and Islam, 1968–2003: Ba'thi Iraq from Secularism to Faith* (Baltimore: Johns Hopkins University Press, 2014).

Barzegar, Abbas, "The Persistence of Heresy: Paul of Tarsus, Ibn Saba' and Historical Narrative in Sunni Identity Formation," *Numen*, 58:2/3 (2011): 207–231.

Bashkin, Orit, "'Religious Hatred Shall Disappear from the Land': Iraqi Jews as Ottoman Subjects, 1864–1913," *International Journal of Contemporary Iraqi Studies*, 4:3 (2010): 305–323.

Batatu, Hanna, *The Old Social Classes and the Revolutionary Movements of Iraq: A Study of Iraq's Old Landed and Commercial Classes and of Its Communists, Ba'thists and Free Officers* (Princeton: Princeton University Press, 1978).

Batatu, Hanna, "Some Observations on the Social Roots of Syria's Ruling Military Group and the Causes for Its Dominance," *Middle East Journal*, 35:3 (Summer 1981): 331–344.

Batatu, Hanna, "Syria's Muslim Brethren," *MERIP*, 12:110 (Nov.–Dec. 1982): http://www.merip.org/mer/mer110/syrias-muslim-brethren#4.

Bayart, Jean-Francois, *The Illusion of Cultural Identity* (London: Hurst & Co., 2005).

Bazzaz, Sahar, "The Discursive Mapping of Sectarianism in Iraq: The 'Sunni Triangle' in the Pages of the *New York Times*," in *Imperial Geographies in Byzantine and Ottoman Space*, ed. Sahar Bazzaz et al. (Cambridge: Harvard University Press, 2013).

BBC Arabic, *Freedom to Broadcast Hate*, Sept. 18, 2014, https://www.bbc.com/news/av/world-middle-east-29257524/freedom-to-broadcast-hate.

Behravesh, Maysam, "How Iran Justifies Its Costly Syria Intervention," *Middle East Eye*, March 23, 2017, https://www.middleeasteye.net/columns/how-iran-justifies-its-costly-syria-intervention-home-643289507.

Belge, Ceren and Karakoc, Ekrem, "Minorities in the Middle East: Ethnicity, Religion and Support for Authoritarianism," *Political Research Quarterly*, 68:2 (2015): 280–292.

Bell, Duncan S.A., "Mythscapes: Memory, Mythology and National Identity," *British Journal of Sociology*, 54:1 (March 2003): 63–81.

Ben-Dor, Gabriel and Bengio, Ofra, "The State and Minorities toward the Twenty-First Century: An Overview," in *Minorities and the State in the Arab World*, ed. Ofra Bengio and Gabriel Ben-Dor (London: Lynne Rienner, 1999).

Bengio, Ofra, "Shi'is and Politics in Ba'thi Iraq," *Middle Eastern Studies*, 21:1 (Jan. 1985): 1–14.

Bengio, Ofra and Litvak, Meir (eds), *The Sunna and Shi'a in History: Division and Ecumenism in the Middle East* (New York: Palgrave Macmillan, 2011).

Berger, J.M., "The Turner Legacy: The Storied Origins and Enduring Impact of White Nationalism's Deadly Bible," International Centre for Counter-Terrorism – The Hague, Sept. 2016.

Berinsky, Adam J., "Can We Talk? Self-Presentation and the Survey Response," *Political Psychology*, 25:4 (Aug. 2004): 643–659.

Bilqiz, Abd al-Ilah (ed.), *Al-Ta'ifiyya wa-l-Tasamuh wa-l-Adala al-Intiqaliyya: Min al-Fitna ila Dawlat al-Qanun* (Sectarianism, Tolerance and Transitional Justice: From Discord to the State of Law) (Beirut: Centre for Arab Unity Studies, 2013).

Bin Ghanisa, Nasr al-Din, "Muqaraba Simya'iyya li-Surat al-Akhar fi Makhyalat al-Ana Bayn al-Sunna wa-l- Shi'a" (Semiotic Comparison of the Portrayal of the Other in Imaginations of Self between Sunnis and Shi'as), in *Al-Ta'ifiyya fi-l-Alam al-Islami: al-Khitab al-Qadim wa-l-Mashhad al-Jadid* (Sectarianism in the Islamic World: Old Discourse and New Scene), ed. Fu'ad Kathim (London: The Centre for Academic Shi'a Studies, 2015).

Bishara, Azmi, "Madkhal li-Fahm al-Mas'ala Ta'ifiyya wa Sina'at al-Aqaliyat fi-l-Mashriq al-Arabi al-Kabir" (An Introduction to Understanding the Sectarian Question and the Creation of Minorities in the Greater Arab Mashriq), *Omran*, 11 (2015): 7–18.

Blake, John, "This is what 'whitelash' looks like," CNN, Nov. 30, 2016, https://edition.cnn.com/2016/11/11/us/obama-trump-white-backlash/index.html.

Blanga, Yehuda U., "Saudi Arabia's Motives in the Syrian Civil War," *Middle East Policy*, 24:4 (Winter 2017), https://www.mepc.org/journal/saudi-arabias-motives-syrian-civil-war.

Blaydes, Lisa, *State of Repression: Iraq under Saddam Hussein* (Princeton: Princeton University Press, 2018).

Blight, Garry et al., "Arab Spring: An interactive timeline of Middle East protests," *The Guardian*, Jan. 5, 2012, https://www.theguardian.com/world/interactive/2011/mar/22/middle-east-protest-interactive-timeline.

Blok, Anton, "The Narcissism of Minor Differences," *European Journal of Social Theory*, 1 (1998): 33–56.

Bond, David, "Tunisia's Minority Mosaic: Constructing a National Narrative," in *Minorities and the Modern Arab World*, ed. Robson, 2016.

Boyle, Michael J., "Bargaining, Fear and Denial: Explaining Violence Against Civilians in Iraq 2004–2007," *Terrorism and Political Violence*, 21 (2009): 261–287.

Bozarslan, Hamit, "Rethinking the Ba'thist Period," in *Writing the Modern History of Iraq: Historiographical and Political Challenges*, ed. Jordi Tejel et al. (Singapore: World Scientific Publishing, 2012).

Braude, Benjamin, "Foundation Myths of the Millet System," in *Christians and Jews in the Ottoman Empire, vol. I: The Central Lands*, ed. Benjamin Braude and Bernard Lewis (New York: Holmes and Meier, 1982).

Breuilly, John, *Nationalism and the State* (Manchester: Manchester University Press, 1983).

Brewer, Marilynn B., *Intergroup Relations*, 2nd edn (Maidenhead: Open University Press, 2003).

Brooke, Steven, "Sectarianism and Social Conformity: Evidence from Egypt," *Political Research Quarterly*, 70:4 (2017): 848–860.

Brubaker, Rogers, "Religion and Nationalism: Four Approaches," *Nations and Nationalism*, 18:1 (2012): 2–20.

Brubaker, Rogers, "Religious Dimensions of Political Conflict and Violence," *Sociological Theory*, 33:1 (2015): 1–19.

Brubaker, Rogers et al., "Ethnicity as Cognition," *Theory and Society*, 33:1 (2004): 31–64.

Bruce, Steve et al., *Sectarianism in Scotland* (Edinburgh: Edinburgh University Press, 2011).

Bruce, Steve, "Scottish sectarianism? Let's lay this myth to rest," *The Guardian*, Apr. 24, 2011, https://www.theguardian.com/commentisfree/belief/2011/apr/24/scotland-sectarianism-research-data.

Brunner, Rainer and Ende, Werner (eds), *The Twelver Shia in Modern Times: Religious Culture and Political History* (Leiden: Brill, 2001).

Brunner, Rainer, *Islamic Ecumenism in the 20th Century: The Azhar and Shiism Between Rapprochement and Restraint* (Leiden: Brill Academic Publishers, 2005).

Brunner, Rainer, "Sunnites and Shiites in Modern Islam: Politics, Rapprochement and the Role of al-Azhar," in *The Dynamics of Sunni–Shia Relationship*, ed. Marechal and Zemni, 2012.

Buchta, Wilfred, "Tehran's Ecumenical Society (*Majma' Al-Taqrib*): A Veritable Ecumenical Revival or a Trojan Horse of Iran?" in *The Twelver Shia in Modern Times*, ed. Brunner and Ende, 2001.

Bunzel, Cole, "The Kingdom and the Caliphate: Saudi Arabia and the Islamic State," in *Beyond Sunni and Shia*, ed. Wehrey, 2017.

Buruma, Ian, "The Joys and Perils of Victimhood," *New York Review of Books*, Apr. 8, 1999.

Bustamam-Ahmad, Kamaruzzaman, "From Power to Cultural Landscapes: Rewriting History of Shi'ah in Aceh," *Journal of Indonesian Islam*, 11:2 (Dec. 2017): 509–530.

Buyukkara, Mehmet Ali, "Al-Ma'mun's Choice of Ali al-Ridha as His Heir," *Islamic Studies*, 41:3 (Autumn 2002): 445–466.

Buyuksarac, Guldem Baykal, "Unheard Voices: State-Making and Popular Participation in Post Ottoman Iraq," *Ethnic and Racial Studies*, 38:14 (2015): 2551–2568.

Byman, Daniel, "Let Iraq Collapse," *National Interest*, 45 (Fall 1996): 48–60.

Byman, Daniel, "Sectarianism Afflicts the New Middle East," *Survival*, 56:1 (2014): 79–100.

Casanova, Julian, *A Short History of the Spanish Civil War* (London: I.B. Tauris, 2013).

Cetinsaya, Gokhan, "The Caliph and Mujtahids: Ottoman Policy towards the Shiite Community of Iraq in the Late Nineteenth Century," *Middle Eastern Studies*, 41:4 (July 2005): 561–574.

Cetinsaya, Gokhan, *Ottoman Administration of Iraq, 1890–1908* (London: Routledge, 2011).

Cockburn, Patrick, *Muqtada al-Sadr and the Fall of Iraq* (London: Faber and Faber, 2008).

Cockburn, Patrick, "Muslim sectarianism will halt democracy in its tracks," *The Independent*, Oct. 2, 2011, http://www.independent.co.uk/opinion/commentators/patrick-cockburn-muslim-sectarianism-will-halt-democracy-in-its-tracks-2364259.html.

Cole, Juan R.I., "'Indian Money' and the Shi'i Shrine Cities of Iraq, 1786–1850," *Middle Eastern Studies*, 22:4 (1986): 461–480.

Cole, Juan R.I., "Shaikh al-Ra'is and Sultan Abdulhamid II: The Iranian Dimension of Pan-Islam," in *Histories of the Modern Middle East*, ed. Gershoni et al., 2002.

Cole, Juan R.I., "Shiite Religious Parties Fill Vacuum in Southern Iraq," Middle East Research and Information Project, Apr. 22, 2003, http://www.merip.org/mero/mero042203.

Cook, Michael, "Weber and Islamic Sects," in *Max Weber and Islam*, ed. Toby E. Huff and Wolfgang Schluchter (New Jersey: Transaction, 1999).

Cook, Michael, *Ancient Religions, Modern Politics: The Islamic Case in Comparative Perspective* (Princeton: Princeton University Press, 2014).

Corboz, Elvire, "Islamisk enhedsdiskurs: Et studie af Sunni–Shiarelationer fra britiske shiamuslimers perspektiv" (Islamic Unity Discourse: A Study of Sunni–Shi'i Relations from the Perspective of British Shi'i Muslims), *Tidsskrift for Islamforskning*, 13:1 (2019): 62–86.

Corstange, Daniel, "Ethnicity on the Sleeve and Class in the Heart," *British Journal of Political Science*, 43:4 (Oct. 2013): 889–914.

Davis, Eric, "Introduction: The Question of Sectarian Identities in Iraq," *International Journal of Contemporary Iraqi Studies*, 4:3 (Dec. 2010): 229–242.

Daw, Antun, "al-Munaqashat" (Debates), in *Al-Ta'ifiyya wa-l-Tasamuh wa-l-Adala al-Intiqaliyya* (Sectarianism, Tolerance and Transitional Justice), ed. Bilqiz, 2013.

Delgado, Richard and Stefancic, Jean, *Critical Race Theory: An Introduction*, 3rd edn (New York: New York University Press, 2017).

Deringil, Selim, "The Struggle against Shiism in Hamidian Iraq: A Study in Ottoman Counter-Propaganda," *Die Welt des Islams*, 30:1/4 (1990): 45–62.

Devine, Thomas Martin (ed.), *Scotland's Shame? Bigotry and Sectarianism in Modern Scotland* (Edinburgh: Mainstream Publishing, 2000).

al-Dini, Yusuf, "Mafhum al-Ta'ifiyya bayn al-Tajathub al-Dini wa-l-Siyasi" (An Understanding of Sectarianism between Religious and Political Dynamics), in *Al-Ta'ifiyya: Sahwat al-Fitna al-Na'ima*, al-Mesbar Studies and Research Centre, 2010.

Dodge, Toby, "State Collapse and the Rise of Identity Politics," in *Iraq: Preventing Another Generation of Conflict*, ed. Markus Bouillon et al. (Boulder: Lynne Rienner, 2007).

Dodge, Toby, *Iraq: From War to a New Authoritarianism* (London: International Institute for Strategic Studies, 2012).

Dodge, Toby, "Seeking to Explain the Rise of Sectarianism in the Middle East: The Case Study of Iraq," POMEPS, March 9, 2014, https://pomeps.org/2014/03/19/seeking-to-explain-the-rise-of-sectarianism-in-the-middle-east-the-case-study-of-iraq/.

Dodge, Toby, "'Bourdieu Goes to Baghdad': Explaining Hybrid Political Identities in Iraq," *Journal of Historical Sociology*, 31 (2018): 25–38.

Dudoignon, Stephane A., "Sunnis and Shiites in Iran since 1979: Confrontations, Exchanges, Convergences," in *The Dynamics of Sunni–Shia Relationships*, ed. Marechal and Zemni, 2012.

Dudoignon, Stephane A., *The Baluch, Sunnism and the State in Iran* (London: Hurst & Co., 2017).

al-Dulaimi, Taha, "Hathihi Hiya al-Haqiqa: al-A'dad wa-l-Nisab al-Sukaniyya li-Ahl al-Sunna wa-l-Shi'a fi-l-Iraq" (This is the Truth: Population Numbers and Percentages of Sunnis and Shi'as in Iraq), published online Aug. 2003, republished in 2009, https://ia601608.us.archive.org/19/items/adel-0044/Aqidah05778.pdf.

Dyer, Richard, "The Matter of Whiteness," in *Theories of Race and Racism*, ed. Back and Solomos, 2000.

Enayat, Hamid, *Modern Islamic Political Thought* (New York: I.B. Tauris, 2005).

Ende, Werner, "Sunni Polemical Writings on the Shi'a and the Iranian Revolution," in *The Iranian Revolution and the Muslim World*, ed. David Menashri (Boulder: Westview Press, 1990).

Eriksen, Stein Sundstøl, "State Effects and the Effects of State-Building: Institution Building and the Formation of State-Centered Societies," *Third World Quarterly*, 38:4 (2017): 771–786.

Esman, Milton J., *Ethnic Politics* (Ithaca: Cornell University Press, 1994).

European Council on Foreign Relations, *The Gulf and Sectarianism*, Gulf Analysis, Nov. 2013.

Faramarzi, Scheherezade, "Iran's Sunnis Resist Extremism, but for How Long?" Atlantic Council, South Asia Center, April 2018, https://www. atlanticcouncil.org/images/Iran_s_Sunnis_WEB.pdf.

Farha, Mark, "Global Gradations of Secularism: The Consociational, Communal and Coercive Paradigms," *Comparative Sociology*, 11 (2012): 354–386.

Farha, Mark, "Searching for Sectarianism in the Arab Spring: Colonial Conspiracy or Indigenous Instinct," *Muslim World*, 106:1 (Jan. 2016): 8–60.

Farouk-Alli, Aslam, "The Genesis of Syria's Alawi Community," in *The Alawis of Syria*, ed. Kerr and Larkin, 2015.

Farouk-Sluglett, Marion and Sluglett, Peter, *Iraq since 1958: From Revolution to Dictatorship* (London: I.B. Tauris, 2001).

Fields, Barbara J., "Whiteness, Racism and Identity," *International Labor and Working-Class History*, 60 (Fall 2001): 48–56.

Fields, Karen E. and Fields, Barbara J., *Racecraft: The Soul of Inequality in American Life* (London: Verso, 2014).

Formichi, Chiara, "Shaping Shi'a Identities in Contemporary Indonesia between Local Tradition and Foreign Orthodoxy," *Die Welt des Islams*, 54 (2014): 212–236.

Formichi, Chiara, "Violence, Sectarianism and the Politics of Religion: Articulations of Anti-Shi'a Discourses in Indonesia," *Indonesia*, 98 (Oct. 2014): 1–27.

Foster, Dennis M. et al., "There Can Be No Compromise: Institutional Inclusiveness, Fractionalization and Domestic Terrorism," *British Journal of Political Science*, 43:3 (July 2013): 541–557.

Fragiskatos, Peter, "The Stateless Kurds in Syria: Problems and Prospects for the Ajanib and Maktumin Kurds," *International Journal of Kurdish Studies*, 21:1 (2007): 109–122.

Freer, Courtney, "Challenges to Sunni Islamism in Bahrain since 2011," Carnegie Middle East Center, March 6, 2019, https://carnegie-mec. org/2019/03/06/challenges-to-sunni-islamism-in-bahrain-since-2011-pub-78510.

Friedland, Roger, "Religious Nationalism and the Problem of Collective Representation," *Annual Review of Sociology*, 27 (2001): 125–152.

Friedland, Roger and Moss, Kenneth B., "Thinking through Religious Nationalism," in *Words: Religious Language Matters*, ed. Ernst van den Hemel and Asja Szafraniec (New York: Fordham University Press, 2016).

Friedman, Yaron, "Ibn Taymiyya's Fatawa against the Nusayri-Alawi Sect," *Der Islam*, 82:2 (2005): 349–363.

Froio, Caterina, "Race, Religion or Culture? Framing Islam between Racism and Neo-Racism in the Online Network of the French Far Right," *Perspectives on Politics*, 16:3 (2018): 696–709.

Gaiser, Adam, "A Narrative Identity Approach to Islamic Sectarianism," in *Sectarianization*, ed. Hashemi and Postel, 2017.

Gallagher, Tom, *Divided Scotland: Ethnic Friction and Christian Crisis* (Glendaruel: Argyll Publishing, 2013).

Gallie, Walter Bryce, "Essentially Contested Concepts," *Proceedings of the Aristotelian Society*, 56 (1955–1956): 167–198.

Garner, Steve, "A Moral Economy of Whiteness: Behaviours, Belonging and Britishness," *Ethnicities*, 12:4 (2012): 445–464.

Garrison, James, "Popular Mobilization Messaging," International Centre for Counter-Terrorism, The Hague, Apr. 2017, https://icct.nl/wp-content/uploads/2017/04/ICCT-Garrison-Popular-Mobilization-Messaging-April-2017-1.pdf.

Gasper, Michael, "Sectarianism, Minorities and the Secular State in the Middle East," *International Journal of Middle East Studies*, 48 (2016): 767–778.

Gat, Azar, *Nations: The Long History and Deep Roots of Political Ethnicity and Nationalism* (Cambridge: Cambridge University Press, 2013).

Gause, Gregory, III, "Beyond Sectarianism: The New Middle East Cold War," Brookings Doha Center, Analysis Paper no. 11 (July 2014).

Gellner, Ernest, *Nationalism* (London: Weidenfeld and Nicolson, 1997).

Gengler, Justin J., "Understanding Sectarianism in the Persian Gulf," in *Sectarian Politics in the Persian Gulf*, ed. Potter, 2013.

Gengler, Justin J., *Group Conflict and Political Mobilization in Bahrain and the Arab Gulf: Rethinking the Rentier State* (Bloomington: Indiana University Press, 2015).

Gengler, Justin J., "The Political Economy of Sectarianism: How Gulf Regimes Exploit Identity Politics as a Survival Strategy," in *Beyond Sunni and Shia*, ed. Wehrey, 2017.

Gershoni, Israel, Erdem, Hakan and Wokock, Ursula (eds), *Histories of the Modern Middle East: New Directions* (Boulder: Lynne Rienner, 2002).

al-Gharbi, Musa, "The myth and reality of sectarianism in Iraq," Al Jazeera America, Aug. 18, 2014, http://america.aljazeera.com/opinions/2014/8/iraq-sectarianismshiassunniskurdsnourialmalaki.html.

Ghobadzdeh, Naser and Akbarzadeh, Shahram, "Sectarianism and the Prevalence of 'Othering' in Islamic Thought," *Third World Quarterly*, 36:4 (2015): 691–704.

Goldsmith, Leon T., *Cycle of Fear: Syria's Alawites in War and Peace* (London: Hurst & Co., 2015).

Goldsmith, Leon T., "Alawi Diversity and Solidarity: From the Coast to the Interior," in *The Alawis of Syria*, ed. Kerr and Larkin, 2015.

Goody, Jack, "Bitter Icons," *New Left Review*, no. 7 (Jan.–Feb. 2001): 5–15.

Gordon, Anna and Parkinson, Sarah E., "How the Houthis Became 'Shi'a'," Middle East Research and Information Project, Jan. 27, 2018. http://merip.org/mero/mero012718.

Greengrass, Mark, *Christendom Destroyed: Europe 1517–1648* (London: Penguin Books, 2015).

Grehan, James, *Twilight of the Saints: Everyday Religion in Ottoman Syria and Palestine* (New York: Oxford University Press, 2014).

Haddad, Fanar, *Sectarianism in Iraq: Antagonistic Visions of Unity* (London: Hurst & Co., 2011).

Haddad, Fanar, "Political Awakenings in an Artificial State: Iraq, 1914–1920," *International Journal of Contemporary Iraqi Studies*, 6:1 (2012): 3–26.

Haddad, Fanar, "Sectarian Relations in Arab Iraq: Contextualizing the Civil War of 2006–2007," *British Journal of Middle Eastern Studies*, 40:2 (2013): 115–138.

Haddad, Fanar, "Sectarian Relations and Sunni Identity in Post-Civil War Iraq," in *Sectarian Politics in the Persian Gulf*, ed. Potter, 2013.

Haddad, Fanar, "The Language of Anti-Shi'ism," *Foreign Policy*, Aug. 9, 2013. http://foreignpolicy.com/2013/08/09/the-language-of-anti-shiism/.

Haddad, Fanar, "A Sectarian Awakening: Reinventing Sunni Identity after 2003," *Current Trends in Islamist Ideology*, 17 (2014): 70–101.

Haddad, Fanar, "Secular Sectarians," Middle East Institute, Middle East–Asia Project, Sectarianism in the Middle East and Asia, June 17, 2014, www.mei.edu/content/map/secular-sectarians.

Haddad, Fanar, "Shi'a-Centric State-Building and Sunni Rejection in Post-2003 Iraq," Carnegie Endowment for International Peace, Jan. 2016.

Haddad, Fanar, "Competing Victimhoods in a Sectarian Landscape," *Jadaliyya*, Nov. 1, 2016, http://www.jadaliyya.com/Details/33690/Competing-Victimhoods-in-a-Sectarian-Landscape.

Haddad, Fanar, "'Shia Forces', 'Iraqi Army' and the Perils of Sect-Coding," *Jadaliyya*, Sept. 8, 2016, http://www.jadaliyya.com/pages/index/25064/shia-forces-iraqi-army-and-the-perils-of-sect-codi.

Haddad, Fanar, "Sectarian Relations before 'Sectarianization' in pre-2003 Iraq," in *Sectarianization*, ed. Hashemi and Postel, 2017.

Haddad, Fanar, "Understanding Iraq's Hashd al-Sha'bi," Century Foundation, March 5, 2018, https://tcf.org/content/report/understanding-iraqs-hashd-al-shabi/.

Haddad Kreidie, Lina and Renwick Monroe, Kristen, "Psychological Boundaries and Ethnic Conflict: How Identity Constrained Choice and Worked to Turn Ordinary People into Perpetrators of Ethnic Violence during the Lebanese Civil War," *International Journal of Politics, Culture and Society*, 16:1 (2002): 5–36.

al-Hadrawi, Majid Hamid Abbas, "Dawr al-Marji'iyya al-Diniyya fi-l-Difa' 'an al-Iraq: Khutab al-Jum'ah al-Siyasiyya li-'Am 2014 Namuthaj" (The Role of the Religious *Marji'iyya* in the Defence of Iraq: The Case of the Political Friday Sermons of 2014), *Al-Ameed Journal*, 7:1 (2018): 22–83.

Hagan, Johan et al., "The Theory of Legal Cynicism and Sunni Insurgent Violence in Post-Invasion Iraq," *American Sociological Review*, 81:2 (2016): 316–346.

al-Haidari, Nabil, *Al-Tashayu' al-Arabi wa-l-Tashayu' al-Farisi: Dawr al-Furs al-Tarikhi fi-Inhiraf al-Tashayu'* (Arabic Shi'ism and Persian Shi'ism: The Historic Persian Role in the Perversion of Shi'ism) (London: Dar al-Hikma, 2014).

Haider, Najam, *The Origins of the Shi'a: Identity, Ritual and Sacred Space in Eighth-Century Kufa* (Cambridge: Cambridge University Press, 2014).

al-Haj, Abd al-Rahman, *Al-Ba'th al-Shi'i fi-Syria* (The Shi'a Ba'th in Syria) (London: International Institute for Syrian Studies, 2008).

al-Haj Salih, Yassin, "al-Ta'ifiyya wa-l-Siyasa fi Syria" (Sectarianism and Politics in Syria), in *Nawasib wa Rawafidh*, ed. Saghiya, 2009.

Hamid, Ala', "Al-Ayquna al-Shi'iyya: Qira'ah fi-Dala'il al-Suwar al-Ramziyya li-A'immat al-Shi'a" (The Shi'a Icon: Analysing the Symbolic Images of the Shi'a Imams), *Masarat*, 15 (2011): 116–220.

Hammond, Andrew, "Saudi Arabia: Cultivating Sectarian Spaces," in European Council on Foreign Relations, *The Gulf and Sectarianism*, 2013.

Hanf, Theodore, *Coexistence in Wartime Lebanon: Decline of a State and Rise of a Nation* (London: I.B. Tauris, 2015).

Hanson, Jim, "To Bring Peace to Syria and Iraq, Allow Them to Break Apart," Fox News, Feb. 18, 2018, http://www.foxnews.com/opinion/2018/02/16/to-bring-peace-to-syria-and-iraq-allow-them-to-break-apart.html.

Harmes, Adam, "Political Marketing in Post-Conflict Elections: The Case of Iraq," *Journal of Political Marketing* (2016), DOI: 10.1080/15377857.2016.1193834.

al-Hasani, Abd al-Razzaq, *Tarikh al-Wizarat al-Iraqiyya* (The History of the Iraqi Cabinets) (Baghdad: Dar al-Shu'un al-Thaqafiyya al-Ama, 1988).

Hashemi, Nader and Postel, Danny (eds), *Sectarianization: Mapping the New Politics of the Middle East* (London: Hurst & Co., 2017).

Hastings, Adrian, *The Construction of Nationhood: Ethnicity, Religion and Nationalism* (Cambridge: Cambridge University Press, 1997).

Hazleton, Lesley, *After the Prophet: The Epic Story of the Shia–Sunni Split* (New York: Anchor Books, 2010).

Healy, Kieran, "Fuck Nuance," *Sociological Theory*, 35:2 (2017): 118–127.

Hinnebusch, Raymond, "Syria's Alawis and the Ba'ath Party," in *The Alawis of Syria*, ed. Kerr and Larkin, 2015.

Hinnebusch, Raymond, "The Sectarianization of the Middle East: Transnational Identity Wars and Competitive Interference," in *Transnational Diffusion and Cooperation in the Middle East*, POMEPS Studies 21, Aug. 24, 2016.

Hinnebusch, Raymond, "The Sectarian Surge in the Middle East and the Dynamics of the Regional States-System," *Tidsskrift for Islamforskning*, 13:1 (2019): 35–61.

Hiro, Dilip, *Cold War in the Islamic World: Saudi Arabia, Iran and the Struggle for Supremacy* (London: Hurst & Co., 2018).

Hobsbawm, Eric and Ranger, Terence (eds), *The Invention of Tradition* (Cambridge: Cambridge University Press, 1983).

Hodgson, Marshall G. S., "How Did the Early Shia Become Sectarian?" *Journal of the American Oriental Society*, 57:1 (Jan.-March, 1955): 1–13.

Holmes, Oliver, "Assad's Devious, Cruel Plan to Stay in Power by Dividing Syria – and Why It's Working," *The New Republic*, Aug. 15, 2011, https://newrepublic.com/article/93286/syria-assad-shabbiha-sectarianism.

Horowitz, Donald L., "Three Dimensions of Ethnic Politics," *World Politics*, 23:2 (Jan. 1971): 232–244.

Human Rights Watch, "Egypt: Lynching of Shia Follows Months of Hate Speech," June 27, 2013, https://www.hrw.org/news/2013/06/27/egypt-lynching-shia-follows-months-hate-speech.

Human Rights Watch, "Saudi Arabia: Religion Textbooks Promote Intolerance," Sept. 13, 2017, https://www.hrw.org/news/2017/09/13/saudi-arabia-religion-textbooks-promote-intolerance.

Human Rights Watch, "'They Are Not Our Brothers': Hate Speech by Saudi Officials," Sept. 26, 2017, https://www.hrw.org/report/2017/09/26/they-are-not-our-brothers/hate-speech-saudi-officials#.

Hurvitz, Nimrod, "Early Hanbalism and the Shi'a," in *The Sunna and Shi'a in History*, ed. Bengio and Litvak, 2011.

Husain, Rahat, "Malaysian 'Confronting the Shia Virus' Seminar was Precursor to Anti-Shia Alliance Meeting," *Communities Digital News*, May 2, 2014, http://www.commdiginews.com/world-news/middle-east/malaysian-confronting-the-shia-virus-seminar-was-precursor-to-anti-shia-alliance-meeting-16310/#HDE78HVBvde5Uerw.99.

Hussain, Abd al-Khaliq, *Al-Ta'ifiyya al-Siyasiyya wa Mushkilat al-Hukum fi-l-Iraq* (Political Sectarianism and the Problem of Governance in Iraq) (Baghdad: Dar Mesopotamia, 2011).

al-Hussain, Abd al-Satir, *Tahthir al-Bariyya min Nashat al-Shi'a fi Syria* (Warning Creation of Shi'a Activity in Syria) (Cairo: Dar al-Muhadithin, 2007).

Ibrahim, Farhad, *Al-Ta'ifiyya wa-l-Siyasiyya fi-l-Alam al-Arabi: Namudhaj al-Shi'a fi-l-Iraq* (Sectarianism and Politics in the Arab World: The Example of the Shi'a in Iraq) (Cairo: Madbouly, 1996).

Ibrahim, Fu'ad, "Al-Su'udiyya: al-Hiwar al-Masmum" (Saudi Arabia: The Poisoned Discourse), in *Nawasib wa Rawafidh*, ed. Saghiya, 2009.

Ida, Rachmah, "Cyberculture and Sectarianism in Indonesia: The Rise of Shia Media and Anti-Shia Online Movements," *Jurnal Komunikasi Islam*, 6:2 (2016): 194–215.

Ihsan, Mohammed, "Arabization as Genocide: The Case of the Disputed Territories of Iraq," in *The Kurdish Question Revisited*, ed. Gareth Stansfield and Mohammed Shareef (London: Hurst & Co., 2017).

International Crisis Group, "The Next Iraqi War? Sectarianism and Civil Conflict," *Middle East Report* no. 52, Feb. 27, 2006.

International Crisis Group, "Iraq's Civil War, the Sadrists and the Surge," *Middle East Report* no. 72, Feb. 7, 2008.

International Crisis Group, "Iraq's Uncertain Future: Elections and Beyond," *Middle East Report* no. 94, Feb. 25, 2010.

International Crisis Group, "Iraq's Secular Opposition: The Rise and Decline of al-Iraqiya," *Middle East Report* no. 127, July 31, 2012.

International Crisis Group, "Make or Break: Iraq's Sunnis and the State," *Middle East Report* no. 144, Aug. 14, 2013.

International Crisis Group, "Saudi Arabia: Back to Baghdad," *Middle East Report* no. 186, May 22, 2018.

Isenberg, Nancy, *White Trash: The 400-Year Untold History of Class in America* (New York: Viking, 2016).

Iskander, Elizabeth, *Sectarian Conflict in Egypt: Coptic Media, Identity and Representation* (London: Routledge, 2012).

Ismael, Tareq Y. and Ismael, Jacqueline S., "The Sectarian State in Iraq and the New Political Class," *International Journal of Contemporary Iraqi Studies*, 4:3 (Dec. 2010): 339–56.

Ismael, Tareq Y. and Ismael, Jacqueline S., *Iraq in the Twenty-First Century: Regime Change and the Making of a Failed State*, Durham Modern Middle East and Islamic World Series 34 (Oxford: Routledge, 2015).

Ismail, Raihan, "The Saudi Ulema and the Shi'a of Saudi Arabia," *Journal of Shi'a Islamic Studies*, 5:4 (Autumn 2012): 403–422.

Itani, Husam, "Khutut al-Fasl wa-Khuyut al-Wasl" (Lines of Separation and Threads of Connection), in *Nawasib wa Rawafidh*, ed. Saghiya, 2009.

Jabar, Faleh A., "The Genesis and Development of *Marja'ism* versus the State," in *Ayatollahs, Sufis and Ideologues: State, Religion and Social Movements in Iraq*, ed. Faleh A. Jabar (London: Saqi, 2002).

Jabar, Faleh A., *The Shi'ite Movement in Iraq* (London: Saqi, 2003).

Jabar, Faleh A., "The Iraqi Protest Movement: From Identity Politics to Issue Politics," LSE Middle East Centre Paper Series no. 25, 2018, http://eprints.lse.ac.uk/88294/1/Faleh_Iraqi%20Protest%20Movement_Published_English.pdf.

Jabar, Faleh A., Mansour, Renad, and Khaddaj, Abir, "Maliki and the Rest: A Crisis within a Crisis," Iraq Institute for Strategic Studies, June 2012, http://iraqstudies.com/books/featured3.pdf.

Jaffrelot, Christophe, *Religion, Caste and Politics in India* (London: Hurst & Co., 2011).

Jamail, Dahr, "The Myth of Sectarianism: The Policy Is Divide to Rule," *International Socialist Review*, 57 (Jan.–Feb. 2008), www.isreview.org/issues/57/rep-sectarianism.shtml.

Jam'iyat al-Tajdid al-Thaqafiyya, *Al-Ta'ifiyya: Radda ila al-Jahiliyya* (Sectarianism: A Return to Jahiliyya) (Manama: Jam'iyat al-Tajdid al-Thaqafiyya, 2010).

Jones, Marc Owen, "Automated Sectarianism and Pro-Saudi Propaganda on Twitter," *Exposing the Invisible*, 2016, https://exposingtheinvisible.org/resources/obtainingevidence/automated-sectarianism.

Jones, Marc Owen, "Contesting the Iranian Revolution as a Turning-Point Discourse in Bahraini Contentious Politics," in *Gulfization of the Arab World*, ed. Marc Owen Jones, Ross Porter and Marc Valeri (Berlin: Gerlach Press, 2018).

Jones, Marc Owen, "Propaganda, Fake News and Fake Trends: The Weaponization of Twitter Bots in the Gulf Crisis," *International Journal of Communication*, 13 (2019): 1389–1415.

Joseph, Suad, "Working-Class Women's Networks in a Sectarian State: A Political Paradox," *American Ethnologist*, 10:1 (Feb. 1983): 1–22.

Kadhim, Abbas, "Efforts at Cross-Ethnic Cooperation: The 1920 Revolution and Sectarian Identities in Iraq," *International Journal of Contemporary Iraqi Studies*, 4:3 (Dec. 2010): 275–294.

Kadhim, Abbas, "The Hawza under Siege: A Study in the Ba'th Party Archive," Institute for Iraqi Studies, Boston University, IISBU Occasional Paper no. 1, June 2013.

Kadhum, Oula, "The Transnational Politics of Iraq's Shia Diaspora," *Diwan*, Carnegie Middle East Center, March 1, 2018. https://carnegie-mec.

org/2018/03/01/transnational-politics-of-iraq-s-shia-diaspora-pub-75675.

Kakar, Sudhir, *The Colors of Violence: Cultural Identities, Religion and Conflict* (Chicago: University of Chicago Press, 1996).

Kaufman, Stuart J., *Modern Hatreds: The Symbolic Politics of Ethnic War* (New York: Cornell University Press, 2001).

Kazimi, Nibras, "Zarqawi's Anti-Shi'a Legacy: Original or Borrowed?" *Current Trends in Islamist Ideology*, no. 1 (2006): 53–72, https://www.hudson.org/content/researchattachments/attachment/1351/kizimi_vol4.pdf.

Kazimi, Nibras, *Syria through Jihadist Eyes: A Perfect Enemy* (Stanford: Hoover Institution Press, 2010).

Kern, Karen, *Imperial Citizen: Marriage and Citizenship in the Ottoman Frontier Provinces of Iraq* (Syracuse: Syracuse University Press, 2011).

Kerr, Michael and Larkin, Craig (eds), *The Alawis of Syria: War, Faith and Politics in the Levant* (New York: Oxford University Press, 2015).

Kerr, Michael, "Introduction: For 'God, Syria, Bashar and Nothing Else'?" in *The Alawis of Syria*, ed. Kerr and Larkin, 2015.

Keynoush, Banafsheh, *Saudi Arabia and Iran: Friends or Foes?* (New York: Palgrave Macmillan, 2016).

Khan, Yasmin, *The Great Partition: The Making of India and Pakistan* (New Haven: Yale University Press, 2008).

al-Khayyun, Rashid, "al-Iraq: Tawdhif al-Ta'ifiyya Siyasiyyan," in *Al-Ta'ifiyya: Sahwat al-Fitna al-Na'ima*, al-Mesbar Studies and Research Centre, 2010.

al-Khayyun, Rashid, *Dhid al-Ta'ifiyya: Al-Iraq — Jadal ma Ba'd Nisan 2003* (Against Sectarianism: Iraq –The Post-April 2003 Debate) (Beirut: Madarek, 2011).

Khoury, Dina Rizk, "The Security State and the Practice and Rhetoric of Sectarianism in Iraq," *International Journal of Contemporary Iraqi Studies*, 4:3 (Dec. 2010): 325–338.

Khoury, Dina Rizk, "The 1991 *Intifada* in Three Keys: Writing the History of Violence," in *Writing the Modern History of Iraq: Historiographical and Political Challenges*, ed. Jordi Tejel et al. (Singapore: World Scientific Publishing, 2012).

Khoury, Dina Rizk, *Iraq in Wartime: Soldiering, Martyrdom and Remembrance* (Cambridge: Cambridge University Press, 2013).

Kinnvall, Catarina, "Globalization and Religious Nationalism: Self, Identity and the Search for Ontological Security," *Political Psychology*, 25:5 (2004): 741–767.

al-Kirami, Abu Suhaib (ed.), *Al-Kamil fi Tarikh Ibn al-Athir* (The Complete History of Ibn al-Athir) (Amman: Beit al-Afkar al-Duwaliyya, n.d.).

Kohlberg, Etan, "From Imamiya to Ithna-Ashariyya," *Bulletin of the School of Oriental and African Studies, University of London*, 39:3 (1976): 521–534.

Kohlberg, Etan, "The Term 'Rafida' in Imami Shi'i Usage," *Journal of the American Oriental Society*, 99:4 (Oct.–Dec. 1979): 677–679.

Kolsto, Pal, "The 'Narcissism of Minor Differences' Theory: Can it Explain Ethnic Conflict?" *Filozofija I Drustivo*, 2 (2007): 153–171.

Krisna, Yuli, "Calls for Jihad, Purges Emerge at Hate-Filled Anti-Shiite Gathering in Indonesia," *Jakarta Globe*, April 20, 2014, http://www.thejakartaglobe.com/news/calls-jihad-purges-emerge-hate-filled-anti-shiite-gathering/.

Krohley, Nicholas, *The Death of the Mehdi Army: The Rise, Fall and Revival of Iraq's Most Powerful Militia* (London: Hurst & Co., 2015).

al-Kubaisi, Yahya, "Al-Iraq: al-Ihtijajat wa Azmat al-Nidham al-Siyasi" (Iraq: The Protests and the Crisis of the Political System), Arab Center for Research and Policy Studies, Case Analysis, Feb. 2013.

al-Kubaisi, Yahya, "Iraq: Recent Protests and the Crisis of a Political System," Arab Center for Research and Policy Studies, Feb. 2013.

Kumar, Krishan, *The Making of English Identity* (Cambridge: Cambridge University Press, 2003).

Kuttab, Daoud, "The Media and Iraq: A Blood Bath for and Gross Dehumanization of Iraqis," *International Review of the Red Cross*, 89:868 (Dec. 2007): 879–891.

Landis, Joshua, "Islamic Education in Syria: Undoing Secularism," *Insania*, 13:3 (Sept.–Dec. 2008): 534–549.

Lefevre, Raphael, *Ashes of Hama: The Muslim Brotherhood in Syria* (London: Hurst & Co., 2013).

Lefevre, Raphael, "The Sociopolitical Undercurrent of Lebanon's Salafi Militancy," Carnegie Middle East Center, March 26, 2018, https://carnegie-mec.org/2018/03/27/sociopolitical-undercurrent-of-lebanon-s-salafi-militancy-pub-75744.

Leoussi, Athena S. and Grosby, Steven (eds), *Nationalism and Ethnosymbolism: History, Culture and Ethnicity in the Formation of Nations* (Edinburgh: Edinburgh University Press, 2007).

Lewis, Amanda E., "'What Group?' Studying Whites and Whiteness in the Era of 'Color-Blindness'," *Sociological Theory*, 22:4 (Dec. 2004): 623–646.

Liebhaber, Samuel, "From Minority to Majority: Inscribing the Mahra and Touareg into the Arab Nation," in *Minorities and the Modern Arab World*, ed. Robson, 2016.

Lindemann, Stefan, "Do Inclusive Elite Bargains Matter? A Research Framework for Understanding the Causes of Civil War in Sub-Saharan Africa," Development Studies Institute (LSE), Crisis States Discussion Papers no. 15, Feb. 2008.

Linge, Marius, "Sunnite–Shiite Polemics in Norway," *FLEKS: Scandinavian Journal of Intercultural Theory and Practice*, 3:1 (2016), https://doi.org/10.7577/fleks.1684.

Litvak, Meir, *Shi'i Scholars of Nineteenth Century Iraq: The Ulama of Najaf and Karbala* (Cambridge: Cambridge University Press, 1998).

Litvak, Meir, "Money, Religion, and Politics: The Oudh Bequest in Najaf and Karbala, 1850–1903," *International Journal of Middle East Studies*, 33:1 (2001): 1–21.

Litvak, Meir, "Encounters between Shi'i and Sunni Ulama in Ottoman Iraq," in *The Sunna and Shi'a in History*, ed. Bengio and Litvak, 2011.

Locke, John, *A Letter Concerning Toleration*, ed. James H. Tully (Indianapolis: Hackett Publishing Co., 1983).

Loomis, Louise R., "Nationality at the Council of Constance: An Anglo-French Dispute," *American Historical Review*, 44:3 (April 1939): 508–527.

Louer, Laurence, *Transnational Shia Politics: Religious and Political Networks in the Gulf* (New York: Columbia University Press, 2008).

Louer, Laurence, "The Rise and Fall of Revolutionary Utopias in the Gulf Monarchies," in *The Shi'a Worlds and Iran*, ed. Mervin, 2010.

Louer, Laurence, "Sectarianism and Coup-Proofing Strategies in Bahrain," *Journal of Strategic Studies*, 36:2 (2013): 245–260.

Lu'aibi, Shakir, *Tasawir al-Imam Ali* (Depictions of Imam Ali) (Beirut: Riad al-Rayyes Books, 2011).

Luomi, Mari, "Sectarian Identities or Geopolitics? The Regional Shia–Sunni Divide in the Middle East," Finnish Institute of International Affairs, Working Paper 56, Feb. 2, 2008.

Lynch, Marc, "New Iraq, New Arab Public," in *Voices of the New Arab Public: Iraq, Al Jazeera, and Middle East Politics Today* (New York: Columbia University Press, 2006).

Lynch, Marc, "The War for the Arab World," in *The Politics of Sectarianism*, POMEPS Briefing 21, Nov. 13, 2013, https://pomeps.org/wp-content/uploads/2014/06/POMEPS_Studies4_Sectarianism.pdf.

Lynch, Marc, "Sectarianism and the Campaign to Retake Fallujah," *Diwan*, Carnegie Middle East Center, June 17, 2016, https://carnegie-mec.org/diwan/63834?lang=en.

Lynch, Marc, "The New Arab Order: Power and Violence in Today's Middle East," *Foreign Affairs*, Sept.–Oct. 2018, https://www.foreignaffairs.com/articles/middle-east/2018-08-13/new-arab-order.

Mabon, Simon, *Saudi Arabia and Iran: Power and Rivalry in the Middle East* (London: I.B. Tauris, 2016).

Mabon, Simon (ed.), *Saudi Arabia and Iran: The Struggle to Shape the Middle East*, The Foreign Policy Centre, 2018, https://fpc.org.uk/wp-content/uploads/2018/11/Saudi-Arabia-and-Iran-The-Struggle-to-Shape-the-Middle-East-Report.pdf.

Mabon, Simon and Gause, Gregory, III, "SEPAD Pod with Gregory Gause," Sectarianism, Proxies and De-sectarianization, Richardson Institute, Dec. 2018, https://soundcloud.com/richardsoninstitute/sepadpod-with-gregory-gause.

Mabon, Simon and Phillips, Christopher, "SEPAD Pod: Chris Phillips," Sectarianism, Proxies and De-sectarianization, Dec. 2018, https://www.sepad.org.uk/announcement/sepadpod-chris-phillips.

Machlis, Elisheva, *Shi'i Sectarianism in the Middle East: Modernisation and the Quest for Islamic Universalism* (London: I.B. Tauris, 2014).

Mackintosh-Smith, Tim, *Arabs: A 3,000 Year History of Peoples, Tribes and Empires* (New Haven: Yale University Press, 2019).

Maghen, Ze'ev, "Unity or Hegemony? Iranian Attitudes to the Sunni–Shi'i Divide," in *The Sunna and Shi'a in History*, ed. Bengio and Litvak, 2011.

Maher, Shiraz, *Salafi-Jihadism: The History of an Idea* (London: Penguin, 2017).

Mahfuz, Muhammad, *Dhid al-Ta'ifiyya* (Against Sectarianism) (Casablanca: al-Markaz al-Thaqafi al-Arabi, 2009).

Mahmood, Saba, *Religious Difference in a Secular Age: A Minority Report* (Princeton: Princeton University Press, 2016).

Makdisi, Ussama, *The Culture of Sectarianism: Community, History, and Violence in Nineteenth-Century Ottoman Lebanon* (Berkeley: University of California Press, 2000).

Makdisi, Ussama, "Pensee 4: Moving beyond Orientalist Fantasy, Sectarian Polemic and Nationalist Denial," *International Journal of Middle East Studies*, 40:4 (Nov. 2008): 559–560.

Makdisi, Ussama, "The Problem of Sectarianism in the Middle East in an Age of Western Hegemony," in *Sectarianization*, ed. Hashemi and Postel, 2017.

Makiya, Kanaan, *Cruelty and Silence* (New York: W. W. Norton & Co., 1993).

Al-Maktaba al-Takhasusiyya fi-l-Red ala al-Shi'a al-Rawafidh (The Specialist Library on Responding to the Rawafidh Shi'a), http://azahera.net/showthread.php?p=69901.

Malekzadeh, Shervin, "What Iran's textbooks can teach us about sectarianism and ancient hatreds," *Washington Post*, Monkey Cage Blog, Jan. 25, 2016, https://www.washingtonpost.com/news/monkey-cage/wp/2016/01/25/how-irans-view-of-sectarianism-has-evolved-since-its-revolution/?noredirect=on&utm_term=.2ba309025744.

Malik, Cyrus, "Washington's Sunni Myth and the Middle East Undone," Aug. 23, 2016, https://warontherocks.com/2016/08/washingtons-sunni-myth-and-the-middle-east-undone/.

Mallat, Chibli, *The Renewal of Islamic Law: Muhammad Baqir as-Sadr, Najaf and the Shi'i International* (Cambridge: Cambridge University Press, 1993).

Mango, Andrew, "Minorities and Majorities: Review Article," *Middle Eastern Studies*, 23:4 (Oct. 1987): 512–528.

Mansour, Renad, "Protests Reveal Iraq's New Fault Line: The People vs. the Ruling Class," *World Politics Review*, July 20, 2018, https://www. worldpoliticsreview.com/articles/25161/protests-reveal-iraq-s-new-fault-line-the-people-vs-the-ruling-class.

Mansour, Renad and Jabar, Faleh A., "The Popular Mobilization Forces and Iraq's Future," Carnegie Middle East Center, April 2017, http://carnegie-mec.org/2017/04/28/popular-mobilization-forces-and-iraq-s-future-pub-68810.

Mansour, Renad and van den Toorn, Christine, "The 2018 Iraqi Federal Elections: A Population in Transition?" LSE Middle East Centre, July 2018, http://eprints.lse.ac.uk/89698/7/MEC_Iraqi-elections_Report_2018. pdf.

Marechal, Brigitte and Zemni, Sami (eds), *The Dynamics of Sunni–Shia Relationships: Doctrine, Transnationalism, Intellectuals and the Media* (London: Hurst & Co., 2012).

Marechal, Brigitte and Zemni, Sami, "Introduction: Analysing Contemporary Sunnite–Shiite Relations; Changing Identities, Political Projects, Interactions and Theological Discussions," in *The Dynamics of Sunni–Shia Relationships*, ed. Marechal and Zemni, 2012.

Marechal, Brigitte and Zemni, Sami, "Conclusion: Analysing Contemporary Sunnite–Shiite Relationships" in *The Dynamics of Sunni–Shia Relationships*, ed. Marechal and Zemni, 2012.

Marr, Phebe, "Iraq's New Political Map," United States Institute for Peace, Special Report no. 179, Jan. 2007.

Masters, Bruce, *Christians and Jews in the Ottoman Arab World: The Roots of Sectarianism* (Cambridge: Cambridge University Press, 2001).

Matthiesen, Toby, "A 'Saudi Spring?' The Saudi Protest Movement in the Eastern Province 2011–2012," *Middle East Journal*, 66:4 (Autumn 2012): 628–659.

Matthiesen, Toby, *Sectarian Gulf: Bahrain, Saudi Arabia and the Arab Spring That Wasn't* (Stanford: Stanford University Press, 2013).

Matthiesen, Toby, *The Other Saudis: Shiism, Dissent and Sectarianism* (Cambridge: Cambridge University Press, 2015).

Matthiesen, Toby, "Transnational Diffusion between Arab Shi'a Movements," in *Transnational Diffusion, Cooperation and Learning in the Middle East and North Africa*, POMEPS Studies 28, 2016, http://pomeps.org/2016/08/16/transnational-diffusion-between-arab-shia-movements/.

Matthiesen, Toby, "Sectarianization as Securitization: Identity Politics and Counter Revolution in Bahrain," in *Sectarianization*, ed. Hashemi and Postel, 2017.

McHugo, John, *A Concise History of Sunnis and Shi'is* (London: Saqi Books, 2017).

al-Mdaires, Falah, "Shi'ism and Political Protest in Bahrain," *DOMES: Digest of Middle East Studies*, 1 (Spring 2002): 20–44.

Meijer, Roel and Wagemakers, Joas, "The Struggle for Citizenship of the Shiites of Saudi Arabia," in *The Dynamics of Sunni–Shia Relationships*, ed. Marechal and Zemni, 2012.

Mervin, Sabrina (ed.), *The Shi'a Worlds and Iran* (London: Saqi, 2010).

Al-Mesbar Studies and Research Centre, *Al-Ta'ifiyya: Sahwat al-Fitna al-Na'ima* (Sectarianism: Awakening the Dormant Discord) (Beirut: Madarek, 2010).

Messarra, Antoine, "Ma Ma'na al-Ta'ifiyya wa Kayfa Nadrusuha al-Yawm" (What Is the Meaning of Sectarianism and How Can We Study It Today?), in *Al-Ta'ifiyya wa-l-Tasamuh wa-l-Adala al-Intiqaliyya* (Sectarianism, Tolerance and Transitional Justice), ed. Bilqiz, 2013.

Modood, Tariq, "Majorities, Minorities and Multiculturalism," *Discover Society*, Dec. 4, 2018, https://discoversociety.org/2018/12/04/majorities-minorities-and-multiculturalism/.

Momen, Moojan, *An Introduction to Shi'i Islam: History and Doctrines of Twelver Shi'ism* (New Haven: Yale University Press, 1985).

Monier, Elizabeth, "Egypt, Iran and the Hizbullah Cell: Using Sectarianism to 'De-Arabize' and Regionalize Threats to National Interests," *Middle East Journal*, 69:3 (Summer 2015): 341–357.

Muasher, Marwan, *The Second Arab Awakening – and the Battle for Pluralism* (New Haven: Yale University Press, 2014).

Muhammad, Amira, "Al-Su'udiyya tal'ab bi-l-waraqa al-Shi'iyya … wa-l-Islamiyyun fazza'at al-hukkam" (Saudi Arabia Plays the Shi'a Card and the Islamists are the Rulers' Scarecrow), *DeutscheWelle*, March 11, 2011, https://www.dw.com/ar/الشيعيةو الإسلاميون-فزاعة-الحكام السعودية-تلعب-بالورقة/a-14906452.

al-Mu'min, Ali, *Min al-Mathhabiyya ila al-Ta'ifiyya: Al-Mas'ala al-Ta'ifiyya fi-l-Waqi' al-Islami* (From Schools of Thought to Sectarianism: The Sectarian Question in Islamic Reality) (Beirut: Dar al-Kawakib, 2007).

Muttar, Salim, *Al-Dhat al-Jariha: Ishkalat al-Hawiyya fi-l-Iraq wa-l-Alam al-Arabi 'al-Sharqmutawasiti'* (The Wounded Self: The Problems of Identity in Iraq and in the 'Middle Eastern' Arab World) (Beirut: Al-Mu'asasa al-Arabiyya li-l-Dirasat wa-l-Nashr, 1997).

Muttar, Salim, *Jadal al-Hawiyat: Arab, Akrad, Turkuman, Siryan, Yezidiyya – Sira' al-Intima'at fi-l-Iraq wa-l-Sharq al-Awsat* (The Identity Debate: Arabs, Kurds,

Turkmens, Syriacs, Yezidis – The Struggle of Belongings in Iraq and the Middle East) (Beirut: Arab Institute for Research and Publishing, 2003).

Nakash, Yitzhak, *The Shi'is of Iraq* (Princeton: Princeton University Press, 1994).

Nasr, Vali R., "International Politics, Domestic Imperatives, and Identity Mobilization: Sectarianism in Pakistan, 1979–1998," *Comparative Politics*, 32:2 (Jan. 2000): 171–190.

Nasr, Vali R., *The Shia Revival: How Conflicts within Islam Will Shape the Future* (New York: W.W. Norton & Co., 2006).

Niens, Ulrike et al., "Prejudiced or Not? Hidden Sectarianism among Students in Northern Ireland," *Journal of Social Psychology*, 144:2 (2005): 163–180.

al-Nifis, Ahmed Rasim, "al-Ta'ifiyya al-Unsuriyya" (Racist Sectarianism), *Shu'un Mashriqiyya*, 1:1 (Summer 2008): 43–72.

Novick, Peter, *The Holocaust in American Life* (New York: First Mariner Books, 2000).

Nu'man, Issam, "al-Munaqashat" (Debates), in *Al-Ta'ifiyya wa-l-Tasamuh wa-l-Adala al-Intiqaliyya* (Sectarianism, Tolerance and Transitional Justice), ed. Bilqiz, 2013.

Nusseira, Hani, "Hawl Kharitat al-Aqaliyat fi-l-Alam al-Arabi" (On the Map of Minorities in the Arab World), in *Al-Ta'ifiyya: Sahwat al-Fitna al-Na'ima*, al-Mesbar Studies and Research Centre, 2010.

al-Omar, Nasir, *Waqi' al-Rafidha fi Bilad al-Tawhid* (The Reality of the Rafidha [Shi'a] in the Land of Monotheism), self-published, available at https://eldorar.net/science/article/13802.

Oren, Neta, "Israeli Identity Formation and the Arab Israeli Conflict in Election Platforms, 1969–2006," *Journal of Peace Research*, 47:2 (2010): 193–204.

Osman, Khalil F., *Sectarianism in Iraq: The Making of a Nation since 1920* (London: Routledge, 2015).

Ostovar, Afshon, "Sectarian Dilemmas in Iranian Foreign Policy: When Strategy and Identity Politics Collide," Carnegie Endowment for International Peace, Nov. 30, 2016, http://carnegieendowment.org/2016/11/30/sectarian-dilemmas-in-iranian-foreign-policy-when-strategy-and-identity-politics-collide-pub-66288.

Ostovar, Afshon, "Iran, Its Clients, and the Future of the Middle East: The Limits of Religion," *International Affairs*, 94:6 (Nov. 2018): 1237–1255.

Owen, Roger, *State, Power and Politics in the Making of the Modern Middle East* (London: Routledge, 2000).

Ozkirimli, Umut, *Theories of Nationalism: A Critical Introduction* (London: Macmillan Press, 2000).

Panjwani, Imranali (ed.), *The Shi'a of Samarra: The Heritage and Politics of a Community in Iraq* (New York: I.B. Tauris, 2012).

Pardo, Eldad J., "Iranian Education: The Continuous Revolution," IMPACT-se, 2016, http://www.impact-se.org/wp-content/uploads/Iranian-Education_The-Continuous-Revolution-2016.pdf.

Parker, Ned and Salman, Raheem, "Notes from the Underground: The Rise of Nouri al-Maliki," *World Policy Journal*, 30:1 (2013): 63–76.

Pelham, Nicolas, *A New Muslim Order: The Shia and the Middle East Sectarian Crisis* (London: I.B. Tauris, 2008).

Pew Research Center, *Mapping the Global Muslim Population: A Report on the Size and Distribution of the World's Muslim Population*, Oct. 2009, http://www.pewresearch.org/wp-content/uploads/sites/7/2009/10/Muslimpopulation.pdf.

Pew Research Center, *The World's Muslims: Unity and Diversity*, Aug. 9, 2012.

Pew Research Center, *Europe's Growing Muslim Population*, Nov. 29, 2017, http://www.pewforum.org/2017/11/29/europes-growing-muslim-population/.

Phillips, Christopher, "Sectarianism and Conflict in Syria," *Third World Quarterly*, 36:2 (2015): 357–376.

Phillips, Christopher, *The Battle for Syria: International Rivalry in the New Middle East* (New Haven: Yale University Press, 2016).

Phillips, Christopher, "Sectarianism as Plan B: Saudi–Iranian Identity Politics in the Syria Conflict," The Foreign Policy Centre, Nov. 12, 2018, https://fpc.org.uk/sectarianism-as-plan-b-saudi-iranian-identity-politics-in-the-syria-conflict/.

Phillips, Christopher and Valbjorn, Morten, "'What Is in a Name?' The Role of (Different) Identities in the Multiple Proxy Wars in Syria," *Small Wars and Insurgencies*, 29:3 (2018): 414–433.

Picard, Elizabeth, "Conclusion: Nation-Building and Minority Rights in the Middle East," in *Religious Minorities in the Middle East: Domination, Self-Empowerment, Accommodation*, ed. Anne Sofie Roald and Anh Nga Longva (Leiden: Brill, 2012).

Pierret, Thomas, "Karbala in the Umayyad Mosque: Sunni Panic at the 'Shiitization' of Syria in the 2000s," in *The Dynamics of Sunni–Shia Relationships*, ed. Marechal and Zemni, 2012.

Pierret, Thomas, *Religion and State in Syria: The Sunni Ulama from Coup to Revolution* (Cambridge: Cambridge University Press, 2013).

Pierret, Thomas, "The Reluctant Sectarianism of Foreign States in the Syrian Conflict," United States Institute of Peace, Peace Brief 162, Nov. 18, 2013.

Pierret, Thomas, "On Nir Rosen's Definitions of 'Sectarian' and 'Secular'," *Pulse*, Dec. 23, 2014, https://pulsemedia.org/2014/12/23/on-nir-rosens-definitions-of-sectarian-and-secular/.

Pinto, Paulo Gabriel Hilu, "The Shattered Nation: The Sectarianization of the Syrian Conflict," in *Sectarianization*, ed. Hashemi and Postel, 2017.

Pollock, Katherine and Wehrey, Frederic, "The Sufi–Salafi Rift," *Diwan*, Carnegie Middle East Center, Jan. 23, 2018. http://carnegie-mec.org/diwan/75310.

Potter, Lawrence G. (ed.), *Sectarian Politics in the Persian Gulf* (London: Hurst & Co., 2013).

Project on Middle East Political Science, "Iraq between Maliki and the Islamic State," July 9, 2014, https://pomeps.org/wp-content/uploads/2014/07/POMEPS_BriefBooklet24_Iraq_Web.pdf.

Provence, Michael, *The Last Ottoman Generation and the Making of the Modern Middle East* (Cambridge: Cambridge University Press, 2017).

Pursley, Sara, "'Lines Drawn on an Empty Map': Iraq's Borders and the Legend of the Artificial State," *Jadaliyya*, June 2, 2015, http://www.jadaliyya.com/Details/32140/%60Lines-Drawn-on-an-Empty-Map%60-Iraq%E2%80%99s-Borders-and-the-Legend-of-the-Artificial-State-Part-1.

al-Qarawee, Harith Hasan, "Heightened Sectarianism in the Middle East: Causes, Dynamics and Consequences," *Italian Institute for International Political Studies*, Analysis no. 205, Nov. 2013.

al-Qarawee, Harith Hasan, "Ab'ad al-ihtijajat al-ijtima'iyya bi-l-Iraq wa mu'tayat al-khilaf al-Shi'i" (The Parameters of Social Protests in Iraq and the Nature of Shi'a Division), Al Jazeera Center for Studies, Aug. 17, 2015, http://studies.aljazeera.net/mritems/Documents/2015/8/17/201581712140930734Iraq-Shi'ite.pdf.

al-Qarawee, Harith Hasan, "The Basra Exception," *Diwan*, Carnegie Middle East Center, Sept. 19, 2018, http://carnegie-mec.org/diwan/77284?lang=en.

Rahim, Taufiq, "Is Hypernationalism the New Islamism?" *Al-Monitor*, Aug. 23, 2013, http://www.al-monitor.com/pulse/originals/2013/08/violence-arab-nationalism.html#.

Rahimah, Badr Eddin, "The Class Oriented Rationale: Uncovering the Sources of the Syrian Civil War," *Muslim World*, 106:1 (Jan. 2016): 169–186.

Ramadani, Sami, "The sectarian myth of Iraq," *The Guardian*, June 16, 2014, www.gu.com/commentisfree/2014/jun/16/sectarian-myth-of-iraq.

al-Rasheed, Madawi, "Sectarianism as Counter-Revolution: Saudi Responses to the Arab Spring," in *Sectarianization*, ed. Hashemi and Postel, 2017.

Ra'uf, Adil, *Al-Amal al-Islami fi-l-Iraq: Bayn al-Marji'iyya wa-l-Hizbiyya, Dirasa Naqdiyya li-Masirat Nisf Qirin (1950–2000)* (Islamic Activism in Iraq: Between the Marji'iyya and Party Affiliation – A Critical Study of a Half-Century Journey (1950–2000)) (Damascus: Al-Markaz al-Iraqi li-l-I'lam wa-l-Dirasat, 2000).

Rayburn, Joel, *Iraq after America: Strongmen, Sectarians, Resistance* (Stanford: Hoover Institution Press, 2014).

Reicher, Stephen, "The Context of Social Identity: Domination, Resistance and Change," *Political Psychology*, 26:6 (2004): 921–945.

Reilly, Patrick, "Kicking with the Left Foot: Being Catholic in Scotland," in *Scotland's Shame?*, ed. Devine, 2000.

Rieff, David, "History Resumes: Sectarianism's Unlearned Lessons," *World Affairs*, 175:2 (July–Aug., 2012): 29–38.

Robson, Laura (ed.), *Minorities and the Modern Arab World: New Perspectives* (Syracuse: Syracuse University Press, 2016).

Roccas, Sonia and Brewer, Marilynn B., "Social Identity Complexity," *Personality and Social Psychology*, 6:2 (2002): 88–106.

Roe, Paul, "Securitization and Minority Rights: Conditions of Desecuritization," *Security Dialogue*, 35:3 (Sept. 2004): 279–294.

Rogan, Eugene, "Sectarianism and Social Conflict in Damascus: The 1860 Events Reconsidered," *Arabica*, 51:4 (Oct. 2004): 493–511.

Rogerson, Barnaby, *The Heirs of Muhammad: Islam's First Century and the Origins of the Sunni–Shia Split* (New York: Overlook Press, 2008).

Rosen, Nir, "Assad's Alawites: The guardians of the throne," Al Jazeera, Oct. 11, 2011. http://www.aljazeera.com/indepth/features/2011/10/20111-1-122434671982.html.

Rougier, Bernard, *The Sunni Tragedy in the Middle East: Northern Lebanon from al-Qaeda to ISIS* (Princeton: Princeton University Press, 2015).

Roy, Olivier, *The Politics of Chaos* (London: Hurst & Co., 2007).

Roy, Olivier, "The Impact of the Iranian Revolution on the Middle East," in *The Shi'a Worlds and Iran*, ed. Mervin, 2010.

Roy, Olivier, *Jihad and Death: The Global Appeal of Islamic State* (London: Hurst & Co., 2017).

al-Rubay'ie, Fadhil and Kawtharani, Wajih, *Al-Ta'ifiyya wa-l-Harb* (Sectarianism and War) (Damascus: Dar al-Fikr, 2011).

Rudolf, Inna, "From Battlefield to Ballot Box: Contextualising the Rise and Evolution of Iraq's Popular Mobilisation Units," International Centre for the Study of Radicalisation and Political Violence, May 2018, https://icsr.info/wp-content/uploads/2018/05/ICSR-Report-From-Battlefield-to-Ballot-Box-Contextualising-the-Rise-and-Evolution-of-Iraq%E2%80%99s-Popular-Mobilisation-Units.pdf.

Sabahi, Farian, "Iran, Iranian Media and Sunnite Islam," in *The Dynamics of Sunni–Shia Relationships*, ed. Marechal and Zemni, 2012.

Sadeghi-Boroujerdi, Eskandar, "Strategic Depth, Counterinsurgency and the Logic of Sectarianization: The Islamic Republic of Iran's Security

Doctrine and Its Regional Implications," in *Sectarianization*, ed. Hashemi and Postel, 2017.

al-Sadr, Muhammad, *Al-Ta'ifiyya fi Nadhar al-Islam* (Sectarianism in the Eyes of Islam) (Beirut: Dar wa Maktabat al-Basa'ir, 2013).

Saeed, Haider, *Siyasat al-Ramz: 'An Nihayat Thaqafat al-Dawla al-Wataniyya fi-l-Iraq* (The Politics of the Symbol: On the End of the Culture of the National State in Iraq) (Beirut: Al-Mu'asasa al-Arabiyya, 2009).

al-Saffar, Hasan bin Musa, *Al-Ta'ifiyya Bayn al-Siyasa wa-l-Din* (Sectarianism between Politics and Religion) (Casablanca: al-Markaz al-Thaqafi al-Arabi, 2009).

Safouan, Moustapha, *Why Are the Arabs Not Free? The Politics of Writing* (Oxford: Wiley-Blackwell, 2007).

Saghiya, Hazim (ed.), *Nawasib wa Rawafidh* (Beirut: Dar al-Saqi, 2009).

Salamandra, Christa, *A New Old Damascus: Authenticity and Distinction in Urban Syria* (Bloomington: Indiana University Press, 2004).

Salamandra, Christa, "Sectarianism in Syria: Anthropological Reflections," *Middle East Critique*, 22:3 (Oct. 2013): 303–306.

Saleem, Zmkan Ali et al., "Security and Governance in the Disputed Territories under a Fractured GoI: The Case of Northern Diyala," LSE Middle East Centre Blog, Nov. 14, 2018, http://blogs.lse.ac.uk/mec/2018/11/14/security-and-governance-in-the-disputed-territories-under-a-fractured-goi-the-case-of-northern-diyala/.

Saleh, Alam and Kraetzschmar, Hendrik, "Politicized Identities, Securitized Politics: Sunni–Shi'a Politics in Egypt," *Middle East Journal*, 69:4 (Autumn 2015): 545–562.

Salih, Qasim Hussain, *Al-Mujtama' al-Iraqi: Tahlil Sikosociology lima Hadath wa Yahduth* (Iraqi Society: A Psycho-Sociological Analysis of What Happened and Is Happening) (Beirut: Arab Scientific Publishers: 2008).

Salloukh, Bassel F. et al., *The Politics of Sectarianism in Postwar Lebanon* (London: Pluto Press, 2015).

Salloukh, Bassel, "The Sectarianization of Geopolitics in the Middle East," in *Sectarianization*, ed. Hashemi and Postel, 2017.

Salloum, Saad, "Ziyara ila Qabr Saddam Hussain" (A Visit to Saddam Hussain's Grave), *Niqash*, Aug. 2009, http://www.niqash.org/articles/?id=2501&lang=ar.

al-Samarra'i, Sa'id, *Saddam wa-Shi'at al-Iraq* (Saddam and the Shi'a of Iraq) (London: Mu'asasat al-Fajr, 1991).

al-Samarra'i, Sa'id, *Al-Ta'ifiyya fi-l-Iraq: Al-Waqi' wa-l-Hal* (Sectarianism in Iraq: The Reality and the Solution) (London: Mu'asasat al-Fajr, 1993).

Sassoon, Joseph, *Anatomy of Authoritarianism in the Arab Republics* (Cambridge: Cambridge University Press, 2016).

Scott, James C., *The Art of Not Being Governed: An Anarchist History of Upland Southeast Asia* (New Haven: Yale University Press, 2009).

Seale, Patrick, *Asad: The Struggle for the Middle East* (Berkeley: University of California Press, 1992).

Sha'ban, Abd al-Hussain, *Jadal al-Hawiyat fi-l-Iraq: al-Dawla wa-l-Muwatana* (The Identity Debate in Iraq: The State and Citizenship) (Beirut: Arab Scientific Publishers, 2010).

Shaery-Eisenlohr, Roschanack, *Shi'ite Lebanon: Transnational Religion and the Making of National Identities* (New York: Columbia University Press, 2011).

Shakman Hurd, Elizabeth, "Politics of Sectarianism: Rethinking Religion and Politics in the Middle East," *Middle East Law and Governance*, 7:1 (2015): 61–75.

al-Shar', Mahdi, "al-Mukawinat al-Siyasiyya li-l-Ta'ifiyya fi-l-Iraq" (The Political Components of Sectarianism in Iraq), *Shu'un Mashriqiyya*, 1:1 (Summer 2008): 95–131.

Sherberger, Max, "Confrontations between Sunni and Shi'i Empires: Ottoman–Safavid Relations between the Fourteenth and the Seventeenth Century," in *The Sunna and Shi'a in History*, ed. Bengio and Litvak, 2011.

Shields, Sarah D., *Fezzes in the River: Identity Politics and European Diplomacy in the Middle East on the Eve of World War II* (New York: Oxford University Press, 2011).

al-Shimmari, Hadif, *Al-Khutta al-Khamsiniyya al-Sirriyya li-Ayat Qom wa-In'ikasatiha ala Waqi' Mamlakat al-Bahrain* (The Secret Fifty Year Plan of the Ayat[ollas] of Qom and Its Reflection on the Reality of the Kingdom of Bahrain), 2nd edn (self-published, 2008).

Shuman, Abd al-Khaliq Nasir, *Al-Ta'ifiyya al-Siyasiyya fi-l-Iraq: al-Ahd al-Jumhuri, 1958–1991* (Political Sectarianism in Iraq: The Republican Era, 1958–1991) (London: Dar al-Hikma, 2013).

Sindawi, Khalid, "Jawla fi-Ma'jam Mustalahat al-Shi'a" (A Journey through the Dictionary of Shi'a Phrases), The Arabic Language Academy, http://www.arabicac.com/content.asp?id=97.

Sindawi, Khalid, "The Shiite Turn in Syria," *Current Trends in Islamist Ideology*, 8 (2009): 82–107.

Sluglett, Peter, *Britain in Iraq: Contriving King and Country, 1914–1932* (New York: Columbia University Press, 2007).

Sluglett, Peter, "The British, the Sunnis and the Shi'is: Social Hierarchies of Identity under the British Mandate," *International Journal of Contemporary Iraqi Studies*, 4:3 (Dec. 2010): 257–273.

Sluglett, Peter and Sluglett, Marion Farouk, "Some Reflections on the Sunni/Shi'i Question in Iraq," *British Society for Middle Eastern Studies Bulletin*, 5:2 (1978): 79–87.

Smith, Anthony, *The Ethnic Origins of Nations* (Oxford: Blackwell, 1986).

Smith, Anthony, *Chosen Peoples: Sacred Sources of National Identity* (Oxford: Oxford University Press, 2003).

Smith Diwan, Kirstin, "Saudi Nationalism Raises Hopes of Greater Shia Inclusion," The Arab Gulf States Institute in Washington, May 3, 2018, http://www.agsiw.org/saudi-nationalism-raises-hopes-greater-inclusion-shias/.

Steinberg, Guido, "Jihadi-Salafism and the Shi'is: Remarks about the Intellectual Roots of Anti-Shi'ism," in *Global Salafism: Islam's New Religious Movement*, ed. Roel Meijer (New York: Columbia University Press, 2009).

Stephenson, Lindsey, "Ahistorical Kuwaiti Sectarianism," *Foreign Policy*, April 29, 2011, https://foreignpolicy.com/2011/04/29/ahistorical-kuwaiti-sectarianism/.

Strobl, Staci, "The Roots of Sectarian Law and Order in the Gulf: Bahrain, the Eastern Province of Saudi Arabia and the Two Historical Disruptions," in *Beyond Sunni and Shia*, ed. Wehrey, 2017.

Strobl, Staci, *Sectarian Order in Bahrain: The Social and Colonial Origins of Criminal Justice* (New York: Lexington Books, 2018).

Al-Suri, Abu Mus'ab, "Ahl al-Sunna fi-l-Sham fi Muwajahat al-Nusayriyya wa-l-Salibiyya wa-l-Yahud" (The Sunnis in Syria in Confronting the Nusayriyya, the Crusaders and the Jews), https://www.cia.gov/library/abbottabad-compound/1D/1D8B8465CBFC9E8BA7CB1DE89DCB8B25_ANUSIREA.pdf.

Taher, Ali, "Harakat al-ihtijajat al-madani fi-l-Iraq ba'd 31 July 2015: aliyat al-tashakul wa ma'alat al-mustaqbal" (The Social Protest Movement in Iraq after 31 July 2015: Mechanisms of Formation and Future Implications), King Faisal Center for Research and Islamic Studies, Oct. 2015.

Tajfel, Henri and Turner, John C., "The Social Identity Theory of Intergroup Behavior," in *Political Psychology: Key Readings*, ed. John T. Jost and James Sidanius (New York: Psychology Press, 2004).

Talhamy, Yvette, "The Fatwas and the Nusayri/Alawis of Syria," *Middle Eastern Studies*, 46:2 (2010): 175–194.

Taqi al-Din, Sulayman, "al-Ta'ifiyya wa-l-Mathhabiyya wa Atharuhuma al-Siyasiyya" (Sectarianism, *Mathhabiyya* and Their Political Influences), in *Al-Ta'ifiyya wa-l-Tasamuh wa-l-Adala al-Intiqaliyya* (Sectarianism, Tolerance and Transitional Justice), ed. Bilqiz, 2013.

Tarabishi, George, *Hartaqat II* (Heresies II) (Beirut: Dar al-Saqi, 2008).

Taub, Ben, "Iraq's Post-ISIS Campaign of Revenge," *New Yorker*, Dec. 24, 2018, https://www.newyorker.com/magazine/2018/12/24/iraqs-post-isis-campaign-of-revenge.

Terzioglu, Derin, "Sufis in the Age of State-Building and Confessionalization," in *The Ottoman World*, ed. Christine Woodhead (New York: Routledge, 2012).

The Day After, "Sectarianism in Syria: Survey Study," 2016, http://tda-sy.org/en/content/215/279/latest-news/syrian-opinions-and-attitudes-towards-sectarianism-in-syria-survey-study.

Thompson, A.C., "Katrina's hidden race war," *The Nation*, Dec 17. 2008, https://www.thenation.com/article/katrinas-hidden-race-war/.

Ting-Toomey, Stella, "Identity Navigation Theory," in *Sage Encyclopedia of Intercultural Competence*, vol. 1, ed. Janet M. Bennett (Los Angeles: Sage Publishing, 2015).

Tomass, Mark, *The Religious Roots of the Syrian Conflict: The Remaking of the Fertile Crescent* (New York: Palgrave Macmillan, 2016).

Torpey, John, *The Invention of the Passport: Surveillance, Citizenship and the State* (Cambridge: Cambridge University Press, 2000).

Tsugitaka, Sato, *State and Rural Society in Medieval Islam: Sultans, Muqta's and Fallahun* (Leiden: E.J. Brill, 1997).

Tucker, Ernest S., *Nadir Shah's Quest for Legitimacy in Post-Safavid Iran* (Gainesville: University Press of Florida, 2006).

United Nations Economic and Social Commission for Western Asia, "The Demographic Profiles of the Arab States, 2017," https://www.unescwa.org/sites/www.unescwa.org/files/publications/files/demographic-profiles-2017.pdf.

al-Uzri, Abd al-Kareem, *Mushkilat al Hukum fi-l-Iraq* (The Problem of Governance in Iraq) (London: self-published, 1991).

Valbjorn, Morten, "Arab Nationalism(s) in Transformation: From Arab Interstate Societies to an Arab-Islamic World Society," in *International Society and the Middle East: English School Theory at the Regional Level*, ed. Barry Buzan and Ana Gonzalez-Pelaez (London: Palgrave Macmillan, 2009).

Van Dam, Nikolaos, "Middle Eastern Political Cliches: 'Takriti' and 'Sunni Rule' in Iraq; 'Alawi Rule' in Syria; A Critical Appraisal," *Orient: German Journal for Politics and Economics of the Middle East*, 21:1 (Jan. 1980): 42–57.

Van Dam, Nikolaos, *The Struggle for Power in Syria: Sectarianism, Regionalism and Tribalism in Politics, 1961–1980* (London: Croom Helm, 1981).

Van Dam, Nikolaos, *Destroying a Nation: The Civil War in Syria* (London: I.B. Tauris, 2017).

Vatanka, Alex, "The Islamic Republic's Cross-Sectarian Outreach," *Current Trends in Islamist Ideology* (April 2011): 25–39.

Volkan, Vamik, *Blood Lines: From Ethnic Pride to Ethnic Terrorism* (Boulder: Westview Press, 1998).

Wagemaker, Joas, "Anti-Shi'ism without the Shi'a: Salafi Sectarianism in Jordan," *Maydan*, Sept. 30, 2016.

al-Wardi, Ali, *Dirasa fi-Tabi'at al-Mugtama' al-Iraqi* (A Study of the Nature of Iraqi Society) (Baghdad: Matba'at al-Ani, 1965).

al-Wardi, Ali, *Lamahat Ijtima'iyya min Tarikh al-Iraq al-Hadith* (Social Aspects of the Modern History of Iraq), vol. 4, 2nd edn (Beirut: Dar al-Rashid, 2005).

Warner, John, "Questioning Sectarianism in Bahrain and Beyond: An Interview with Justin Gengler," *Jadaliyya*, April 17, 2013, www.jadaliyya. com/pages/index/11267/questioning-sectarianism-in-bahrain-and-beyond_an-n.

Wehrey, Frederic, *Sectarian Politics in the Gulf: From the Iraq War to the Arab Uprisings* (New York: Columbia University Press, 2014).

Wehrey, Frederic (ed.), *Beyond Sunni and Shia: The Roots of Sectarianism in a Changing Middle East* (London: Hurst & Co., 2017).

Wehrey, Frederic et al., "Saudi-Iranian Relations since the Fall of Saddam: Rivalry, Cooperation and Implications for U.S. Policy," RAND Corporation, 2009, https://www.rand.org/content/dam/rand/pubs/monographs/2009/RAND_MG840.pdf.

Weiss, Max, *In the Shadow of Sectarianism: Law, Shiism, and the Making of Modern Lebanon* (Cambridge: Harvard University Press, 2010).

Wells, Madeleine, "Sectarianism, Authoritarianism and Opposition in Kuwait," in *Sectarianization*, ed. Hashim and Postel, 2017.

White, Benjamin Thomas, *The Emergence of Minorities in the Middle East: The Politics of Community in French Mandate Syria* (Edinburgh: Edinburgh University Press, 2011).

Wicken, Stephen, "Iraq's Sunnis in Crisis," Institute for the Study of War, Middle East Security Report II, May 2013.

Williams, Thomas Chatterton, "How Ta-Nehisi Coates gives whiteness power," *New York Times*, Oct. 6, 2017, https://www.nytimes.com/2017/10/06/opinion/ta-nehisi-coates-whiteness-power.html.

Williams, Thomas Chatterton, "The French Origins of 'You Will Not Replace Us'," *New Yorker*, Dec. 4, 2017, https://www.newyorker.com/magazine/2017/12/04/the-french-origins-of-you-will-not-replace-us.

Wimmen, Heiko, "Divisive Rule: Sectarianism and Power Maintenance in the Arab Spring – Bahrain, Iraq, Lebanon and Syria," German Institute for International and Security Affairs, Research Paper no. 4, March 2014.

Wing, Joel, "Understanding Iraq's Protest Movements: An Interview with Kirk H. Sowell, Editor of *Inside Iraqi Politics*," May 7, 2013, *Musings on Iraq*, http://musingsoniraq.blogspot.sg/2013/05/understanding-iraqs-protest-movements.html.

Winter, Stefan, *The Shiites of Lebanon under Ottoman Rule, 1516–1788* (Cambridge: Cambridge University Press, 2010).

Winter, Stefan, "The Kizilbas of Syria and Ottoman Shiism," in *The Ottoman World*, ed. Christine Woodhead (New York: Routledge, 2012).

Winter, Stefan, "The Alawis in the Ottoman Period," in *The Alawis of Syria*, ed. Kerr and Larkin, 2015.

Yassin-Kassab, Robin and al-Shami, Leila, *Burning Country: Syrians in Revolution and War* (London: Pluto Press, 2016).

Yousif, Bassam, "The Political Economy of Sectarianism in Iraq," *International Journal of Contemporary Iraqi Studies*, 4:3 (Dec. 2010): 357–367.

Zaman, Muhammad Qasim, "Sectarianism in Pakistan: The Radicalization of Shi'a and Sunni Identities," *Modern Asian Studies*, 32:3 (July 1998): 689–716.

Zertal, Idith, *Israel's Holocaust and the Politics of Nationhood* (Cambridge: Cambridge University Press, 2005).

Zubaida, Sami, "Contested Nations: Iraq and the Assyrians," *Nations and Nationalism*, 6:3 (2000): 363–382.

al-Zu'bi, Ahmed, "al-Ta'ifiyya wa Mushkilat Bina' al-Dawla fi Lubnan" (Sectarianism and the Problem of State-Building in Lebanon), in *Al-Ta'ifiyya: Sahwat al-Fitna al-Na'ima*, al-Mesbar Studies and Research Centre, 2010.

INDEX

Note: Page numbers followed by "*n*" refer to notes.

357